POSTMODERN CAREER COUNSELING

A Handbook of Culture, Context, and Cases

edited by
Louis A. Busacca and Mark C. Rehfuss

AMERICAN COUNSELING
ASSOCIATION
6101 Stevenson Avenue, Suite 600
Alexandria, VA 22304
www.counseling.org

POSTMODERN CAREER COUNSELING
A Handbook of Culture, Context, and Cases

American Counseling Association
6101 Stevenson Avenue, Suite 600
Alexandria, VA 22304

Associate Publisher   Carolyn C. Baker

Digital and Print Development Editor   Nancy Driver

Senior Production Manager   Bonny E. Gaston

Copy Editor   Kay Mikel

Cover and text design by Bonny E. Gaston

Library of Congress Cataloging-in-Publication Data
Names: Busacca, Louis A., editor. | Rehfuss, Mark C., editor.
Title: Postmodern career counseling: a handbook of culture, context, and cases / edited by Louis A. Busacca and Mark C. Rehfuss.
Description: Alexandria, VA : American Counseling Association, 2016. | Includes bibliographical references and index.
Identifiers: LCCN 2016020323 | ISBN 9781556203589 (pbk.: alk. paper)
Subjects: LCSH: Vocational guidance. | Cross-cultural counseling. | Career development—Case studies.
Classification: LCC HF5381 .P6727 2016 | DDC 331.702—dc23 LC record available at https://lccn.loc.gov/2016020323

To my late loving father Sam Busacca, Sr., and family.

—*Louis A. Busacca*

To Tracie, Adelyn, Taylor, and Claire, the most incredible women
I have ever known.

—*Mark C. Rehfuss*

Table of Contents

Part III: Procedures

Social Constructionist, Constructivist, and Narrative Models

Variants of Social Constructionist, Constructivist, and Narrative Models

Systemic and Integrative Models

Conclusion

Foreword

Mark Pope[1]

Insecurity is the predominant psychological characteristic of the postmodern historical period. What Drs. Busacca and Rehfuss have done in this book offers career counselors who are facing such issues with their clients an important perspective that enables them to plan their career counseling interventions accordingly. They accomplished this by gathering together the brightest thinkers and practitioners of constructivist and constructionist career counseling, both the new and the more mature, to write about their passion. And this passion comes through in each of the chapters.

Insecurity about precarious work is an inherent part of career choice and job search, but in the postmodern era it is both the quantity and quality of the insecurity that has changed and is changing. During the industrial era, workers moved even further away from having some felt control of the means and outcomes of production. In some cases, benevolent owners tried to compensate for that inherent insecurity by pledges of lifelong employment, but in many cases workers had to fight for such job security with labor unions as their instrument. And fight they did! In fact there were 4,740 labor strikes in 1937 alone.[2] In the modern era, however, the power of U.S. labor unions plateaued, and during the Reagan presidency the utter defeat of the PATCO air traffic controllers union strike of 1981 set in motion the gradual descent of union power, which continues even to this day. This descent coincided with the beginning of the postmodern era, shortening of the capitalist boom or bust economic cycles, and a

---

[1]Mark Pope is a past president of both the National Career Development Association and the American Counseling Association. He is also a former editor of *The Career Development Quarterly* and an Eminent Career Award recipient, curators' professor and chair, Department of Counseling and Family Therapy, University of Missouri–Saint Louis.

[2]Brenner, A., Day, B., & Ness, I. (Eds.). (2009). *The encyclopedia of strikes in American history* (p. ii). Armonk, NY: M. E. Sharpe.

concomitant rise in workforce insecurity for both blue- and white-collar workers. Thus the time is right for this book as postmodern theories and interventions are coming to the forefront of our profession.

What also makes this book unique is the chapter authors' thorough integration of cultural context into the constructionist paradigm in career counseling. Nowhere else in the career counseling and development literature will you find this consistent dedication to such integration. For this reason alone, this book sets a new landmark for our field.

And finally, this book is a very real tribute to the pioneering and continuing work of Dr. Mark Savickas, as both a theoretician and a mentor. His impact on our field is indescribable; in so many ways you can see his soul permeating each chapter. His mentorship is evident in the professional lives of so many of these authors and of the two editors, Louis A. Busacca and Mark C. Rehfuss, as well as in my own.

This is a very special book. A treasure! I hope that you both learn from and enjoy it as much as I have.

Preface

Two colleagues discuss the reduction in hours in their department and the rapid change of assignments over the past year. The company they work for has been going through restructuring due to offshore outsourcing, and it has implemented new computer programs that have replaced the need for some workers. Several employees in their department have already been laid off or had their hours reduced. Leon, a middle-aged African American with a bachelor's degree, has just been informed of a 40% reduction in his part-time hours due to the company's need to comply with the Affordable Care Act. After 4 years with the company, Leon is worried that he may need to find another job or eventually be laid off. He mentions how difficult it will be for his wife and child now that his hours have been cut, and more so if he loses his job. He is despondent and repeats over and over that he just cannot imagine having to look around for another job again after the struggles he experienced when he was laid off from a full-time position 6 years ago. Leon talks to his colleague Ann about how he struggles to focus on his work and how he just lost an account because of his preoccupation with the uncertainty over his job, career, and family.

Ann has been a full-time employee for 2 years. She is 30 years old, a lesbian, and working on her master's degree. She fears she will be downsized or asked to take an unappealing position within the company. Her partner of 5 years is happy living in what they consider a gay-friendly community, and she does not want to move. Ann discloses that she too has been preoccupied and not doing her best work for the department lately. Although Ann has her own concerns, she listens and helps Leon understand how much he has contributed to a series of important projects and how he has demonstrated skills that the company increasingly needs. Leon and Ann acknowledge feeling alone and unable to share their fear and insecurity with other employees or with their supervisor. They both feel a lack of guidance from their supervisor and the company with regard to how to position themselves for possible transition. Leon decides to take advantage of his employee assistance program and seek out counseling services.

Graduate students learning about career counseling and practitioners who provide career services need to know how to assist individuals like Leon and Ann. In the uncertainty of today's workplace, career counselors are increasingly called upon to help clients navigate work and life situations, which are typically in a state of flux. Every client's experience is embedded in a cultural context, which is a factor that makes each client's experience unique. Thus we may also inquire: How might Leon and Ann's culture and context influence their experience at work? The most effective counseling approach for Leon and Ann requires extending the postmodern perspective in general to career counseling in particular. *Postmodern Career Counseling: A Handbook of Culture, Context, and Cases* demonstrates how counselors can holistically apply postmodern career assessment and counseling to clients like Leon and Ann in their social and cultural contexts.

We believe there remains a need for scholarly publications within the counseling profession that highlight the usefulness of the most prominent career counseling models and methods derived from postmodern epistemologies and that also represent a range of diverse populations. For this book, we operationally define the phrase *postmodern career counseling* to include career counseling paradigms and processes derived from the epistemologies of contemporary psychological constructivism, social constructionism, and narrative. We adopt Savickas's (2011a) definition of *career counseling* as "career intervention that uses psychological methods to foster self-exploration as a prelude to choosing and adjusting to an occupation" (p. 151). We conceptualize *culture* as the personal meaning and interpretations clients ascribe to such variables as race, ethnicity, age, sex, sexual orientation, disability, religion/spirituality, socioeconomic status, and intersecting identities. *Context* denotes the influences and interactions that make and remake the individual, such as socioeconomic status, workplace, employment market, educational institutions, geographical location, peers, political decisions, family, historical trends, media, globalization, and community groups (culture, context, and intersecting identities are discussed in more detail in the Introduction). Thus, cultural context becomes essential as the labor force in the United States becomes more diverse, with marked increases in the number of women, non-White, immigrant, and older workers (Arabandi, 2015).

This text demonstrates how postmodern career counseling can meet the needs of individuals preparing for and participating in the new world of work, which has been shaped by the digital revolution and a global economy. The models and methods presented in this book are designed for clients who live in fluid societies, work in flexible organizations, and socialize in multicultural contexts. Within these chapters, you will find theory-based models and methods that students and practitioners may use to counsel clients who have difficulty coping with career transitions, career tasks such as occupational choice, and work traumas (e.g., layoff, illness, and termination).

Purpose of the Book

We have provided practitioner-friendly resources to help counselors, career practitioners, and students provide career counseling with diverse clients. Two foundational issues underlie the need for this book: (a) update existing career assessment and intervention to respond to the occupational landscape of the 21st century, and (b) expand the multicultural scope of career counseling through career models and processes drawing upon psychological constructivist and social constructionist epistemologies.

First, as the world of work has been restructured, there remains a need to help clients build meaning, build purpose, and revise identity by augmenting traditional career counseling with psychological constructivist and social constructionist principles. As Emmett and McAuliffe (2011) noted, "Constructivist career counseling is, in fact, the most relevant approach to contemporary career counseling in the context of current socioeconomic and workplace realities" (p. 210). Twentieth-century theories that helped guide and prepare people for careers, although quite useful for their time, benefit from being supplemented with a pattern of practices that fully address the needs of today's workers.

Second, career counseling must encompass broader conceptions of multicultural career counseling. Multiculturalism has become a potent force, stimulating counselors to understand the unique beliefs and truths people from different cultural groups construct about themselves and their life experiences. The 21st century has witnessed new models of career counseling designed for multicultural contexts. This new force, rooted in constructivism and social constructionism, has gained a substantial presence in career counseling and vocational psychology. Nevertheless, some may wonder about the place of multicultural career counseling models within these epistemologies.

Many of the postmodern career counseling models and methods presented in this book are culturally based because they draw upon constructivist and social constructionist epistemologies. Essentially, postmodern approaches in counseling and therapy inherently support and advance culturally sensitive career counseling and assessment (Leong & Hartung, 2000). To insert multicultural models into postmodern paradigms such as narrative, career construction, life design, systems theory, and relational career theory appears unnecessary because multiculturalism is intrinsically present—if applied within the spirit of the epistemology. Nevertheless, counselors should be alert to infusing cultural models such as cultural theory (e.g., Stead, 2004) into career counseling models and methods that privilege the constructivist or interpersonal dimension of career counseling.

The postmodern models and methods that utilize the constructivist or interpersonal dimension of postmodern career counseling may benefit from using the guiding principles of cultural theory to critique multicultural context. Cultural theory emphasizes the importance of language, meaning making, relationship, and power relations (Stead, 2004). The models and methods in this book are based on either a psychological constructivist or social constructionist epistemology, or both, and in varying degrees. Depending on degree, they pay attention to social context, sexual orientation, race, nationality, disability, age, religion/spirituality, and so on with social constructionism at the extreme. We encourage you to view these two epistemologies on a continuum and determine where the infusion of cultural models would be beneficial.

Postmodern career counseling is a philosophical and psychological framework from which to work. Career counseling becomes not so much a procedure but a philosophical framework for guiding the work of counselor and client. For example, such an expanded view reveals how clients entwine their personal narratives and identities with the stories that saturate their sociohistorical context (Savickas, 2011b). Counselors using postmodern models and methods seek to identify and give voice to the personal story, the local history, the grounded experience, and the marginalized instance. Pope (2010) suggested that "the nuances that lead to assisting adults in mastering their career issues are quite important and can be a detriment in achieving successful outcomes" (p. 731). Thus, we emphasize cultural context, relationship factors, the narrative paradigm, and qualitative assessment to help clients adapt to the changing nature of work in the 21st century. Although we provide examples of career and work issues with clients from various cultures, it is not possible to include examples from all cultures. In-depth discussion of cultures is beyond the scope of this book and can be found in other sources (e.g., Lee, 2013; Sue & Sue, 2016).

In this book, we detail the best practices of postmodern career counseling drawn from case studies and from the experiences of practitioners who apply the models and methods they present. It is important to note that postmodern career counseling is a way of thinking or a set of values, which are illustrated throughout this book as a range of possible approaches and activities that are consistent with psychological constructivist and social constructionist perspectives. In addition, we encourage graduate students, practitioners, and educators to use the models and methods as complementary to traditional career theories rather than as the sole intervention for client career and work-related concerns. The theoretical discussions in Parts I and II provide a foundation for the application chapters in Part III, but they also provide educators with a concise review of concepts and principles highlighted in career counseling courses, making this volume useful as a course text.

Unlike other books on career guidance or vocational behavior, our focus is not on research, nor do we provide a critical analysis of the epistemologies discussed. Practice precedes theory, so career theorists must stay close to practice (Savickas, 2011b). Given the alignment of constructivist and qualitative research, this book offers educators, students, and practitioners the necessary foundation to employ strategies of qualitative inquiry on postmodern career counseling. Because it emphasizes the importance of culture and context embedded in the lives of clients, qualitative research can establish a more empathic and closer connection to participants and provide a deeper understanding of their experiences (Gergen, 2015). We encourage methods of inquiry such as firsthand accounts, conversation analysis, discourse analysis, interviews, and narratives to examine the critical questions about working and career development in a postmodern era (Blustein, Kenna, Murphy, DeVoy, & DeWine, 2005). Our hope is that the procedural case study chapters in Part III provide the impetus toward further empirical inquiry.

We have avoided expressing a perspective rooted in extreme postmodern thought. We view the inclusion of postmodern career counseling as a holistic and integral approach to working with clients' career concerns. An extreme constructivist stance would say that all worldviews are arbitrary, all truth is relative and merely culture bound, and there are no universal truths (Wilber, 2000). But a diamond will cut glass, no matter what words we use for the diamond, and no matter what culture we find them in. Our view values pluralism, which embraces the partial truths contained in both the positivist and postpositivist positions (Wilber, 2000). We agree with Wilber's assertion that the goal of postmodern thought is to arrive at an inclusive, integral, and nonexclusionary embrace.

Overview of the Book

The chapters in this book discuss postmodern career counseling models and methods as ways to augment traditional approaches and enrich career counseling with diverse groups. It offers a fresh perspective. The authors have been vetted, invited, and edited to produce deep and accessible work. This handbook is divided into three parts, with an introductory chapter and a concluding chapter to bookend this material. The Introduction sets the scene for the material you will encounter in the book. Part I, Perspectives, introduces the underpinnings of postmodernism and its implications for career counseling. Part II, Principles, provides an overview of multicultural career counseling, social constructionism, and qualitative career counseling. Part III, Procedures, includes 17 chapters divided into three sections that demonstrate the process of postmodern career assessment and counseling intervention embedded in culture and context, each drawing on a client case vignette. The concluding chapter in the book offers some direction for teaching postmodern principles in career counseling.

Introduction

The introductory chapter helps counselors understand the occupational landscape of the 21st century. It provides a brief overview of postmodern career counseling and orients the reader to the message of postmodern thought for career counselors.

Part I: Perspectives

Part I addresses the underpinnings of postmodernism and its implications for career counseling. Chapter 1 introduces the reader to the necessity for and underlying concepts of postmodern thought in career counseling. Busacca traces the transformation in the social organization of work during the 20th century. In particular, he discusses how societal and organizational narratives within each work era provided external guides to help workers feel secure and also how these narratives have lost credibility. The chapter includes an overview of factors responsible for precarious work and how such work has diminished the standardized job, changed the psychological contract between worker and employer, and affected people's identities. In Chapter 2, McAuliffe and Emmett discuss the call for career counseling in counselor preparation from a postmodernist perspective. This chapter also discusses five dimensions of postmodern/constructivist career counseling and presents several core qualities of counselors who work from a postmodernist stance.

Part II: Principles

Part II offers an overview of the relationship between multicultural career counseling and postmodern perspectives in career counseling, a discussion of social constructionism and discourse analysis, and a discussion of the use of qualitative career assessment in career counseling. In Chapter 3, Evans and Kelchner present the limitations of traditional multicultural models of career counseling and the scope of multicultural training. In Chapter 4, Stead and Davis focus on social constructionism in career counseling. This chapter emphasizes that knowledge is socially constructed through discourse and is contextually embedded. Also discussed are the roles of power and dominant discourses in diverse clients' presenting of problems and how these may offer a springboard for alternative narratives in the co-construction of meaning in the career counseling relationship. In Chapter 5, Wood and Scully provide an overview of qualitative career assessment and discuss the advantages and potential challenges of qualitative career assessments, followed by an examination of the utilization of qualitative career assessments by the counselor and career practitioner.

Part III: Procedures

Part III provides the perspectives of experts who apply the presented models and methods. These 17 application chapters are organized into three sections based on epistemological perspective: social constructionist, constructivist, and narrative models; variants of social constructionist, constructivist, and narrative models; and systemic and integrative models. Each chapter includes a multicultural case vignette to demonstrate the principles and practices of the given assessment or intervention procedure. A "Practical Application Guide" is included at the end of each chapter to provide a quick way for the reader to search for and review a particular postmodern career counseling model of interest.

Chapters 6 through 16 demonstrate social constructionist, constructivist and narrative-based approaches to career counseling. Informed by the narrative method, Chapter 6 explains the application of the *My Career Story* autobiographical workbook with an African American high school student. Chapter 7 presents an application of the My Career Chapter with a Malaysian engineer. This narrative–autobiographical approach is based in psychological constructivism. Chapters 8 and 9 cover group-based modalities. Chapter 8 looks at constructivist group career counseling with low-income, first-generation college students. The method is based on the Life Design Group model and career construction theory. Chapter 9 presents the use of early recollections in providing career counseling interventions to offenders using a group format. Chapter 10 demonstrates narrative counseling through the storied approach to career co-construction with an older female client. Chapter 11 uses the genogram as a narrative-based intervention with an economically disadvantaged client, and Chapter 12 demonstrates the use of constructivist-based Life Role Analysis with a transgender client. Chapters 13 and 14 emphasize human subjectivity, meaning making, and individuality. Chapter 13 discusses an Asian American female in relation to personal construct psychology. Consistent with the personal construct system, Chapter 14 demonstrates the use of vocational card sorts with a Latina client, and Chapter 15 explores Possible Selves Mapping with a Mexican American prospective first-generation college student. Chapter 16 is drawn from life design theory and applies the Life Design Genogram to an Italian female transitioning to the world of work in the United States.

Chapters 17 through 19 demonstrate variants of social constructionist, constructivist, and narrative models. The term *variant* refers to models initially derived from either psychological constructivism or social constructionism but that divert from the more common models in theory integration and application. Chapter 17 illustrates a relational cultural career assessment and provides a holistic approach for gathering information to inform career counseling interventions. This model emphasizes the centrality of culture and other forms of diversity in relationships and is based in constructivist meaning-making principles and the social constructionist perspective. Chapter 18 demonstrates the use of solution-focused career counseling, which originated from constructivist thought, with a male military veteran. Chapter 19 presents an application of the One Life Tools narrative framework with an East Asian woman, using face-to-face and Web-based interactions. The framework is based on constructivist meaning-making principles and draws from various theories and models such as narrative, positive psychology, cognitive methods, happenstance approach, and chaos theory of careers.

Chapters 20 through 22 demonstrate systemic and integrative approaches to postmodern career counseling with an emphasis on contextualism. Chapter 20 presents an application of the My System of Career Influences (MSCI) with a Black South African adult male. The MSCI is metatheoretical, based on systems theory and guided by constructivist and narrative meaning-making principles. Chapter 21 uses the action theory of career assessment with clients with chronic illness and disability. Action theory is informed by the social constructionist perspective and narrative. Informed by constructivist meaning-making principles and systems theory, Chapter 22 applies the chaos theory of careers to the case of a female African American college student.

Conclusion

The concluding chapter, by Busacca and Rehfuss, summarizes the central concepts and themes inherent in postmodern career counseling discussed throughout this book and offers teaching suggestions for counselor educators and others who teach career counseling courses.

Some Final Thoughts

Our hope is that this collection of writings invites and inspires students, practitioners, and instructors of career counseling and those in counselor education to explore, apply, and teach postmodern career counseling in the cultures and contexts in which clients' working lives are embedded. Perhaps one of the case studies in this handbook will resonate with you. Whether you are beginning your journey in the counseling field or are a seasoned practitioner, this handbook will serve as a resource when you begin the task of helping yourself and others build work and career as an integral part of life imbued with meaning and purpose.

References

Arabandi, B. (2015). Globalization, flexibility and new workplace culture in the United States and India. In A. S. Wharton (Ed.), *Working in America: Continuity, conflict, and change in a new economic era* (4th ed., pp. 69–87). Boulder, CO: Paradigm.

Blustein, D., Kenna, A. C., Murphy, K. A., DeVoy, J. E., & DeWine, D. B. (2005). Qualitative research in career development: Exploring the center and margins of discourse about careers and working. *Journal of Career Assessment, 13,* 351–370.

Emmett, J., & McAuliffe, G. J. (2011). Teaching career development. In G. J. McAuliffe & K. Eriksen (Eds.), *Handbook of counselor preparation: Constructivist, developmental, and experiential approaches* (pp. 209–228). Thousand Oaks, CA: Sage.

Gergen, K. J. (2015). *An invitation to social construction* (3rd ed.). London, England: Sage.

Lee, C. C. (2013). *Multicultural issues in counseling: New approaches to diversity* (4th ed.). Alexandria, VA: American Counseling Association.

Leong, F. T. L., & Hartung, P. J. (2000). Adapting to the changing multicultural context of career. In A. Collin & R. A. Young (Eds.), *The future of career* (pp. 212–227). Cambridge, England: Cambridge University Press.

Pope, M. (2010). Career counseling with diverse adults. In J. G. Ponterotto, J. M. Casas, L. A. Suzuki, & C. M. Alexander (Eds.), *Handbook of multicultural counseling* (3rd ed., pp. 731–744). Thousand Oaks, CA: Sage.

Savickas, M. L. (2011a). *Career counseling.* Washington, DC: American Psychological Association.

Savickas, M. L. (2011b). New questions for vocational psychology: Premises, paradigms, and practices. *Journal of Career Assessment, 19,* 251–258.

Stead, G. B. (2004). Culture and career psychology: A social constructionist perspective. *Journal of Vocational Psychology, 64,* 389–406.

Sue, D. W., & Sue, D. (2016). *Counseling the culturally diverse: Theory and practice* (7th ed.). Hoboken, NJ: Wiley.

Wilber, K. (2000). *Integral psychology: Consciousness, spirit, psychology, therapy.* Boston, MA: Shambhala.

Louis A. Busacca, PhD, received his doctorate in counseling and human development from Kent State University and holds licensure as a professional counselor in Ohio and as a national certified counselor. He received special recognition as a master career counselor from the National Career Development Association (NCDA) and is certified in clinical rational hypnotherapy from the National Association of Cognitive-Behavioral Therapists.

He is currently an adjunct assistant professor of counseling and human services at Old Dominion University and college counselor and adjunct professor of psychology at Lakeland Community College. Prior to this, he was adjunct professor of counseling for Youngstown State University and an instructor at Northeast Ohio Medical University. Dr. Busacca has 7 years' experience as an administrator in higher education as program director for the U.S. Department of Education's TRiO Veterans Upward Bound in Cleveland, Ohio.

Dr. Busacca was a member of the board of directors for the Council for Accreditation of Counseling and Related Educational Programs (CACREP). He served as president of the Ohio Career Development Association and served on several committees for CACREP and American Counseling Association. He was on the editorial board of *Counselor Education and Supervision*, and the *Journal of Humanistic Counseling, Education and Development*, served as ad hoc reviewer for *The Career Development Quarterly*, and currently serves on the editorial board for the *Journal of Counselor Practice* of the Ohio Counseling Association. He is an active member of the American Counseling Association, NCDA, and Ohio Counseling Association.

Dr. Busacca's interests include postmodern paradigms in career counseling, counselor trainee development, counselor education and supervision, stress, coping and trauma, and the neurobiology of depression and anxiety. He has peer-reviewed publications in the areas of constructivist career counseling, career assessment and counseling, counselor trainee career development, and neurobiology in counselor preparation.

Mark C. Rehfuss, PhD, received his doctorate in counseling and human development from Kent State University and holds licensure as a professional clinical counselor in Ohio and as a professional counselor in Virginia. He is currently an associate professor and director of the human services distance program in the Department of Counseling and Human Services at Old Dominion University, Norfolk, Virginia.

Dr. Rehfuss is an editorial board member of *The Career Development Quarterly*, the *Journal of Employment Counseling*, and the *Virginia Counselors Journal* and is an ad hoc reviewer for the *Journal of Vocational Behavior*. He has served as chair of the NCDA Research Committee and as president of the Virginia Association for Counselor Education and Supervision, and is currently treasurer of the National Organization of Human Services. He has 21 years of experience in higher education administration, curriculum development, and counselor education. He has over 35 peer-reviewed publications and has delivered numerous professional presentations at international and national conferences.

Dr. Rehfuss's research interests include career counseling and guidance, narrative career interventions, counselor education and supervision, online learning, and the integration of the helping professions within family medicine.

Dr. Rehfuss is an active member of the American Counseling Association, NCDA, Association for Counselor Education and Supervision, and the Virginia Counseling Association.

About the Contributors

Tina Anctil, PhD, is department chair and an associate professor in the Department of Counselor Education at Portland State University. She is a certified rehabilitation counselor and licensed professional counselor. She directs the clinical rehabilitation counseling program and has been a practicing rehabilitation counselor for over 20 years. In her private practice, she specializes in career counseling with individuals with chronic illness and disability.

Susan R. Barclay, PhD, is an assistant professor and coordinator of the college student personnel services and administration graduate program at the University of Central Arkansas. She received her PhD in higher education from the University of Mississippi. Susan holds the GCDF-I certification, is a licensed professional counselor, and is an approved clinical supervisor. Her research interests include student success, career transitions, and the use of career construction techniques in multiple modalities.

Pamelia E. Brott, PhD, is an associate professor and program coordinator for school counseling in the Educational Psychology and Counseling Department at the University of Tennessee at knoxville. Her specific areas of interest are constructivist career counseling and qualitative assessments, the process of learning and becoming a counselor, and demonstrating counselor effectiveness. She has served as president of the Virginia Counselors Association and Virginia Career Development Association.

Janice A. Byrd, MEd, is a doctoral candidate in counselor education and supervision at the University of Iowa. She is a certified school counselor and global career development facilitator. Her research focuses on promoting social justice and multicultural competency in the fields of school counseling and career counseling.

Brittan L. Davis, MEd, is a doctoral candidate in the counseling psychology program at Cleveland State University. Her primary research interests include vocational psychology, relational cultural theory, social constructionist and postmodern feminist thought, sexual and gender transgressive minority concerns, intersectionality and identity politics, social justice, mentoring and supervisory relationships, and feminist multicultural and cross-cultural psychology.

Annamaria Di Fabio, PhD, is a professor of psychology of guidance and career counseling and organizational psychology at the University of Florence, where she is responsible for the Research and Intervention Laboratory of Psychology for Vocational Guidance and Career Counseling. She is editor of the scientific journal *Counseling. Giornale Italiano di Ricerca e Applicazioni* [*Counseling: Italian Journal of Research and Applications*] and coeditor of the French journal *Orientation Scolaire et Professionnelle*. She is general editor of the newsletter of the International Association for Educational and Vocational Guidance. She conducts research and intervention in the areas of counseling psychology, positive psychology, and work and organizational psychology.

Judy Emmett, PhD, is a professor emeritus at the University of Wisconsin–River Falls. She received her doctorate from Northern Illinois University. Her research and teaching have focused on constructivist career counseling and school counseling.

Kathy M. Evans, PhD, is an associate professor and counselor education program coordinator at the University of South Carolina. She is a licensed professional counselor and a national certified counselor. She has published widely in career counseling, including her textbook *Gaining Cultural Competence in Career Counseling*. She is the 2015–2018 trustee for counselor educators and researchers for the National Career Development Association.

Rich Feller, PhD, is a professor of counseling and career development and university distinguished teaching scholar at Colorado State University. He is a past president of the National Career Development Association and a recipient of its eminent award and fellow designation. With the help of many, he is author of numerous publications, assessment tools, and media products and programs.

Mark Franklin, MEd, leads CareerCycles, a career management social enterprise. A Stu Conger leadership award recipient, he developed the CareerCycles narrative method of practice and has authored related articles and book chapters. His MEd in counseling psychology and BSc are from the University of Toronto. He is a Canadian certified counselor and career management fellow.

Donna M. Gibson, PhD, is an associate professor and coordinator of the counselor education program at Virginia Commonwealth University. She also works as a part-time counselor. She earned her doctorate from the University of North Carolina at Greensboro. She is a licensed professional counselor and a national certified counselor.

Seth C. W. Hayden, PhD, is an assistant professor of counseling at Wake Forest University. Dr. Hayden has provided career and personal counseling in community agencies, secondary school, and university settings. Dr. Hayden's research focuses on the career and personal development of military service members, veterans, and their families. In addition, he explores the connection between career and mental health issues and integrated models of clinical supervision designed to facilitate positive growth in counselors' ability to formulate interventions. Dr. Hayden is a licensed professional counselor in North Carolina and Virginia, a national certified counselor, a certified clinical mental health counselor, and an approved clinical supervisor. In addition, Dr. Hayden is the past-president of the Association for Counselors and Educators in Government (ACEG), a division of the American Counseling Association and a cochair of the research committee for the National Career Development Associationn.

Jessica A. Headley, MA, is a licensed professional counselor in the state of Ohio and a doctoral candidate in the Counselor Education and Supervision Program at the University of Akron. She has coauthored numerous publications on women's and gender issues in counseling, serves as an editorial board member for journals that publish works on gender and multiculturalism, and has held numerous leadership positions in counseling organizations at the state and national levels. Her passion for transgender issues as they relate to career development is exemplified in her scholarship, teaching, and clinical practice.

Viki P. Kelchner, PhD, is an assistant professor at the University of Central Florida in the counselor education and school psychology department. She is a licensed professional counselor and licensed marriage and family therapist. Dr. Kelchner's research interest and publications focus on families, couples, and supporting at-risk youth and families through school-based family services and intervention programs.

Garrett J. McAuliffe, EdD, is a university professor of counselor education at Old Dominion University in Norfolk, Virginia. He has been a career counselor. He wrote his dissertation on social learning and career decision making, for which he won the national outstanding dissertation award. He is the author of six books on topics ranging from cultural dimensions of counseling to the teaching of counseling.

Peter McIlveen, PhD, teaches and researches career development and vocational psychology at the University of Southern Queensland, Australia. He is a psychologist and a member of the Australian Psychological Society's College of Counselling Psychologists and the Career Development Association of Australia.

Mary McMahon, PhD, is a senior lecturer in the school of education at the University of Queensland, Brisbane, Australia, where she teaches career development theory and narrative career counseling. Professor McMahon has published several books, book chapters, and refereed journal articles nationally and internationally. She researches how people construct their careers across the life span and has a particular interest in the use of storytelling and qualitative career assessment in career counseling.

Rebecca E. Michel, PhD, is an assistant professor within the division of psychology and counseling at Governors State University, where she teaches and conducts research on career development. She is a licensed clinical professional counselor. As a strengths-based educator, she is passionate about helping people discover and capitalize on their unique personal strengths to enhance educational and career success across the life span.

Delila Lashelle Owens, PhD, is an associate professor and coordinator of school counseling at the University of Akron. She received her doctorate in counselor education from Michigan State University. Dr. Owens is a licensed school counselor in Ohio and a licensed professional counselor. She is a member of the National Career Development Association's editorial board.

Wendy Patton, PhD, is an executive dean in the faculty of education at Queensland University of Technology, Brisbane, Australia. Dr. Patton has taught and researched in the areas of career development and counseling for more than 20 years. She has coauthored and coedited a number of books and is currently series editor of the Career Development Series with Sense Publishers. She has published widely, with more than 150 refereed journal articles and book chapters. She serves on a number of national and international journal editorial boards.

Sneha Pitre, MA, is a counseling psychology doctoral student at Cleveland State University. She received her MA in counseling psychology from the University of Mumbai, India. Her research interests include multicultural counseling, vocational psychology, advisory and mentoring relationship within academia, international students, and immigrant-related issues.

Varunee Faii Sangganjanavanich, PhD, is an associate professor in the Department of Counseling at the University of Akron and a licensed professional clinical counselor with supervisor endorsement in the state of Ohio. She has authored and coauthored numerous peer-reviewed journal articles, encyclopedia entries, and book chapters in the fields of career counseling and development and transgender counseling. She has served as an editorial board member of many peer-reviewed counseling and career development journals and has held multiple leadership positions in state and national counseling organizations.

Mark B. Scholl, PhD, is an associate professor of counseling at Wake Forest University. He has extensive clinical experience in both career and mental health counseling. His primary research interests involve examining culturally responsive approaches to counseling and supervision, existential counseling and psychotherapy, constructivist approaches to counseling, and career counseling with the ex-offender population and individuals with disabilities. He has served as president of the Association for Humanistic Counseling, is an associate editor of the *Journal of College Counseling,* and has served as editor of the *Journal of Humanistic Counseling, Education and Development.*

Donna Schultheiss, PhD, is a professor of counseling psychology at Cleveland State University. She received the John Holland Award for Outstanding Achievement in Career and Personality Research by Division 17 of the American Psychological Association and the award for most outstanding research contribution in *The Career Development Quarterly.*

Zachary Scully, MEd, is a doctoral candidate in the counseling program at Old Dominion University. He has a master's in counseling and career development from Colorado State University. He is currently director of the Career and Academic Resource Center in the Darden College of Education. Previously he was the bilingual career counselor and outreach coordinator at University of Northern Colorado career services, Greeley, Colorado.

Graham B. Stead, PhD, is the director of doctoral studies in the College of Education and Human Services at Cleveland State University, Cleveland, Ohio. His research interests are in vocational psychology, social constructionism, discourse analysis, critical psychology, cultural psychology, statistics, and meta-analysis.

Kevin B. Stoltz, PhD, is an associate professor in the Department of Leadership Studies at the University of Central Arkansas. He is a national certified counselor and approved clinical supervisor. His research interests include career development and counseling, career assessment with early recollections, career transition, and career adaptability.

Cassandra A. Storlie, PhD, is an assistant professor of counselor education and supervision at Kent State University. She earned her doctorate from the University of Iowa. She is a professional clinical counselor-supervisor and a national certified counselor. Her research includes career development and career counseling of marginalized populations, specifically documented and undocumented Latinos/as and those with disabilities.

Jennifer M. Taylor, PhD, is an assistant professor of counseling psychology and counseling at West Virginia University. Her research interests include professional competence, multicultural competence, vocational psychology and career counseling, continuing professional development, mentoring, training issues, continuing education, and lifelong learning. She currently serves as vice chair of the Continuing Education Committee of the American Psychological Association.

Julia V. Taylor, MA, is a licensed school counselor and counselor education and supervision doctoral student at Virginia Commonwealth University. She has published numerous books on relational aggression and body image that have been used by school counselors nationally.

Mark Watson, PhD, is a distinguished professor at the Nelson Mandela Metropolitan University, South Africa. Dr. Watson teaches, researches, and practices in the field of career development, counseling, and assessment. He has coauthored and coedited a number of books and published 85 refereed journal articles and 67 book chapters. He serves on several international journal editorial boards.

Christopher Wood, PhD, is an associate professor in the counseling program at the University of Nevada, Las Vegas. He has been involved in more than a dozen research projects totaling more than $3 million in grants that investigated the efficacy of career development interventions in Kindergarden–Grade 12 settings. Dr. Wood is currently editor of the *Professional School Counseling* journal, and he coedited the fifth and sixth editions of *A Counselor's Guide to Career Assessment Instruments.*

Acknowledgments

We thank all the contributors to this project and the American Counseling Association for making this book a reality. Thank you to Dr. Mark Savickas and Dr. Paul Hartung for their generous and helpful consultations. Our editorial assistants are Charlie Loudin and Suzanne Savickas.

Introduction

Postmodern Career Counseling: A New Perspective for the 21st Century

Louis A. Busacca and Mark C. Rehfuss

"The teller of a story is primarily, none the less, the listener to it,
the reader of it too."

—Henry James

As society has moved from the high modernity of the 20th century to the postmodernity of the 21st century, existing career theories no longer adequately account for the uncertain and rapidly changing occupational structure. The nature of work and the meaning of career have been restructured and reinvented over the last three decades. Shaped by a global economy and propelled by information technology, the new social arrangement is characterized by uncertain, unpredictable, and risky employment opportunities (Kalleberg, 2009). In addition, organizational restructuring has increasingly altered the mutual expectations between employee and employer, making it difficult for workers to adapt to the changing demands of the new psychological contract (Conway & Briner, 2005). Consequently, many companies today expect their employees to take responsibility for the direction and evolution of their own career pathways (M. B. Arthur & Rousseau, 1996). As established paths and societal narratives disappear, individuals are forced to assume increased responsibility for managing their own lives, which leaves some feeling anxious, depressed, and frustrated.

The transformation that has occurred during postmodern times has made career choices more difficult. In a postmodern era, identities no longer provide

1

meaning as they once did, making occupational commitments problematic (Richardson, 2015). Commitment to an occupational choice is difficult due to lack of stability in social structures. As suggested by Savickas et al. (2009), "Clients and counselors should not concentrate on choice in a world where there is much uncertainty and fewer choices. Instead, they should concentrate on meaning-making through intentional processes in the ongoing construction of lives" (p. 246). This requires that young people, with less external guidance, prepare for life based on their own decisions about purpose and values and that they reflect on their interests, goals, and responsibilities. Some individuals lack a stable framework and may benefit from the collaboration of counselors who understand the occupational landscape of the 21st century.

Postmodern career counseling offers a new paradigm with which to understand the diversity in people's careers and vocational behavior. Twentieth-century theories, which helped guide and prepare people for careers and were quite useful in their time, are more useful today when supplemented by a pattern of practices that fully addresses the needs of today's workers. Career counseling informed by psychological constructivism and social constructionism responds to the call to innovate the modern paradigm for career theory and intervention (Savickas, 2011a). The career models and methods presented in this book are designed for workers who live in fluid societies, work in flexible organizations, and socialize in multicultural contexts.

Precarious Work in a Postmodern Era

New social arrangements of work in the United States and in Western Europe during the last few decades have made career progression more difficult for many people. Organizational restructuring for lower costs and greater efficiencies has resulted in layoffs, unanticipated transfers, offshoring (i.e., contracting out the performance of service sector activities to businesses located beyond U.S. borders), career destabilization, and nonstandardized work contracts (Inkson & Elkin, 2008). Yet, for many people, such transformation results in what Kalleberg (2009) denoted as precarious work or "employment that is uncertain, unpredictable, and risky from the point of view of the worker" (p. 2). Standing (1999) described sources of work insecurity to include loss of a job or fear of losing a job, lack of alternative employment opportunities, and diminished freedom to obtain and maintain particular skills and to advance in a position. According to Standing, possible effects of insecurity include a sense of oppression and exploitation, demoralization, demotivation, and ill health. In the past, precarious work was often described in terms of a dual labor market, with unstable and uncertain jobs concentrated in the secondary labor market (low-skilled, low-wage jobs requiring relatively little training with high labor turnover). Today, precarious work and insecurity have spread to the primary sector of the economy (higher grade, higher status, and better paid jobs) and have become much more pervasive and generalized.

According to data from the Current Population Survey, employment in white-collar occupations accounts for more than one half of total U.S. employment. Some 9 out of 10 white-collar workers are employed in the service sector (e.g., as cooks and servers, cleaners and maintenance workers, hairdressers, child care workers, and police and firefighters), and these jobs represent about four fifths of total U.S. employment (Levine, 2005). This has resulted in a changing mix of occupations, reflected in a decline in blue-collar jobs and an increase in high- and low-wage white-collar occupations. Nevertheless, many white-collar workers also have experienced a transformation in secure employment due to organizational restructuring. Whether this uncertainty affects more white- or blue-collar workers, we face a transformation in which occupation and employment no longer serve to grade and group people to the extent or in the same way that was possible under industrialism. Our interest is in understanding the meaning of the postmodern transformation on individuals today and in presenting this as a trend to help counselors comprehend its characteristics.

Three primary features characterize the difficulty individuals encounter with precarious work. First, permanent jobs increasingly are in short supply in the United States, forcing workers to be part of a temporary workforce. For the most part, during the industrial period jobs were characterized by standardized employment contracts: Individuals worked full-time for a single employer and had opportunities to advance gradually in responsibility and pay (Kalleberg & Leicht, 2002). Today many firms are organized around a nonstandardized employment model, which is a form of flexibility that advocates for a small group of core workers in managerial positions who are augmented by an adjustable number of peripheral workers who make up a contingent, part-time, and temporary workforce (Arabandi, 2015; Kalleberg, 2009). This type of flexibility reduces vertical hierarchies while increasing horizontal management practices within an organization, providing fewer workers with an opportunity for advancement (Arabandi, 2015).

The second feature of the transformation of work arrangements describes the general decline in the average length of time workers remain with their employers. Rather than developing a stable life based on secure employment, most workers today change jobs every 5 years (Bureau of Labor Statistics, 2015). The general assumption has been that a "career" consisted of a succession of permanent, full-time, five-days-a-week, 9-to-5 jobs, which was a value held within hierarchical societies. Now individuals can expect to occupy at least 11 jobs during their lifetime, in part because of being a displaced worker. In particular, the average person born in the later years of the baby boom in the United States (1957–1964) held an average of 11.7 jobs between age 18 and age 48, with nearly half of these jobs being held before age 25 (Bureau of Labor Statistics, 2015). Moreover, among jobs started by 40- to 48-year-olds, the Bureau reported that 32% ended in less than a year, and 69% ended in fewer than 5 years. Related to this decline in length of employment is the change in psychological contracts between employee and employer.

A salient trend confronting the contemporary workforce is the new employment relationship between workers and their employers. This has been referred to by organizational psychologists as the *psychological contract* (Rousseau, 1998). Long-term employment with one organization has become increasingly rare and is characterized by individuals willing to move from job to job. In the 1950s, there was a relational implicit contract (legal in the case of unions) between employee and employer. Workers traded their work hours, labor, and commitment for what was frequently a lifetime job or at least the steady income and job security geared to seniority. Today the psychological contract has been steadily replaced by the transactional explicit contract, and fewer workers can count on guaranteed job security, regardless of their occupational status (Conway & Briner, 2005). For many peripheral workers today, hiring is based in an "at-will" employment relationship, which is predominant in almost all states within the United States. An employer can terminate an at-will employee at any time for any reason, except an illegal one, or for no reason without incurring legal liability; also an employer can change the terms of the employment relationship with no notice and no consequences (Stone, 2007). Workers increasingly feel like independent contractors, having to chart their own career paths. As a result, fewer workers now offer total loyalty to their employers.

The third primary feature involves a change in standardized work hours. Paid work is no longer based on holding a position but on producing a project (Savickas, 2011b). As workers shift from one assignment to another, work schedules change as well, and workers are expected to adjust their hours accordingly. This work role unpredictability has had subsequent effects on family, community, and leisure. Technology and flexibility have intensified work to such an extent that overwork is valued in American culture (Sweet & Meiksins, 2008). For example, if employees do not spend long hours in the office, they fear it might be interpreted as a lack of commitment to the job and might reflect negatively on their aspirations for promotion. Job insecurity and nonstandardized work contracts have heightened anxiety about job loss and unemployment, placing increased demands on workers' performance and productivity (Crowley, Tope, Chamberlain, & Hodson, 2010). These new 21st-century workplace arrangements require career interventions to help people keep pace with the changing structure of work.

The Postmodern Turn in Career Counseling

The postmodern turn in career counseling involves a fundamental change in direction that follows a logical path through its history. In response to the massive changes taking place in the world of work, by the beginning of the 21st century many of the core concepts in vocational psychology were being reexamined and broadened, and new theories were being proposed. The importance of individuals becoming more self-directed in making meaning of the role of work in their lives and managing their careers increased (Richardson, 1996). Career theories and interventions have evolved over time to keep pace with the changing needs of society.

Career counseling paradigms emanated from a perspective taken by society during particular historical periods. As suggested by Guichard (2015), the dominant theories and interventions of career counseling reflect contemporary societal, political, and economic conditions. Yet, as counselors attempted to apply these patterns of practice in their work with clients, career interventions proved insufficient as social, technological, and global changes affected people's working lives. Given the changes in work, career and vocational scholars have proposed a redefinition of the word *career* to fit the postmodern economy.

To understand the turn to postmodern career counseling, we need to look briefly at three major waves of career theory and intervention (see Hartung, 2013, for a discussion of the major waves). The first wave, initiated in the early 1900s, concerned matching people to jobs (Holland, 1959; Parsons, 1909; Roe, 1956). The second wave, beginning in the mid-20th century, focused on managing worker and other life roles over the life span (Super, 1957, 1980). The third wave, introduced toward the end of the first decade of the 21st century, involves career counseling models and methods with a central focus on meaning making (e.g., Savickas, 2005). The turning point for the third wave of career services was marked by a key event in the history of career counseling and vocational psychology.

In 1994, at the inaugural conference of the Society for Vocational Psychology, Arnold Spokane posed this question: Where is the counseling in career counseling? Two major paradigms for career intervention were in use in the 20th century: vocational guidance and career education. Holland's (1959) congruence theory of vocational personality types and work environments brought the matching model to its peak. Vocational guidance rests on enhancing self-knowledge, increasing occupational information, and securing occupational fit. The overriding goal of vocational guidance was to promote the adjustment outcomes of success, satisfaction, and stability (Savickas, 2011b). Career education rests on a predictable trajectory of developmental tasks. Educational methods orient students, young adults, and groups to imminent tasks of vocational development and ways to cope with them (Savickas, 2011b). The Career Maturity Inventory–Revised (Crites & Savickas, 1996) was designed to measure career attitudes and competencies (Busacca & Taber, 2002), or readiness to engage in career tasks. For example, teaching and fostering the mature attitudes and competencies required to prepare students for a career can help in the transition from high school to college or to the work world. Although useful for preparing individuals for imminent and predictable career tasks, career education cannot be expanded to address the needs of flexible organizations and fluid societies (Savickas, 2011b).

Vocational guidance and career education interventions were successful solutions to the pressing social needs of their times. Vocational guidance met a societal need in the early to mid-20th century as a result of the changes in work organization and in the scientific models within which research questions were formulated (Guichard, 2015). Career education, based on Super's (1957) theory of vocational development, emerged in the mid-20th century to address the question of how to advance a career in one hierarchical organization or profession. Career education relates to predictability, stability, and societal expectations. When Super approached the relationship between individuals and work from a developmental perspective, a new form of work organization appeared as a consequence of production automation. That is, long-standing work teams formed a functional network (Dubar, 1998), and employers offered their loyal employees a career within a hierarchical organization wherein they could climb the ladder of success.

Because developmental career theory is rooted in assumptions of stability of personal characteristics and secure jobs in bounded organizations, a career was conceptualized as a progressive sequence of stages. Concepts such as vocational identity, career planning, career development, and career stages were each used to help people advance in work environments with relatively high stability and clear career paths. Although valuable and effective for their intended purpose, these theories do not adequately account for the uncertain and rapidly changing occupational structure today—nor do they address the needs of peripheral workers (Savickas, 2011b). A focus on career counseling rather than on career development became the distinguishing feature of the postmodern move in career theory and intervention.

Career counseling, the third wave, began to distinguish itself from vocational guidance and career education primarily through the integration of a process-oriented, subjective, and emotional domain. Vocational scholars such as Miller-Tiedeman and Tiedeman (1990) began to challenge the objective views of career development evident in earlier theories. Tiedeman has been described as the first postmodern career counselor (Richmond, Savickas, Harris-Bowlsbey, Feller, & Jepsen, 2006). The subjective process of career development focuses more on the characteristics of a quality counseling relationship (Bedi, 2004; Granvold, 1996). Because emotions are embedded in all aspects of the client's experiences, the subjective nature of emotion is particularly suited to career theory and to the emphasis on intervention in psychological constructivism and social constructionism (Hartung, 2011). Emotions show prominently in motivational processes related to career counseling methods such as narrative career counseling, use of early recollections, career construction counseling, and areas of life designing. The move from individual differences and resemblance of types to individuality, uniqueness, and context has begun. The emphasis on the subjective aspects of career choice and development became known as *career counseling*, and it generated a paradigm shift in vocational guidance.

As a result of this shift in the career field, new theories, propositions, and discussions emerged. An identifiable collection of career counseling models infused with narrative, psychological constructivism, and social constructionism can be organized into three categories. One category contains models based in psychological constructivism, such as sociodynamic counseling (Peavy, 2010), career construction theory (Busacca, 2007; Savickas, 2005), narrative career counseling (Cochran, 1997), personal constructs (G. J. Neimeyer, 1992), and active engagement (Amundson, 2003). A second category contains social constructionist and systemic models, such as life designing (Savickas et al., 2009), the systems theory framework of careers (Patton & McMahon, 2006), the relational theory of working (Blustein, 2011), chaos theory (Pryor & Bright, 2011), and the action theory of careers (Young & Valach, 2004). A third category contains models primarily based in narrative, such as Savickas's (2011b) career counseling, the storied approach (Brott, 2001), and narrative career counseling (Cochran, 1997). Many of these models are demonstrated in Part III of this book. Table I.1 highlights and contrasts the conceptual and pragmatic shifts from traditional career services provided during the modern era to the postmodern career counseling of today.

The Message of Postmodern Thought for Career Counseling

Postmodernism has, in part, influenced psychological constructivist and social constructionist epistemology in career counseling and vocational psychology. The message of postmodern thought provides the assumptions underlying postmodern career counseling. In this section, we first provide a brief contrast between two epistemologies: realism and constructivism. Second, we discuss the concept of meaning and how it is personally and socially constructed. Last, we explain how cultural context has become increasingly essential as individuals have become disconnected from the established paths and narratives that once guided their career progression.

Underlying Assumptions

An important aspect of philosophical inquiry as it applies to career counseling concerns the study of how ideas and meaning are generated. Each of the career models discussed previously originates from a point of view that encompasses shared assumptions, common understandings, and collective values (Savickas, 2015). This epistemology validates the source of knowledge or what we know about career issues, counseling orientations, and interventions. Writers tend to refer to epistemologies when discussing postmodern career counseling. A brief look at two epistemological foundations—realism and constructivism—illustrates the assumptions underlying the constructivist and social constructionist perspectives.

For most of the 20th century, the career field embraced realism. The foundational assumption of realism (also called *modernism*) is that an actual reality, with particular enduring properties, exists that is independent from those who observe it (Erwin, 1999). That is, reality represents what we know. Realism, as applied to counseling, denotes that counselors can objectively observe clients and come to know particular truths about them. A counselor uses a map or a theory, hypothesis, idea, table, or representation in general of the objective world. Once a client's experience is understood, the coun-

Table I.1

*Parameters for Distinguishing Career Counseling
During Modern and Postmodern Eras*

Parameter	Modernity	Postmodernity
Era	1900–1980s (late modernity)	1980s–present
Philosophy		
Worldview	Mechanism; organicism	Contextualism, postmodernism
Epistemology	Realism	Psychological constructivism, social constructionism
Truth	Objectivity; verifiable, demand singular truths	Perspectivity; viable, appreciate multiple realities
View of self	Separate, isolated	Embedded, situated
View of culture	Monocultural	Pluralistic, contextual, relational
Language	Representational, language reflects reality	Formative, language produces reality
Employment		
Socioeconomic era	Industrial and corporate	Information and global
Labor market	Permanent workers	Contingent workers
Jobs	Standardized jobs	Nonstandardized assignments
Psychological contracts	Implicit	Explicit
Elements of Career Counseling		
Career service area	Vocational guidance; career education; career development; career placement; career coaching	Career counseling
Cultural stance	Multicultural counseling, monolithic, universal	Culture centered; context sensitive, intersecting identities
Core facets of counseling	Career maturity, occupational fit, decision making, developmental tasks	Adaptability, meaning, purpose, usefulness, life stories, themes, identities, reflexivity, active agency, relationship
Nature of assessment	Quantitative; norms referenced, interpreting scores, statistical, linear	Qualitative; idiographic, clinical judgment, nonstatistical, flexible, holistic
Forms of assessment	Interest inventories and ability tests	Card sorts, timelines, reptest, genograms, early recollections, story, narrative, metaphor
Phases of counseling	Clear cut, linear	Overlapping, holistic
Counselor use of language	Conventional	Relational
Motivational process	Reason	Emotion
Counselor role	Prescriptive; expert	Dialogue; shared meaning
Client role	Passive	Collaborative
Therapeutic relationship	Content oriented	Process oriented
Ethical decision making	Responsibility of the counselor	Dialogue between counselor and client

selor can draw on a map to impart an intervention. For example, vocational guidance emphasizes norm-based inventories such as the STRONG and Self-Directed Search. Realism in counseling and psychology also relies on quantitative research and psychometrics. The critique of modernism does not challenge its validity but the omission of the process. That is, it leaves out the mapmaker (the subject) who may bring something to the picture (Wilber, 2000). Consequently, the postmodern movement has increasingly challenged the basic assumptions of modernism (Sexton, 1997).

The way the term *postmodern* is used has become so convoluted that confusion may exist regarding its meaning. In general, postmodernists believe that individuals construct meaning or perceive their own reality or truth (R. A. Neimeyer & Stewart, 2000). This contrasts with the modernist assumption that an external and objective meaning can be discovered. Postmodernism is at the leading edge of today's cultural evolution, and the goal of postmodernity in the social and behavioral sciences can be summarized as an attempt to be more inclusive and to avoid marginalizing the many voices and viewpoints that modernity has often overlooked (Wilber, 2000). Career and vocational scholars have turned to the counseling and psychotherapy literature, where the influence of various offshoots of postmodern thought such as psychological constructivism (e.g., Maturana & Varela, 1988) and social constructionism (e.g., Berger & Luckmann, 1966) has gained significance in recent years.

Since the 1980s, career counseling has increasingly infused its theories and practices with the epistemologies of psychological constructivism and social constructionism. These perspectives emphasize subjectivity, appreciate multiple perspectives, acknowledge multiple truths, value interpretive or qualitative research, and emphasize context (Watson & McMahon, 2004). As a response to the modernist tradition, which highlighted the notion of the self-contained individual with measureable traits, the postmodern conceptualization of career represents a unique interaction of self and social experience (Young & Collin, 2004). Both constructivism and social constructionism emphasize certain features of postmodern thought.

The similarities between psychological constructivism and social constructionism are much greater than their differences. The postmodern era describes a world that is in part a construction or an interpretation in which meaning is context dependent. Both view reality as relative to social interaction and the social context rather than as completely objective and waiting to be discovered. The words *constructivism* and *constructionism* frequently have been used interchangeably in the literature, with constructivism often referring to both. Constructivism is a perspective that arose in developmental and cognitive psychology, whereas constructionism is derived from multidisciplinary sources such as sociology, literary studies, and postmodern approaches. Constructivism focuses on meaning making and construing the social and psychological worlds through individual cognitive processes, or how we develop meaning. Constructivism posits a highly individualistic approach with minimal reference to social interaction, context, and discourse, which Young and Collin (2004) asserted are important factors that make self-reflection and meaning making possible. This limitation is being addressed by social constructionism, which emphasizes that the social and psychological worlds are made real (constructed) through social processes and interaction.

It may be useful to think of psychological constructivism and social constructionism as windows or perspectives for how counselors view and approach a client's experience and reality. These two perspectives have emerged relatively recently and are still evolving (Young & Collin, 2004); they can be placed on a continuum from constructivist to social constructionist with offshoots and variations. We do not recommend viewing these perspectives as mutually exclusive because ambiguity exists. The postmodern career models and methods in this book may be rooted in one of these perspectives or in both. Although each of the career counseling models focuses on different aspects and has a different name, they all originate from either a constructivist or social constructionist epistemology, or both, or may be classified as a variant. Given these assumptions, both perspectives concentrate on meaning making.

The Construction of Meaning

Individuals build their careers by imposing meaning on their vocational behavior. Certainly, many individuals identify the work role as an important source of meaning in their lives (Baum & Stewart, 1990). For individuals who view their work as having more than just an economic value, purpose is considered to be at the center of their career satisfaction (Kosine, Steger, & Duncan, 2008). To succeed in a postmodern world of work, personal meaning must be present because it structures an individual's career as it plays out across the various jobs a worker can expect to occupy during her or his work life. Individuals must identify a purpose for doing the work they do to maintain their motivation. As Savickas (2011b) noted, meaning is embedded within intentions, and intention denotes having a purpose in mind as one acts. At a general level, *meaning* can be defined as "the sense made of, and significance felt regarding, the nature of one's being and existence" (Dik & Duffy, 2012, p. 65). The models and methods in this book value the concept of meaning at their core and demonstrate how meaning is personally construed and socially constructed.

The emphasis on personal meaning draws inspiration and support from the constructivist perspective. According to Young and Collin (2004), meaning making results from constructing the social and psychological worlds through individual cognitive processes. Likewise, the social constructionists emphasize that the social and psychological worlds are made real through social processes and interaction. Postmodern career models and methods informed by these epistemologies facilitate the meaning-making process for clients. The counselor explores how clients can elaborate on and evaluate their meanings relative to their intentions, rather than attempting to match people to occupations based on their decisions.

Postmodern career counseling also distinguishes meaning making from matchmaking. From a postmodern perspective, individual difference variables do not exist for the client; they exist within the counselor's objective view. For example, postmodern career counselors rely more on autobiography, meaning making, and qualitative assessment than on interest inventories and guidance techniques (Savickas, 1993). Qualitative career assessment as an idiographic subjective process is the preferred method of assessment. Qualitative career assessment is grounded in constructivism, with a focus on meaning making and an understanding that the client's contextual experiences are continually evolving (Whiston & Rahardja, 2005). Many of the dominant career models in the positivist tradition do not support the individual's meaning-making process and personal constructs. These interventions aim to help clients discover meaning that they are not yet aware of but that is already present.

In contrast, postmodern career models and methods help clients create personal meaning. Meaning making, through dialogue and relationship with a counselor, becomes an objective framed in terms of how it can be useful for the client. The central intervention goal of career counseling is narratability, helping clients reflect on and retell their own stories to foster meaning (Savickas, 2011b). Narrative helps clients create alternative meanings and new knowledge that open up possibilities. The postmodern concepts of personal meaning making extend to language as well.

Use of Language

The power of language in constructing meaning offers an important contribution to postmodern career counseling. Counselors view language not as a tool for uncovering a client's true self, or solely as a reflection of clients' subjective perceptions, but as an active process in constructing identity and meaning in therapeutic conversations (Watson, 2011). As such, language is viewed in a relational rather than a conventional sense. The strategic use of language to elicit new meanings, expand perspectives, and encourage change is central to the postmodern perspective. Bird's (2004) concept of relational language making positions the self of the client in relation to his or her feelings, thoughts, characteristics, personality traits, and actions. For example, when externalizing a problem, a client may use totalizing language: "I am a failure at work." The traditional counselor would help the client view failure as a separate problem with a life of its own. In relational externalizing, however, the counselor helps move the client's words and phrases from individual contexts of meaning toward a relational language in a collaborative way. The counselor may respond, "The failure, letdown feelings you notice in relation to your employer not providing you with an interview for the full-time position. . . ." In this case, a shift from meaning construed by self to meaning construed in relationship provides a form of inquiry that locates the client's interaction and experiences within the contextual environment that has shaped the self (Watson, 2011). Thus, the use of language goes from reflecting reality to producing reality and meaning.

Culture and Context

Postmodern career counseling embraces all expressions of diversity. Whether clients are from ethnic minority populations, are immigrants from other countries, live in the Little Italy of a major city, are military veterans, or are transgender students attending a university, career counseling needs to take place within the individual's cultural context. Cultural context becomes increasingly essential as the labor force becomes more diverse, with marked increases in the number of women, non-White and immigrant workers, and older workers (Arabandi, 2015). It is important to understand four features of culture and context in postmodern career counseling, as these features provide a unique perspective from which to counsel clients who experience difficulty in work and career.

First, the dialogue in multicultural career counseling has evolved from a monocultural to a pluralistic perspective of culture. The postmodern perspective includes not only race and ethnicity but also gender, sexual orientation, disability, age, religion, and spirituality—along with multiple or intersectional identities. *Intersectionality* refers to the assumption that one cannot understand any one of these identities in isolation; they must be considered in combination (Cole, 2009). This draws attention to diversity within categories. Nevertheless, both the constructivist and social constructionist principles go beyond group membership. Although the influence of social and political forces on clients' lives and careers is important, the focus of counseling emphasizes the meaning and interpretations of culture rather than the experiences of clients fixed to group membership (N. Arthur, 2006). Thus, career counselors take a universalistic stance, which assumes that every client has a unique cultural background embedded in and influenced by context.

The second feature views individual career behavior as relative to the contexts in which it occurs. Psychological constructivism and social constructionism have made inroads in career counseling, but many career theories have been informed by organicism or mechanism, or both (Collin & Young, 1986). The mechanistic worldview attempts to explain phenomena in mechanical terms, and the organismic worldview sees human development as an orderly, maturational, unfolding process. Counselors ascribing to these views believe individuals can be studied separately from their environments, and, consequently, the contexts within individuals' work become less important than their actions (Watson, 2006). Contextualism opposes these views.

The contextualist worldview is reflected in social constructionist epistemology. It considers knowledge about ourselves that is derived from social interaction and the active nature of individuals. This differs from the organismic model, which takes a passive view of people, claiming that some unfolding developmental process underlies change. Contexts provide the influences and interactions that make and remake the individual. Contextual variables that can have an influence on a client include socioeconomic status, workplace, employment market, educational institutions, geographical location, peers, political decisions, family, historical trends, media, globalization, and community groups. For example, two clients may grow up in the same town and culture but have vastly different contextual exposures, expectations, and perspectives. Context also consists of multiple complex connections and interrelationships, the significance of which is interpreted from the client's perspective (Young, Valach, & Collin, 2002). Career counselors who value a contextual worldview understand development and change as resulting from an ongoing process of interaction between the client and his or her environment (Ford, 1987; Steenbarger, 1991).

The third feature examines the linkages between culture and social justice through discourse analysis. Discourse analysis moves beyond social constructionism, not only acknowledging the construction of phenomena through language but underscoring how language is ruled by the hierarchies of discourse, including structures of power, ideology, and knowledge (Stead & Bakker, 2010). This view of culture moves from the dominant social discourse concerned with power relations to more contextual processes concerned with local occurrences of behavior. That is, counselors shift the focus from society's story for how people should live and work in the United States to the client's individual story (see Chapter 1). Blustein (2006) postulated that many traditional career theories and models appear irrelevant to some groups because they remain based on cultural assumptions that emphasize freedom of choice, affluence, the centrality of the work role, and notions of career success. The social justice perspective requires that counselors encourage clients to give voice to their experiences of oppression and to examine how dominant discourses have framed their career experiences (Blustein, Schultheiss, & Flum, 2004). For example, approaches that use narrative or autobiographical methods empower clients from traditionally oppressed groups, because this exploration broadens and validates their perspective. Some of the postmodern career models and methods in this book emphasize the development of narratives in one's local context.

The fourth feature explores the ways work is rooted in a relational context. Relational theory builds on the social constructionist perspective, which proposes that people learn about themselves, their social world, and culture through relationships (Blustein, 2011). The relational understanding of work and career enriches traditional career counseling practice by acknowledging the potential adaptive function of interpersonal connection in approaching career transitions, career choice, and work traumas (e.g., Schultheiss, 2003). Yet some multicultural theories have persisted in their use of value orientation models, which are deeply entrenched in individualistic dominant discourses. For example, postmodernists have challenged constructs such as locus of control and the Western concept of individualism and self-reliance in the workplace (Kvale, 1992). According to Jordan (1991), an appreciation of the importance of relational interdependence provides recognition and acknowledgment of the importance of turning to others for support rather than relying solely on self-reliance and independence expected from society's new metanarrative (this discussion continues in Chapter 1 and in Chapter 15).

A Relational View of Ethical Decision Making

An in-depth discussion of postmodern ethics is beyond the scope of this introduction. In this section, we briefly describe the social constructionist position in counseling in relation to ethical decision making (see Cottone, 2001; Guterman & Rudes, 2008, for further discussion). Counselors operating from a modernist perspective tend to seek a single, correct interpretation of any given ethics code, whereas counselors who adhere to a postmodern perspective tend to see information in ethics codes as intersubjective, changeable, and open to interpretation (Guterman & Rudes, 2008). Social constructionism recognizes that knowledge is social, intersubjective, and language based. Viewing ethical dilemmas in a traditional way can be problematic and often results in using language that is embedded in one's culture and in society. Stead and Perry (2012) have contended that "career psychology needs to focus less on its largely individualistic, reductionist, and positivist focus toward research and practice and address inequities in communities through ethically based social justice and community work" (p. 68). Thus, a postmodern career counselor would take context, meaning, and relationship into consideration when making ethical decisions.

Scholars who embrace postmodern career counseling believe there is a need for an ethical decision-making process—but from a relational viewpoint. Essentially, decision making is based on a relational view of reality rather than being the responsibility of the individual decision maker (Cottone, 2001). Although fully aware of ethical guidelines, postmodern career counselors rely on ethical decision making through a process of dialogue between counselor and client (and supervisors and others in the client's world). Guterman and Rudes (2008) suggested that "a code of ethics not be considered a fixed text but, rather, a fluid and socially constructed document" (p. 143).

Conclusion

Postmodern career counseling offers a new paradigm with which to comprehend the diversity in people's careers and vocational behavior. The new social arrangements of work in the United States during the last few decades have made career progression for many people more difficult. The turn to postmodern career counseling keeps up with the pace of this transformation and the needs of clients through psychological constructivist and social constructionist models and methods that emphasize meaning making and purpose. Four important features of postmodern career counseling include individual behavior as relative to the contexts in which it occurs; the linkages between culture and social justice; working as being rooted in a relational context; and a postmodern view of the ethical decision-making process, which focuses on contextual issues. In our changing world or work, we advise counselors to acknowledge a third paradigm for career services that addresses the needs of adults who must make frequent transitions among jobs, occupations, and organizations.

References

Amundson, N. E. (2003). *Active engagement: Enhancing the career counseling process.* Richmond, British Columbia, Canada: Ergon Communications.

Arabandi, B. (2015). Globalization, flexibility and new workplace culture in the United States and India. In A. S. Wharton (Ed.), *Working in America: Continuity, conflict, and change in a new economic era* (4th ed., pp. 69–87). Boulder, CO: Paradigm.

Arthur, M. B., & Rousseau, D. M. (Eds.). (1996). *The boundaryless career: A new employment principle for a new organizational era.* Oxford, England: Oxford University Press.

Arthur, N. (2006). Infusing culture in constructivist approaches to career counseling. In M. McMahon & W. Patton (Eds.), *Career counseling: Constructivist approaches* (pp. 57–68). New York, NY: Routledge.

Baum, S. K., & Stewart, R. B. (1990). Sources of meaning through the lifespan. *Psychological Reports, 67,* 3–14.

Bedi, R. P. (2004). The therapeutic alliance and the interface of career counseling and personal counseling. *Journal of Employment Counseling, 41,* 126–135.

Berger, P., & Luckmann, T. (1966). *The social construction of reality.* Garden City, NY: Doubleday.

Bird, J. (2004). *Talk that sings: Therapy in a new linguistic key.* Auckland, New Zealand: Edge Press.

Blustein, D. L. (2006). *The psychology of working: A new perspective for career development, counseling, and public policy.* Mahwah, NJ: Erlbaum.

Blustein, D. L. (2011). A relational theory of working. *Journal of Vocational Behavior, 79,* 1–17.

Blustein, D. L., Schultheiss, D. E. P., & Flum, H. (2004). Toward a relational perspective of the psychology of careers and working: A social constructionist analysis. *Journal of Vocational Behavior, 64,* 423–440.

Brott, P. E. (2001). The storied approach: A postmodern perspective for career counseling. *The Career Development Quarterly, 49,* 304–313.

Bureau of Labor Statistics. (2015). *Number of jobs held, labor market activity, and earnings growth among the youngest baby boomers: Results from a longitudinal survey.* Retrieved from http://www.bls.gov/news.release/pdf/nlsoy.pdf

Busacca, L. A. (2007). Career construction theory: A practitioner's primer. *Career Planning and Adult Development Journal, 23,* 57–67.

Busacca, L. A., & Taber, B. J. (2002). The Career Maturity Inventory-Revised. A preliminary psychometric investigation, *Journal of Career Assessment, 4,* 441–455.

Cochran, L. (1997). *Career counseling: A narrative approach.* Thousand Oaks, CA: Sage.

Cole, E. R. (2009). Intersectionality and research in psychology. *American Psychologist, 64,* 170–180.

Collin, A., & Young, R. A. (1986). New directions for theories of career. *Human Relations, 39,* 837–853.

Conway, N., & Briner, R. B. (2005). *Understanding psychological contracts at work: A critical evaluation of theory and research.* New York, NY: Oxford University Press.

Cottone, R. R. (2001). A social constructivism model for ethical decision making in counseling. *Journal of Counseling & Development, 79,* 39–45.

Crites, J. O., & Savickas, M. L. (1996). Revision of the Career Maturity Inventory. *Journal of Career Assessment, 4,* 131–138.

Crowley, M., Tope, D., Chamberlain, L. J., & Hodson, R. (2010). Neo-Taylorism and work: Occupational change in the post-Fordist era. *Social Problems 57,* 421–447.

Dik, B. J., & Duffy, R. D. (2012). *Make your job a calling: How the psychology of vocation can change your life at work.* West Conshohocken, PA: Templeton Press.

Dubar, C. (1998). *La socialisation: Construction des identities sociales et professionnelles* [Socialization: Construction of social and occupational identities] (2nd rev. ed.). Paris, France: Armand Colin.

Erwin, E. (1999). Constructivist epistemologies and the therapies. *British Journal of Guidance & Counselling, 27,* 353–365.

Ford, D. (1987). *Humans as self-constructing living systems.* Hillsdale, NJ: Erlbaum.

Granvold, D. K. (1996). Constructivist psychotherapy. *Families in Society, 77,* 345–359.

Guichard, J. (2015). From vocational guidance and career counseling to life design dialogues. In L. Nota & J. Rosier (Eds.), *Handbook of life design: From practice to theory and from theory to practice* (pp. 11–25). Boston, MA: Hogrefe.

Guterman, J. T., & Rudes, J. (2008). Social constructionism and ethics: Implications for counseling. *Counseling and Values, 52,* 136–144.

Hartung, P. J. (2011). Barrier or benefit? Emotion in life-career design. *Journal of Career Assessment, 19,* 296–305.

Hartung, P. J. (2013). Career as story: Making the narrative turn. In W. B. Walsh, M. L. Savickas, & P. J. Hartung (Eds.), *Handbook of vocational psychology* (4th ed., pp. 33–52). New York, NY: Routledge.

Holland, J. L. (1959). A theory of vocational choice. *Journal of Counseling Psychology, 6,* 35–45.

Inkson, K., & Elkin, G. (2008). Landscape with travelers: The context of careers in developed nations. In J. A. Athanasou & R. van Esbroeck (Eds.), *International handbook of career guidance* (pp. 69–94). Dordrecht, The Netherlands: Springer.

Jordan, J. V. (1991). Empathy, mutuality and therapeutic change: Clinical implications of a relational model. In J. V. Jordan et al. (Eds.), *Women's growth in connection: Writings from the Stone Center* (pp. 283–290). New York, NY: Guilford Press.

Kalleberg, A. L. (2009). Precarious work, insecure workers: Employment relations in transition. *American Sociological Review, 74,* 1–22.

Kalleberg, A. L., & Leicht, K. (2002). The United States. In D. Cornfield & R. Hodson (Eds.), *Worlds of work: Building an international sociology of work* (pp. 87–110). New York, NY: Kluwer Academic/Plenum.

Kosine, N. R., Steger, M. F., & Duncan, S. (2008). Purpose-centered career development: A strengths-based approach to finding meaning and purpose in careers. *Professional School Counseling, 12,* 133–136.

Kvale, S. (Ed.). (1992). *Psychology and postmodernism.* London, England: Sage.

Levine, L. (2005). *Offshoring (a.k.a. offshore outsourcing) and job insecurity among U.S. workers.* Washington, DC: Congressional Research Service. Retrieved from http://digitalcommons.ilr.cornell.edu/cgi/viewcontent.cgi?article=1243&context=key_workplace

Maturana, H. R., & Varela, F. J. (1988). *The tree of knowledge: The biological roots of human understanding.* Boston, MA: New Science Library.

Miller-Tiedeman, A., & Tiedeman, D. (1990). Career decision-making: An individualistic perspective. In D. Brown, L. Brooks, & Associates (Eds.), *Career choice and development* (2nd ed., pp. 308–337). San Francisco, CA: Jossey-Bass.

Neimeyer, G. J. (1992). Personal constructs in career counseling and development. *Journal of Career Development, 18,* 164–173.

Neimeyer, R. A., & Stewart, A. E. (2000). Constructivist and narrative psychotherapies. In C. R. Snyder & R. E. Ingram (Eds.), *Handbook of psychological change: Psychotherapy processes and practices for the 21st century* (pp. 337–357). New York, NY: Wiley.

Parsons, F. (1909). *Choosing a vocation.* Boston, MA: Houghton-Mifflin.

Patton, W., & McMahon, M. (2006). *Career development and systems theory: Connecting theory and practice* (2nd ed.). Rotterdam, The Netherlands: Sense.

Peavy, R. V. (2010). *Sociodynamic counseling: A practical approach to meaning making.* Chagrin Falls, OH: Taos Institute.

Pryor, R. G. L., & Bright, J. E. H. (2011). *The chaos theory of careers: A new perspective on working in the 21st century.* Hoboken, NJ: Taylor & Francis.

Richardson, M. S. (1996). From career counselling to counseling/psychotherapy and work, jobs, and career. In M. L. Savickas & W. B. Walsh (Eds.), *Handbook of career counseling theory and practice* (pp. 347–360). Palo Alto, CA: Davies-Black.

Richardson, M. S. (2015). Agentic action in context. In R. A. Young, J. F. Domene, & L. Valach (Eds.), *Counseling and action: Toward life-enhancing work, relationships, and identity* (pp. 51–68). New York, NY: Springer.

Richmond, L., Savickas, M., Harris-Bowlsbey, J., Feller, R., & Jepsen, D. (2006, July). *In honor of David Tiedeman: The first post-modern career counselor.* Paper presented at the National Career Development Association Global Conference, Chicago, IL.

Roe, A. (1956). *The psychology of occupations.* New York, NY: Wiley.

Rousseau, D. M. (1998). The problem of the psychological contract considered. *Journal of Organizational Behavior, 19,* 665–671.

Savickas, M. L. (1993). Career counseling in the postmodern era. *Journal of Cognitive Psychotherapy, 7,* 205–215.

Savickas, M. L. (2005). The theory and practice of career construction. In R. W. Lent & S. D. Brown (Eds.), *Career development and counseling: Putting theory and research to work* (pp. 42–70). Hoboken, NJ: Wiley.

Savickas, M. L. (2011a). New questions for vocational psychology: Premises, paradigms, and practices. *Journal of Career Assessment, 19,* 251–258.

Savickas, M. L. (2011b). *Career counseling.* Washington, DC: American Psychological Association.

Savickas, M. L. (2015). Career counseling paradigms: Guiding, developing, and designing. In P. Hartung, M. Savickas, & W. Walsh (Eds.), *The APA handbook of career interventions* (pp. 129–143). Washington, DC: APA Press.

Savickas, M. L., Nota, L., Rossier, J., Dauwalder, J. P., Duarte, M. E., Guichard, J., . . . van Vianen, A. E. M. (2009). Life designing: A paradigm for career construction in the 21st century. *Journal of Vocational Behavior, 75,* 239–250.

Schultheiss, D. E. P. (2003). A relational approach to career counseling: Theoretical integration and practical application. *Journal of Counseling & Development, 81,* 301–310.

Sexton, T. (1997). Constructivist thinking within the history of ideas: The challenge of a new paradigm. In T. Sexton & B. Griffin (Eds.), *Constructivist thinking in counseling practice, research, and training* (pp. 3–18). New York, NY: Teachers College Press.

Standing, G. (1999). *Global labour flexibility: Seeking distributive justice.* New York, NY: St. Martin's Press.

Stead, G. B., & Bakker, T. M. (2010). Discourse analysis in career counseling and development. *The Career Development Quarterly, 59,* 72–86.

Stead, G. B., & Perry, J. C. (2012). Practice trends, social justice and ethics. In M. Watson & M. McMahon (Eds.), *Career development: Global issues and challenges* (pp. 59–71). New York, NY: Nova Science.

Steenbarger, B. N. (1991). All the world is not a stage: Emerging contextualist themes in counseling and development. *Journal of Counseling & Development, 70,* 288–296.

Stone, K. V. W. (2007). Revisiting the at-will employment doctrine: Imposed terms, implied terms, and the normative world of the workplace. *Industrial Law Journal, 36,* 84–101.

Super, D. E. (1957). *The psychology of careers: An introduction to vocational development.* New York, NY: Harper & Row.

Super, D. E. (1980). A life-span, life-space approach to career development. *Journal of Vocational Behavior, 16,* 282–298.

Sweet, S., & Meiksins, P. (2008). *Changing contours of work: Jobs and opportunities in the new economy.* Thousand Oaks, CA: Pine Forge Press.

Watson, M. B. (2006). Career counseling theory, culture and constructivism. In M. McMahon & W. Patton (Eds.), *Career counseling: Constructivist approaches* (pp. 45–56). New York, NY: Routledge.

Watson, M. B. (2011). Postmodern career counseling and beyond. In K. Maree (Ed.), *Shaping the story: A guide to facilitating career counseling* (pp. 73–86). Pretoria, South Africa: Van Schaik.

Watson, M. B., & McMahon, M. (2004). Postmodern (narrative) career counseling and education. *Perspectives in Education, 22,* 169–170.

Whiston, S. C., & Rahardja, D. (2005). Qualitative career assessment: An overview and analysis. *Journal of Career Assessment, 13,* 371–380.

Wilber, K. (2000). *Integral psychology: Consciousness, spirit, psychology, therapy.* Boston, MA: Shambhala.

Young, R. A., & Collin, A. (2004). Introduction: Constructivism and social constructionism in the career field. *Journal of Vocational Behavior, 64,* 373–388.

Young, R. A., & Valach, L. (2004). The construction of career through goal-directed action. *Journal of Vocational Behavior, 64,* 499–514.

Young, R. A., Valach, L., & Collin, A. (2002). A contextualist explanation of career. In D. Brown & Associates (Eds.), *Career choice and development* (4th ed., pp. 206–252). San Francisco, CA: Jossey-Bass.

Part I

PERSPECTIVES

Chapter 1

Career Counseling in Postmodern Times: Emergence and Narrative Conceptions

Louis A. Busacca

"I define postmodern as incredulity toward meta-narratives."
—J. F. Lyotard, *The Postmodern Condition:*
A Report on Knowledge

For several decades, social, economic, and political forces have aligned to make work more unstable in Western societies, including in the United States. Shaped by a global economy and propelled by information technology, the new social arrangement has been characterized by uncertain and precarious employment opportunities (Kalleberg, 2009). This restructuring has diminished the standardized job, changed the relationship between worker and employer, and posed a threat to personal meaningfulness. As society moves from high modernity to postmodern times, existing career theories do not adequately account for today's unpredictable and rapidly changing occupational structure (Savickas, 2011a). Established paths and narratives that once guided many people's career progression have eroded. New demands require individuals to repeatedly revise their identities, accept more responsibility for managing their own lives, and invest in their families and communities for stability. Client questions such as "How do I fit in?" or "How do I advance my career?" have transformed into concerns such as "Who am I?" or "Where can I find purpose?" Postmodern career counseling emphasizes the importance of meaningful work and of holding oneself together while developing a career (Savickas, 2011b). Counselors now ask themselves an implicit question: How do we counsel clients when security and stability in the workplace are no longer guaranteed?

In this chapter, I provide an overview of how postmodern career counseling answers this question. Drawing on sociological theory and thought, I first discuss how societal and organizational narratives within each work era provided external guides for people to help them feel secure in an increasingly precarious work environment. I examine some factors responsible for how work in a postmodern era has diminished the standardized job, changed the psychological contract between worker and employer, and affected people's identities. Then I propose a new metanarrative for postmodern society, highlight implications for culturally diverse groups, and conclude with a brief discussion on narrative career counseling in culture and context.

The Changing Nature of Work Narratives

In most Western societies, a large majority of individuals uniformly followed an established and accepted sequence of events in their transition to adulthood. To know the expectations of the community in which one lived and worked provided a familiar script or dominant narrative that led to a predictable environment and a sense of security during times of change. Metanarratives denote the societal scripts (Lyotard, 1979/1984) that include the collective norms and values of family and social institutions that intentionally shape and state expectations for how people live their lives (Savickas, 2011b). Typical scripts included (and in some cultures still do include) such things as when to take over the family business or trade, when to go to college, whether or not to join the military, and when to get married and have children. During the 20th century, when most employees had a permanent job, typical organizational narratives provided workers with expectations about how their careers would unfold and how they could advance in their positions. As you will see later in this chapter, postmodern thought primarily represents a broad challenge to and a cultural shift away from fixed metanarratives, privileged discourses, and universal truths.

To help you appreciate the revolutionary character of a postmodern conception of work, I first briefly describe how work lives were shaped by agrarian, artisan, industrial, and postindustrial economies. I also explain the metanarratives that prevailed during these different eras. The shared assumptions, implicit values, and ideals presented by these metanarratives guided adaptation to the changing conditions of technology and work during each era.

Agrarian Society

During the colonial period, which began with the arrival of the first English settlers in North America and lasted into the 18th century, country life and the Puritan ethic largely shaped American values. During this era, "work was not a special subject; it was part of the general social and spiritual framework" (Anthony, 1977, p. 37). The Puritan ethic emphasized hard work, frugality, and diligence as constant displays for a person seeking salvation in the Christian faith. People progressed in work through self-motivation and individual efforts that led to success and personal fulfillment. Work was shaped into chores, and men predominantly held occupations that typically followed family traditions, such as being a farmer or a craftsperson.

For many people during this period, family, religion, and the Puritan ethic provided structure and predictability. Personal relationships and collectivist values unified agricultural communities. Individuals defined the self by social function and the way in which they contributed to the shared social order (Savickas, 2008). The community expected everyone to be of good character: honest, moral, and hardworking in ways that were consistent with Calvinistic teachings. Because people had been assigned a work role (e.g., children inherited their parent's craft), to choose a life's work did not pose a problem for many people. The metanarrative during this era rested in a community that valued and expected moral order through one's personal character. This began to change with the advent of the artisan era.

Artisan Society

During the late 18th and early 19th centuries, artisans or craftsmen worked independently. They refined their skills, owned their own tools, and served an apprenticeship to learn their trade (Applebaum, 1998). More than 80% of workers were farmers, craftspeople, and small business owners (Maccoby, 1983). As a secular version of the Puritan ethic, the value of work began to be based on pride in workmanship and the maintenance of self-reliance in one's own work, along with the provision of economic independence for the family. Although workers felt a responsibility to serve their communities, they "performed work for its own sake, beyond the ulterior motivation as a means to livelihood" (Applebaum, 1998, p. 21).

Like the Puritans, many artisans worked in crafts because their fathers and grandfathers had worked as craftsmen. Applebaum (1998) stated, "A craftsman knew his role in life, and in following this path he was anchored to a way of life" (p. 21). A sense of purpose through tradition and social responsibility provided a great deal of structure and predictability for artisan workers during this time. The metanarrative rested in the community that expected them to follow the path of their forebears. With the arrival of the 19th century, however, an enormous change in social organization took place.

Industrial Society

With the advent of the American industrial revolution, cultural changes occurred in the institutions of work. The War of 1812 made it apparent that America needed more economic independence. There was now a conflict between the traditional values associated with holding a craft and the new model of industrial factory work, and these two approaches to work struggled for supremacy (Applebaum, 1998). Agricultural society offered freedom of activity and the joys of craftsmanship. When people moved from the farm or village to the city, they had to choose one major job or focus on a single task in a manufacturing industry rather than do the variety of chores they had done at home. For many workers, the assembly line in machine-aided production factories provided a career. Working life went from the leisurely style of the colonial period to a standardized one with clearly delineated rules, procedures, boundaries, and requirements. As Applebaum (1998) noted, workers no longer found themselves as self-employed producers providing a service to customers but as wageworkers dealing with owners of capital. It was at this point that a new form of organization, called *modernism*, occurred.

By the second half of the industrial revolution (c. 1870–1914), views of success espoused by corporations, educational institutions, and the family served as socializing agents to prepare people for lifelong jobs. In the early 20th century, expectations regarding one's life course became institutionalized, as industrial work and corporate careers imposed strong discipline on the order and the timing of life events. Jobs became standardized for efficiency and uniformity, making advancement in a career possible. The metanarrative of this order, uniformity, and predictability helped people to envision their career and ultimately shaped the path that they took. Although this brought people and groups closer together, sociopolitical limitations and resistances in the form of stratification, inequality, and differentiation by gender, ethnicity, race, and social class remained (Savickas, 2015). During the first half of the 20th century, Western society's dominant work philosophy transformed from agricultural collectivism to industrial individualism.

The subsequent decades of increased individualism in the world of work resulted in an erosion of the life course script that had previously provided the framework with which to build one's life. During the 1950s, the United States was a nation of political individualism that still promoted social conformity. The 1960s ushered in radical individualism, broadening it from the political domain to the realm of personal lifestyle. The life course became more complex and less conformist, and by the early 1970s the formerly popular narrative of a linear path (i.e., complete school, live on one's own, obtain a full-time job, get married, develop a career within one organization, retire) had lost a great deal of ground. During the 1970s and 1980s, new options led many people to reconsider the social script; they began to feel uneasy about normative pressures around role sequencing and timing (Savickas, 2015). As a response, people began to create their own story or biography about how to live their lives. Individualistic values and high levels of achievement motivation moved to the forefront.

Postindustrial Society

Forces that propelled postindustrial change during the 1980s included digitalization and globalization. To adjust to a new market economy, many organizations needed to reduce costs and increase flexibility, which led to major changes in the strategies and structures of most employing organizations (Inkson & Elkin, 2008). Downsizing, outsourcing, flattening of managerial hierarchies, and general restructuring were some of the strategies that helped companies deal with these changes; these strategies affected both blue- and white-collar jobs. As an example, employers came to believe that uniformity in work was not the best way to get work done because it involved employees doing similar or routine tasks (Savickas, 2015). Projects and assignments that involved completing diverse tasks came to be preferred by many employers. Distinctions can be made about the impact of these transformations between blue- and white-collar workers, and Sweet and Meiksins (2013) provided information on this topic. My purpose here is limited to illuminating the 21st-century trends in work for the counselor.

During the late 20th century, ambiguity and tension became part of contemporary postmodern life. The term *postmodern* refers to the cultural shift in postindustrial society (Savickas, 1993). From a sociological perspective, culture had become fragmented, tentative, experimental, discontinuous, and ever changing (Elliott, 2014). Rather than follow the values imposed by institutions, as had happened during the industrial era, a deinstitutionalization of the life course occurred. Institutions no longer provided temporal security for employees, which made long-term career progression more difficult (Blatterer, 2007). Although some freedom of choice resulted from deinstitutionalization, it came with the burden of searching for meaning in life (Baumeister, 1987). This shift in the social arrangement of work transformed to the point that our current narrative about work life has grown less useful in today's society (Savickas, 2011b).

A Postmodern Metanarrative

The loss of the legitimacy of established metanarratives from the industrial era has implications for culturally diverse groups. Although it deconstructs the metanarratives of former times, the new metanarrative still tells a story of how people should live and work in the United States. As Savickas (2008) pointed out, the new story is that each person is the chief executive officer of her or his own career, with a return to investment in family and community providing meaning and stability. This metanarrative attacks the multicultural homogenization of groups that attributes fixed characteristics to each group (e.g., race, ethnicity, disability, religion/spirituality, and sexual orientation). This is especially relevant as the United States moves to affirm its multiculturalism. This breakdown in identity is akin to what Beck (2002) described as the cosmopolitan society and which sociologists call *hybridity theory* (Nederveen Pieterse, 2004). Group-based identities have begun to be challenged by the metanarrative of individualization because it deprives cultural groups of the context in which they live (Burr, 2015). I address this narrative turn through individualization of the life course, the expectation for self-reliance, and how seeking relationships creates "holding environments" that help individuals cope with work-related transitions.

Individualization of the Life Course

Individualization is seen as the core characteristic of postmodern society. Individualism indicates a shift from standardized, institutionalized life course patterns to an individualized biography. The life course denotes the pathways or transition markers leading to adulthood. Beck and Beck-Gernsheim (2002) used the term *individualization of the life course* to refer to the loss of stable structures and predictable trajectories resulting from life in a postmodern world. As a consequence, Mills (2007) denoted a shift in responsibility for navigating the life course from organizations to individuals. To understand the trend toward individualization and its implications, it is necessary to discuss some changes in the timing and sequence of the transitions.

Although the 21st century has seen an erosion of traditional ways of life, there has been an evolution of individualization. Modern society fostered adaptation by offering individuals metanarratives, or life course scripts, that conferred social meaning. Families and social institutions used these scripts to deliberately shape individuals and to produce similarity among people in society. To understand one's life course was uncommon before the 19th century because life had been shaped by the expectations of family and religion. A normatively imposed life course predominated. By 1960 in most Western societies, a large majority of individuals followed the scripted order and timetable of events in their transition to adulthood. In posttraditional society, however, the transition to adulthood is viewed less as a discrete set of experiences and more as a series of nonnormative transitions often in the roles of school, work, and family (Buchmann, 1989; Shanahan, 2000). Thus, a person's life course today depends less on the normatively imposed life course and more on an individually shaped life.

Far from cutting people loose from social expectations, institutionalized individualism has placed employees in precarious arrangements with their employers. As nonstandard work arrangements become more common and organizations assign people the responsibility of shaping their own lives, individuals may find it difficult to identify a secure place in the world (Savickas, 2011b). Such a shift encourages counselors to reevaluate objective interventions that focus on interpreting scores and move toward subjective interventions that focus on assisting clients in narrating their own stories and uncovering their uniqueness.

A Shift to Self-Reliance

Individualization of the life course stresses that employers no longer have much obligation with regard to the career trajectories of their employees. Mirvis and Hall (1996) suggested that workers must prove their value to justify continued employment in organizations that face severe competition. Organizational scholars describe this as a shift away from psychological contracts, which embody the values of mutuality and reciprocity, to trans-actional contracts, which represent a more calculative and instrumental relationship between employee and employer (Doyle, 2000). The once accessible and secure career in many organizations has been replaced by the expectation that employees will take responsibility for the direction and evolution of their own career pathways (Arthur & Rousseau, 1996).

Rather than developing in a stable work environment, people must now actively plan and implement self-management behaviors. Because metanarratives have eroded, individualization calls for the development of competencies to anticipate changes in changing contexts. This parallels Savickas et al.'s (2009) concept of career adaptability. Employers require their employees to assume greater personal responsibility for understanding their own needs, determining their goals, and managing their careers. For example, organizations seem to place value on self-reliant characteristics in workers, valuing employees who are emotionally intelligent, attuned to the dynamics of a temporary work group, sensitive to cultural differences, and flexible enough to satisfy diverse and sometimes competing demands within cross-functional and self-directed teams that navigate broad organizational networks (Savickas, 2008). Although this may provide opportunities for self-expression, it also contributes to pressure to ensure success (Mirvis & Hall, 1996).

The necessary qualities for self-reliance require people to acquire agency and relational interdependence. Active agency is a core assumption of personal constructivism (Mahoney, 2003); it implies that individuals are actively engaged in constructing their lives and patterning their experiences so that they provide meaning (Watson, 2006). People become capable of being self-reliant when they feel securely attached to others they trust (Bowlby, 1988). Relational interdependence provides recognition and acknowledgment of the importance of turning to others for support rather than relying solely on a utopian view of self-reliance and independence (Jordan, 1991). Self-reliant workers look for sources of security and reaffirmation when they experience a loss of traditional security (Flum, 2015).

Holding Environments

The holding environment concept, initially developed by the British psychoanalyst D. W. Winnicott (1956/1975), described the nature of effective caregiving relationships between mothers and infants. To expand the scope of this concept, Winnicott (1961/1986) proposed an ecosystem model that extends one's holding environment beyond the immediate holding environments early in life, such as parents, home, and school. According to Kahn (2001), relationships become temporary holding environments in which people flounder in anxiety, then become calmed, appreciated, understood, and helped, until they are able to regain their stability. In the context of work, Kahn defined *holding environments* as "interpersonal or group-based relationships that enable self-reliant workers to manage situations that trigger potentially debilitating anxiety" (p. 260). In the past, work organizations served as holding environments for many people.

Traditionally, work, family, and community created personal and social meaning in people's lives. In agricultural societies, people connected to others because of personal ties and traditions. During the industrial era, organization members were supported by hierarchical superiors, mentors, and departmental coworkers who were more or less able to provide resources, protection and buffering, solutions, training, and advice with some assurance of successful outcomes (Kotter, 1995). The hierarchical structure managed workers' anxiety through the provision of predictability and certainty (Hirschhorn, 1990). When holding environments at work erode, however, individuals can no longer depend on colleagues or supervisors to provide rules, goals, clear promotional ladders, or protection (Kahn, 2001). Without strong institutional holding environments, individuals must adapt and organize their lives by scripting their own stories through active agency or career counseling.

Toward a Postmodern Conception of Identity

The construct of identity in vocational psychology and career counseling has been transformed and now focuses on interpersonal relations rather than intrapersonal possession. In the major positivist career theories, identity as an intrapersonal construct mostly describes the relatively stable aspects of one's psychological experiences, but it often lacks connection to one's culture and context. In vocational guidance, counselors focus on the client's personality and vocational personality type and rely on the stability of occupations. For example, before providing vocational guidance, a counselor may assess a client's identity to determine whether the client displays confidence in her or his ability to make good decisions and thus is ready for career guidance interventions (Busacca, 2002). Holland (1997) referred to this as *vocational identity* and defined it as "possession of a clear and stable picture of one's goals, interests, and talents" (p. 5). In contrast, postmodern career counseling parallels the changes in the working world by considering identity in an uncertain world. The counselor now focuses on the uniqueness of clients rather than on scores that indicate whom clients resemble (Lamiell, 2003). Such a contemporary view of identity can be conceptualized as something that is constructed and reconstructed within relationships and across multiple contexts (Collin & Young, 2000).

Identity is co-constructed by the individual within a social context. From a postmodernist view, identity is not constructed by the individual alone (i.e., constructivist) but can only emerge and exist as a result of interaction with others (i.e., constructionist; LaPointe, 2010). For example, a client who is a part-time employee and who complains of viewing herself as having a minimal voice in her department's objectives may state to the counselor that she will feel better when she knows how her colleagues feel. Alternatively, in the context of career choice, a student who seeks career counseling may state that he will be happy and satisfied in a career in which he can help others with their alcohol addiction. In addition, an individual's identity is communicated to others through language and is historically and socially embedded and culturally shaped (Savickas, 2008). As Erikson (1968) eloquently stated, identity formation is the key "process 'located' in the core of the individual and yet also in the core of his communal culture" (p. 22). Identity is found in the interaction between the individual and her or his social environment.

From a social constructionist perspective, each person has multiple identities. Multiple stories or truths are formed through relationships and internalized through experience in various cultural contexts (Stead, 2004). Savickas's (2011b) parsimonious definition of identity as the self that is invested in a social role (e.g., vocational identity, parenthood identity, marriage identity, and leisure identity) captures this notion. Each person has a story that encompasses the salient roles in her or his life. When an individual invests in the work role, it forms an identity, provides meaning, and creates a story of who the individual is in relation to work. In time, a sense of continuity develops as the individual organizes and integrates new experiences into her or his identity. The development of an individual's work identity can be thwarted, however, by the demands imposed by a destandardized and individualized life course.

People often seek career counseling when the content of their identity is insufficient or unable to support them when confronting a new set of demands imposed by society. Giddens (1991) stressed that the demand on the individual to construct him- or herself has become a major social fact and a characteristic of our societies. When confronted by developmental career tasks (e.g., occupational choice), occupational transition (e.g., new work arrangements), or a work trauma (e.g., reduced hours, layoff, termination, and illness), individuals may find that their story concerning who they are and where they fit in, in relation to occupation and work, loses continuity. Individuals adapt by repeatedly revising their identity to integrate new experiences into their ongoing life story (Savickas, 2012).

Identity has increasingly been viewed as a narrative concept. "When we want someone to know who we really are, we tell them our life story" (Polkinghorne, 1988, p. 29). Identity is formed by and expressed in narratives (McAdams, 2001). According to Giddens (1991), the self must be explored and constructed in a self-defining process called *reflexivity*. That is, we actively shape, reflect on, and monitor ourselves to build our biographical narratives as we go through life. The counselor enhances client reflexivity and clarifies identity through interventions such as narrative career counseling, life design, card sorts, and Possible Selves Mapping. In the past, one's job or career fixed one's identity, virtually for life (Ibarra, 2004). Today individualization calls for career interventions that help clients use their own stories to revise their identity and to produce a sense of coherence and distinctiveness. Narrative methods provide a powerful framework to gather client information, to understand a client's worldview, and to help clients express their identity and infuse their life with meaning.

Micronarratives in Context

As the metanarrative of individualization evolves, people search for direction when they confront career choices and negotiate work transitions.

Narrative identity is a personalized interpretation of the self in a social world (Savickas, 2011b). Although people tend toward and often achieve a unifying story of life (Cochran, 2011), when they feel lost and believe that they are encountering novel situations without a script that tells them who they are and what to do, they need to construct their own stories. As Beck and Beck-Gernsheim (2002) noted, individualization "compel[s] the self-organization and self-schematization of people's biographies" (p. 24). Career stories reveal the themes that clients tend to utilize when they evaluate their choices, take on meaningful roles, and begin the process of work adjustment (Savickas, 2011a). To help clients redefine their career issue through narrative expression confers meaning, purpose, and an integrated sense of self.

At a basic level, there are three stages of the story development in narrative work: construction, deconstruction, and reauthoring. Counselors help clients elicit stories to create meaning and direction or a sense of causality and continuity about their career path (Linde, 1993; Wijers & Meijers, 1996). The client reveals information to the counselor (construction), the counselor identifies a series of small stories or micronarratives (Savickas, 2011b) in collaboration with the client and attempts to replace the problematic metanarrative (deconstruction), and then counselor and client reconstruct or create a new narrative or story (reauthoring). From a cultural context view, individual life stories reflect cultural values and norms, including assumptions about gender, race, and class (McAdams, 2001). The goal of narrative counseling, according to Chope and Consoli (2011), "is to help clients deconstruct the oppressive stories that have consumed their thoughts and behavior and facilitate their constructing, and at times co-constructing with the counselor, of new stories and models that are more empowering and appropriate" (p. 90). The goal of the narrative career counselor is to help clients actively seek expression of their local, social, and historically situated reality.

Micronarratives are smaller stories of the individual that are embedded within their social role and local context. Positioned outside the metanarrative, micronarratives serve as the genre that gives metanarratives their context (Savickas, 2011b). According to social constructionists, the dominant, broader metanarratives are always accompanied by resistant, marginal, local narratives (Stead & Bakker, 2012). Hancock and Tyler (2001) argued that dominant narratives can function as technologies of marginalization, suppressing certain voices within the organizational and career domain. Additionally, postmodern career counselors do not help clients to think about their lives from the perspective of the current social or broader norms because these norms can contain particular cultural agendas (Stead & Bakker, 2012); instead, through dialogue, clients define their own norms (i.e., micronarratives) from which they can give meaning to their lives (Guichard, 2015). When counseling culturally diverse clients, it is important that counselors help them create meaning and purpose, cope, and maintain a sense of self and coherence as they encounter and manage the restructuring of occupations in the 21st century.

Conclusion

In a world in which career planning has become precarious and employment more contingent, postmodern career counselors help clients define the self, create meaning, and act within their social context. Today's workers feel more anxious, discouraged, and frustrated because of perceived job insecurity, coping with multiple transitions, and multicultural imperatives. Career counseling requires counselors to consider the impact of dominant narratives, the degree of institutionalized individualization experienced within an occupation, and how individuals construct their own ideas about their world as they try to make meaning out of the career transitions confronting them. Postmodern career counseling complements the more positivistic approaches found in vocational guidance and updates the normative expectations found in career education. Counseling in a postmodern era requires more career counselors who are trained to help clients shape their stories and to supply a sense of continuity, coherence, and commitment as they confront career tasks, occupational transitions, and work traumas.

References

Anthony, P. D. (1977). *Ideology of work.* London, England: Routledge.

Applebaum, H. (1998). *The American work ethic and the changing work force: An historical perspective.* Westport, CT: Greenwood Press.

Arthur, M. B., & Rousseau, D. M. (Eds.). (1996). *The boundaryless career: A new employment principle for a new organizational era.* Oxford, England: Oxford University Press.

Baumeister, R. F. (1987). How the self became a problem: A psychological review of historical research. *Journal of Personality and Social Psychology, 52,* 163–176.

Beck, U. (2002). The cosmopolitan society and its enemies. *Theory, Culture and Society, 19,* 17–40.

Beck, U., & Beck-Gernsheim, E. (2002). *Individualization: Institutionalized individualism and its social and political consequences.* Thousand Oaks, CA: Sage.

Blatterer, H. (2007). *Coming of age in times of uncertainty.* New York, NY: Berghahn Books.

Bowlby, J. (1988). *The secure base.* New York, NY: Basic Books.

Buchmann, M. (1989). *The script of life in modern society: Entry into adulthood in a changing world.* Chicago, IL: University Chicago Press.

Burr, V. (2015). *Social constructionism* (3rd ed.). London, England: Routledge.

Busacca, L. A. (2002). Career problem assessment: A conceptual schema for counselor training. *Journal of Career Development, 29,* 129–146.

Chope, R. C., & Consoli, A. J. (2011). A storied approach to multicultural career counseling. In K. Maree (Ed.), *Shaping the story: A guide to facilitating career counseling* (pp. 83–96). Pretoria, South Africa: Van Schaik.

Cochran, L. (2011). The promise of narrative career counseling. In K. Maree (Ed.), *Shaping the story: A guide to facilitating narrative career counseling* (pp. 7–19). Rotterdam, The Netherlands: Sense.

Collin, A., & Young, R. A. (2000). The future of career. In A. Collin & R. A. Young (Eds.), *The future of career* (pp. 276–300). Cambridge, England: Cambridge University Press.

Doyle, M. (2000). Managing careers in organizations. In A. Collin & R. A. Young (Eds.), *The future of career* (pp. 228–242). Cambridge, England: Cambridge University Press.

Elliott, A. (2014). *Concepts of the self* (3rd ed.). Malden, MA: Polity Press.

Erikson, E. H. (1968). *Identity: Youth and crisis.* New York, NY: Norton.

Flum, H. (2015). Career and identity construction in action: A relational view. In R. A. Young, J. F. Domene, & L. Valach (Eds.), *Counseling and action: Toward life-enhancing work, relationships, and identity* (pp. 115–133). New York, NY: Springer.

Giddens, A. (1991). *Modernity and self identity: Self and society in the late modern age.* Cambridge, MA: Polity Press.

Guichard, J. (2015). From vocational guidance and career counseling to life design dialogues. In L. Nota & J. Rosier (Eds.), *Handbook of life design: From practice to theory and from theory to practice* (pp. 11–25). Boston, MA: Hogrefe.

Hancock, P., & Tyler, M. (2001). *Work, postmodernism and organization: A critical introduction.* Thousand Oaks, CA: Sage.

Hirschhorn, L. (1990). Leaders and followers in a postindustrial age. *Journal of Applied Behavioral Science, 26,* 529–542.

Holland, J. L. (1997). *Making vocational choices: A theory of vocational personalities and work environments* (3rd ed.). Englewood Cliffs, NJ: Prentice Hall.

Ibarra, H. (2004). *Working identity: Unconventional strategies for reinventing your career.* Boston, MA: Harvard Business School.

Inkson, K., & Elkin, G. (2008). Landscape with travelers: The context of careers in developed nations. In J. A. Athanasou & R. van Esbroeck (Eds.), *International handbook of career guidance* (pp. 69–94). Dordrecht, The Netherlands: Springer.

Jordan, J. V. (1991). Empathy, mutuality and therapeutic change: Clinical implications of a relational model. In J. V. Jordan et al. (Eds.), *Women's growth in connection: Writings from the Stone Center* (pp. 283–290). New York, NY: Guilford Press.

Kahn, W. A. (2001). Holding environments at work. *Journal of Applied Behavioral Science, 37,* 260–279.

Kalleberg, A. L. (2009). Precarious work, insecure workers: Employment relations in transition. *American Sociological Review, 74,* 1–22.

Kotter, J. (1995). *The new rules.* New York, NY: Free Press.

Lamiell, J. T. (2003). *Beyond individual and group differences: Human individuality, scientific psychology, and William Stern's critical personalism.* Thousand Oaks, CA: Sage.

LaPointe, K. (2010). Narrating career, positioning identity: Career identity as a narrative practice. *Journal of Vocational Behavior, 77,* 1–9.

Linde, C. (1993). *Life stories: The creation of coherence.* New York, NY: Oxford University Press.

Lyotard, J. F. (1984). *The postmodern condition: A report on knowledge* (G. Bennington & B. Massumi, Trans.). Minneapolis: University of Minnesota. (Original work published 1979)

Maccoby, M. (1983). *The leader: A new face for American management.* New York, NY: Ballantine Books.

Mahoney, M. J. (2003). *Constructive psychotherapy.* New York, NY: Guilford Press.

McAdams, D. P. (2001). The psychology of life stories. *Review of General Psychology, 5,* 100–122.

Mills, M. (2007). Individualization and the life course: Towards a theoretical model and empirical evidence. In C. Howard (Ed.), *Contested individualization: Debates about contemporary personhood* (pp. 61–79). London, UK: Palgrave Macmillan.

Mirvis, P. H., & Hall, D. T. (1996). Psychological success and the boundaryless career. In M. B. Arthur & D. M. Rousseau (Eds.), *The boundaryless career* (pp. 237–255). New York, NY: Oxford University Press.

Nederveen Pieterse, J. (2004). *Globalization and culture: Global mélage.* Lanham, MD: Rowman and Littlefield.

Polkinghorne, D. E. (1988). *Narrative knowing and the human sciences.* Albany, NY: SUNY Press.

Savickas, M. L. (1993). Career counseling in the postmodern era. *Journal of Cognitive Psychotherapy, 7,* 205–215.

Savickas, M. L. (2008). Helping people choose jobs: A history of the guidance profession. In J. A. Athanasou & R. van Esbroeck (Eds.), *International handbook of career guidance* (pp. 97–113). Dordrecht, The Netherlands: Springer.

Savickas, M. L. (2011a). Prologue: Reshaping the story of career counseling. In K. Maree (Ed.), *Shaping the story: A guide to facilitating narrative career counseling* (pp. 1–3). Rotterdam, The Netherlands: Sense.

Savickas, M. L. (2011b). *Career counseling.* Washington, DC: American Psychological Association.

Savickas, M. L. (2012). Life design: A paradigm for career intervention in the 21st century. *Journal of Counseling & Development, 90,* 13–19.

Savickas, M. L. (2015). Life designing with adults: Developmental individualization using biographical bricolage. In L. Nota & J. Rosier (Eds.), *Handbook of life design: From practice to theory and from theory to practice* (pp. 135–149). Boston, MA: Hogrefe.

Savickas, M. L., Nota, L., Rossier, J., Dauwalder, J. P., Duarte, E., Guichard, J., . . . van Vianen, A. E. M. (2009). Life designing: A paradigm for career construction in the 21st century. *Journal of Vocational Behavior, 75,* 239–250.

Shanahan, M. J. (2000). Pathways to adulthood in changing societies: Variability and mechanisms in life course perspective. *Annual Review of Sociology, 26,* 667–692.

Stead, G. B. (2004). Culture and career psychology: A social constructionist perspective. *Journal of Vocational Behavior, 64,* 389–406.

Stead, G. B., & Bakker, T. M. (2012). Self in work as a social/cultural construction. In P. McIlveen & D. E. Schultheiss (Eds.), *Social constructionism in vocational psychology and career development* (pp. 29–43). Rotterdam, The Netherlands: Sense.

Sweet, S. A., & Meiksins, P. F. (2013). *Changing contours of work: Jobs and opportunities in the new economy.* Thousand Oaks, CA: Sage.

Watson, M. B. (2006). Career counseling theory, culture and constructivism. In M. McMahon & W. Patton (Eds.), *Career counseling: Constructivist approaches* (pp. 45–56). New York, NY: Routledge.

Wijers, G., & Meijers, F. (1996). Career guidance in the knowledge society. *British Journal of Guidance and Counselling, 24,* 185–198.

Winnicott, D. W. (1975). The antisocial tendency. In *Through paediatrics to psychoanalysis* (pp. 306–315). New York, NY: Basic Books. (Original work published 1956)

Winnicott, D. W. (1986). Varieties of psychotherapy. In *Home is where we start from* (pp. 101–111). New York, NY: Norton. (Original work published 1961)

Chapter 2

The Postmodern Impulse and Career Counselor Preparation

Garrett J. McAuliffe and Judy Emmett

"What is done is done, but nothing is settled.
And if nothing is settled, then everything matters."
—Robert Walsh, Noisy Stones:
A Meditation Manual

"Nothing is settled." That phrase captures the postmodern ethos. Postmodernism has emerged as a guiding worldview for counseling in the 21st century. This worldview invites counselors and counselor educators to recognize the pervasive subjectivity of all human meaning making. Postmodernism asks individuals to be skeptical of any truth claims. The central focus of counseling shifts from "What is true?" to "What is helpful for clients under these circumstances?" Postmodernism is an invitation for counselors to be self-reflective, to be culturally alert, and to take multiple perspectives on the stories they are telling. It is a reminder that all understandings are subject to revision.

A "career," as Super (1990) would have it, consists of the life roles, including occupation, that a person constructs throughout the life span. This expression of the fluidity of all life careers contrasts with a static perspective on human endeavors. In postmodern terms, career can be viewed as a continuously emerging story of one's life experiences and roles. This unsettled, and unsettling, perspective is one of the foundational ideas for postmodern career counseling and counselor education.

If nothing is settled, what do counselor educators rely on to provide students with the understanding and methods needed to be good career counselors? Robert Walsh says that everything matters. In this chapter, we examine what matters for the postmodern career counseling project.

Traditionalism and Modernism: Alternate Epistemologies

Postmodernism can be contrasted with two other major epistemologies, or ways of knowing (Kegan, 1998). The first is traditionalism, wherein deference to external authority and adherence to cultural norms is ultimate, dictating by conformity to social norms what is good, true, and beautiful. In career terms, this adherence to received knowledge (Belenky, Clinchy, Goldberger, & Tarule, 1997) may be expressed in clients' rigid rules about gender roles, family dictates, and other inherited expectations. In Western intellectual history, traditionalism dominated thought in medieval times, as the authority of inherited doctrine was an unquestioned guide to life. In psychological terms, such a stance can be called *conventional knowing* (Kohlberg, 1969), in which adherence to external social norms is assumed to be the definitive guide to living. In the place of traditionalism, the great modernist intellectual enterprise emerged with the European Enlightenment of the 17th and 18th centuries. Modernism broke the code of traditionalism, instead seeking evidence-based truth. In psychological terms, modernism represents permission to "think for oneself," to use personalized methods to make decisions, such as career plans. However, modernism was a captive of its own scientific-rational paradigm. Modernists did not account for their Western perspective on how to find truth and live well.

In career terms, modernism relied on reason and scientific methods for guidance in choosing a life career path. That reliance translated into vocational guidance that used such methods as career testing and "right reasoning" (Parsons, 1909) for matching clients with occupations. In its best sense, modernism freed individuals from ultimate allegiance to social convention and authority. It contributed greatly to the notion that the individual was free to make a good career choice based on her or his own authority.

It can be argued that the modernist career counselor and client are captives of their somewhat fixed, nonreflexive paradigms for making good career decisions. Modernism relies on the notion that truth can be known if rational procedures for knowing can be used. Modernism set about fixing methods that are objectively "right" for good career–life decision making.

In the process of doing so, modernist career counseling theorists and educators pursue a truth outside of context about how to make career choices, looking for standards beyond culture and time, or geography and chronology (Gergen, 2009). Modernist educators, counselors, and researchers have ignored their own location in gender, social class, and ethnicity, to name a few elements of the social context. This approach fails to account for other versions of what to study and what to practice.

Postmodernism does not reject modernism. Thus it is "post," not "anti," modernism (Burbules & Rice, 1991). For example, postmodernism recognizes science as a path to understanding but challenges its premise as a totally objective, contextless pursuit. Postmodernism tempers the hubris of modernism with the recognition that meaning making is subjective and contextual. Postmodernism honors culture as an ineluctable presence in human meaning making, thereby mitigating the single-mindedness of objectivist science.

Postmodernism, Social Constructionism, Psychological Constructivism, and Narrative

A number of intellectual traditions come together under the aegis of postmodernism. These terms are related, and sometimes conflated, and you may benefit from some clarification.

Social Constructionism

One highly related cousin of postmodernism is social constructionism. Social constructionism emphasizes the inevitably social, or communal, context of human meaning making. Another way to describe social construction is to say that all meaning is saturated in culture, history, place, and time in the form of discourses such as social class, gender, ethnicity, race, disability, and religion.

Constructivism

Social constructionism is often confused with the more global notion of constructivism. Constructivism can be considered a *metatheory* (Raskin, 2002), which is an umbrella term that refers to locating the meaning of all experience in a person's subjective world. Constructivism rejects the notion of a purely objective, knowable reality. Instead, personal cognitive structures are emphasized as vehicles with which to make meaning of experience (Kelly, 1955). Constructivists seek to understand the lenses that people use to make meanings of experience. Technically speaking, psychological constructivism concentrates on reality as made individually through beliefs formed about self and the world, whereas social constructionism focuses on reality as made collectively through and within human experience and sensemaking (Hartung, 2013).

Despite the specialized meaning of psychological constructivism, for simplicity's sake *constructivism* will sometimes be used in this chapter as an umbrella term for postmodernism, and *social constructionism* will sometimes be used to represent the overall recognition of subjectivity in human affairs.

Narrative

The notion of narrative is an expression of this postmodern turn in thinking. The emergence of narrative in counseling and psychotherapy in the mid-1980s can be found in works by McAdams (1985), Bruner (1986), and Polkinghorne (1988), and later in the writings of White (2004). People compose their actions and events into a narrative structure, "an understandable composite" (Polkinghorne, 1988, p. 13). Through these narratives, they make meaning of their work, relationships, and leisure lives. They tell themselves what they are good at, what they value, and how they should accordingly act.

The notion of narrative can serve as an alert. No matter what the career inventories or experts seem to say, clients will still construct their own career-related narratives. Therefore, it behooves the career counselor to help the client express the most helpful narrative. How that translates into career counselor education is discussed later in this chapter.

Implications of Postmodernist Thinking

A constructivist approach is an invitation to a humbler, more inclusive, and more skeptical enterprise relative to the objectivist position on a knowable, neutral truth. Constructivism challenges people to acknowledge the basis for their constructions, to deconstruct their assumptions, and to take multiple perspectives on their supposed certainties.

One implication of postmodernism and social construction is egalitarianism. The counselor and client are fundamentally equals who are engaged in a mutual search for a helpful life narrative. The notion of the unquestionable expert is challenged by a recognition that there are many sources for meaning making.

Fluidity reigns in postmodern thinking. If all is story, as postmodernism suggests, there is no permanent foundation for human constructions such as science, religion, values, and career (Rorty, 1989). Instead, these are unstable beliefs that either work or do not work for a given situation. The opposite is a rigid obeisance to the idea of a permanent, lifelong occupation. Each individual, whether counselor or client, constructs and is constructed by her or his "storying." This gerund, with its emphasis on the "ing," implies that the individual is engaged in shifting, ongoing meaning making rather than being locked into a permanent condition dictated by, for example, predicted career interests or personality types.

Postmodernism and social constructionism ask career counselors to be inclusive and dialogical—that is, to consider all understandings by both counselors and clients to be socially constructed and in process—rather than to look for correct and permanent truths.

From a Modernist to a Postmodernist View of Career Counseling

Viewed through the postmodernist lens, a career is much more than a job or an objective chronology of one's job history. It can be described as a fluid storying of a life, an emerging and subjective narrative (Bateson, 1990; Cochran, 1992; Peavy, 1993) that is saturated with context, or what Kegan (1998) referred to as the social "surround." This subjectivist emphasis is iterated, for instance, by Peavy (1995), who has described career as an "evolving biographical narrative under continuous revision" (p. 2). Similarly, both

Miller-Tiedeman (1987) and Super (1990) have suggested the nonstatic view that everyone has a career (or is "careering"). It is their life. As mentioned previously, modernist models of career behavior relied largely on the assumption of the stability of personal characteristics throughout the life span (Savickas et al., 2009), yet individuals' "interests are never completely fixed, and the self is continuously reconstituted" (p. 242).

With exceptions (e.g., Super, 1990), modernist career counseling focused on work career, leaving out the intersection of life domains such as relationships, location, and health. However, with the pervasiveness of relative affluence and cultural changes (e.g., in gender roles), individuals have to carve out a satisfactory lifestyle under more tenuous circumstances. Work cannot be decontextualized, as was often done in modernist career counseling. For example, the Self-Directed Search (Holland, 1994b) focuses on occupations. That type of single focus is limited; it cannot account for the fact that life conditions change, interests evolve, and once quiescent aptitudes emerge. Occupation-focused career inventories, although potentially useful, are static.

Postmodernist career counseling offers a more dynamic, multiperspective take on life career. It also recognizes context. For example, postmodernist career counseling disaggregates social class–related career experiences that affect how consistent one's career path can be (i.e., whether one's work life is relatively steady, transitional, or sporadic). This contextual and dynamic emphasis requires related counseling sensibilities.

Career has not always been viewed this way. For three quarters of a century, career counseling relied on Parsons's (1909) matching model for vocational guidance. It was presented as a process of "true reasoning" by which a person's traits were matched to the requirements of an occupation. Counselors primarily viewed people as combinations of psychometric traits to be measured and matched to single best occupations for life. The counselor served the role of expert guide. In this view, counselors alone had the knowledge, hence the power, to enable clients to identify the best occupational choices (Peavy, 1993; Savickas, 1993).

This static, content-oriented approach to vocational guidance was eventually supplemented by a process approach to career education (e.g., Figler, 1993; Krumboltz, Mitchell, & Jones, 1976). The process model concentrated on how to make decisions, not on which occupation to choose. In applying the process model, practitioners help clients cope with the developmental career task of exploration by teaching them the attitudes, beliefs, and competencies that lead to realistic decisions (Busacca, 2002; McAuliffe & Fredrickson, 1990). Similar to vocational guidance, this process model of teaching developmental attitudes was often used with secondary school students. However, vocational guidance and career education do not have a significant relationship dimension; therefore, they are not considered to be career *counseling* as such (Crites, 1981).

Postmodernist Career Counseling

Postmodernists, in contrast to modernists, emphasize the role of clients as culturally anchored meaning makers who design (not discover) their own realities through continuous reflection on their unique life experiences and social contexts. Thus, postmodernist career counseling assumes a more facilitative, more collaborative, and less directive focus. It recognizes the need for adaptability and flexibility throughout the life span. In the process, the counselor is a companion with the client, one who shares the power and expertise with the client to design her or his life (Hoskins, 1995). The counselor needs to help the client construct a life story based on what matters at this time to the client (Giddens, 1991). Those "matterings" include concerns like care for others, evolving social justice commitments, changing lifestyle choices, and volatility in the job market.

Postmodernist career counselors help clients discern patterns, and consequently meaning, from previous life experiences and assist them in understanding and giving voice to their current life stories. A current story might presume a particular primacy, superiority, privilege, or importance, excluding other constructions. If the current story is unhelpful, the counselor helps the client "deconstruct" (Derrida, 1967) that story, probing for its foundations. In the current unhelpful story, gender, social class, family, or other cultural assumptions might dominate. These assumptions can be questioned. Instead of the client being beholden to "received" messages from authorities (Belenky et al., 1997), the postmodern career counseling process encourages the client to "author" her or his own career story (Kegan, 1998). In this sense, the current stories become interesting narratives, not imperatives.

Through this process, clients become able to make decisions and to extend or modify their life stories because of new understandings about what has influenced their choices and about what meaning they have ascribed to past experiences. Cochran (1992) described postmodernist career counselors as "coauthors of stories in progress." Those stories are evolving and unsteady; they are not fixed in an isolated universe of discrete, permanent life roles. Instead, postmodernism invites openness to competing interpretations. The central theme is meaning making in a discontinuous life span, with the understanding that meaning making is a product of self-reflection. The hoped-for result is a client's relatively self-directed or "self-authorized" (Kegan, 1998) life career.

Five dimensions can be considered in postmodern constructivist career counseling. They are characteristic of all of the epistemologies that are the foundations for this book. These five dimensions are dynamic processes, nonlinear progression, multiple perspectives, personal patterns, and dialogue (Savickas et al., 2009). Each can be honored in postmodern career counseling.

Dynamic Processes

Individuals face a lifetime of changing occupations, jobs, and roles within an occupation or job. "Temporary fit" is a more useful metaphor for occupation–person match than is the notion of a static lifelong occupation. Therefore, a person is involved in ongoing career storying, in contrast to the illusory notion of a permanent or semipermanent life career role. "Managing" might be a better notion than "matching" concerning career construction. In this view, the counselor helps a client manage "how" to engage in a life career rather than "what" to do (Savickas et al., 2009).

Nonlinear Progression

The simple formula of assessment–interpretation that characterized much modernist career counseling does not fit the complexity of the life career. Instead, a counseling relationship might incorporate happenstance, shifting aptitudes and interests, and changing relationship circumstances. This counseling process reflects the nonlinear nature of a life career. Teaching clients how to make decisions under changing, uncertain conditions is likely to be superior to trying only to predict a long-term person–environment match.

Multiple Perspectives

Rather than relying on scientific generalizations, postmodern career counselors invite clients to identify their own narratives about their career lives, incorporating multiple elements. The counselor can prompt the client to consider such factors as cultural imperatives, family expectations, accuracy of self-constructions, socioeconomic understandings, age-related considerations, relationship changes, and internalized gender rules. These factors can emerge from a client's narrative rather than in a single-perspective generalization about a lifelong suitable career match.

Personal Patterns

Overwhelming all generalizations is the idiosyncratic nature of the emerging life career for any one person. No standardized career counseling mode can do justice to the unique construction of the life career of an individual.

It should be noted that postmodern career counseling does not entirely discard the modernist constructions of occupation–person matching and testing (e.g., Holland, 1994a) or of plotting career phases and tasks (e.g., Super, 1990). Instead, it builds on those achievements while casting a skeptical eye on their ultimate coherence for any one individual. Thus the modernist career formulations are interesting possibilities to be incorporated into the storying of career.

Dialogue

Dialogue is the sine qua non of postmodern career counseling. According to Peavy (1992, 1993), postmodernist career counselors value multiple realities, believing that there is no "one right way" to see the world and no one best way to go about constructing or interpreting one's life story. Postmodernist counselors value dialogue that enhances both their own understanding of the client's perspective as well as the client's understanding of his or her own world. During such dialogue, the counselor listens for and reflectively questions the internal meaning-making processes of the client. Counselors help clients recognize the impacts, including both opportunities and constraints, of their individual contexts and cultures upon their experiences and their interpretation of those experiences. During such dialogue, postmodernist career counselors remain authentically present with their clients. They create counseling environments that balance both the support and the challenge necessary for growth. This dialogue promotes the understanding that empowers and informs future choice.

Postmodernist Career Counselor Qualities

Peavy (1994) proposed that effective postmodernist career counselors possess three key competencies. The first is *mindfulnesss,* or reflexivity. In this quality lies the ability to observe oneself and consequently understand oneself as a constructed(ing) person, with a personal "life career" story of one's own. That story is composed of the counselor's personally and socially constructed interpretations, assumptions, and biases. To the extent that counselors are mindful, they attend to clients without imposing their own meanings or direction onto a client's emerging life story.

The second competency is *receptive inquiry.* This stance consists of creating a climate in which clients feel safe while being respectfully questioned about their assumptions and interpretations of experiences. Through inquiry, sometimes called *being curious* in narrative therapy terms, counselors empower clients to critically examine their actions, their beliefs, and the contextual influences on their thinking, their choices, and their lives.

The third competency is *meaning-making facilitation.* Through deconstructive inquiry, counselors help clients derive readings of their "texts" (their storying of life career matters). The counselor must possess a repertoire of strategies and skills to assist clients in discovering themes, patterns, and meanings ascribed to their life stories and in creating alternative, more helpful stories.

Narrative-Constructivist Career Counseling Practice

One expression of postmodernism is narrative/constructivist career counseling (NCCC). (*Narrative* and *constructivist* are used interchangeably here.) NCCC is an approach to accompanying people in understanding their life stories and in designing their life careers. It represents a shift from career guidance as matching to career counseling as meaning making. Narrative-oriented career counseling is personal counseling in a full sense.

The counselor is an inquiring companion who helps the client know the lenses (e.g., ethnicity, gender) through which she or he is storying her or his career life. The hope is that revealing themes, preoccupations, and aspirations will help to drive the story forward. The counselor helps the client look for presuppositions, asks about the basis for such presuppositions, and helps the client examine them and determine if they are helpful. As mentioned previously, and by contrast, modernist career theory proposes that a career truth (in the form of a matching occupation) can be found by some method (e.g., "true reasoning"). Instead, the NCCC counselor explores meanings with the client but does not interpret meanings. The counselor assists the client in discovering the meanings, often using questions.

Narrative postmodern career counseling is not a rejection of modernist methods. In practice, the narrative career counselor can use so-called objective measures, such as person–occupation matching instruments.

However, NCCC treats the inventories as interesting data, or "processes that have possibilities" (Savickas, 2005, p. 42), instead of as objective predictions of a person's career path. The way these theories and tools are used defines postmodern career counseling. Instead of using instruments to interpret and guide, the narrative career counselor is a companion to the client as she or he constructs her or his career life through dialogue. The narrative career counselor might help the client discover how the inventories evoke other stories, as we describe in the next section. In all, the key to NCCC is that the client is helped to embrace the most helpful current life career narrative.

Career Counselor Training and Postmodernism

Given the shift toward a postmodern career counseling ethos, counselor education now needs to instigate experiences that are likely to encourage future counselors to be mindful of the process of career construction. In particular, the counselor educator should facilitate the development in future counselors of mindfulness, receptive inquiry, and meaning-making facilitation.

Training in constructivist career counseling is reflexive and experiential. In general, the counselor educator provides a safe but challenging learning environment in which students can reflect on their own career stories. They would be encouraged to understand the experiences and influences that have shaped and will continue to shape them as counselors. In the learning process, they can themselves come to be more mindful and thus become able to encourage future clients to do the same.

In addition to examining their personal career stories, students also need opportunities to experience actual career counseling work and then reflect on the meanings of those experiences. Through that dual process, students will become more intentional as career counselors.

Two dimensions of a constructivist career counseling education course illustrate these general notions. One is an initial course activity, and the other is the constructivist teaching of career development theories.

Initial Constructivist Activity: StoryTech

A grounding activity that sets the tone for a constructivist career counselor education course is called StoryTech (Harkins & Kubik, 2012). This model was created by professor and futurist Arthur Harkins of the University of Minnesota to describe a structured visioning process. It requires students to examine their own narratives about career, thereby attuning them to the subjectivist foundation for postmodernist career counseling.

The process is introduced early in a career counseling course and continues throughout the term. Each StoryTech instrument consists of a series of open-ended lead statements. Students respond to these leads by creating visualized stories. These stories feature the student writer telling her or his own life story, enjoying a perfect day, identifying troublesome career beliefs, confronting personal feelings about the career future and the overwhelming array of career information available, and functioning effectively as a career counselor with clients. This technique and its use in a career counseling class has been described in detail elsewhere (Emmett & Harkins, 1997).

Throughout the course, students complete written visualizations. They then respond to a series of reflective questions designed to illuminate themes or patterns in their stories. The aim is for students to realize that projecting their personal beliefs may both help and hinder their work with some clients.

Students examine their stories for insights into their personal views on life, on work, and on career. They reflect on how their unique life experiences of race, gender, class, culture, sexual orientation, or age have influenced those views. In addition, they consider how their particular experiences and viewpoints influence how they view career counseling and how they imagine they will practice career counseling. Finally, students identify areas in which to seek feedback from their classmates.

In the initial StoryTech experience, students describe themselves as children, recalling how they dealt with significant life events. They then characterize their approach to life as the title of a book. In reflecting on their stories, students look for central themes and for indications of contexts in which they will likely be helpful (or not) to their future clients. Classmates meet every 2 to 3 weeks in the same reflection group of two to four students to share their StoryTechs. In these sessions, they both give and receive feedback about how they view the role of career counselor and how they are likely to interact with clients in a career counseling setting.

At the end of the semester, students write essays in which they synthesize their life career stories. They reflect on how their own life stories will affect how they practice as career counselors, incorporating what they have learned about themselves as counselors throughout the semester.

Teaching Career Theory

A central feature of a career counseling course is teaching career theory. Theories about career patterns, decision making, planning, self-efficacy, and development attempt to explain patterns that students might look for in counseling individuals and designing programs. However, a postmodern perspective on teaching career theories has a particular slant. Consistent with postmodernism, career theories are not taught as objective givens but are instead deconstructed for their location in time (era), place (culture), and theorists' biographies. Deconstructing theories can illustrate the constructed nature of knowledge.

When comparing career theorists' ideas and explanations about people's career lives, students become aware that no one "best" or "perfect" explanation exists for how people make career decisions or integrate their life roles. Furthermore, when students examine the historical and individual contexts in which the career theorists developed their theories, they find out how the varied life experiences of the theorists and the theorists' varied interpretations of those experiences resulted in the construction of different career theories. Each theory potentially offers some important understandings; no theory completely explains career choice or career development for all people. Each theory is both skewed and incomplete.

The postmodern recognition of how careers and career theories are constructed can affect how students go about counseling practice in at least three ways. First, they can treat career theories as potentially helpful tools but not certainties. Second, future counselors can also become aware of the career theory (or theories) by which they themselves operate. Finally, they can become alert to the informal career theories that have already been constructed by their clients. An example of using a personalized, experiential approach to teaching career theories is the career interview.

Discovering Theory Through Career Interviews
The career interview process, consisting of at least three interviews, begins inductively, with the instructor directing students to ask a family member, friend, neighbor, or classmate how she or he thinks about career. Instructors may further ask interviewees additional questions or engage in any topic of discussion that seems relevant to career. Students then bring the results of these interviews back to class and share them with classmates. Students discuss and reflect on similarities and differences in interviewees' responses to similar questions. They also speculate on what those replies might mean about both the questioner and the person questioned.

Students subsequently examine these interviews through the lenses of different career theories (e.g., typological, trait and factor, differential, developmental, existential, decision making, behavioral, social cognitive) to determine the usefulness of their theories to their work with particular clients. Students discover that they almost always favor some theoretical views over others. They also begin to understand that clients also operate from belief systems that more closely resemble those of one theory over another.

Finally, when students examine the interview questions they selected or the topics of discussion they chose to pursue, they begin to see how their choice of focus reveals their implicit career theories. When they intentionally change focus in successive interviews, students begin to appreciate how they are selecting particular career theories with which to work. They are in the process of constructing working theories based on their current experiences.

The final assignment for the theory section of the course is for students to tell the life story of one of their interviewees. They "explain" in an essay the client's career development from the point of view of several theorists and how a counselor would apply each theory with the client. Finally, students name elements of two theories that might direct their work with that client, reflecting on how their own social identity (i.e., race, gender, age, class) might influence their choice of theories and their work with that client. Thus, they synthesize and evaluate the various career theories and integrate selected elements of the theories with strategies for using them in a postmodern narrative manner with clients.

Conclusion

Career counselors assist clients with the examination of the beliefs and other constructs they have used to create meaning in their lives. In addition, counselors help clients hypothesize alternative constructs, test those constructs, and develop action plans for implementing the constructs that promise to be useful in extending or rewriting their life stories.

The constructivist teaching of career counseling follows a parallel process. Students of counseling examine the beliefs and the constructs that they themselves have as career counselors. They experience the diversity of constructs about career counseling held by their peers. They have the opportunity to hypothesize alternative constructs and to test the effects those alternate constructs have on their conducting of career counseling sessions. As students learn to examine their own career-related constructs, they learn the process for helping clients to do likewise.

Postmodernist constructivist career counseling has a particular advantage in its synchronicity with the demands of the dominant 21st-century ethos, in which intellectual and cultural diversity are pervasive. In that vein, postmodernism encourages counselors to become competent with clients who hold differing worldviews, a necessity in meeting today's mental health needs. A postmodernist education that values multiple perspectives and that teaches the skills of mindfulness and receptive inquiry makes that more likely.

References

Bateson, M. C. (1990). *Composing a life*. New York, NY: Penguin.

Belenky, M. F., Clinchy, B. M., Goldberger, N. R., & Tarule, J. M. (1997). *Women's ways of knowing*. New York, NY: Basic Books.

Bruner, J. (1986). *Actual minds, possible worlds*. Cambridge, MA: Harvard University Press.

Burbules, N. C., & Rice, S. (1991). Dialogue across differences: Continuing the conversation. *Harvard Educational Review, 61*, 393–417.

Busacca, L. A. (2002). Career problem assessment: A conceptual schema for counselor training. *Journal of Career Development, 29*, 129–146.

Cochran, L. (1992). The career project. *Journal of Career Development, 18*, 187–198.

Crites, J. O. (1981). *Career counseling: Models, methods, and materials*. New York, NY: McGraw-Hill.

Derrida, J. (1967). *L'Écriture et la différence*. Paris, France: Éditions du Seuil.

Emmett, J. D., & Harkins, A. M. (1997). StoryTech: Exploring the use of a narrative technique for training career counselors. *Counselor Education and Supervision, 37*, 60–73.

Figler, H. E. (1993). *PATH: A career workbook for liberal arts students*. Cranston, RI: Carroll Press.

Gergen, K. J. (2009). *An invitation to social construction*. Thousand Oaks, CA: Sage.

Giddens, A. (1991). *Modernity and self-identity: Self and society in the late modern age.* Cambridge, UK: Polity Press.

Harkins, A. M., & Kubik, G. H. (2012). *StoryTech: A personalized guide to the 21st century.* Minneapolis, MN: Education Futures.

Hartung, P. J. (2013). Career as story: Making the narrative turn. In W. B. Walsh, M. L. Savickas, & P. J. Hartung (Eds.), *Handbook of vocational psychology: Theory, research and practice* (4th ed., pp. 33–52). New York, NY: Routledge.

Holland, J. L. (1994a). *Self-Directed Search (SDS).* Odessa, FL: Psychological Assessment Resources.

Holland, J. L. (1994b). *Self-Directed Search Form R: 1994 edition.* Odessa, FL: Psychological Assessment Resources.

Hoskins, M. (1995). *Postmodernist approaches for career counselors.* Unpublished manuscript, ERIC Digest ED401505.

Kegan, R. (1998). *In over our heads: The mental demands of modern life.* Cambridge, MA: Harvard University Press.

Kelly, G. (1955). *The psychology of personal constructs.* New York, NY: Norton.

Kohlberg, L. (1969). Stage and sequence: The cognitive-developmental approach to socialization. In D. A. Goslin (Ed.), *The handbook of socialization theory and research* (pp. 347–480). Chicago, IL: Rand McNally.

Krumboltz, J. D., Mitchell, A. M., & Jones, G. B. (1976). A social learning theory of career selection. *The Counseling Psychologist, 6,* 71–81.

McAdams, D. P. (1985). *Power, intimacy, and the life story: Persononological inquiries into identity.* New York, NY: Guilford Press.

McAuliffe, G. J., & Fredrickson, R. H. (1990). The effects of program length and participant characteristics on group career counseling outcomes. *Journal of Employment Counseling, 27,* 19–23.

Miller-Tiedeman, A. (1987). *How to not make it . . . and succeed: The truth about your lifecareer.* Los Angeles, CA: LIFECAREER Foundation.

Parsons, F. (1909). *Choosing a vocation.* Boston, MA: Houghton Mifflin.

Peavy, R. V. (1992). A postmodernist model of training for career counselors. *Journal of Career Development, 18,* 215–228.

Peavy, R. V. (1993). Envisioning the future: Worklife and counselling. *Canadian Journal of Counselling, 27,* 123–139.

Peavy, R. V. (1994). Postmodernist counselling: A prospectus. *Guidance and Counseling, 9,* 3–12.

Peavy, R. V. (1995). *Postmodernist career counseling.* Unpublished manuscript, ERIC Digest ED401504.

Polkinghorne, D. E. (1988). *Narrative knowing and the human sciences.* Albany, NY: SUNY Press.

Raskin, J. D. (2002). Constructivism in psychology: Personal construct psychology, radical constructivism, and social constructionism. In J. D. Raskin & S. K. Bridges (Eds.), *Studies in meaning: Exploring constructivist psychology* (pp. 1–25). New York, NY: Pace University Press.

Rorty, R. (1989). *Contingency, irony, and solidarity.* Cambridge, UK: Cambridge University Press.

Savickas, M. L. (1993). Career counseling in the postmodern era. *Journal of Cognitive Psychotherapy, 7,* 205–215.

Savickas, M. L. (2005). The theory and practice of career construction. In S. D. Brown & R.W. Lent (Eds.), *Career development and counseling: Putting theory and research to work* (pp. 42–70). Hoboken, NJ: Wiley.

Savickas, M. L., Nota, L., Rossier, J., Dauwalder, J., Duarte, M. E., Guichard, J., . . . Van Vianen, A. E. (2009). Life designing: A paradigm for career construction in the 21st century. *Journal of Vocational Behavior, 75,* 239–250.

Super, D. E. (1990). A life-span, life-space approach to career development. In D. Brown, L. Brooks, & Associates (Eds.), *Career choice and development: Applying contemporary theories to practice* (2nd ed., pp. 197–261). San Francisco, CA: Jossey-Bass.

Walsh, R. R. (1991). *Noisy stones: A meditation manual.* Boston, MA: Skinner House Books.

White, M. (2004). Folk psychology and narrative practice. In L. E. Angus & J. McLeod (Eds.), *The handbook of narrative and psychotherapy: Practice, theory, and research* (pp. 15–51). Thousand Oaks, CA: Sage.

Part II

PRINCIPLES

Chapter 3

Multicultural Career Counseling: Limitations of Traditional Career Theory and Scope of Training

Kathy M. Evans and Viki P. Kelchner

Traditional career counseling approaches adhere to a single worldview. Today multicultural career counselors need to be skilled at understanding and negotiating multiple realities, or pluralistic perspectives. Macro cultural beliefs about individualism versus collectivism need to be interpreted differently within the micro world of the client (Savickas, 2003). These and other challenges call for career counselors to move out of their comfort zone, deconstruct how they have perceived career barriers and the counseling process, and reconstruct their theoretical and assessment frameworks (Watson, 2006). This stance requires counselors to move from applying "one grand narrative to everyone" (Savickas, 1993, p. 211) to helping clients construct the local narrative as they perceive it. In this chapter, we explore how diverse clients fit into existing career development theories and consider how well these theories explain and support the experiences of clients.

Traditional Career Approaches

Traditional career theories were developed prior to the rise of the multicultural "fourth force" (Pedersen, 2013) and reflect the modernistic scientific approach to theory fashioned by the hard sciences. Modernism is grounded in the belief that knowledge is generalizable to all populations through a "grand narrative"—what is true for one is true for all (Savickas, 2012). These theories espouse the idea that there is only one real answer, one truth, one way to think about career development and that this one way is measurable, is researchable, and can be proven. Many of the traditional modernist theories used by career counseling professionals were developed in the early to mid-20th century and reflected the culturally encapsulated and paternalistic views of that time. The focus was on middle- to upper class White males for whom opportunities were limitless, career advancement was linear, and jobs were stable and secure (Arthur, 2006). This narrow ethnocentric approach to career counseling can no longer be supported as the sole approach to helping clients in the diverse world of today. Even with updates and revisions to make them more inclusive, most modernist theories do not adequately address the needs of today's culturally diverse populations (Richardson, 2012).

In recent years, modernist theories also have been criticized because they fail to reflect the changing world of work in the 21st century. Career development has evolved beyond simply helping clients plan a linear movement from career choice to stable employment in the same occupation. Today's clients face a work world in which jobs are consistently changing. Postmodern career approaches have gained favor in the career field because they more closely reflect the everyday lives of today's workers (Young & Collin, 2004). In contrast to the "one real truth" perspective of modernist theories, postmodern career approaches embrace multiple perspectives, embrace multiple truths, and view clients in the context of their lives (D'Andrea, 2000; McMahon & Watson, 2007). Postmodern approaches that value seeing the world through multiple perspectives are gaining favor in the multicultural arena as well. Career counselors are increasingly integrating postmodern techniques not only to meet the needs of their culturally different clients but to more accurately reflect the unpredictable world of work clients face today (Savickas, 2003).

Multicultural Limitations of Traditional Career Theories

The traditional theories of career counseling are long-standing. Although research on the modernist perspective has been extensive, understanding how these theories can be used with multicultural populations remains unclear (Evans, 2008; Peterson & González, 2005). In this section, we look at three of these theories in more detail: trait and factor theory, Holland's personality theory of vocational choice, and developmental theory.

Trait and Factor Theory

Frank Parsons's concept of vocational guidance and its propositions evolved into what is known as trait and factor theory, and it is one of the cornerstones of career counseling and development (Sharf, 2013). The essence of the theory is that individuals possess measureable characteristics, or traits, and abilities that match the requirements of certain occupations, and when the match is appropriate, the end result is a lifetime of occupational satisfaction (O'Brien, 2001; Parsons, 1909). Some common assessment tools include interest inventories, personality inventories, values inventories, and achievement and ability/aptitude tests. Trait and factor theory provides an easily understood and effective guide for counselors to help clients explore their interests, abilities, values, and personality factors. There are more negatives than positives to traditional trait and factor theory, however, when it is applied to culturally different clients. Krumboltz (1993) pointed out that, in its simplicity, trait and factor theory neglects other factors that shape an individual, such as family involvement, religion and community pressures, gender stereotyping, and status considerations. In addition, trait and factor theory does not account for the fact that certain traits that are desirable for one group may not be as desirable for other groups. For example, characteristics desirable in male managers are not necessarily desirable in female managers (Duehr & Bono, 2006). Multicultural theorists have also criticized the trait and factor approach because of its dependence on normative samples: (a) Diverse groups are not identified; (b) insufficient numbers of diverse groups are sampled; and (c) within-group diversity is not acknowledged. The result is that the normative group is representative of the dominant White, middle class, heterosexual population, and cultural test bias cannot be determined (Leong & Serafica, 2001). Thus, counselors find it necessary to compare culturally diverse clients to a set of norms that may or may not apply to them (Evans, 2008).

Holland's Theory

John Holland's theory of vocational choice is a trait and factor approach based on personality factors (Gottfredson & Johnstun, 2009). Holland postulated that individuals are drawn to work environments that best match their personalities. His typology outlines six different personality types among individuals and six corresponding work environments to which each personality type is drawn. In using this theory, counselors employ personality testing and classification of employment environments. Holland's theory is helpful in organizing information about individuals and career alternatives and in understanding individuals' entry persistence in occupational and other environments (Gottfredson & Johnstun, 2009). It is a clear, well-organized theory that is easily interpreted by others, making it one of the most popular and most widely used career counseling theories (Gottfredson & Johnstun, 2009; Ohler & Levinson, 2012). Holland's Self-Directed Search enables clients to organize factors about themselves much like the Strong Interest Inventory, which also uses Holland's codes. In 1997, Holland updated his work by elaborating on the person–environment fit and providing research to support his additions to the theory (Gottfredson & Johnstun, 2009).

From a multicultural standpoint, Holland's theory of vocational choice misses the link to the cultural context of clients' lives. In fact, modernist paradigm researchers tend to view culture and diversity as nuisance variables that have to be controlled so the one real truth or universal knowledge can be discovered (Stead, 2004; Young, Marshall, & Valach, 2007). Holland's theory also has been criticized for being too heavily dependent on standardized testing; for assuming that it is acceptable to stereotype careers with clients because careers are stereotyped in society in terms of gender and ethnicity; and for failing to address the impact of race, gender, socioeconomic status, sexual orientation, and ability status (Evans, 2008; Peterson & González, 2005).

Developmental Theory

Donald Super (1994) developed one of the most comprehensive theories of career development, and he updated it continuously throughout his lifetime. His developmental theory describes the process individuals employ to learn about, gain, maintain, and leave their careers. Super viewed careers as unfolding in a series of developmental stages, with each stage being characterized by an appropriate task (Patton & Lokan, 2001). From this developmental premise arose the concept of *career maturity*, which refers to the individual's ability to achieve developmental tasks within a predicted timeline. However, when it became apparent that many people were not remaining in one occupation for their entire work lives, Super reimagined this concept to account for the fact that individuals had to recycle through the stages when changing careers (Super, 1994).

According to Super, career exploration begins in childhood and is expressed through curiosity and exploration, which contribute to one's sense of self (Sharf, 2013). A cornerstone of Super's theory is the importance of choosing a career that fulfills one's self-concept. Self-concept is the perception individuals have of themselves coupled with how others perceive them. Self-concept may include traits such as self-esteem, self-efficacy, and role self-concept, and these traits help to craft one's personality (Sterner, 2012).

Super, Savickas, and Super (1996) identified six major roles people play throughout their lives: child, student, worker, citizen, homemaker, and leisurite. The life space concept involves these roles (Sterner, 2012). Individuals inaugurate values and meaning through life roles. The life space element of this theory is readily adapted to ethnic minority and other oppressed groups because it acknowledges the individual's perception of his or her world and the importance of defining roles based on the individual's culture.

The concept of career maturity has been questioned in relation to some diverse groups because of the lack of attention it gives to cultural influences and the high correlation of the cognitive scales of the instrument, which measures maturity (e.g., Career Development Inventory), and intelligence tests, socioeconomic status, and the absence of cultural influences (Patton & Creed, 2001). As measured, career maturity depends on individuals having career information, but poverty limits access to those resources. The overrepresentation of ethnic minority groups among the poor, therefore, means that the concept of career maturity is not easily transferable to these populations. The tasks that need to be completed at each stage are relevant even if the age specification for completion of these tasks is not.

Finally, the idea that occupations satisfy one's self-concept may not apply to ethnic minorities and members of oppressed groups. Many individuals who live in poverty work for survival and not necessarily as a means to fulfill their lives. Discrimination and poverty may prohibit individuals from fulfilling their self-concept through job choices (Evans, 2008). It is likely, though, that counselors can help clients find fulfillment outside of their jobs—for example, in religious, community, and fraternal organizations.

Summary

In general, career counselors who adhere solely to the modernist perspective may find the following limitations when working with culturally diverse clients:

- One real truth, or a "grand narrative," cannot explain career development for all people.
- Cultural differences and environmental influences affect people's lives.
- Career development is no longer linear, and all opportunities are not open to all people.
- Counselors must adjust their theoretical framework to match clients' needs in today's world of work.
- Focusing on personal variables without regard to race/ethnicity, gender, socioeconomic status, and other factors limits counselors' effectiveness with diverse clients.

Boundaries of Modernist Career Assessment

One of the criticisms of traditional theories, especially trait and factor and Holland's theory of vocational choice, is a dependence on standardized testing that is inappropriate for many culturally different clients (Worthington, Flores, & Navarro, 2005). Several problems arise when testing culturally diverse clients in this way:

- A lack of appropriate norms for specific racial/ethnic groups for many of the most widely used instruments
- The influence of English language proficiency and the need for appropriate translations of tests into different languages
- The potential conflicts that may arise when using tests for purposes that may be culturally incongruent for people of color
- The need for multicultural counseling training to promote appropriate test use and interpretation for people of color (p. 236)

Counselors are sometimes compelled to use standardized instruments given their employment setting (e.g., in K–12 schools). When that is the case, researchers and professional organizations have suggested helpful strategies that include (a) knowing one's self and one's biases toward assessment and deconstructing them (Evans, 2013), (b) knowing the cultural limitations of the instruments being used (Association for Assessment in

Research and Counseling, 2012; Worthington et al., 2005), (c) beginning with qualitative assessments to understand the client's culture and his or her story (Flores, Spanierman, & Obasi, 2003), (d) choosing tests appropriately by following published guidelines such as those recommended by the Association for Assessment and Research in Counseling (2012), and (e) including cultural information and integrating qualitative and standardized results when interpreting the results (Comas-Díaz, 1996; Flores et al., 2003; Ridley, Li, & Hill, 1998). Assessment issues are discussed in detail in Chapter 5.

Career counselors who are culturally competent are aware of the adjustments they need to make to the traditional theories and to career assessments to meet the needs of their diverse clients. Unfortunately, multicultural training, as it is currently taught, often falls short in developing career counselors who are culturally competent.

The Scope of Multicultural Training for Career Counseling

The shortcomings of multicultural training have limited career counselors' abilities to adjust traditional career theories to better assist current clients. Training in multicultural counseling has been offered for decades, and it has grown and evolved over the years. Initially, the focus was on teaching counselors about culturally different populations, or "the other." The target population was mostly White students, so training involved helping counselors learn about groups that differed from them. It was thought that this knowledge would help change any negative attitudes and beliefs students might hold about "the other."

Over the years, multicultural training expanded to include diversity training (which took into greater consideration the experiences of sexual minorities, people with disabilities, religious minorities, etc.), but the focus was still on learning about "the other." Researchers have found, however, that knowledge-based exposure (book learning) alone regarding diverse populations may lead to resistance, to even more strongly held prejudices and biases, or to avoidance of intergroup interaction (Jayaratne et al., 2006). This limited exposure, intended to provide knowledge of "the other" and increase sensitivity, often had the opposite effect. Career counselors who reacted to multicultural training in this way might refuse to work with culturally diverse clients or might provide inadequate assistance for the career needs of culturally diverse clients.

With findings like these, many multicultural trainers expanded their focus from just learning about other groups to emphasizing self-knowledge of the trainees' own prejudices, biases, and values. Once these attitudes were brought to the surface and processed, it was hoped that bias and prejudice would be reduced. Chao, Okazaki, and Hong (2011) pointed out that this approach may be viewed as accusatory, increasing the possibility of "reactance and resistance, reducing individuals' motivation to engage in cultural competence trainings" (p. 268). This resistance to training leaves the career counselor unprepared to work with clients who are culturally different.

Multicultural training rarely goes beyond the intellectual understanding of differences to the actual exposure of trainees to culturally different populations. Lewis, Bethea, and Hurley (2009) suggested that multicultural training should be infused into all courses, that trainees should participate in experiential activities in those courses, and that they should also be required to intern at sites with a diverse clientele. Just as Savickas (2015) critiqued the traditional career theorists for failing to provide the "how" of implementing theories, it seems that multicultural training hasn't gone far enough into the "how" of learning multicultural skills with actual clients.

Arredondo et al. (1996) described three areas of multicultural counseling competence: cultural self-awareness, awareness of the client's worldview, and culturally appropriate intervention strategies. Lewis and colleagues (2009) believed training has been inadequate in terms of intervention. When career counseling trainees receive their field training, it is important for them to work with a culturally diverse clientele to understand the "how" of culturally competent career counseling. Even if career counseling trainees do not experience the negative reactions to training previously mentioned, they will not develop the skills necessary to work effectively with culturally diverse clients unless their multicultural training extends to practicum and internship training sites (Lewis et al., 2009).

Diversity and the Postmodern Perspective for Career Counseling

A postmodern perspective provides a foundation for improved multicultural training and delivery of culturally appropriate career counseling. As Leong and Hartung (2000) noted, postmodern approaches in counseling and therapy inherently support and advance culturally sensitive career counseling and assessment. Inserting multicultural models into career paradigms that draw on constructivist and social constructionist epistemologies is unnecessary because these models are intrinsically present (Busacca & Rehfuss, 2017). Sue and Sue (2013) asked us to reflect on an old Asian saying: "All individuals, in many respects are (a) like no other individuals, (b) like some individuals, and (c) like all individuals" (p. 41). Multiple perspectives are needed to adequately serve multiple populations. A postmodern or, more specifically, a constructionist perspective helps counselors and trainees understand that "it is not group membership per se that imbues understanding, rather it is the meanings and interpretations of culture derived by individuals" (Arthur, 2006, p. 59).

Career counselors who integrate postmodern principles into career counseling paradigms help clients gain a deeper understanding of the meaning of their life experiences as well as the meaning they assign to their problems. Counselor and client work together to discover the meaning clients assign to their experiences and to deconstruct problem stories. In a constructivist approach to career counseling, clients are empowered to develop a cognitive shift from feeling defeated to feeling in charge (Grier-Reed, Skaar, & Parson, 2009). Clients are actively involved in their counseling and are encouraged to act as agents in building their own lives. This approach to understanding careers is helpful to diverse populations because it validates their view of the microaggressions, discrimination, and other daily challenges they experience. It also relieves counselors from having to fit their clients into a preconceived category as is common when using a modernist approach.

When counseling diverse clients, keep the following points in mind:

- Cultural diversity includes race and ethnicity, but it also encompasses gender, sexual orientation, disability, age, socioeconomic class, and other marginalized groups along with their intersectional identities (Arthur & Collins, 2010; Sue & Sue, 2008).
- Every client has a unique cultural background, and that background has some level of importance to the client (Pedersen, 1991).
- An individual's experience is not tied to a single cultural identity that is bounded by group membership (Arthur, 2006).
- Counselors encourage clients' active agency, or self-helpfulness (Peavy, 1992).
- The influence of culture on a client's career development depends on the meaning that individual ascribes to these influences (Watson, 2006).
- Over time, individuals build belief systems that help them understand themselves and the world; counselors can help in this discovery process by attending to the unique and personal accounts of clients' lives (Peterson & González, 2005).

Conclusion

The postmodern perspective for career counseling offers a number of advantages to multicultural counselors. These approaches release counselors from having to fit their clients into a traditional theoretical model and from using standardized instruments that may not be applicable to the populations they serve. They also relieve the counselor from having to be the expert. By encouraging clients to participate fully in the counseling process, counselors see the world through their clients' eyes. Counselors' understanding and acceptance of their clients' truths is empowering to both parties.

References

Arredondo, P., Toporek, R., Brown, S. P., Jones, J., Locke, D. C., Sanchez, J., & Stadler, H. (1996). Operationalization of the multicultural counseling competencies. *Journal of Multicultural Counseling and Development, 24*, 42–78.

Arthur, N. (2006). Infusing culture in constructivist approaches to career counselling. In M. McMahon & W. Patton (Eds.), *Career counseling: Constructivist approaches* (pp. 57–68). New York, NY: Routledge.

Arthur, N., & Collins, S. (2010). Social justice and culture-infused counselling. In N. Arthur & S. Collins (Eds.), *Culture-infused counselling* (2nd ed., pp. 139–164). Calgary, Alberta, Canada: Counselling Concepts.

Association for Assessment in Research and Counseling. (2012). *Standards for multicultural assessment: Fourth revision.* Retrieved from http://www.theaaceonline.com/AACE-AMCD.pdf

Busacca, L. A., & Rehfuss, M. C. (2017). Preface. In L. A. Busacca & M. C. Rehfuss (Eds.), *Postmodern career counseling: A handbook of culture, context, and cases* (pp. xi–xix). Alexandria, VA: American Counseling Association.

Chao, M. M., Okazaki, S., & Hong, Y. Y. (2011). The quest for multicultural competence: Challenges and lessons learned from clinical and organizational research. *Social and Personality Psychology Compass, 5,* 263–274.

Comas-Díaz, L. (1996). Cultural considerations in diagnosis. In F. W. Kaslow (Ed.), *Handbook of relational diagnosis and dysfunctional family patterns* (pp. 152–168). Oxford, England: Wiley.

D'Andrea, M. (2000). Postmodernism, constructivism, and multiculturalism: Three forces reshaping and expanding our thoughts about counseling. *Journal of Mental Health Counseling, 22,* 1–6.

Duehr, E. E., & Bono, J. E. (2006). Men, women, and managers: Are stereotypes finally changing? *Personnel Psychology, 59,* 815–846.

Evans, K. (2008). *Gaining cultural competence in career counseling.* Boston, MA: Lahaska Press.

Evans, K. M. (2013). Multicultural considerations in career assessment. In C. Wood & D. G. Hayes (Eds.), *A counselor's guide to career assessment instruments* (6th ed., pp. 49–61). Broken Arrow, OK: National Career Development Association.

Flores, L. Y., Spanierman, L. B., & Obasi, E. M. (2003). Ethical and professional issues in career assessment with diverse racial and ethnic groups. *Journal of Career Assessment, 11,* 76–95.

Gottfredson, G. D., & Johnstun, M. L. (2009). John Holland's contributions: A theory-ridden approach to career assistance. *The Career Development Quarterly, 58,* 99–107.

Grier-Reed, T., Skaar, N., & Parson, L. (2009). A study of constructivist career development, empowerment, indecision, and certainty. *Career and Technical Education Research, 34,* 3–20.

Jayaratne, T. E., Ybarra, O., Sheldon, J. P., Brown, T. N., Feldbaum, M., Pfeffer, C. A., & Petty, E. M. (2006). White Americans' genetic lay theories of race differences and sexual orientation: Their relationship with prejudice toward Blacks, and gay men and lesbians. *Group Processes and Intergroup Relations, 9,* 77–94.

Krumboltz, J. D. (1993). Integrating career and personal counseling. *The Career Development Quarterly, 42,* 143–148.

Leong, F. T. L., & Hartung, P. J. (2000). Adapting to the changing multicultural context of career. In A. Collin & R. A. Young (Eds.), *The future of career* (pp. 212–227). Cambridge, UK: Cambridge University Press.

Leong, F. T. L., & Serafica, F. C. (2001). Cross-cultural perspectives on Super's career development theory: Career maturity and cultural accommodation. In F. T. Leong & A. Barak (Eds.), *Contemporary models in vocational psychology: A volume in honor of Samuel H. Osipow* (pp. 167–205). Mahwah, NJ: Erlbaum.

Lewis, A., Bethea, J., & Hurley, J. (2009). Integrating cultural competency in rehabilitation curricula in the new millennium: Keeping it simple. *Disability & Rehabilitation, 31*, 1161–1169.

McMahon, M., & Watson, M. (2007). An analytical framework for career research in the post-modern era. *International Journal for Educational and Vocational Guidance, 7*, 169–179.

O'Brien, K. M. (2001). The legacy of Parsons: Career counselors and vocational psychologists as agents of social change. *The Career Development Quarterly, 50*, 66–76.

Ohler, D. L., & Levinson, E. M. (2012). Using Holland's theory in employment counseling: Focus on service occupations. *Journal of Employment Counseling, 49*, 148–159.

Parsons, F. (1909). *Choosing a vocation.* Boston, MA: Houghton Mifflin.

Patton, W., & Creed, P. A. (2001). Developmental issues in career maturity and career decision status. *The Career Development Quarterly, 49*, 336–351.

Patton, W., & Lokan, J. (2001). Perspectives on Donald Super's construct of career maturity. *International Journal for Educational & Vocational Guidance, 1*, 31–48.

Peavy, R. V. (1992). A constructivist model of training for career counselors. *Journal of Career Development, 18*, 215–229.

Pedersen, P. B. (1991). Multiculturalism as a generic approach to counseling. *Journal of Counseling & Development, 70*, 6–12.

Pedersen, P. (2013). *Multiculturalism as a fourth force.* Philadelphia, PA: Brunner/Mazel.

Peterson, N., & González, R. C. (2005). *The role of work in people's lives: Applied career counseling and vocational psychology* (2nd ed.). Belmont, CA: Thomson Brooks/Cole.

Richardson, M. S. (2012). A critique of career discourse practices. In P. McIlveen & D. E. Schultheiss (Eds.), *Social constructionism in vocational psychology and career development* (pp. 87–104). Rotterdam, The Netherlands: Sense.

Ridley, C. R., Li, L. C., & Hill, C. L. (1998). Multicultural assessment: Reexamination, reconceptualization, and practical application. *The Counseling Psychologist, 26*, 827–910.

Savickas, M. L. (1993). Career counseling in the postmodern era. *Journal of Cognitive Psychotherapy, 7*, 205–215.

Savickas, M. L. (2003). Advancing the career counseling profession: Objectives and strategies for the next decade. *The Career Development Quarterly, 52*, 87–96.

Savickas, M. L. (2012). Life design: A paradigm for career intervention in the 21st century. *Journal of Counseling & Development, 90*, 13–19.

Savickas, M. L. (2015). Designing projects for career construction. In R. A. Young, J. F. Domene, & L. Valach (Eds.), *Counseling and action* (pp. 13–31). New York, NY: Springer.

Sharf, R. S. (2013). *Applying career development theory to counseling* (6th ed.). Pacific Grove, CA: Brooks/Cole.

Stead, G. B. (2004). Culture and career psychology: A social constructionist perspective. *Journal of Vocational Behavior, 64,* 389–406.

Sterner, W. R. (2012). Integrating existentialism and Super's life-span, life-space approach. *The Career Development Quarterly, 60,* 152–162.

Sue, D. W., & Sue, D. (2008). *Counseling the culturally diverse: Theory and practice* (5th ed.). Hoboken, NJ: Wiley.

Sue, D. W., & Sue, D. (2013). *Counseling the culturally diverse: Theory and practice* (6th ed.). Hoboken, NJ: Wiley.

Super, D. E. (1994). A life span, life space perspective on convergence. In M. Savickas & R. W. Lent (Eds.), *Convergence in career development theories* (pp. 63–74). Palo Alto, CA: CPP Books.

Super, D. E., Savickas, M. L., & Super, C. M. (1996). A life-span, life-space approach to career development. In D. Brown, L. Brooks, & Associates (Eds.), *Career choice and development* (3rd ed., pp. 121–178). San Francisco, CA: Jossey-Bass.

Watson, M. B. (2006). Career counseling theory, culture and constructivism. In M. McMahon & W. Patton (Eds.), *Career counseling: Constructivist approaches* (pp. 45–56). New York, NY: Routledge.

Worthington, R. L., Flores, L. Y., & Navarro, R. L. (2005). Career development in context: Research with people of color. In S. D. Brown & R. W. Lent (Eds.), *Career development and counseling: Putting theory and research to work* (pp. 225–252). Hoboken, NJ: Wiley.

Young, R. A., & Collin, A. (2004). Introduction: Constructivism and social constructionism in the career field. *Journal of Vocational Behavior, 64,* 373–388.

Young, R. A., Marshall, S. K., & Valach, L. (2007). Making career theories more culturally sensitive: Implications for counseling. *The Career Development Quarterly, 56,* 4–18.

Chapter 4

Culture and Context in Constructionist Approaches to Career Counseling

Graham B. Stead and Brittan L. Davis

Social constructionist ideas can be found in texts as early as Niccolò Machiavelli's (1469–1527) *The Prince,* a political treatise that expressed the view that rulers do not possess power but preserve power through relationships with others via strategizing and negotiating. Another Italian, Giambattista Vico (1668–1744), thought that shared understandings of a phenomenon construct that phenomenon. He believed our knowledge of the world doesn't come about because we understand it as it is but because we create it (Lock & Strong, 2010). Social constructionism and discourse analysis are postmodernist epistemologies (i.e., knowing is achieved through the recognition that there is no singular truth but multiple realities, or ontologies). There is a critical and suspicious stance toward received or taken-for-granted knowledge. Social constructionists and discourse analysts ask "How else could it be?" or "What other ways can we try to understand the problem?" Both approaches view psychology as a constructed enterprise, so they do not believe in core or foundational truths. Common statements such as "core personality traits" and so-called proofs and facts based on statistical probabilities and inductive reasoning are viewed with suspicion.

In this chapter, we primarily focus on social constructionism and on discourse analysis to the extent that it informs social constructionism. We explore how these constructionist approaches may assist in understanding culture and context in relation to multicultural career counseling. We begin with a case vignette illustrating constructivist career counseling and how it contrasts with other epistemological approaches to career counseling.

The neglected focus on culture and context in career psychology research and the limitations of traditional multicultural career counseling are discussed. We conclude with a look at how discourse analysis informs a social constructionist approach to postmodern career counseling.

Social constructionism is not monolithic or identified with a single author; rather, it comprises a variety of approaches that have a familial resemblance. More recently, social constructionism has been given impetus in the sociological and psychological literature through works by Berger and Luckmann (1966), Burr (2003), Gergen (1985, 2009a, 2009b), Holstein and Gubrium (2008), and many others. This impetus is partly the result of social constructionist's critique of positivism and its hegemony in the social sciences, as positivism is widely seen as the only paradigm for acceptable scientific research.

The Case of Jennifer

Jennifer, a 34-year-old, partnered, working-class, African American woman, has a bachelor's degree in psychology from a state university. Jennifer is able bodied and a socially accepted size, and Christianity plays an important role in her life. She identifies as lesbian and has one 14-year-old son from a previous relationship with a man. Her partner has passed the general educational development tests and has a $30,000 salary as a secretary at a local business. Since she comleted her bachelor's degree 2 years ago, the economic recession has impaired Jennifer's ability to secure employment. Jennifer has now returned to her state university's career center for help. She presents as tearful, irritated, and discouraged because she cannot obtain employment that she believes she "deserves"—that is, a job in which she can utilize her education. The staff at the career center do not perceive Jennifer as employable in the corporate world. They believe she lacks the attitudes, knowledge, skills, experience, and professional appearance that would make her successful.

We next introduce three epistemologies: positivism and postpositivism, social constructionism, and discourse analysis. Examples of how these approaches would be applied to the case of Jennifer are provided.

Positivism and Postpositivism

Positivism is a paradigm that purports that one "true" reality exists, that complete objectivity can be achieved, and that a value-free and unbiased stance in research constitutes good science (Guba & Lincoln, 1994). Postpositivism is an adaption of positivism. Although it assumes the existence of only one reality, this reality can be understood only incompletely, objectivity is merely a model to guide research, and hypotheses can be disproven but not confirmed (Guba & Lincoln, 1994). Both positivism and postpositivism are *reductionistic* in that they assume that the best understanding of phenomena comes from studying their essential parts.

For example, a counselor with reductionistic and essentialist counseling perspectives may use an interest inventory to explore Jennifer's core personality traits, how these traits interact with one another, and how they may cause difficulties in finding work.

Positivism and postpositivism are both *deterministic* in that there is a belief that specific causes of events can be identified, and they seek to determine universal laws and theories (Mouton, 1993). Positivism and postpositivism are modernist epistemologies: They maintain that knowing is achieved by "discovering truths," and they presume that essences of objects in the material world can be either correctly or incorrectly exemplified by the immateriality of human minds (Rorty, 1979). Social constructionists question these approaches and offer alternative ways to understand human behaviors.

Social Constructionism

The fundamental assumptions underlying social constructionism (see Burr, 2003; Holstein & Gubrium, 2008; Lock & Strong, 2010) are briefly described here. Our understanding of the world is our understanding of the world(s) we construct. The constructions are shared and provided through interactions with others for mutually agreed-upon and negotiated understandings. For example, all of the terms and their meanings commonly used in career counseling (*intervention, self-efficacy, empathy, culture*, etc.) are constructed.

Social constructionism emphasizes language and discourse and explores how they are used to construct phenomena, such as career theories and counseling. Language may be viewed as consisting of structure and grammar and the relationships they share between statements. According to Foucault (1972), discourse is viewed as a set of representations or statements situated in a well-bounded set of knowledge that provide a perspective on what is being described. For example, economists, philosophers, politicians, and psychologists have different discourses in describing work, unemployment, or culture. Not only may their language differ regarding the terms and meanings they use, but their discourses may also differ. In a similar vein, the English philosopher Wittgenstein (1953) referred to "language games" that are used to construct what is being described. Language has meaning dependent on the uses to which it is put; hence, it may be likened to moves in a game.

Language and all of our senses are removed from perceiving an absolute reality. The phenomena we describe are dependent on language and discourse and do not have meaning prior to language. Hence, everything we reflect on or communicate is a perspective or a viewpoint. What we understand of career counseling is based on our interactions with others in culture, time, and context and is not an objective truth. Language is active, not passive, as words *do* things when we put into practice what we have spoken about. For example, diagnostic labels are not discovered but are constructed, and the terms and their meanings are in flux. Diagnostic labels may result in actions on people, such as therapy, interventions, labeling, discrimination, and aggression. Parker (2002) pointed out that it is important "to challenge the discipline's claims to have 'discovered' an essential and universal characteristic of mental functioning," when the discipline then proceeds to "pathologise those who do not then display it" (p. 59). Rose (1985) referred to the *psy-complex* as a network of theories, terms, and procedures psychologists use to diagnose human behavior. This network is a specific discourse that psychologists use (see also Stead & Bakker, 2010). However, other discourses with similar and sometimes very different theories and terms describing human behavior are used by, for example, sociologists, political scientists, economists, and lawyers.

The existence, stability, and internality of personality is questioned because not all cultures subscribe to personality as it is described in psychology. Rather, social constructionists view personality as being dependent on cultural, historical, and relational events and therefore not being stable but in constant flux (Burr, 2003). Social constructionists have an antiessentialist perspective—namely, that people do not have inner, discoverable essences, natures, or personality traits. In this way, social constructionists differ from social constructivists, who adhere to essentialist views of an inner core self and who are interested in cognitive processes (Young & Collin, 2004). Sometimes these two approaches are conflated under the terms *constructionism* or *constructivism*, which adds to the confusion of their similarities and differences.

For example, a social constructionist may explore the narrative Jennifer uses that explains her difficulty in finding employment. The counselor may assist Jennifer in identifying inconsistencies in her narrative, and this may result in an alternative narrative that helps Jennifer resolve her unemployment problems.

Discourse Analysis

Although discourse analysis comprises various approaches, we refer to discourse analysis as described by Foucault (1972, 1977, 1980). Discourse analysis is comparable to social constructionism in that it is profoundly antiessentialist and concentrates on the ways language and social relationships inform personal identities (Stead & Bakker, 2010). Discourse analysis differs from social constructionism in its explicit focus on power, ideology, and politics in relationships between people, institutions, and structures. Discourse analysis moves beyond social constructionism by not only acknowledging the construction of phenomena through language but also underscoring how such language is ruled by the hierarchies of discourse, including structures of power, ideology, and knowledge (Stead & Bakker, 2010). Discourse is viewed as an institutionalized form of communicating, in which a network of terms is used to construct and interpret a phenomenon, such as counseling theories or counseling skills (Rose, 1985; Stead & Bakker, 2010).

Of special interest to Foucauldian discourse analysts is power, which is viewed as being inseparable from knowledge (Foucault, 1980; the term *power/knowledge* is sometimes used). It is commonly understood that power is hierarchical and is situated primarily in governments, military complexes, and large corporations, but Foucault (1980) pointed out that power is more pervasive and subtle than that and exists almost every-where—including in our everyday discourses. People are viewed not as possessing power, which is essentialist, but rather as employing power through discourse, which constructs and provides knowledge. Power can be positive in that it constructs knowledge, and accepted knowledge provides power. Power is also seductive, and insofar as one subscribes to knowledge claims, one is being subjugated to the power one accepts in a discourse. And so language, discourse, knowledge, and power are integrally connected (Stead & Bakker, 2012), with each being situated in culture and context.

For example, Jennifer may be encouraged to examine and deconstruct the ways in which powerful discourses provided by the media, her parents, or her friends influence her view of unemployment. These discourses may help or hinder her in finding alternative narratives with which to construct her unemployment experiences.

Infusing Culture and Context in Career Counseling

In the field of psychology, less interest has been shown in studying culture and context than in seeking to provide universal laws of human behavior, a search that was undertaken when positivism and experimental methods were embraced (Danziger, 1990). The outcome of much career psychology research has largely provided ahistorical, acultural, and acontextual research infused with reductionist findings. Career theories are primarily U.S. career theories, and these theories seldom take into account cultural variations within the United States or beyond it. In fact, there is little discussion on how context and culture inform theory or what their implications are for career counseling. Qualitative research has sought to counteract this trend by providing data that are more holistic, contextual, and culturally based than has been the case with much of positivist science. However, inroads into career psychology's body of knowledge have been minimal. Stead et al. (2012) examined 3,279 career psychology journal articles from 1990 to 2009 and found that qualitative research methods provided only 6.3% of career research, with quantitative research methods providing 55.9%. However, social constructionists support research methods that are based on research goals rather than those fixated on one research method (e.g., Gergen, 1999).

Social constructionists do not favor one research method over another, but they support research that is relational, contextual, and culturally based. Social constructionism and discourse analysis call attention to the ways in which cultures have been created, how they perpetuate powers of inclusion and exclusion, and how the dominant discourses of a given society place rank and value on identities in a hierarchical fashion (Robinson, 1999). Thus, dominant discourses neutralize the identities of the most privileged members of a given society (e.g., White, heterosexual, able-bodied, Christian, middle-class, male-identified man). Social categories are employed to categorize the "other" while failing to recognize the culture of the status quo. For example, Euro-Americans are not seen as racialized, nor are men considered to be gendered beings. This type of nonseeing is perilous because it preserves structures of sexism, racism, and other acts of oppression (Robinson, 1999).

For example, cultural discourses, some of which may promote dysfunctional beliefs, can be examined in relation to work and Jennifer's unemployment. Such beliefs could include gender and work, types of work to consider, and women's work roles and their relation to the family.

Multicultural Counseling

Pedersen (1990) acknowledged the complexity and power of culture and recognized its absence in psychological theory and research; therefore, he introduced multicultural counseling as the "fourth force" (p. 93) of psychology. Multicultural counseling was argued to be a "generic approach" (Pedersen, 1991, p. 6). Some definitions of culture in multicultural counseling scholarship have attempted to be more inclusive (including race, ethnicity, nationality, sex, age, sexual orientation, social class, religion, gender, etc.) and have a foundation in anthropology (e.g., Carter & Qureshi, 1995; Ponterotto, Casas, Suzuki, & Alexander, 2001; Sodowsky, Wai Ming Lai, & Plake, 1991; Sue & Sue, 2016), and other approaches have adopted a narrower definition of culture to include only racial and ethnic minority groups (see Sue, Arredondo, & McDavis, 1992), arguing that a broad definition of culture decreases its meaning and focus. Such narrow definitions of culture sometimes equate race and ethnicity with culture; refer to Western, Eastern, and non-Western cultures as if they were monoliths, and exclude the dominant culture as constituting a "culture" (Stead, 2004).

Gergen and Kaye (1992) posited that therapeutic theories contain assumptions concerning the following: "(1) the underlying cause or basis of pathology, (2) the location of this cause within clients or their relationships, (3) the means by which such problems can be diagnosed, and (4) the means by which the pathology may be eliminated" (p. 169). Despite all the potential lived experiences of individuals in the world, therapy focuses on specific concepts (e.g., interests, self-actualization, cognitions, ego strength, emotional expressiveness, and relationships) that depend on the socially constructed assumptions held by the therapist and the therapeutic theories chosen. Theories are constructed within relationships in specific temporal and spatial locations in which people live. The understanding of counseling theories, and their corresponding interventions, "needs to have a local or cultural appreciation rather than simply a monolithic and universal perspective" (Jencius & West, 2003, p. 346). Further, discourses are not simply conversations about understandings of the world; they are also embedded in the ways in which people act in or engage with the world. Even the construct "career" has been deeply influenced by the dominant discourse of a linear employment trajectory based on personal capacities, interests, and personality traits.

People from marginalized cultures have been silenced in the career psychology field, and career theories have been inappropriately applied to clients whose lived experiences have been ignored. For example, those individuals who work to survive or whose work is unpaid or in the personal sphere (e.g., care work) have been disregarded by a society that questions their worth. Social constructionism can serve as a basis for a departure from the traditional study of careers among the middle class as a homogeneous group and toward a more inclusive understanding of work and working across various cultures (see Blustein, 2001; Richardson, 2000).

Multicultural theories have added to the field's understanding of the impact of social, economic, historical, and political factors on cultural identity, particularly for people from marginalized groups (Arrendondo et al., 1996). These theories have challenged the dominant Eurocentric discourse in counseling theories, which has given privilege to White, heterosexual, middle-class men and the traits associated with masculinity (e.g., objectivity, individualism, personal agency) as signs of mental health (Williams, 2005). However, multicultural theories have limitations, such as failing to move beyond an essentialist view of social identity, inadequately integrating multiple or intersecting identities into theories, and continuing to stay firmly rooted in postpositivism with the goal of generalizability. Thus, multicultural research and theories have often fragmented individuals with multiple identities by compartmentalizing each identity while failing to recognize the interplay between them (Williams, 2005). Furthermore, multicultural counseling theories have continued to use stage models of cultural/racial identities that aim to reduce identity to a series of traits that need to be developed; apply a deterministic account of how individuals move through their identity development; and adopt a version of self-actualization or a sense of "wholeness" once one reaches the final stage of identity development. Multicultural theories also have persisted in their use of value orientation models that do not make the absent standard or dominant discourse of such values an object of awareness and also in their use of the constructs of "locus of control" and "locus of responsibility," which are deeply entrenched in individualistic dominant discourses.

For example, a traditional multicultural approach to career counseling would likely place high emphasis on social identities, would tend to minimize or ignore how intersecting identities influence Jennifer's social location and career concerns, and would probably utilize theories and interventions that have been based on a generalized understanding of each of her traditionally marginalized identities. A multicultural approach may use an identity development model, possibly coupled with a developmental model of career, to better understand Jennifer's career concerns and would likely perpetuate the dominant discourse values of individualism (e.g., locus of control, self-efficacy, locus of responsibility, self-concept, trait factors).

These common flaws notwithstanding, some multicultural theoretical models have emphasized the sociopolitical context. Gonzalez, Biever, and Gardner (1994) proposed a social constructionist approach to multicultural counseling that recognizes some of the previously mentioned limitations of this type of counseling. They acknowledged the inappropriateness of authoritatively applying a socially constructed diagnostic system like the *Diagnostic and Statistical Manual of Mental Disorders, Fifth Edition* (American Psychiatric Association, 2013) to individuals from cultures who are being further oppressed by such conceptualizations of "symptom," and those from cultures that do not even recognize such conditions. Social constructionists would encourage the counselor to depart from the notion of expert status and more equally distribute power in the therapeutic relationship through a conscientious exploration and continuous reexamination of social and cultural contextual influences (Gerstein, Rountree, & Ordonez, 2007). Rather than being wedded to any one therapy, social constructionism provides suggestions for understanding one's self in the therapeutic relationship. Gonzalez et al. (1994) offered the following suggestions as an approach to uniting social constructionism and multicultural counseling: (a) Understand the counselor's role as necessitating the exploration of the client's view of self, attitudes, beliefs, and resources; (b) create a space for clients from marginalized groups to feel valued and heard; (c) continue to demonstrate interest in the client's narratives; (d) strive for a collaborative therapeutic relationship; (e) silence essentialist interpretations of the presenting concern by continuing to focus on what the client presents without the imposition of the counselor's personal constructs; (f) recognize that the counselor's interpretation of the client's narrative is tentative and not factual; (g) acknowledge that the narratives of clients from marginalized cultures can be significantly influenced by the dominant discourses of society; and (h) emphasize client strengths and opportunities rather than focusing on barriers.

Discourse Analysis Informs Career Counseling

Like social constructionism, discourse analysis focuses on language and social relationships; however, discourse analysis further acknowledges the intimate connection between discourses and power in almost all interactions between people. Discourse analysis also acknowledges prevailing allocations of power in society, as it is beneficial for the comparatively more powerful groups to uphold some discourses and to suppress others. Therefore, the everyday subtle use of discourse can be used by the most privileged to preserve power by silencing groups of people, especially those who have the capability to disrupt the status quo (Gergen, 1999). Drewey and Winslade (1997) posited that discourse is advantageous to the counseling process because of the inherently social way in which discourses shape behavior patterns and provide structure to the ways individuals make meaning of the world. For example, a client's familial and ethnic cultures may provide a framework that only occupations in health care or the sciences are acceptable, and cultural expectations for behavior stress the importance of hard work and self-sacrifice for others; however, the client is experiencing distress due to having a passion for art. Discourse analysis can serve as a useful tool in therapy to increase cognizance and conceptualization of these competing discourses by supporting clients to position themselves in relation to opposing discourses in their lives. Discursive positioning and deconstruction are especially helpful in this regard.

Discursive positioning claims that individuals assume positions regarding discourse in every utterance within conversations because discursive material (words and their meanings) is needed to make sense of the dialogue (Winslade, 2005). Through participation in a conversation, people receive, produce, and reproduce the influences of social discourse. Positioning in counseling, therefore, can help to uncover how discourses function in the production of relationships (including the therapeutic relationship) and in the production of individual subjective reactions to such discourses. Furthermore, positioning makes visible the cultural influences in discourses and focuses on the ways in which individuals challenge, reject, or take up the discursive positions they are offered during social exchanges. Through an emphasis on the subtle nuances of incongruity and disjointedness, positioning allows space for individuals to take stands, exercise agency, and demonstrate against injustice in ways that create more power than the generalized concepts of cultural identity within multicultural counseling scholarship (Winslade, 2005).

Deconstruction (Derrida, 1981) may be useful in multicultural counseling because it disentangles the discourses that clients have constructed to examine how they are arranged, and it can also offer clients other worldviews and possibilities (Stead & Bakker, 2010). Furthermore, deconstruction seeks to understand disconnectedness between and within clients' discourses that could be contributing to their presenting concerns and to reconstruct clients' narratives in preferred alternative forms. In this way, deconstruction becomes particularly important in career counseling because clients often need to uncover different narratives to address the dominant discourses in their lives and to encourage change (Stead & Bakker, 2010). In this sense, discourse analysis may be more beneficial than social constructionism. Not only does it deconstruct the dominant discourses in clients' lives, but it also creates the opportunity to reconstruct narratives, or alternative discourses, in ways that challenge problematic discourses and construct liberatory space for change.

For example, the counselor would encourage Jennifer to construct her narrative of work, paying particular attention to the ways in which social discourse and her relationships with others have contributed to her current career concerns. Working together in session, the counselor and Jennifer would deconstruct Jennifer's previous narrative by exploring any disconnections between and within Jennifer's discourses that could be contributing to her career concerns. As a result of this, Jennifer may bring to light how her marginalized identities have contributed to minimal power in relationship to others, which has had a negative effect on her career. Jennifer and the counselor also may work together to deconstruct the meaning of *career* because this term is culturally loaded. Finally, they would mutually reconstruct Jennifer's work narrative to allow for alternative discourses that give Jennifer a sense of empowerment, validation in her narrative of work rather than career, and scripts to use when confronting the oppressive systems and structures that limit her access to work.

Conclusion

Social constructionism and discourse analysis provide promising alternative perspectives on career counseling in culture and context. By focusing on relationships through the lenses of language and discourse, they provide tools for multicultural career counseling. With increased levels of immigration and globalization, it is imperative for career counselors to pay attention to the implications of context and culture to effectively and ethically assist clients.

References

American Psychiatric Association. (2013). *Diagnostic and statistical manual of mental disorders* (5th ed.). Washington, DC: Author.

Arredondo, P., Toporek, R., Brown, S. P., Jones, J., Locke, D. C., Sanchez, J., & Stadler, H. (1996). Operationalization of the multicultural counseling competencies. *Journal of Multicultural Counseling and Development, 24,* 42–78.

Berger, P., & Luckmann, T. (1966). *The social construction of reality.* New York, NY: Doubleday.

Blustein, D. L. (2001). Extending the reach of vocational psychology: Toward an inclusive and integrative psychology of working. *Journal of Vocational Behavior, 59,* 171–182.

Burr, V. (2003). *Social constructionism* (2nd ed.). New York, NY: Routledge.

Carter, R., & Qureshi, A. (1995). A typology of philosophical assumptions in multicultural counseling and training. In J. G. Ponterotto, J. M. Casas, L. A. Suzuki, & C. M. Alexander (Eds.), *Handbook of multicultural counseling* (pp. 239–262). Thousand Oaks, CA: Sage.

Danziger, K. (1990). *Constructing the subject: Historical origins of psychological research.* Cambridge, UK: Cambridge University Press.

Derrida, J. (1981). *Positions* (A. Bass, Trans.). Chicago, IL: University of Chicago Press.

Drewey, W., & Winslade, J. (1997). The theoretical story of narrative therapy. In G. Monk, J. Winslade, K. Crocket, & E. Epston (Eds.), *Narrative therapy in practice: An archaeology of hope* (pp. 32–52). San Francisco, CA: Jossey-Bass.

Foucault, M. (1972). *The archaeology of knowledge.* London, England: Tavistock.

Foucault, M. (1977). *Discipline and punish: The birth of the prison.* New York, NY: Pantheon Books.

Foucault, M. (1980). *Power/knowledge: Selected interviews and other writings, 1972–1977* (C. Gordon, Ed.). Brighton, England: Harvester Press.

Gergen, K. J. (1985). The social constructionist movement in modern psychology. *American Psychologist, 40,* 266–275.

Gergen, K. J. (1999). *An invitation to social construction*. London, England: Sage.

Gergen, K. J. (2009a). *An invitation to social construction* (2nd ed.). Thousand Oaks, CA: Sage.

Gergen, K. J. (2009b). *Relational being. Beyond self and community.* New York, NY: Oxford University Press.

Gergen, K. J., & Kaye, J. (1992). Beyond narrative in the negotiation of therapeutic meaning. In S. NcNamee & K. J. Gergen (Eds.), *Therapy as social construction* (pp. 166–185). Thousand Oaks, CA: Sage.

Gerstein, L. H., Rountree, C., & Ordonez, A. (2007). An anthropological perspective on multicultural counselling. *Counselling Psychology Quarterly, 20,* 375–400.

Gonzalez, R., Biever, J. L., & Gardner, G. T. (1994). The multicultural perspective in therapy: A social constructionist approach. *Psychotherapy, 31,* 515–524.

Guba, E., & Lincoln, Y. S. (1994). Competing paradigms in qualitative research. In N. K. Denzin & Y. S. Lincoln (Eds.), *Handbook of qualitative research* (pp. 105-117). Thousand Oaks, CA: Sage Publications.

Holstein, J. A., & Gubrium, J. F. (Eds.). (2008). *Handbook of constructionist research.* New York, NY: Guilford Press.

Jencius, M., & West, J. (2003). Traditional counseling theories and cross-cultural implications. In F. D. Harper & J. McFadden (Eds.), *Culture and counseling: New approaches* (pp. 339–349). Boston, MA: Allyn & Bacon.

Lock, A., & Strong, T. (2010). *Social constructionism. Sources and stirrings in theory and practice.* Cambridge, UK: Cambridge University Press.

Mouton, J. (1993). Positivism. In J. Snyman (Ed.), *Conceptions of social inquiry* (pp. 1–28). Pretoria, South Africa: Human Sciences Research Council.

Parker, I. (2002). *Critical discursive psychology.* New York, NY: Palgrave Macmillan.

Pedersen, P. (1990). The multicultural perspective as a fourth force in counseling. *Journal of Mental Health Counseling, 12,* 93–95.

Pedersen, P. B. (1991). Multiculturalism as a generic approach to counseling. *Journal of Counseling & Development, 70,* 6–12.

Ponterotto, J. G., Casas, J. M., Suzuki, L. A., & Alexander, C. M. (2001). *Handbook of multicultural counseling* (2nd ed.). Thousand Oaks, CA: Sage.

Richardson, M. S. (2000). A new perspective for counsellors: From career ideologies to empowerment through work and relationship practices. In A. Collin & R. A. Young (Eds.), *The future of career* (pp. 197–211). Cambridge, UK: Cambridge University Press.

Robinson, T. L. (1999). The intersections of dominant discourses across race, gender, and other identities. *Journal of Counseling & Development, 77,* 73–79.

Rorty, R. (1979). *Philosophy and the mirror of nature.* Princeton, NJ: Princeton University Press.

Rose, N. (1985). *The psychological complex. Psychology, politics and society in England 1869–1939.* London, England: Routledge & Kegan Paul.

Sodowsky, G. R., Wai Ming Lai, E., & Plake, B. S. (1991). Moderating effects of sociocultural variables on acculturation attitudes of Hispanics and Asian Americans. *Journal of Counseling & Development, 70*, 194–204.

Stead, G. B. (2004). Culture and career psychology: A social constructionist perspective. *Journal of Vocational Behavior, 64*, 389–406.

Stead, G. B., & Bakker, T. M. (2010). Discourse analysis in career counseling and development. *The Career Development Quarterly, 59*, 72–86.

Stead, G. B., & Bakker, T. M. (2012). Self in work as a social/cultural construction. In P. McIlveen & D. E. Schultheiss (Eds.), *Social constructionism in vocational psychology and career development* (pp. 29–43). Rotterdam, The Netherlands: Sense.

Stead, G. B., Perry, J. C., Munka, L. M., Bonnett, H. R., Shiban, A. P., & Care, E. (2012). Qualitative research in career development: Content analysis from 1990 to 2009. *International Journal for Educational and Vocational Guidance, 12*, 105–122.

Sue, D. W., Arredondo, P., & McDavis, R. J. (1992). Multicultural counseling competencies and standards: A call to the profession. *Journal of Counseling & Development, 70*, 477–486.

Sue, D. W., & Sue, D. (2015). *Counseling the culturally diverse: Theory and practice* (7th ed.). New York, NY: Wiley.

Williams, C. B. (2005). Counseling African American women: Multiple identities-multiple constraints. *Journal of Counseling & Development, 83*, 278–283.

Winslade, J. M. (2005). Utilising discursive positioning in counselling. *British Journal of Guidance & Counseling, 33*, 351–364.

Wittgenstein, L. (1953). *Philosophical investigations*. Oxford, England: Blackwell.

Young, R. A., & Collin, A. (2004). Introduction: Constructivism and social constructionism in the career field. *Journal of Vocational Behavior, 64*, 373–388.

Chapter 5

Postmodern Career Assessment: Advantages and Considerations

Christopher Wood and Zachary Scully

"There is no greater agony than bearing an untold story inside you."
—Maya Angelou

Applying a postmodernist epistemology to career counseling is not a new phenomenon. Whenever a helper has listened to the lived experience of a person as a component of career decision making, it is likely that a postmodern approach to career assessment was being used. In this chapter, we provide an overview of postmodern or qualitative career assessment. We begin by defining some key terms and follow that with a discussion of the advantages of qualitative career assessments along with the potential challenges. In the final section we focus on a variety of qualitative career assessments and how they are used by career counselors.

Definitions of Terms

Shared definitions are important to understanding postmodern career assessment, and we begin by defining these key terms: *career development, positivist* and *postpositivist, postmodernism, epistemological tradition, qualitative (nontraditional) career assessment,* and *traditional career assessment.* Sears (1982) defined *career development* as "the total constellation of economic, sociological, psychological, educational, physical, and chance factors that combine to shape one's career" (p. 139). The comprehensive nature of career development and the important consideration of sociopolitical context within which this shaping occurs are central to this definition. The task of career assessment—to capture so many factors operating in such idiosyncratic ways—is fraught with shortcomings.

The terms *positivist* and *postpositivist* refer to a system of beliefs based in a logical, objective reality that is best learned through direct observation (and the rigors of the scientific method). The origins of the career counseling profession are largely based in this positivistic tradition (Patton & McMahon, 1999). *Postmodernism* changes that focus and assumes that knowledge is not static and that there are no universal or absolute truths to be objectively identified by scientific inquiry. Moreover, most of what we refer to as "truth" or "fact" is socially constructed through language and dialogue. The primacy of the context within which knowledge is created is essential to postmodern thought. The term *epistemology* refers to "ways of knowing," and, more specifically, the *epistemological tradition* refers to organized schools of thought or common understandings of how we come to learn and know.

Qualitative career assessment refers to instruments and activities that use qualitative research methods (e.g., open-ended questions, thick/rich description of context, and prolonged engagement) to gather information for the purpose of assisting individuals or groups in the process of career development. Examples of qualitative career assessments include card sorts, Life Role Analysis, Life Design Genogram, and My Career Chapter. In qualitative career assessments, the way in which the assessment is administered can be tailored to context, constituents, or both, and the subsequent results will be responsive to greater shaping by both counselor and client. McMahon, Patton, and Watson (2003) noted that in the interpretation of qualitative assessments there is an emphasis on the meaning of personal traits and events within the context of a person's life circumstances. Personal meaning on the part of the career counseling client/student is more important than the counselor's interpretation in qualitative career assessments.

Traditional career assessments use quantitative measures with standardized formats (e.g., true/false questions, multiple-choice answer options, and short answer questions) with a protocol for administration based on the instrument itself rather than a format made to fit the client's needs. These quantitative career assessments are often standardized with some number of psychometric properties emerging from the test's construction as well as from any subsequent empirical research (Wood & Hays, 2013).

These are simplistic definitions of complicated concepts, and we use *qualitative career assessment* and *nontraditional career assessment* somewhat synonymously here. Moreover, although some authors view formal or informal categories of career assessment as being synonymous with quantitative or qualitative approaches, we do not. We distinguish qualitative career assessment from the broader category of informal career assessment based on the following factors: They are holistic, existentialist, constructivist, change generating (McMahon et al., 2003), subjective, personal/social, meaningful, oriented to a client's real life, humanistic, and interpersonal.

Although little had been written about qualitative assessments until the past decade, qualitative assessments are not new to professional practice. Qualitative career assessments may have been more pervasive in practice than is represented in the scholarly literature and may indeed have a more extensive history than many of the more traditional quantitative career assessments.

Advantages of Qualitative Career Assessments

Qualitative career assessments are interventions intended to assist an individual in increasing self-awareness and meaning while attending to the contextual dimensions of her or his life (Gysbers, 2006; McMahon & Patton, 2006; Whiston & Rahardja, 2005). This approach to career assessment is most consistent with the epistemological tradition of constructivism. Drawing on a constructivist learning perspective, these assessments can be tailored to meet a client's individual needs and life circumstances. Schultheiss (2005) noted that qualitative career assessments are more holistic in nature and tend to foster greater client involvement in the career assessment process. They also can be more useful in helping clients generate new meanings about all aspects of life in relation to career planning. Qualitative career assessments are inclusive of a client's life context, are well-suited for working with diverse populations, and support a social justice approach to working with marginalized groups.

McMahon and Patton (2006) pointed to the earlier work of Goldman (1990, 1992) in describing additional advantages of qualitative assessment:

- Encourages the client to be engaged and actively involved in collecting information and discerning meaning
- Is more holistic and systemic
- Contextualizes learning about oneself within a developmental framework
- Encourages a collaborative relationship between counselor and client
- Is suitable for groups focused on learning and growth
- Is flexible and adaptable when used with clients from diverse backgrounds

Savickas (1992) maintained that qualitative career assessment puts an emphasis on the counseling relationship as opposed to viewing career assessment as the delivery of a service. Busacca (2007) noted that engagement and collaboration ultimately call for different roles to be enacted by counselors and clients using qualitative career assessments within the career construction approach. These different counselor and client roles emphasize the counseling process: Meaning is articulated as the process unfolds rather than being presented after the final results of the assessment are evident. As with other qualitative approaches to counseling, the role of the client moves from passive to active, and the position of the counselor moves from that of expert to one of an interested, curious, and tentative inquirer.

The flexibility and adaptability of qualitative career assessments also allow for the consideration of sociopolitical and economic context. Maree (2013) noted the role of the changing global economy in increased utilization of constructivist approaches to career assessment when serving the unique needs of 21st-century career counseling clients. Career information and occupational outlook data increasingly take globalization into consideration, but quantitative career assessments such as interest inventories fail to incorporate these considerations in the assessment results.

Access to career resources and services is a social justice issue (Sampson, Dozier, & Colvin, 2011; Sampson, McClain, Musch, & Reardon, 2011), as is access to career assessments (Sampson, 2009). Qualitative career assessments are more oriented toward social justice in several ways. First, as many qualitative career assessments are available for free, the cost-prohibitive nature of commercially offered quantitative career assessments is eliminated for clients. Second, as alternative models of staffing and delivery of career services are explored (Sampson, 2009), some qualitative career assessments offer self-guided activities that can be done before or after career counseling sessions (see Chapter 6, *My Career Story Workbook*). Further, the infusion of counseling for social justice and advocacy competencies can be a part of career counseling processes (Butler, 2012; Pope & Pangelinan, 2010), as can be the promotion of prosocial values (Dik, Duffy, & Steger, 2012) and the infusion of advocacy competencies in career development programs (Gysbers, Lapan, & Cato, 2013).

Potential Challenges

The use of qualitative career assessments is not without tensions or potential challenges that practitioners must consider. Time, client expectations relating to culture and context, procedures, and the conjoint use of qualitative and quantitative career assessments are all important considerations for users of qualitative career assessments. These considerations are addressed separately.

Time

Facilitating the use of a qualitative career assessment and helping a client apply personal meaning to her or his life may not adhere to a prescribed administration time. Qualitative career assessments often take longer than quantitative career assessments. Career practitioners may need to adjust the traditional therapeutic hour of a counseling session to allow enough time for a client to take full advantage of the benefits of qualitative career assessments and postmodern career counseling.

Within the practice of individual career counseling, and when designing and delivering career development programs, the counselor should allow individuals or groups adequate time for the following: (a) time to complete the requisite actions, (b) time to discuss and process emerging personal and social awareness with a competent career counselor, and (c) time to reflect on personal learning and new meaning. Addressing these concerns is essential to ethical and effective practice.

Client Expectations, Culture, and Context

Addressing client/student expectations is another challenge in the application of qualitative career assessments and techniques. These expectations are shaped by clients' worldviews and cultural backgrounds and perhaps are influenced by the cultural lens through which clients perceive the helping professions. Sociopolitical influences and pressing life demands may shape client/student expectations in ways that are not conducive to the investment of time and engagement necessary for effective qualitative career assessment. Whiston and Rahardja (2005) pointed out that the collaborative counselor–client relationship endemic to many qualitative career assessments may be culturally inconsistent with clients' expectations: "Clients from certain cultures may perceive the clinician's view as having greater validity than their own, whereas other clients may simply acquiesce to the counselor's analysis of meaning to avoid any type of dissonance" (p. 377). The practitioner using qualitative assessments should be mindful of being culturally responsive and adhering to the requisite principles of shared power and collaboration in processing qualitative career assessments.

Procedures

Although a career counselor has the flexibility to tailor a qualitative assessment specifically for an individual client, the lack of a prescriptive assessment protocol may pose a threat to the fidelity of the intended goals and the theoretical grounding of the assessment. McMahon et al. (2003) recommended several suggestions for developers of qualitative assessments (and these suggestions might also be conceptualized as guidelines for users of quantitative assessments).

Developers of qualitative career assessments should position the qualitative career assessment within its theoretical foundation. Likewise, users of qualitative career assessments should understand the theory and epistemology behind the creation of the assessment and utilize it in a fashion consistent with its theoretical orientation and epistemological tradition.

Qualitative career assessment developers should "test the career assessment process" (McMahon et al., 2003, p. 198) through application with multiple individuals and groups from diverse backgrounds and in different career counseling environments. An important part of this testing is to seek feedback from career counselors and clients regarding the application and adaptation of the qualitative career assessment. Similarly, practitioners should understand the application of qualitative career assessments with a diverse range of clients and consistently explore the client's input on the personal relevance and usefulness (or lack thereof) of the qualitative career assessment and any related activities.

As mentioned previously, it is important to attend to time in the use of qualitative career assessments. For developers, this may mean constructing a qualitative career assessment in a form that allows use across multiple counseling sessions giving the practitioner/client the opportunity to choose one or more sections/units rather than the entire qualitative career assessment. Practitioners need to be mindful of informing clients of the time necessary for the use of qualitative career assessments (in light of client expectations that may be for fewer sessions than is most effective) as well as affording clients the opportunity to choose between alternatives.

McMahon et al. (2003) suggested that processes for qualitative career assessments should facilitate holism, the exploration of a comprehensive consideration of all the systems operating within the client's life. "Holism is fundamental to the constructivist worldview and, as such, needs to be reflected in the development of qualitative career assessment instruments" (p. 199). Moreover, career counselors should utilize holistic processes in helping clients tailor qualitative career assessment results to their career goals.

Because qualitative career assessments frequently call for greater client involvement and increased collaboration between client and counselor, information and guidance on assessment administration need to be adequately shared with the client. McMahon et al. (2003) suggested that instructions be written as directed toward the client (as opposed to administration manuals of quantitative assessments directed toward the practitioner/career counselor). Again, this suggestion can be used by practitioners and can be applied in career counseling practice as well as in test development. Practitioners can share written instructions with the client and supplement any published instructions with additional information and activities that facilitate the client's involvement in the process. Moreover, the practitioner can explain instructions in the client's language so the activity purpose and procedures can be readily understood. Instructions and tasks in qualitative career assessments can be structured in a logical sequence and broken down into small steps or tasks that are likely achievable for an individual or group. This approach is important to assist clients in feeling mastery over the assessment process and "can instill a sense of hope in clients" (p. 200).

Finally, any procedure for developing or using qualitative career assessments can make use of a debriefing process that is a supplement to the learning and meaning occurring throughout the process itself (McMahon et al., 2003). This is a sort of "metaprocessing" whereby client and counselor step out of the qualitative career assessment (and related activities) to reflect and debrief (i.e., engage in a dialogue on the experience and the new learning or meaning). Debriefing as an aspect of experiential learning is discussed in depth within the scholarly literature in the field of education (see Pearson & Smith, 1986; Rudolph, Simon, Rivard, Dufresne, & Raemer, 2007).

Integration of Qualitative and Quantitative Assessments

Epistemological arguments aside, it is possible to use qualitative assessments in conjunction with quantitative assessments to meet client needs.

Sampson (2009) discussed the problematic view of quantitative career assessments and qualitative career assessments as mutually incompatible and suggested that both approaches may be used in integrated ways to enhance the efficacy of career development interventions. Whiston and Rahardja (2005) criticized the conceptualization of qualitative and quantitative career assessment as a mutually exclusive and incompatible dichotomy as being an overly simplistic view of both approaches. They called for the integration of both into a complementary process that is a part of new models of career counseling. Moreover, both qualitative and quantitative career assessments can be used systematically in career development programs to help meet program objectives and to better serve the program constituency.

Qualitative Career Assessment in Practice

Chope (2015) described four basic models of qualitative career assessment: card sorts, sentence completions, career genograms, and life lines. We incorporate career genograms into a category we call "social patterns" and place life lines into a category we call "narrative-systemic approaches." The social patterns category of career assessment describes the goal of qualitative career assessments that are designed to explore the influence of family, racial/ethnic heritage, and socialization on an individual's career development. Narrative-systemic approaches describe qualitative career assessments that explore "the complexity of individuals' lives through dynamic, recursively connected individual, social and environmental-societal systems of influence" (McMahon & Watson, 2013, p. 281). The interconnectedness of time (with past and present influencing the future) is also an important aspect of approaches in this category.

In the following sections, we describe some examples of qualitative career assessments used in practice in the following categories: card sorts, sentence completions, social patterns, and narrative-systemic approaches. We reference various chapters within this text that provide more in-depth discussion or description of these applications, and we encourage you to consult those chapters as well.

Card Sorts

Card sorts are kinetic tools that allow clients to cognitively process constructs such as values, interests, and skills by having them read and sort definitions represented on cards. Card sorts are more structured than many qualitative career assessments and maintain elements of a positivist/postpositivist epistemology (with standard form and procedures), but they afford users many of the benefits of postmodern qualitative assessments (engagement and personal meaning) as well. Two examples of card sorts are the Career Values Card Sort and the Motivated Skills Card Sort (Knowdell, 2005a, 2005b).

The Career Values Card Sort (Knowdell, 2005a) requires clients/ students to rank 54 career values on a 5-point Likert scale ranging from *always valued* to *never valued* and then to prioritize a delineated number of values in ascending order of importance. A skilled career helper then facilitates student/client awareness of how these values can be used to enhance career decision making, including exploration of values conflicts (such as "high earnings" and "helping others").

The Motivated Skills Card Sort (Knowdell, 2005b) asks individuals to rate their desire to utilize 51 skills (defined on the cards) on a Likert scale ranging from *totally delight in using* to *strongly dislike using*. Users then rate their self-efficacy for each skill as highly proficient, competent, or lacking desired skill level. Assisted by a career helping professional, clients/students use the information and insight gained from the activity to deliberate on how the knowledge relates to career decision making and career planning, including recognition of potential *burnout skills* (skills they possess proficiency in but prefer not to use).

Although there is an administration protocol for card sorts, they maintain the essential qualities of postmodern assessments because interpretation of the assessment results is highly contextualized within the individual's life, and most of the "results" are generated in discussion between the student/client and the career helper. This flexibility enables career counselors to use card sorts in ways that are culturally responsive with diverse clients (see Chapter 14 for their use with a Latina client).

McMahon and Patton (2002) suggested that card sorts can be based on a client's specific personal narrative, and Whiston and Rahardja (2005) pointed out that using personalized card sorts "serve[s] as a means to elicit life themes, values, and beliefs" (p. 375). Similarly, a client's personal narratives could be used to design a personal sentence completion assessment.

Sentence Completions

Sentence completions assessments provide a dialogue prompt or sentence stem that requires clients/students to cognitively process and then articulate a written or verbal response. By design these responses are highly contextualized to the person's life and may focus the person on reflecting on the past, present, or future.

One classic version of the sentence completion is the sentence stem "If I had a million dollars I would. . . ." This is intended to tap into interests and values beyond financial reward and standards of living. Another example includes completing these three sentence stems: "If all careers were possible for me I would . . . ," "Given my situation I will probably . . . ," and "Several things that would need to happen for me to get from B to A are . . . ." Chope (2015) placed My Career Chapter/My Career Future (McIlveen Ford, & Dun, 2005; McIlveen & Patton, 2010) in the sentence completion category because these measures also use multiple sentence stems. We, however, place My Career Chapter in the narrative-systemic approaches category to emphasize the systems perspective and the narrative approach inherent in that particular qualitative assessment.

Social Patterns

The career genogram is a qualitative career assessment in the social patterns category. A genogram is a graphical depiction of the student/client's familial history/lineage that emphasizes the relationships within the family (McGoldrick, Gerson, & Shellenberger, 1999). A career genogram is a graphic representation of a student/client's family of origin expanded to include the careers of respective family members (Okiishi, 1987). The emphasis is on the patterns of careers, messages about the world of work, and, most important, what may have influenced (or currently be influencing) the student/client's conceptualization of work and career options, career decision making, and life planning. (See Chapter 11 for an illustration of how genograms can be used in career assessment and intervention with an economically disadvantaged client.)

Another example of a qualitative career assessment that explores patterns of social roles and influences is Life Role Analysis. Life Role Analysis is an approach theoretically grounded in Super's life span and life spaces concepts (Gysbers, Heppner, & Johnston, 2014; Gysbers & Moore, 1973, 1987). Practitioners using Life Role Analysis prompt clients to choose among roles presented to them and then to draw the respective influence of each role at three points in time during their life (in 5-year increments, for example). The client is asked to graphically represent the significance (by size) and the intersection (through overlap) of each respective role 5 years ago, today, and 5 years from now (the timeline can be tailored to be developmentally appropriate for the client). In processing the activity, the career helping practitioner can help the client process life role connections, role conflict, and the influence of these roles on individual career decision making and planning. (See Chapter 12 for an application of Life Role Analysis in working with a transgender client.)

Narrative-Systemic Approaches

Qualitative career assessments in the narrative-systemic approaches category draw from positive psychology and narrative approaches, as well as from social constructivism. The purpose of assessments in this category is increased understanding of a person's life (comprehensively and contextually), including cultural and sociopolitical influences and articulation of a self-constructed life plan (Guichard, 2005). Two approaches that exemplify this category are the My Career Chapter/My Career Future (McIlveen et al., 2005; McIlveen & Patton, 2010) and the Career Style Interview (Savickas, 2005). The *My Career Story Workbook* is a self-guided application built in part on questions and themes from the Career Style Interview (Savickas & Hartung, 2012). Examples of the narrative-systemic approaches can be found in Chapter 16, where the Life Design Genogram, an approach building on the Career Style Interview, helps an Italian client. The *My Career Story Workbook* is applied to career development work with an African American high school student in Chapter 6, and in Chapter 7 the counselor employs My Career Chapter to help a Malaysian client tell a career story.

Conclusion

Qualitative career assessments have many advantages when counselors work with diverse populations. Goldman (1994) predicted an increased use of qualitative assessments by a majority of counselors because these assessments have greater compatibility with the counseling process. Savickas (2015) described the postmodern influence on career counseling in the following way: "The 21st century perspective on career counseling moves from empiricism of objective vocational guiding and the humanism of subjective career developing to the social constructionism of projective life designing" (p. 136). It may very well be that practitioner utilization of qualitative career assessments follows a similar trend.

References

Busacca, L. A. (2007). Career construction theory: A practitioner's primer. *Career Planning and Adult Development Journal, 23,* 57–67.

Butler, S. K. (2012). Issues of social justice and career development. *Career Planning and Adult Development Journal, 28,* 140–151.

Chope, R. C. (2015). Card sorts, sentence completions, and other qualitative assessments. In P. J. Hartung, M. L. Savickas, & B. W. Walsh (Eds.), *APA handbook of career intervention, Volume 2: Applications. APA handbooks in psychology* (pp. 71–84). Washington, DC: American Psychological Association.

Dik, B. J., Duffy, R. D., & Steger, M. F. (2012). Enhancing social justice by promoting prosocial values in career development interventions. *Counseling and Values, 57,* 31–57.

Goldman, L. (1990). Qualitative assessment. *The Counseling Psychologist, 18,* 205–213.

Goldman, L. (1992). Qualitative assessment: An approach for counselors. *Journal of Counseling & Development, 70,* 616–622.

Goldman, L. (1994). The marriage is over . . . for most of us. *Measurement and Evaluation in Counseling and Development, 26,* 217–218.

Guichard, J. (2005). Life-long self-construction. *International Journal for Educational and Vocational Guidance, 5,* 111–124.

Gysbers, N. C. (2006). Using qualitative career assessments in career counseling with adults. *International Journal for Educational and Vocational Guidance, 6,* 95–108. doi:10.1007/s10775-0069102-4

Gysbers, N. C., Heppner, M. J., & Johnston, J. A. (2014). *Career counseling: Process, issues, and techniques* (4th ed.). Alexandria, VA: American Counseling Association.

Gysbers, N. C., Lapan, R. T., & Cato, S. (2013). Using assessments for personal, program, and policy advocacy. In C. Wood & D. G. Hays (Eds.), *A counselor's guide to career assessment instruments* (6th ed., pp. 75–84). Broken Arrow, OK: National Career Development Association.

Gysbers, N. C., & Moore, E. J. (1973). *Life career development: A model.* Columbia: University of Missouri.

Gysbers, N. C., & Moore, E. J. (1987). *Career counseling: Skills and techniques for practitioners.* Englewood Cliffs, NJ: Prentice Hall.

Knowdell, R. (2005a). *Career values: Card sort card deck.* San Jose, CA: Career Research & Testing.

Knowdell, R. (2005b). *Motivated skills: Card sort card deck.* San Jose, CA: Career Research & Testing.

Maree, J. (2013). Latest developments in career counselling in South Africa: Towards a positive approach. *South African Journal of Psychology, 43,* 409–421.

McGoldrick, M., Gerson, R., & Shellenberger, S. (1999). *Genograms: Assessment and intervention.* New York, NY: Norton.

McIlveen, P., Ford, T., & Dun, K. (2005). A narrative sentence completion process for systems career assessment. *Australian Journal of Career Development, 14,* 30–39.

McIlveen, P., & Patton, W. (2010). My Career Chapter as a tool for reflective practice. *International Journal for Educational and Vocational Guidance, 10,* 147–160. doi:10.1007/s10775-010-9181-0

McMahon, M., & Patton, W. (2002). Using qualitative assessment in career counseling. *International Journal of Educational and Vocational Guidance, 2,* 51–66.

McMahon, M., & Patton, W. (2006). Qualitative career assessment. In M. McMahon & W. Patton (Eds.), *Career counselling: Constructivist approaches* (pp. 164–174). London, England: Routledge.

McMahon, M., Patton, W., & Watson, M. (2003). Developing qualitative career assessment processes. *The Career Development Quarterly, 51,* 194–202.

McMahon, M., & Watson, M. (2013). Story telling: Crafting identities. *British Journal of Guidance & Counselling, 41,* 277–286.

Okiishi, R. W. (1987). The genogram as a tool in career counseling. *Journal of Counseling & Development, 66,* 139–143. doi:10.1002/j.1556-6676.1987.tb00820.x

Patton, W., & McMahon, M. (1999). *Career development and systems theory: A new relationship.* Pacific Grove, CA: Brooks/Cole.

Pearson, M., & Smith, D. (1986). Debriefing in experience-based learning. *Simulation Games for Learning, 16,* 155–172.

Pope, M., & Pangelinan, J. S. (2010). Using the ACA Advocacy Competencies in career counseling. In M. J. Ratts, R. L. Toporek, & J. A. Lewis (Eds.), *ACA Advocacy Competencies: A social justice framework for counselors* (pp. 209–223). Alexandria, VA: American Counseling Association.

Rudolph, J. W., Simon, R., Rivard, P., Dufresne, R. L., & Raemer, D. B. (2007). Debriefing with good judgment: Combining rigorous feedback with genuine inquiry. *Anesthesiology Clinics, 25,* 361–376.

Sampson, J. P., Jr. (2009). Modern and postmodern career theories: The unnecessary divorce. *The Career Development Quarterly, 58,* 91–96.

Sampson, J. P., Dozier, V. C., & Colvin, G. P. (2011). Translating career theory to practice: The risk of unintentional social injustice. *Journal of Counseling & Development, 89,* 326–337.

Sampson, J. P., McClain, M. C., Musch, E., & Reardon, R. C. (2011, November). *The supply and demand for career interventions as a social justice issue.* Paper presented at the 10th Biennial Conference: Forging Career Policy for the Greater Good, Society for Vocational Psychology, Boston, MA.

Savickas, M. L. (1992). New directions in career assessment. In D. H. Montross & C. J. Shinkman (Eds.), *Career development: Theory and practice* (pp. 336–355). Springfield, IL: Charles C Thomas.

Savickas, M. L. (2005). The theory and practice of career construction. In S. D. Brown & R. W. Lent (Eds.), *Career development and counseling: Putting theory and research to work* (pp. 42–70). Hoboken, NJ: Wiley.

Savickas, M. L. (2015). Career counseling paradigms: Guiding, developing, and designing. In P. J. Hartung, M. L. Savickas, & B. W. Walsh (Eds.), *The APA handbook of career intervention* (Vol. 1, pp. 129–143). Washington, DC: APA Books.

Savickas, M. L., & Hartung, P. J. (2012). *My career story: An autobiographical workbook for life-career success.* Retrieved from http://www.vocopher.com/CSI/CCI_workbook.pdf

Schultheiss, D. (2005). Qualitative relational career assessment: A constructivist paradigm. *Journal of Career Assessment, 13,* 381–394.

Sears, S. (1982). A definition of career guidance terms: A national vocational guidance association perspective. *Vocational Guidance Quarterly, 31,* 137–143.

Whiston, S. C., & Rahardja, D. (2005). Qualitative career assessment: An overview and analysis. *Journal of Career Assessment, 13,* 371–380.

Wood, C., & Hays, D. G. (2013). *A counselor's guide to career assessment instruments* (6th ed.). Broken Arrow, OK: National Career Development Association.

Part III

PROCEDURES

Chapters 6–16
**Social Constructionist, Constructivist,
and Narrative Models**

Chapters 17–19
**Variants of Social Constructionist,
Constructivist, and Narrative Models**

Chapters 20–22
Systemic and Integrative Models

Chapter 6

Using the *My Career Story Workbook* With an African American High School Student

Mark C. Rehfuss

Youth today face multiple challenges at societal, cultural, institutional, and economic levels when considering their career futures. Career instruments that are accessible and free can facilitate and empower individuals encountering these diverse barriers when implementing their careers or facing career transitions. In this chapter I discuss the use of *My Career Story: An Autobiographical Workbook for Life-Career Success* (Savickas & Hartung, 2012) as a tool for assisting youth with limited access to other career choice and development resources. Literature related to the development of the workbook and its approach to career assessment and storytelling is reviewed, and the helpfulness of the model for working with youth is addressed. A case study of a young high school-age African American male is presented to illustrate the use of this instrument in the life of one individual.

My Career Story Workbook

The development of the *My Career Story (MCS) Workbook* had its origins in Savickas's Career Construction Interview (Savickas, 1989, 1998, 2005, 2011a). Savickas developed his initial tool, the Career Story Interview, in the early 1990s and has been using and refining it ever since (Savickas, 1989). The MCS workbook (Savickas & Hartung, 2012) was developed to adapt the Career Construction Interview, which is applied in a one-on-one setting, to use with multiple individuals in group or educational settings. The MCS is utilized in much the same way as the Self-Directed Search (Holland, 1985, 1997); both enable career counselors to work with large numbers of diverse individuals while still guiding each one to information that may help address the next challenge in his or her career development. The narrative or qualitative nature of the interview is its greatest strength, enabling the individual alone or with assistance from others to gain needed direction about the future. The concept that the self is a story that can empower individuals is at the heart of the workbook; it is important to give voice and clarity to one's story to guide and construct a fuller narrative of one's life moving forward (Bujold, 2004; McAdams, 1997; McAdams, Josselson, & Lieblich, 2006; Savickas, 2011a, 2011b).

Because the MCS is based on a narrative or story, the learning experience for each individual is different. The concrete outcomes of the assessment are not a set of objective letters or numbers needing to be organized on some grid but rather a subjective collection of everyday phrases, mottos, and words that clearly communicate their meaning. This dynamic difference underlies the need for the MCS because it is our own language that we use to communicate the stories of our lives. The MCS draws those stories out and lets the storyteller pull back and gain a new perspective. Such a new view highlights themes across the story and may lead to the construction of a unifying story of the self that can inform and guide career-related decisions. Individuals' stories are deeply embedded in their culture and life, and encouraging them to tell their own unique stories creates opportunities to transcend cultural norms and enables a broader diversity of stories to be voiced, reflected upon, validated, and embraced (Clark, Severy, & Sawyer, 2004; Taber, Hartung, Briddick, Briddick, & Rehfuss, 2011). The MCS provides a platform for diverse clients to share and hear their stories in their own words, often for the first time. Clients create additional occupational options based on their stories, and when working on the MCS with a counselor or others, oppressive or restrictive voices can be identified and challenged.

Using the MCS Workbook

The MCS workbook (Savickas & Hartung, 2012) can be used with individuals or groups in clinical or educational settings. It can be completed by individuals on their own, without feedback from others, or with some one-on-one guidance and discussion. Although the design of the MCS workbook allows the individual to complete it working alone, when clients chooses to process their story with others, the benefits can be greater. The exercise itself takes some time to thoughtfully complete (1 to 2 hours or longer, depending on the number of tasks completed in a single sitting). It can be helpful to complete the workbook over several sittings with reflection in between, but the workbook is designed to be flexible and can be adjusted to meet the participant's time constraints. Clients may also go back and add things they had forgotten; these stories are not permanent but fluid, and different experiences encountered in life may trigger different memories.

In a group setting, be it clinical or educational, the MCS workbook has proved to be beneficial for individuals seeking career guidance (Di

Fabio & Maree, 2012; Savickas & Hartung, 2012). Members of a group should complete sections of the workbook weekly and then meet to share their stories with one another. Many of the stories revealed through the workbook are very personal; therefore, when used in a group setting, it is important to impress upon group members that personal storytelling is a gift that one person shares with another, and sharing deserves the utmost respect. Group work is appropriate for students in a career exploration class or with a select group of high school students who want to understand themselves and their careers and are supportive of others going through the same process.

To understand the benefits and challenges of the MCS, counselors and practitioners who plan on using the workbook should complete it on their own prior to using it with clients (Rehfuss, 2009). The case study illustrates how to use the workbook in a single session with a client, but first a brief overview of the workbook may be helpful. The *My Career Story* workbook (Savickas & Hartung, 2012) can be accessed and printed for free through vocopher.com. The tables and page numbers referenced in the following descriptive sections refer to pages and tables in the workbook itself.

Introduction

The workbook is intended to help participants to better understand themselves and their stories, providing them with a new resource in facing current and future challenges in life and career. The workbook is 18 pages long and begins with a statement of purpose. Referencing the Purpose, Uses, and General Directions sections prior to using the tool will help you know how to apply the workbook with individuals or groups or in an educational setting.

Individuals may choose to include important others in their discussion and reflection, but it is not necessary to do so for individuals to gain insight into themselves. The critical points for individuals completing the workbook are that they write in a manner that is reflective and that they apply what they have written at the end of the workbook. Participants actively engaged in the written tasks while completing the workbook will gain the most benefit. Brief or short answers to the questions are not as effective as fuller and more reflective responses. Encouraging thoughtful and complete answers will aid clients when they are asked to review and rework some of the initial tasks later in the workbook. The Case of Jacob section later in the chapter illustrates each step of the MCS method described here.

The workbook is composed of three sections that guide the storytelling process. In Part 1 participants tell their story, in Part 2 they hear their story, and in Part 3 they enact their story.

Telling the Story

Part 1 begins with clients describing the transition they now face and how they hope the workbook will be useful to them. Clients are then asked to create a list of occupations that they have considered pursuing throughout the course of their life; this list provides some direction to the possible selves of the individual. Clients then are asked to identify and describe examples for each of the following four categories: role models whom they admired while growing up, favorite magazines or television shows, a current favorite story (this can be a book or a movie), and a favorite saying or motto that they can recall.

Hearing the Story

Part 2 of the workbook focuses on drawing together the separate stories described in Part 1 to create a larger, more cohesive narrative of clients' life careers and provides an opportunity for clients to hear their stories. The goal of this section is to clarify clients' full life story and make it more readily available to be used in facing their current career situation. There is a narrative explanation of the three goals and objectives for Part 2 as well as a description of the concepts of self and story that are being used in this process. Essentially, it explains that the self contains the qualities that make us who we are, and knowledge of the self can help us to identify both the setting we would prefer to work in and the core script that motivates us in our life and work. The exercises in Part 2 focus on highlighting the Self, the Setting, and the Script.

Part 2 begins with examining the Self by reviewing the separate stories that were told in Part 1. Clients are asked to reflect on their identified role models and to recall key words used to describe these individuals (e.g., the first adjective, words used more than once in the descriptions, things they have in common, and any other significant words used in the descriptions). Clients are then asked to weave these things together, resulting in a two- to four-sentence description of the core self—who they are and who they are becoming.

The second section of Part 2 focuses on the Setting, or where clients like to be. Here clients are asked to review their favorite magazines and TV shows and to write down the following: words used to describe them, the kinds of activities included in them, what is happening in them, and what the people are doing in them. The instructions go on to explain that TV shows and magazines can be grouped by work setting as shown in Table 1: Six Types of Work Settings With Examples (p. 12). The table includes four columns (Sample Magazines, Sample TV Shows, Description, Work Setting) and six rows for different types of Work Settings, which reflect the Realistic (R), Investigative (I), Artistic (A), Social (S), Enterprising (E), and Conventional (C) model of John Holland (1985, 1997). The Description column in the table expands on what these various Work Settings look like. Clients are asked to identify two out of the six Work Settings that are most like the settings of their favorite shows. Then they choose their favorite words from the Description column for those two Work Settings and the people they like the most. After these steps, clients write two to four sentences that summarize the Settings they most enjoy.

The last item in Part 2 is the My Career Story, Summary Portrait (p. 13). This form provides a concise way to condense the stories and words from Parts 1 and 2 onto a single page, which enables clients to hear their story in a clear manner. The first three sections of this summary draw on clients' responses to the Self, Setting, and Script exercises previously completed. The fourth section is labeled the Success Formula, and it draws from the three previous sections and provides four prompts for writing a one-sentence personal life-career mission statement. The fifth and last section deals with Self-Advice. Clients are instructed to reflect on their favorite saying or motto (from p. 8) and to write it down as the best advice they have for themselves to apply to their Success Formula. Clients review the initial transition and choices they had written down and then rewrite their stories, applying their Success Formula and Self-Advice to explain how they will make that transition and those choices.

Part 2 concludes with an opportunity for clients to apply what they have learned from their Summary Portrait to the occupational choices they had first listed and to identify occupations they now see as potential choices. If they want to add more occupations to their list, they can Explore More Occupations by looking up other occupations on O*NET, a free online resource that describes and details occupations. Clients are encouraged to list any newly identified occupations and to explore them further.

Enacting the Story

The final section of the workbook, Part 3, provides a detailed, three-part plan to move clients' stories into action. The first step, Reflect, prompts clients to select a goal that will enable them to enact and bring to life their career story. The second step, Tell, urges clients to tell their story by planning how they would share it with other people whom they trust. The last step, Perform, instructs clients to perform their story by taking actions that will move them from their current situation toward the goals they have set. The workbook provides several examples to select from relating to committing to, trying, and moving toward the chosen occupation. There is also an opportunity to write in a more specific goal.

The MCS workbook focuses on process and reflection. Each part of the workbook builds on the previous parts to accomplish the goals individuals set at the beginning. It must be stressed that to get the most out of the workbook adequate time and effort are required—the workbook cannot be completed in less than 1 hour.

Now that the basic elements of the workbook have been explained, let's move on to the case study and see the MCS in action. Although not every individual will benefit in the same manner as Jacob in this case study, the approach has much to offer clients facing career-related decisions. As McAdams (1997) stated, the power of story is in its telling. In other words, when we give voice to our story, we cannot help but be changed by it.

The Case of Jacob

Jacob is a 17-year-old African American male who lives in a metropolitan area. He attends a local city high school and is the older of two children.

His sister is 2 years younger and both are being raised by their single mother. His mother works full time for the city in a low-level administrative position. Jacob is active on his high school's football and basketball teams. Although he is not a starter, he enjoys the camraderie he shares with his teammates. Jacob is an average student and hopes to attend a nearby 4-year state university two of his friends also plan to attend after graduation. He is unsure about the type of degree he would like to pursue or what he wants to do for a living, but Jacob has some ideas and wants help clarifying them.

Jacob only has time to meet for one session. Therefore, the MCS workbook is reviewed with the counselor verbally, and the counselor takes notes in the workbook as they go through the questions. The workbook is handed back and forth several times during the session so that exact words, phrases, and sentences can be reviewed while completing the workbook tasks. The workbook is finished relatively quickly (in just over 1 hour) and with assistance of the counselor, but Jacob's responses are typical enough to highlight the process and demonstrate how the questions, words, and exercises all work together to clarify, strengthen, and enact Jacob's story.

Jacob initially responds to the workbook by expressing that it isn't what he is expecting to help with his decision. He wants something like a test that "can just tell me what to do and what to study at college." The counselor reminds Jacob that he took a test like that and didn't think it was helpful. The counselor suggests that this new approach could help in a different way. Jacob is encouraged to think of the MCS as a process that may help him gain clarity regarding the decision he is facing. He agrees and states that he is willing to go through the process if "it doesn't take too much time."

Part 1

When given the first task, "Write a brief essay telling about the transition you now face and how you hope this workbook will be useful," Jacob replies:

> I'm leaving high school and want to go to college. I know I have to study something in college, and since it will cost a lot, I want to know what to study and what I can be successful at so I can get a good job.

The counselor encourages Jacob by supporting his goal and stating that they will try to use the MCS to make additional progress on his goal together. When asked what occupations he is considering or has considered in the past, Jacob indicates that he had wanted to be a pro athlete or a coach but knows that isn't going to happen. He mentions that his mom works for the city in an office building, and he likes the woman who works as her manager. Jacob also expresses that lawyers make good money. That's all he can think of.

When asked who he admired or saw as a hero when growing up, Jacob says, "Batman from the *Batman* movies. Even though he wasn't perfect, he was tough and he got the job done when no one else wanted to." He expresses admiration for Michael Jordan, too, but less as a basketball player than "as a man who uses his money to make more and bought and runs several companies. He had focus and determination to do better and keep doing it." Jacob also mentions his grandfather, who worked as a mechanic and would take Jacob fishing when he visited: "He was tough but always nice to me, and he knew how to catch some fish and cook them up. He was a good man."

When asked about his favorite television shows or books, Jacob remembers a short biography about Michael Jordan that he read, but mainly he likes watching ESPN's SportsCenter. When asked what he likes most about it he says, "Catching up on some of my favorite athletes and seeing what they are doing to get better." He likes getting updates on the professional sports teams he follows and learning what they are doing to improve and win each season. He also likes watching his favorite teams' games and rooting for them. He states that he really enjoys the TV show *Shark Tank* as well. He likes how "the contestants come up with ideas and how the business people or 'sharks' battle over the best ones." He also loves how they don't always go for the person's product, but they have made many people rich. One of his favorite movies is *The Express*. His grandfather had taken him to the theater to see that movie when he was a little boy. He really likes that Ernie Davis fought hard to become the first African American Heisman Trophy winner. He is inspired by the fact that Ernie Davis won despite great obstacles and opposition. "He showed everyone, worked hard and did it." When prompted to think of a saying that means something to him, Jacob remembers his mother saying, "Don't take it, give it." For Jacob, this means both "don't take crap from others without giving some back" but also, more positively, "pass something up so that my little sister can have it."

Part 1 of the MCS enables diverse individuals to identify and reflect on the influences in their lives. Sharing and beginning to reflect on their life stories fosters a sense of consistency across the past that can be used when considering the future. This process is highlighted in Part 2 and applied in Part 3. Regardless of background or environment, all individuals develop and embrace heroes that provide the model for how to live life successfully. Likewise, all individuals repeat sayings that resonate with them and that can provide them with great power, focus and direction. These role models and resonant statements can empower the self when confronted with difficult or oppressive situations. This is clearly seen in Jacob's narratives. As a member of a minority group, he has selected powerful representatives from his own culture that characterize the resolve and dedication needed to be successful in a hostile world. He has seen these strong, good men and embraces their good qualities as helpful building blocks of his own self. As he reflects and shares his story and sees his own words on the page, his narrative becomes more whole, real, and a greater resource for him in facing his decisions. As he continues this process, Jacob discovers that the wisdom needed to confront and handle life and career decisions already resides within his own narratives. Part 2 of the workbook draws the words off the page, which helps Jacob hear and clearly define his own self.

Part 2

In Part 2 Jacob begins to hear the story that has just been told. It is important that the participant understand the concepts of the section. In Jacob's case, these concepts are discussed but not read in their entirety because of the time limitations. When reviewing his statements about Self, several adjectives and phrases stand out to Jacob: "tough, got the job done, focus, determination, kind, and good." Several of these words or concepts repeat in each of his descriptions. When thinking about what they have in common, Jacob indicates that they are "all tough but kind people who got the job done and were successful." He believes these characteristics accurately describe him too, but he isn't sure what job he should do. He wants to be successful and knows he is tough enough to make it happen. He also says that he wants "to be kind along the way—but not too kind."

Next, in exploring Setting, Jacob and the counselor review his media preferences. Several things that he likes stand out: hearing about what athletes and teams are doing to improve their competitive performances, people coming up with ideas, the business leaders battling and helping others become rich. Looking at the Work Settings column in Table 1: Six Types of Work Settings With Examples, Jacob indicates that "Enterprising" is a potential one for sure because both of his TV shows fall in the category. From the Description column, he especially likes the picture of "powerful people using leadership skills to solve business problems and be competitive." He also likes the Social category in Work Settings and the descriptive terms *teamwork* and *caring*. Jacob concludes the Setting section of Part 2 by saying, "I would like to be in a business setting where I can be a leader and help the business and its clients to be successful, and where there is competition but also teamwork to accomplish goals and get the job done."

Summary Page

The Summary Portrait form condenses everything that has been discussed on one page. It starts with summarizing the Self and Setting from the previous discussion. A Script or plot is then created to illustrate the way in which Jacob wants the action in his story to unfold. Working on the Script, Jacob goes back to his favorite movie and summarizes the plot as he did before. "He showed everyone, worked hard and did it." He clarifies by stating that he wants to do the same thing; he wants to show everyone he can work hard and be successful, he hopes in a business career setting. Using these three summaries, Jacob completes his Success Formula:

I will be most happy and successful when I am able to be "a tough but kind leader" in places where people are "competitive but work as a team to solve business problems" so that I can "be rich and show everyone I did it."

He finishes the summary page by clarifying his Self-Advice: "Don't take it, give it." Jacob interprets this as "Don't take any crap about going to college! I can do it and be successful, and after that I can give to others through work and success like the *Shark Tank* bosses." The Summary Portrait is then used to rewrite Jacob's initial story about his transition and choices.

In going back to the beginning of the session and rewriting his story, Jacob now says, "I want to go to college and study business so that I can become a tough leader who solves problems as a part of a team and become rich." Returning to his potential occupations and those he is now considering, he says he will probably be fulfilled by "something in business, like a manager of employees." Careers in management and human resources are discussed, but there are many paths to success in business. Jacob needs to remember his success formula when thinking about choosing a business-related major at college. Part 2 of the MCS ends with the Exploring More Occupations page. Jacob writes down *Enterprising* and *Social* as work settings he wants to explore, and he is instructed to take some time to look at other jobs on O*NET OnLine (n.d.) that would fit with his interests. Part 2 works with individuals from diverse cultures and backgrounds, but the additional occupational resource of O*NET may only be helpful for clients in Western cultures. When considering career options across more diverse settings, other more appropriate resources should be utilized.

Part 2 of the MCS works well with diverse participants because they are drawing on their own stories to create and hear advice they will give to themselves. Jacob's advice to himself is as strong as the role models he has selected. As a member of a minority group, he clearly knows what he is facing, and his words to himself are powerful and pinpoint how he must be to be successful. Jacob has used his own story to find purpose and meaning within work and life. In Part 3 Jacob will be asked to take steps to apply this learning to his current life and career situation.

Part 3

Part 3, Enacting My Story, provides an action plan in three sections: Reflect, Tell, and Perform. Jacob reflects on his career story and decides that his new goal is to meet with an advisor from the business school at the university he is going to attend and decide on a business major. He is going to tell his mother and sister about what he has learned from this process and about his new plans. He will also speak to his college-bound friends when he sees them next. He chooses to perform his story by trying to meet with his mom's boss, a woman who holds a management position in a business setting. The possibility of Jacob learning more about business by getting involved with a student business group at college once he arrives there is also discussed. Jacob is encouraged to contact the counselor again if needed, but also to remember to review the MCS workbook he has just completed when facing future career decisions.

Part 3 of the MCS helps diverse individuals put their stories into action by providing multiple options for reflecting, telling, and performing.

These actions are not limited to culture or setting, and they are focused on the self, others, and the environments in which the individual lives. As a member of a minority group, it is important for Jacob to identify and gain guidance from others who can help him be successful, whether they are advisors, professionals, or peers just a little ahead of him in school. Sharing his learning and plans with those closest to him will make his plans more concrete and enable those in his support system to remind him of his story when he confronts the many obstacles on the path to his goal. Regardless of circumstance, background, or position in life, the MCS process enables the participant to share, hear, and enact his or her personal success story. See Table 6.1 for an application guide.

Conclusion

The *My Career Story Workbook* provides a comprehensive set of steps and the guidance necessary to help an individual tell, hear, and author her or his life and career story (Savickas & Hartung, 2012). It can be used by the individual alone, in partnership with a counselor, or in a group or educational setting. This tool is helpful for those making career decisions who need a perspective that differs from traditional career tests and measures. When fully completed, the MCS provides a narrative framework the individual can use in the present and in the future when facing career and life-related decisions.

Recommended Resources

Busacca, L. (2007). Career construction theory: A practitioner's primer. *Career Planning and Adult Development Journal, 23*, 57–67.

McAdams, D. P., Josselson, R., & Lieblich, A. (Eds.). (2006). *Identity and story: Creating self in narrative.* Washington, DC: American Psychological Association.

O*NET OnLine. (n.d.). *Interests.* Retrieved from https://www.onetonline.org/find/descriptor/browse/Interests

Savickas, M. L. (2015). *Life-design counseling manual.* Retrieved from http://vocopher.com/LifeDesign/LifeDesign.pdf

Savickas, M. L., & Hartung, P. J. (2012). *My Career Story: An autobiographical workbook for life-career success.* Retrieved from http://www.vocopher.com/CSI/CCI_workbook.pdf

References

Bujold, C. (2004). Constructing career through narrative. *Journal of Vocational Behavior, 64*, 470–484.

Clark, M. A., Severy, L., & Sawyer, S. A. (2004). Creating connections: Using a narrative approach in career group counseling with college students from diverse cultural backgrounds. *Journal of College Counseling, 7*, 24–31.

Di Fabio, A., & Maree, J. G. (2012). Group-based life design counseling in an Italian context. *Journal of Vocational Behavior, 80*, 100–107.

Table 6.1
Practical Application Guide

Topic	Using the My Career Story Workbook
General goals and purposes	1. Promote one's understanding of the relationship between personal interests and career interests 2. Explore the ways in which personal stories and narratives influence self-identity and what is needed from work for the individual 3. Identify life and career themes that emerge during the writing and discussion 4. Describe how the emergent themes can be used to address one's career decisions
Applicable modality	Individual, dyadic, group, classroom settings
Applicable counselor settings	Junior and senior high schools, college/university career services, community agency, private practice
Recommended time to complete	One session for group and classroom settings, with a second session offered to those having difficulty with assessment; 45 to 90 minutes
Materials/equipment needed	Copy of free handbook from vocopher.com
Step-by-step outline of the process	Individuals write out or discuss their stories using three parts of the workbook. Each section has detailed directions and explanations, but for the most part clients are answering questions and then using those answers to tell their story and act on it. Part 1. Telling My Story. A. Identify the current transition B. List possible occupations C. Answer four questions related to 　1. Those they admired growing up 　2. Favorite magazines or television shows 　3. Current favorite story 　4. Favorite saying Part 2. Hearing My Story summarizes the information from Part 1. A. Self: identifying words and phrases used that describe who they are and who they want to become. B. Setting: identifying the plots they relate to and linking those to the RIASEC model for more descriptive words related to work setting and using those words in determining the type of work environments they would like to be in. C. Summary Portrait: A single summary page of their story including 　1. Self 　2. Setting

(Continued)

Table 6.1 *(Continued)*
Practical Application Guide

Topic	Using the My Career Story Workbook
Step-by-step outline of the process *(Continued)*	3. Script/plot: work on the script takes place on this page, but there are no real directions for it. They simply use the plot from their favorite story or movie and apply that to what they want to do in the setting described previously. 4. Success Formula: this draws from the first three summaries (Self, Setting, and Script) to fill in and make a one-sentence personal life career mission statement. 5. Self-Advice: this uses the favorite saying, which is the best advice they have for themselves when facing their current career concern. D. Rewriting My Story: rewriting the initial concern using their success formula and self-advice. E. Exploring Occupations: reviewing the initial occupations considered and choosing some and clarifying others. F. Exploring More Occupations: details the process of how to look up more occupations on O*NET related to their interests identified earlier. Part 3. Enacting My Story focuses on developing a plan to put their story into action. A. Reflect: focusing on their career story and using it to set specific goals for the next part of their life. B. Tell: identifying important individuals to whom they want to tell their story and explain the conclusions they have drawn from the workbook. C. Perform: listing two to four objectives or small steps they will take to move toward the goals they have developed.

Holland, J. L. (1985). *The Self-Directed Search professional manual.* Odessa, FL: Psychological Assessment Resources.

Holland, J. L. (1997). *Making vocational choices: A theory of vocational personalities and work environments* (3rd ed.). Odessa, FL: Psychological Assessment Resources.

McAdams, D. P. (1997). *The stories we live by: Personal myths and the making of the self.* New York, NY: Guilford Press.

McAdams, D. P., Josselson, R., & Lieblich, A. (Eds.). (2006). *Identity and story: Creating self in narrative.* Washington, DC: American Psychological Association.

O*NET OnLine. (n.d.). *Interests.* Retrieved from https://www.onetonline.org/find/descriptor/browse/Interests

Rehfuss, M. C. (2009). Teaching career construction and the career style interview. *Career Planning and Adult Development Journal, 25,* 58–71.

Savickas, M. L. (1989). Career-style assessment and counseling. In T. J. Sweeney (Ed.), *Adlerian counseling: A practitioner approach for a new decade* (3rd ed., pp. 289–320). Muncie, IN: Accelerated Development.

Savickas, M. L. (1998). Career-style assessment and counseling. In T. J. Sweeney (Ed.), *Adlerian counseling: A practitioner's approach* (4th ed., pp. 329–359). Bristol, PA: Accelerated Development.

Savickas, M. L. (2005). The theory and practice of career construction. In S. D. Brown & R. W. Lent (Eds.), *Career development and counseling* (pp. 42–70). Hoboken, NJ: Wiley.

Savickas, M. L. (2011a). *Career counseling.* Washington, DC: American Psychological Association.

Savickas, M. L. (2011b). The self in vocational psychology: Object, subject and project. In P. J. Hartung & L. M. Subich (Eds.), *Developing self in work and career: Concepts, cases and contexts* (pp. 17–33). Washington, DC: American Psychological Association.

Savickas, M. L., & Hartung, P. J. (2012). *My Career Story: An autobiographical workbook for life-career success.* Retrieved from http://www.vocopher.com/CSI/CCI_workbook.pdf

Taber, B. J., Hartung, P. J., Briddick, H., Briddick, W. C., & Rehfuss, M. (2011). Career style interview: A contextualized approach to career counseling. *The Career Development Quarterly, 59,* 274–287.

Chapter 7

Using My Career Chapter With a Malaysian Engineer to Write and Tell a Career Story

Peter McIlveen

Stories are universal. Cultures include stories; cultures are stories—incomplete stories, always evolving. Every person has a story; a person is a story—an incomplete story, always evolving. At their confluence, the stories of cultures manifest through individuals, and individuals express themselves through the stories of their cultures. Thus, one is a story of the other, with each reflecting on the other. Indeed, on this planet, there are 7 billion stories and counting, incomplete and evolving, as diverse as all the peoples on Earth, yet somehow very similar to one another. How these many stories are told, heard, and created is very much the domain of counseling.

Story is fundamental to constructivist and social constructionist approaches to career counseling, but storytelling does not come naturally to clients in the peculiar situation and dialogue that is "counseling." Not all clients know how to tell their stories, and not all clients know how to write their stories. My Career Chapter is a semistructured career assessment and counseling procedure that facilitates a client writing a story and telling a story about his or her life in relation to career. The client produces a written manuscript by completing a range of sentence completion activities directed at the myriad influences that constitute his or her life. Client and counselor interpret the written story together in a process of co-construction.

Stories are so intrinsically human that the intellectual arts and social sciences, such as literature, anthropology, and sociology, have subjected story to their methods and ways of knowing. Psychology, too, has brought story into its research gaze to observe how people make and tell stories. In recent years, McAdams (1993) widened psychology's perspective to better understand that story is more than a tale told by one person to another. McAdams has taught others in the field that the story is much more: Story constitutes identity. Grasping this significant idea is germane to understanding narrative approaches to career counseling. In this chapter, I outline the theory and procedures that underpin My Career Chapter, describe how it can be used with adult clients, and provide a case study to illustrate the model. I begin with a brief review of the main theoretical ideas that constitute the narrative career counseling procedure (McIlveen, 2006).

An Epistemological and Ontological Perspective

Social constructionism holds that there is no one truth in psychological reality; each and every person experiences his or her own reality. A story must be true to its context; it cannot be created in a fantasy world lest it be regarded as little more than a daydream. This in no way, however, degrades the benefits of dreaming, fantasizing, and hoping for an imagined future. What would any life be without such dreams? The crux of this caveat is the central tenet of social constructionism. It defies the critique of social constructionism that labels it relativist. Therein lies the existential paradox of social constructionism: I can only become that which is bound by the parameters of the discourse that makes my reality. I cannot exist outside the text of the discourse that constitutes my psychological reality.

To understand the first dimension of the conundrum, imagine yourself as an English-speaking migrant in a new country where the people speak a language that is completely foreign to your ears. There are no traces of language that are familiar, no accents, no Latin or Greek roots that transfer across languages. You cannot hear anything meaningful, and you cannot speak anything meaningful. The symbols you see make no sense. You are surrounded by noise. Those ostensibly normal, taken-for-granted activities, such as saying hello, are no longer part of your psychological reality. You see people reading newspapers, talking with one another, gesticulating and flashing facial expressions at one another, but you are completely uncomprehending of their meanings. You can only look on, feeling very much on the outside of life. Soon enough you feel the pangs of loneliness. The only English-language dialogue you hear are the voices of conversations you remember, of conversations you create to keep you company in the hours that go by without someone calling your name in words that you recognize as familiar and meaningful.

The second dimension of this conundrum is that beyond knowledge of yourself, you have neither knowledge of nor any way of ever gaining knowledge of the social world around you. Your frantic gesticulations soon earn you a drink of water and some food to eat, but you realize that abstract ideas are held and transmitted in language, just as the abstract idea of yourself is constituted in language, and without that language you cannot understand and experience concepts that they—the locals—take for granted.

Thus, from a social constructionist perspective, meaning and truth are not universal givens that are transmissible in immutable form from one person to the next; instead, meaning and truth are negotiable. And, at this juncture, the notion of truth in the social sciences takes on a very different meaning from the notions of truth and laws in the positivist sciences; therefore, it makes no sense to further compare and contrast the two—they are paradigmatically different.

Then what is truth and truthfulness in the social sciences? This question is negotiable too. The very words in the question "what is" imply that a thing, such as truth, is possible and knowable. To avoid descending into an abyss of endless questioning, we must reach out to sanity's salve against relativism, which is found in the ideas of pragmatism (James, 1907/2000; Rorty, 1999). Put in simplistic terms, the proof of the pudding is in the eating. With respect to career counseling, truth is negotiated between client and counselor (and terms such as *co-construction* represent this process, epistemologically); thus, co-construction is the eating—the generative creation of truth. Of course, clients live in worlds beyond the dyad of counseling, but truth is similarly negotiated in dialogue with others in these worlds too, and, as such, the stories a person tells and hears are subject to co-construction and eating among others.

Career as a Story

Humanity marvels at the great storytellers who seem to capture imaginations and draw readers into a story as if it were true. Curious readers are awed by the great writers whose evocative renderings bring one world to another, that of life and lives lived elsewhere. I can smell Charles Dickens's (1854/1969) filthy smog draped like a greasy pall over Victorian towns; I feel Walt Whitman's (1855/2004) wonder at the universe in his words "I believe a leaf of grass is no less than the journey-work of the stars" (p. 35).

The ubiquity of *story* in people's lives (McAdams, 1993) is articulated as a comprehensive theory of *the person* (cf. personology), whereby a person may be holistically and metaphorically conceptualized as an actor, agent, and author (McAdams & McLean, 2013). Within the career development literature, McAdams's theory is best expressed in the segments of career construction theory (Savickas, 2005, 2013): vocational personality—person as *actor*; career adaptability—person as *agent*; and life themes—person as *author*. Furthermore, story is posited as a fundamental *process influence* in the systems theory framework (STF) of career (Patton & McMahon, 2014). From the perspective of the STF, story is the meaningful connection among the myriad *influences* that constitute a person's career. A person does not know him- or herself as his or her abilities, interests, occupation, or social class but rather as the story that connects all of these personalized elements together.

Narrative Career Counseling

Story is the sine qua non of narrative career counseling; without story there cannot be narrative career counseling. What follows is a summary of the definitive features of this approach:

> Narrative career counselling emphasises subjectivity and meaning. It aims to facilitate self-reflection and elaboration of self-concepts toward an enhanced self-understanding that is subjectively and contextually truthful. It entails a collaborative process in which the client is supported in creating an open-ended personal story that holistically accounts for his or her life and career, and enables the person to make meaningfully informed career-decisions and actions. (McIlveen & Patton, 2007b, p. 228)

The various approaches to narrative career counseling, chief among them being the models articulated by Cochran (2000) and Savickas (2011), possess these definitive features: subjectivity, meaningfulness, awareness, collaboration, and movement toward goals.

Narrative career counseling treats story as the product (i.e., the what) and treats storying as the process of telling and editing stories (i.e., the how) with the ultimate aim of generating the meaning necessary for making choices and moving forward toward goals (i.e., the why). Without facilitating the client telling his or her story, without listening and hearing the story, and without the counselor engaging with the client and in the client's story as benevolent editor, there can be no transformation of awareness of the client's identity and there can be no movement toward goals. Thus, narrative career counseling is not so much about the story per se as it is about the process of storying. Indeed, it is the process of storying that is emphasized in My Career Chapter. The writing and telling are separate but inherently valuable processes and are concomitantly confronting to clients, for their stories are their own, written under their own hands, spoken in their own words, and heard in their own ears, perhaps for the first time (McIlveen, Patton, & Hoare, 2008).

Application of Core Theoretical Tenets to My Career Chapter

My Career Chapter is a tool for narrative career counseling rather than an approach such as those articulated by Cochran (2000) and Savickas (2011). A distinctive feature of My Career Chapter is that its design is based on the core tenets of selected theories—namely, the STF (Patton & McMahon, 2014) and the theory of dialogical self (Hermans & Gieser, 2012; Hermans & Kempen, 1993). There is insufficient space here to comprehensively examine the theoretical underpinnings of My Career Chapter, but interested readers may refer to other sources (McIlveen, 2011, 2012; McIlveen & Patton, 2007a). Only the core tenets of these theories are considered in relation to My Career Chapter's application: the decentered career as the confluence of systems of career influences, and dialogical relations with one's selves across time. The way these theories are operationalized in My Career Chapter is briefly outlined in the following paragraphs.

A fundamental aspect of the STF of career is that there is more than one way of knowing a person; thus, it is known as a *framework* for theories. Like an onion, the STF organizes the notion of career as layers of influences that extend from the inner intrapersonal layer (e.g., interests, skills, knowledge, sexuality) outward to the interpersonal (e.g., family, friendships) and social (e.g., workplace, school) layers, and outward again to the societal/environmental layer (e.g., media, government, employment market). This wider perspective is particularly important when ethnic and cultural influences impinge on clients' engagement in career counseling, especially with regard to the establishment of a strong working alliance (Leong & Flores, 2013).

A key process influence in the STF is *change*. Change may be conceived of temporally, as in the past, present, future; and it may be considered as a developmental progression, as in ages and stages. Change also may be considered in terms of fortuitous or ominous events and, as such, may be viewed as a function of *chance*. In light of all of this, the counselor must, through the all-encompassing lens of the STF, endeavor to conceptualize a person's career as being the confluence of all of these influences interacting with one another recursively. Given this wider lens, it is impossible to conceptualize a person's career as a single entity, as if it were a possession owned by the person. Thus, career is decentered in the STF. Through the use of My Career Chapter, counselors can facilitate clients arriving at a view of their careers that enables fresh perspectives: to see sources of influence hitherto unseen, to adopt new potential ideas, and to broaden their view of their career as something more than just a collection of interests, skills, and knowledge.

The main activity of My Career Chapter requires the client to complete sets of sentence stems (cf. Loevinger, 1985). Each of the career influences identified in the spherical model of STF of career (Patton & McMahon, 2014) is written about in a set of sentence stems, and each set is composed of five stems. The first three stems span the past, present, and future; these are followed by a stem that pertains to the emotional salience of the influence on the client's life; and last is a stem that addresses the impact that all of these influence have on the client's life. These last two stems were introduced in response to calls for better integration of emotion in career counseling (Kidd, 2004). These stems invite the client to rate the salience and impact of the influence and then complete the sentence with an explanation. The following sentence stems are examples from the My Career Chapter booklet and show how the career influence, Culture, is addressed:

Sentence Stem	*Specific Career Influence*
My cultural background has given me . . .	Past
In my culture I am . . .	Present
Other cultures could help my career by . . .	Future
I mostly feel [very positive/positive/ indifferent/negative/very negative] in relation to my culture because . . .	Emotional salience
My cultural heritage has a [very positive/ positive/neutral/negative/very negative] impact upon my career life because . . .	Impact

The theory of *dialogical self* (Hermans & Gieser, 2012; Hermans & Kempen, 1993) describes how an individual's identity is created through conversations. Recall the loneliness of yourself imagined as a migrant in a new country, bereft of familiar conversation. Dialogical self explains this experience. But, first, another example is needed to articulate the metaphor more clearly. Imagine yourself to be the character Chuck Noland (originally played by Tom Hanks) in the cinematic blockbuster movie *Cast Away* (Zemeckis, 2000). There you are, marooned, and just like the migrant in the previous example, you are totally alone. But this time is different. Instead of being awash in words you do not understand, you are awash in nothing but the sounds of an island—there are no words, no people. Painfully lonely, psychologically starving for conversation, soon enough you project voices onto an object like Wilson the volleyball. By talking to Wilson you maintain a sense of self; you keep your sanity. But, of course, Wilson is not really talking with you. In reality, you are just talking with yourself. Thus, according to the theory of dialogical self, it is only by keeping your language alive as dialogue with oneself or another person—real or imagined—that you retain your knowledge of your identity (McIlveen, 2012). This dialogical self "mind hack" powers an important process of My Career Chapter, namely, reflexivity.

Dialogical self is conceptualized as an extension of William James's (1890/1952) classical notions of *I* and *Me*; that is, the knowing self and the known self, respectively. Unlike James's singular concept of I, dialogical self is formulated as multiple *I-positions* that are spatially and temporarily placed in relation to one another. Each I-position is endowed with its own voice; it is able to tell its own story from its own position in space and time; and, moreover, the I-positions engage in dialogue with one another. Thus, the normal human phenomenon of constant chatter that a person hears within his or her mind is conceived of as the conversations of I-positions. Hermans (2006) uses the metaphor of self as a theater of voices to capture this dynamic conceptualization of self. This is particularly important when considering the role of I-positions that are culturally bound (Hermans & Hermans-Konopka, 2010).

My Career Chapter uses the theory of dialogical self in two ways. First, as described previously in relation to STF, the client is aided in decentering career as a dynamic of career influences. Each influence can then be taken as an I-position. Second, My Career Chapter facilitates a client engaging in dialogue with him- or herself across time as two distinct I-positions: the client in current time/space and also in a different time/space, usually as him- or herself 5 years younger. Upon completing the bulk of the autobiographical manuscript, the client reads it aloud to the younger version of him- or herself; then the client imaginatively takes the perspective of the younger version of him- or herself and writes feedback to the older version, commenting on how he or she has changed, perhaps how life turned out differently than expected. To complete the manuscript, the client in current time/space provides a response to the younger version, commenting on his or her perspective on the past and the future.

In this way, My Career Chapter is a model of an important three-phase process: (a) present to past, (b) past to present, and then (c) present to past. This iterative process induces the creation of meaning (Hermans & Kempen, 1993). Using the case of Ben, I illustrate the process of working through this model.

The Case of Ben

Ben is a 28-year-old male mechanical engineer who presents concerns about his current work environment. Ben enjoys his work, its complexity and pressure. He enjoys working with his fellow engineers, except the team leader, whom he believes is criticizing his work to force Ben to quit. He does not want to leave the job, but his doubts about long-term prospects with the company are beginning to erode his professional self-esteem. Ben attended company-sponsored career counseling in Djakarta, states, "My boss is a psychopath who undermines everything I do. I don't like him, but I love my job, and I'm thinking about getting out."

Background Information

Ben is a Malaysian national who completed his senior high schooling and university studies in Australia. Since graduating with a Bachelor of Engineering degree at 22 years of age and entering into an elite graduate employment program with an international mining company based in the United States, he has enjoyed a rewarding career in the mining industry, particularly the placements in remote and exotic locations (e.g., Australia, Brazil, South Africa). Ben specializes in the repair of heavy earthworks machinery that operates around the clock. Any downtime due to machinery breakdown is an operational emergency. Wherever and whenever they occur, complex failures in machinery require Ben and other specialist crew members to be flown in to the mine site from the head office in Djakarta. It is a high-pressure and high-paying job: Ben works 12-hour shifts, 3 weeks on duty/3 weeks off, and he "thrives on the pressure to perform." He is conscious of the sacrifices his Chinese middle-class family made for his international education, and he is aware that his parents' pride in his achievement is matched by their expectations for his career success. He returns to Kuala Lumpur to visit his parents during his off-shift weeks. Ben states that he has discussed his problem with his parents, and his father said, "You should get on with the boss and do as he says. He is the boss."

On presentation, Ben's appearance is confident; he has a soft, full handshake and a youthful face with a big smile. His mood is calm and his affect is normal. His speech is slightly accented and quiet, and his answers to questions are spit-fired at a rapid pace. His attention and concentration appear normal; he follows the flow of the interview and does not present any abnormality in thinking or perception. The content of his thinking is directed toward his responsibilities, not knowing what to do in the situation, and his anger at his team leader.

Introducing My Career Chapter

A standard intake interview should precede the application of My Career Chapter. In my practice, I use a semistructured interview schedule, the Career Systems Interview (McIlveen, 2003), because it aligns with the STF that underpins My Career Chapter, and, compared to a standard interview, the Career Systems Interview can produce positive changes in career-related thoughts (McIlveen, McGregor-Bayne, Alcock, & Hjertum, 2003). Other intake interviews can be used just as well. What is most important is that the counselor is able to arrive at a judgment that the client will benefit from a written self-assessment exercise such as My Career Chapter. This judgment should include consideration of the client's interest and capacity to engage in a lengthy self-assessment.

As part of preparing a client to use My Career Chapter, it is important to explain that career is more than the stereotypical factors of interests, skills, and abilities and that career is more than the sum of these parts. This procedure is also included in the Career Systems Interview. To facilitate the process, it is useful to present a copy of the STF diagram (reproduced inside the My Career Chapter booklet) and talk about how influences can change and recursively influence one another, as per the STF's theoretical tenets. This introduction assists the client in adopting a new perspective of career and can loosen tightly held stereotypical views of career. It is also an opportunity to highlight influences that may have particular cultural and ethnic salience, such as class and nationality (Leong & Flores, 2013).

In the case of Ben, his cultural and socioeconomic background places importance on influences such as respect for parents and family (i.e., "filial piety"), respect for authority and institutions, and regard for socioeconomic status. Ben's parents sent their son, a Chinese Malaysian, abroad to be educated at great personal cost, but their sacrifice is not at all unusual in the context of Malaysian culture because of that country's modern history (Pope, Musa, Singaravelu, Bringaze, & Russell, 2002) and its higher education system. Accordingly, in the intake interview with Ben, additional time was devoted to exploring family matters and his conflicted sense of responsibility.

Although clients may use the electronic version of My Career Chapter, it is useful to have a print copy on hand to review with a client. My Career Chapter is composed of seven steps, and explaining the purpose of and how to complete each step of My Career Chapter while flipping through the pages of the print version may better engage clients in their self-exploration and in the writing process. Regardless of whether they choose to write on a print or electronic version, the client is asked to return a print copy for the follow-up session. Refer to the Recommended Resources section in this chapter for materials and guidelines for using My Career Chapter, including a version in Chinese.

Interpreting the Client's Manuscript

During the follow-up session, the counselor engages in rapport-building activities with the client and after doing so asks the client about his or her experience using My Career Chapter. Spending a little time on this exploration is valuable as it may provide ideas of how and why the client wrote the manuscript in certain ways. There is no definitive method for interpreting My Career Chapter with a client, but there are important principles to keep in mind.

First and foremost, the manuscript should be treated as a draft, a work in progress, an open-ended story. It is critical that client and counselor share this understanding of the manuscript as being tentative because this is a quality of a good story (McAdams, 1993). By all means, a life story may involve discrete events or moments of closure, but a life story's author actively narrates and edits his or her story until the author is no more.

The notion of *co-construction* (Del Corso & Rehfuss, 2011) is central to narrative career counseling and the application of My Career Chapter. Co-construction requires active engagement from the client and the counselor. There are numerous effective types of co-construction in My Career Chapter; however, the simplest method involves the counselor speaking the client's story aloud and discussing key themes with the client, all the while drawing on the client's interpretations of his or her own story. In this way, the counselor plays the metaphorical role of a friendly editor who asks questions to clarify the meaning and to advance the transformative quality of the story. A more elaborate approach to co-construction entails a cyclical editorial process between client and counselor, but there is insufficient space to describe the process here (for more information on this, see McIlveen & du Preez, 2012).

In the case of Ben, we agreed that he was feeling the pressure of being "between a rock and a hard place." Although respectful of his father's view and not wanting to contradict or disappoint him, Ben felt conflicted because he believed his father did not understand the complexity and pressure of his work. Throughout the manuscript, there were examples of respect for family and authority, expressed in terms of responsibility and duty, opposed by themes of yearning for independence and autonomy. Together we talked about options for how these two drives might be brought into harmony rather than cause discord.

It is important to note that co-construction is an active process. Accordingly, the counselor (editor) may call on his or her professional skills of listening and interpretation to make pointed comments and suggestions about how the story may involve contradictions or opportunities to create new vistas. The need to actively engage as editor—an interpreter—notwithstanding, the counselor must ensure that his or her own story does not interfere with the client's story; use of My Career Chapter in narrative career counseling demands reflexivity in its practitioners (McIlveen & Patton, 2010). While working with Ben, I had to ensure that my own story of work ethic did not lead to an overemphasis of those traditional values held by Ben's hard-working father.

Narrative career counseling is not just about generating a clearer, revised, or new story; the story should involve self-persuasive arguments that lead toward action. In Ben's case, we discussed how he might better express the themes of independence and autonomy in his work. Ultimately, Ben applied for a promotion and became a team leader. On reflection, he now understands the pressures of leading experts. Although he did not get on well with his previous team leader, Ben no longer thinks of him as a psychopath. Ben also developed the understanding that balancing his values of responsibility/duty and independence/autonomy is a fact of his life; both sets of values are important to him. Thus, Ben came to a resolution that he should carefully monitor how he self-talks when the two sets of values seem to come into conflict.

Integrating With Other Techniques

When used for career counseling, My Career Chapter should be administered in combination with a comprehensive initial interview that prepares a client to develop his or her self-awareness. My Career Chapter is particularly useful for preparing clients to benefit from other narrative or constructivist procedures. Values card sorts (cf. Brott, 2004), for example, may be used to expand on themes in a client's story that need further exploration and elaboration. See Table 7.1 for an application guide.

Conclusion

The fundamental task of counseling is to facilitate a client telling his or her story as a personal account that is authentic to the client's lived reality and is embedded in his or her context. The quality of a personal story is shown by its truth value in the real world, for an authentic story will be created, told, and evolved in dialogue with the world. Stories are inherently cultural and are tied to the nuances of their cultural grounding; ipso facto, the story of an individual—his or her identity—is likewise bound to culture. Any one person's story must be understood in the context of dynamic systems of career influences and as a multiplicity of I-positions. My Career Chapter is a practical model of these theories, and it enables client and counselor to work with one another to co-construct a career story that leads to transformative self-awareness and action.

Recommended Resources

McIlveen, P. (2006). *My Career Chapter: A dialogical autobiography*. Retrieved from http://eprints.usq.edu.au/id/eprint/23797

McIlveen, P. (2015). *My Career Chapter: A dialogical autobiography. Chinese version*. Retrieved from https://www.researchgate.net/publication/283663464_My_Career_Chapter_A_Dialogical_Autobiography._Chinese_Version

McIlveen, P. (2015). 我的生涯篇章 与职业生涯系统访谈 [My Career Chapter and the Career Systems Interview. Chinese version]. In M. McMahon & M. Watson (Eds.), *Career assessment: Qualitative approaches* (pp. 123–128). Rotterdam, The Netherlands: Sense Publishers. Retrieved from https://www.researchgate.net/publication/283663595_My_Career_Chapter_and_the_Career_Systems_Interview._Chinese_Version

Table 7.1

Practical Application Guide

Topic	Using My Career Chapter to Tell a Career Story
General goals and purposes	1. Facilitating a client to write and tell a short career-related autobiography 2. Stimulating the client's autobiography to include career influences that are beyond the individual self, such as family, society, culture, and environment 3. Enabling the client to hear his or her own words spoken aloud with another, as an act of co-construction
Applicable modality	Dyadic with counselor and may include a trusted other person in the process (e.g., spouse)
Applicable counselor settings	Adult counseling, college and university counseling center, mental health center, private practice
Recommended time to complete	Writing time can be up to 2 hours but may be completed over 1 week. Inclusive of an intake interview or preliminary assessment interview, the interpretation process may be completed in one or two sessions.
Materials/equipment needed	The original My Career Chapter booklet is freely available for download at http://eprints.usq.edu.au/23797/ Materials may be printed and then written by hand or typed on a computer.
Step-by-step outline of the process	My Career Chapter involves a series of seven steps that are outlined in the manual: 1. Warm-up questions that promote self-exploration 2. Use of the STF diagram to widen the client's perspective of career 3. Comparing and contrasting the importance of the internal and external influences identified in the STF diagram 4. Writing the bulk of the manuscript 5. Communicating across time as two I-positions 6. Writing the conclusion 7. Final reflections in preparation for counseling

Note. STF = Systems theory framework.

References

Brott, P. (2004). Constructivist assessment in career counseling. *Journal of Career Development, 30,* 189–200. doi:10.1177/089484530403000302

Cochran, L. (2000). *Career counseling: A narrative approach.* Thousand Oaks, CA: Sage.

Del Corso, J., & Rehfuss, M. C. (2011). The role of narrative in career construction theory. *Journal of Vocational Behavior, 79,* 334–339.

Dickens, C. (1969). *Hard times for these times.* London, England: Penguin Books. (Original work published 1854)

Hermans, H. J. M. (2006). The self as a theater of voices: Disorganization and reorganization of a position repertoire. *Journal of Constructivist Psychology, 19,* 147–169. doi:10.1080/10720530500508779

Hermans, H. J. M., & Gieser, T. (Eds.). (2012). *Handbook of dialogical self theory*. Cambridge, UK: Cambridge University Press.

Hermans, H. J. M., & Hermans-Konopka, A. (2010). *Dialogical self theory: Positioning and counter-positioning in a globalizing society*. Cambridge, UK: Cambridge University Press.

Hermans, H. J. M., & Kempen, H. J. G. (1993). *The dialogical self: Meaning as movement*. San Diego, CA: Academic Press.

James, W. (1952). *The principles of psychology*. Chicago, IL: William Benton. (Original work published 1890)

James, W. (2000). *Pragmatism and other writings*. New York, NY: Penguin. (Original work published 1907)

Kidd, J. M. (2004). Emotion in career contexts: Challenges for theory and research. *Journal of Vocational Behavior, 64*, 441–454. doi:10.1016/j.jvb.2003.12.009

Leong, F. T. L., & Flores, L. Y. (2013). Multicultural perspectives in vocational psychology. In B. W. Walsh, M. L. Savickas, & P. J. Hartung (Eds.), *Handbook of vocational psychology: Theory, research, and practice* (4th ed., pp. 53–80). New York, NY: Routledge.

Loevinger, J. (1985). Revision of the sentence completion test for ego development. *Journal of Personality and Social Psychology, 48*, 420–427.

McAdams, D. P. (1993). *The stories we live by: Personal myths and the making of the self*. New York, NY: William Morrow.

McAdams, D. P., & McLean, K. C. (2013). Narrative identity. *Current Directions in Psychological Science, 22*, 233–238. doi: 10.1177/0963721413475622

McIlveen, P. (2003). *Career Systems Interview*. Toowoomba, Australia.

McIlveen, P. (2006). *My Career Chapter: A dialogical autobiography*. Retrieved from http://eprints.usq.edu.au/23797/

McIlveen, P. (2011). Life themes in career counselling. In M. McMahon & M. B. Watson (Eds.), *Career counseling and constructivism: Elaboration of constructs* (pp. 73–85). New York, NY: Nova Science.

McIlveen, P. (2012). Extending the metaphor of narrative to dialogical narrator. In P. McIlveen & D. E. Schultheiss (Eds.), *Social constructionism in vocational psychology and career development* (pp. 59–75). Rotterdam, The Netherlands: Sense.

McIlveen, P., & du Preez, J. (2012). A model for the co-authored interpretation of My Career Chapter. *Cypriot Journal of Educational Sciences, 7*, 276–286.

McIlveen, P., McGregor-Bayne, H., Alcock, A., & Hjertum, E. (2003). Evaluation of a semi-structured career assessment interview derived from systems theory framework. *Australian Journal of Career Development, 12*, 33–41.

McIlveen, P., & Patton, W. (2007a). Dialogical self: Author and narrator of career life themes. *International Journal for Educational and Vocational Guidance, 7*, 67–80. doi:10.1007/s10775-007-9116-6

McIlveen, P., & Patton, W. (2007b). Narrative career counselling: Theory and exemplars of practice. *Australian Psychologist, 42*, 226–235. doi: 10.1080/00050060701405592

McIlveen, P., & Patton, W. (2010). My Career Chapter as a tool for reflective practice. *International Journal for Educational and Vocational Guidance, 10,* 147–160. doi:10.1007/s10775-010-9181-0

McIlveen, P., Patton, W., & Hoare, P. N. (2008). An interpretative phenomenological analysis of clients' reactions to My Career Chapter. *Australian Journal of Career Development, 17,* 51–62.

Patton, W., & McMahon, M. (2014). *Career development and systems theory: Connecting theory and practice.* Rotterdam, The Netherlands: Sense.

Pope, M., Musa, M., Singaravelu, H., Bringaze, T., & Russell, M. (2002). From colonialism to ultranationalism: History and development of career counseling in Malaysia. *The Career Development Quarterly, 50,* 264–276.

Rorty, R. (1999). *Philosophy and social hope.* London, England: Penguin.

Savickas, M. L. (2005). The theory and practice of career construction. In S. D. Brown & R. W. Lent (Eds.), *Career development and counseling: Putting theory and research to work* (pp. 42–70). Hoboken, NJ: Wiley.

Savickas, M. L. (2011). *Career counseling.* Washington, DC: American Psychological Association.

Savickas, M. L. (2013). Career construction theory and practice. In S. D. Brown & R. W. Lent (Eds.), *Career development and counseling: Putting theory and research to work* (2nd ed., pp. 147–183). Hoboken, NJ: Wiley.

Whitman, W. (2004). Song of myself. In M. Warner (Ed.), *The portable Walt Whitman* (pp. 3–67). New York, NY: Penguin. (originally published in 1855)

Zemeckis, R. (Director). (2000). *Castaway.* In T. Hanks, J. Rapke, S. Starkey, & R. Zemeckis (Producers). United States of America: DreamWorks Pictures.

Chapter 8

Constructing a Course: Constructivist Group Career Counseling With Low-Income, First-Generation College Students

Susan R. Barclay

First-generation college students are enrolling in U.S. colleges at increasing rates (Grier-Reed & Ganuza, 2012; Orbe, 2004; Padgett, Johnson, & Pascarella, 2012). These students, for whom neither parent has a bachelor's degree (Engle & Tinto, 2008), face exceptional challenges when compared to continuing generation students. First-generation students classified as low income face even greater challenges.

The government determines income level based on the total annual income for the family unit, and the most recent figures specify *low income* as $17,505 or below for a family unit of one with a range up to $60,135 for a family unit of eight (U.S. Department of Education, 2014a). Engle and Tinto (2008) defined low-income students as those for whom the family income is below $25,000 and noted that most low-income, first-generation (LIFG) students do not have the financial support of their family and are usually financially independent (see also Orbe, 2004). Additional demographic information suggests that LIFG students tend to be female (64%), be from minority backgrounds (54%), and have dependents (38%; Engle & Tinto, 2008).

LIFG college students face unique challenges with college success. They tend to experience lower grades during their first semester and are more likely to drop out during their first year or not return for their second year (Orbe, 2004). Engle and Tinto (2008) presented a dismal comparison of completion rates between LIFG students and students without LIFG risk factors. Depending on the type of institution in which students were enrolled, non-LIFG students had a 66% to 80% 6-year graduation rate, whereas LIFG students had a rate of only 34% to 43%.

In this chapter, I provide an overview of the unique career development needs and risk factors common to LIFG students. Existing efforts being made to meet these needs, few of which include direct career development interventions, are described next. I close with a case study that illustrates how group counseling can meet the unique career development needs of these students.

Risk Factors for LIFG Students

First-generation college students face greater risk factors than students whose parents attended institutions of higher education. One of the most commonly cited risk factors is the lack of college knowledge. Hooker and Brand (2010) highlighted the specific challenges this lack of information presents for first-generation students and, in particular, those who come from low-income backgrounds. LIFG students may have little understanding of the logistics of applying to college, enrolling in classes, and persisting to degree completion. They also may have more difficulty adjusting to college (Engle & Tinto, 2008; Orbe, 2004) and are less likely to seek support services concerning adjustment or career issues (Engle & Tinto, 2008; Hooker & Brand, 2010). There are several likely reasons for this. Typically, LIFG students have to juggle the responsibilities of work, financial obligations, family, and school more so than continuing generation college students (Orbe, 2004). Other risk factors common to LIFG students are diminished levels of self-efficacy (Grier-Reed & Ganuza, 2012), higher levels of dysfunctional career thoughts (Grier-Reed & Conkel-Ziebell, 2009), and difficulty navigating the complexity of layers of identity (Grier-Reed & Ganuza, 2012; Orbe, 2004, 2008).

Identity

In his research investigating identity factors for first-generation students, Orbe (2004, 2008) uncovered multiple layers. The identity of *student* becomes more salient for these students because they are the first in their family to attend college. This can create added pressure for LIFG students as they struggle to be successful in school and make their parents proud. At the same time, they may downplay the student identity to extended family members or to friends because of perceived jealousy or intimidation among those individuals (Olson, 2014).

Although Orbe's (2004) research encompassed first-generation students of various income levels, LIFG students have the added layer of low-income backgrounds, which usually means decreased financial resources for college attendance and persistence. Grier-Reed and Ganuza (2012), Orbe (2008), and Walpole (2007) noted the exceptional challenges faced by LIFG students in developing a coherent sense of identity between the multiple college life identities and home life identities. A coherent sense of identity can bring these multiple layers together to form a more uniform picture of "self" and give respect to the important identity component of career.

Self-Efficacy

As LIFG students navigate multiple identities, they are attempting to ascertain an academic major or career trajectory. Grier-Reed and Ganuza (2012) highlighted the important role of self-efficacy in career decision making and perseverance in degree attainment. Likewise, Bullock-Yowell, Peterson, Wright, Reardon, and Mohn (2011) noted the significance of an individual's self-efficacy when assessing for career interests.

Making career decisions presents problems for LIFG students. Olson (2014) proposed that first-generation students might foreclose prematurely on career options based on their inaccurate perceptions of persisting successfully in college. He stressed the importance of aiding these students in identifying ways in which diminished self-efficacy plays a role in encumbering career decision making. Peabody, Hutchens, Lewis, and Deffendall (2011) highlighted the low educational and degree aspirations of LIFG students and suggested that connecting career interventions with specific campus resource centers might improve LIFG self-efficacy. These researchers advocated career counseling as one of seven promising practices for assisting LIFG college students, and they insisted that career counseling should encompass the ability of a counselor to aid students in cultivating a curiosity about academic major selection and possible career trajectories.

Career Thoughts

The link between dysfunctional career thoughts and career indecision is clear. Saunders, Peterson, Sampson, and Reardon (2000) found that students with negative career thoughts experienced greater challenges in processing career information cogently and methodically. This supports Kilk's (1997) findings on the relationship between dysfunctional career thoughts and academic major selection. Likewise, Grier-Reed and an array of colleagues have found that at-risk (e.g., LIFG) students experience increased levels of dysfunctional and negative career thoughts (see Grier-Reed & Conkel-Ziebell, 2009; Grier-Reed & Ganuza, 2012; Grier-Reed, Skaar, & Conkel-Ziebell, 2009). Multiple studies by these researchers indicate that constructivist career development approaches help decrease dysfunctional career thoughts and increase career decision making.

Existing Culturally Infused Career Programs and Services

Recognizing the unique struggles LIFG students face in attending and completing college, institutions of higher education have been developing programming and services to meet their needs. Peabody et al. (2011) highlighted several promising practices at benchmark institutions across the United States. These included providing students with mentoring programs, offering summer programs to help bridge the high school and college experiences, and requiring students to reside in on-campus living-learning communities.

Some of the best-known programs available for LIFG students are the TRiO programs. The federal government created these eight educational programs to promote scholastic access and quality for students who come from disadvantaged backgrounds (U.S. Department of Education, 2014b). One of the most popular TRiO programs is the Student Support Services (SSS) program (Peabody et al., 2011), which requires colleges and universities to provide academic tutoring and instruction, assistance in course selection, and financial aid information if the institution is receiving federal SSS funds. The Department of Education indicates that TRiO funding recipients may provide individualized services (e.g., personal or career counseling) but that those services are not required components. Grier-Reed and Ganuza (2012) speculated that the SSS program did not extend far enough to be of assistance to LIFG students in selecting an academic major or gaining career traction. They argued that more was needed, and they proposed a constructivist career development approach.

First-year experience (FYE) courses are another tool being used to assist incoming college students. These courses vary from university to university, but their main purpose is to orient first-year students to college life and connect them quickly to university resources to aid in retention (Purdie & Rosser, 2011). Whether required by the university or offered as an elective, FYE courses allow any first-year student to enroll, not just LIFG students. Though FYE courses include general career exploration activities, these courses often offer little in the way of specific career interventions or guidance.

Other efforts currently in place to assist LIFG students include preengineering programs that aim, in part, to raise student awareness of science, technology, engineering, and mathematics career options (Lam, Srivatsan, Doverspike, Vesalo, & Mawasha, 2005), internship programs (Engle & Tinto, 2008), and strategies that involve specific career theoretical approaches (Barclay, Stoltz, & Wolff, 2011; Clark, Severy, & Sawyer, 2004; Garriott, Flores, & Martens, 2013; Mitcham, Greenidge, Bradham-Cousar, Figliozzi, & Thompson, 2012).

Constructivist Career Counseling

Anticipating the work world transition that occurred as the 20th century gave way to the 21st century, Savickas (1993) advocated for changes in career counseling approaches, calling for a shift from "logical positivism, objectivistic science, and industrialism" to "a multiple perspective discourse" (p. 205). Others followed with similar calls. Both Brott (2004) and Clark et al. (2004) encouraged narrative methods. Likewise, Patton (2005) introduced postmodern methodologies to career education (e.g., learning, teaching, and assessment) and acknowledged the use of constructivist career counseling as a way for individuals to construct their identities and gain efficacy in building meaningful lives. He argued that a constructivist approach is vital in the shadow of the "careerquake" (Watts, 1996) of increasing technology and globalization that has transformed the landscape and arrangement of work.

Grier-Reed et al. (2009) and Grier-Reed and Conkel-Ziebell (2009) utilized a constructivist career development curriculum with goals of decreasing dysfunctional career thoughts and increasing career self-efficacy. The curriculum included four critical components of constructivist thought: storying, identity and value exploration, identity construction across contexts, and applying narrative interpretations to career direction. Grier-Reed et al. (2009) reported significant benefits for college students across both sex and race. Results indicated significant decreases in dysfunctional, self-defeating career thoughts; significant increases in career decision self-efficacy; and construction of a stronger sense of identity. As noted previously, these three areas interfere the most with the academic success of LIFG college students.

Grier-Reed and Ganuza (2012) expanded on the work of Grier-Reed et al. (2009) by implementing their constructivist career development curriculum with college students enrolled in TRiO SSS programs. Results indicated improved career decision self-efficacy. Furthermore, the curriculum showed strong potential as a positive supplement to the TRiO program.

Constructivist approaches are gaining popularity and variety in application. They continue the promise of effectiveness as a valuable component to career counseling, given the nature and structure of work in the 21st century. For example, in a study of college undergraduates who took part in a written career narrative class assignment, Barclay and Wolff (2012) reported that the career construction interview might be as effective as objective interest inventories in assessing career interests.

Constructivist approaches have been successful in group career counseling as well as in individual counseling. Many researchers advocate the use and note the benefits of career counseling in group settings. In a small study by Clark et al. (2004), use of a narrative approach in career group counseling with college students showed promise as a useful intervention across gender, race, ethnicity, and social class. Mitcham et al. (2012) proposed a group career counseling curriculum that supports the increased career self-efficacy of a culturally diverse group of high school students. Likewise, Barclay et al. (2011) and Barclay and Stoltz (2016a, 2016b) developed the Life Design Group career counseling model, and it holds promise for decreasing career uncertainty and indecision while increasing academic major and career decision making and career planning among an undergraduate student population.

The case study that follows describes the application of constructivist career counseling in a group format. Although this is a group counseling approach, the focus here is on one group member in particular to illustrate how constructivist career counseling helps individual members gain increases in career self-efficacy, experience decreases in self-defeating career thoughts, and construct a stronger sense of identity. Based on these results, the student is able to gain traction in constructing a career course.

The Case of Mia

Mia is a 19-year-old Latina who is nearing the end of her first year at a local community college. Mia's family emigrated from the Dominican Republic when she and her younger brother were children. Although Mia's father completed high school in the Dominican Republic, Mia's mother left school during her first year of high school to help support the family. Mia is the first member of the family to attend college.

Mia's father works as a security guard at a local bank, and her mother is on the janitorial staff at the community college Mia attends. Mia and her family selected this community college because of its close proximity to their home and because Mia receives a discounted tuition rate due to her mother's employment with the college. To help with additional expenses, such as textbooks and fees, Mia works part time at the day care center located on campus.

During her first year, Mia has taken several courses related to her educational program choice of early childhood development. Mia likes children and thought teaching would provide her with an excellent career. Unfortunately, Mia has found little fulfillment in the courses and has an internal longing for something more meaningful even though she is not sure what that might be. She wants to finish her associate's degree and complete a bachelor's degree in a 4-year institution; however, Mia struggles envisioning a second year of courses in which she finds little meaning. Mia's struggle with what she calls a "muddled identity"—that of a first-generation Latina whose roots lie in a country about which she knows little—confounds her experience. Mia feels both the pressure of being the first in her family to attend college and the well-intended parental pressure of being a role model for her younger brother. Mia decides to speak with her advisor, Winslow, who is a student development specialist. Winslow, an African American man, earned master's degrees in both mental health counseling and college student personnel and holds an added credential in career counseling.

Discussion of the Case

After hearing Mia's concerns, Winslow invited Mia to participate in a career counseling group that he developed and facilitates based on the Life Design Group model (Barclay & Stoltz, 2016a, 2016b). Winslow believed the group setting would be beneficial for Mia for several reasons. Using career construction theory as the foundation (Savickas, 2013), the Life Design Group represents a postmodern career counseling approach based in constructivist epistemology that allows clients to share their life narrative in a peer-supported group environment. As Mia shares her story, Winslow and other members of the group will help Mia recognize and understand the life themes that inform who she wants to become and the work she wants to do (Savickas, 2013). The group is open to first-generation students, and the group participants represent wide diversity in racial and cultural backgrounds. Mia agreed to participate.

During her first group counseling experience, Mia watched to learn about the process. She observed Winslow working with one of the group members through a series of questions and prompts. Furthermore, she gained trust by watching the ways the other group members supported the one who was the focus of the session. When Winslow asked for next week's volunteer, Mia responded quickly and agreed.

As the group got under way the following week, Winslow explained that he would conduct the Career Construction Interview (CCI) with Mia, just as he had done the previous week with another group member (Savickas, 2011, 2013). After the interview, he and the group members would help Mia identify life themes across her responses. Winslow instructed Mia's peers to listen closely and offered that he would be recording Mia's responses on a whiteboard to help with identifying themes.

To begin, Winslow asked Mia to share how he and group members might help her. This important question allowed Mia to begin telling her story about longing to work with children but feeling limited and unfulfilled in both her current courses and her work at the day care facility. Mia offered her perspective that, traditionally, her culture supports domestic-oriented careers for women and that her parents had told her from her youth that she would "make a great teacher." Even though she enjoyed working with children, Mia explained that her coursework and job role did not challenge her to the extent she desired. Winslow recognized that Mia faced career planning barriers of identity moratorium (Marcia, 1966, 1980), decreased self-efficacy, and career thoughts that seemed limited to culturally stereotypical roles for women. Clearly, Mia wanted to gain clarity about a meaningful and enjoyable career trajectory, but she felt limited to her perceived cultural expectations for women.

At Winslow's request, Mia identified the early role models in her life as her maternal grandmother and a nurse who cared for Mia when she was in the hospital with a respiratory virus. She described both women as gentle and caring, and she remembered thinking that both were strong, brave women. She called them "tough."

Next, Winslow asked Mia about her favorite magazines, television shows, and movies. Mia quickly named *Discover* magazine as her favorite. She liked the stories about the latest in medical breakthroughs and application. Mia offered that she enjoyed reruns of *Scrubs* and *ER* but that she did not have any particular favorite movies. She preferred, instead, to follow true-life medical pediatric stories in the news. In particular, she named cases such as the one involving Justina Pelletier of Connecticut.

As Winslow moved through the CCI, Mia identified her preferred elementary school subjects as life science, math, and social studies, stating that these appealed to her strong, curious nature. Mia did not enjoy English grammar or literature. Mia reported two mottos that she had heard all her life. The first was "The colors of the rainbow are our guide," and the second was "Make do with what is available," possibly a tribute to her family's lower socioeconomic status in both the Dominican Republic and the United States.

In closing the CCI with Mia, Winslow asked about early memories. Mia remembered taking walks with her maternal grandmother near the tobacco fields near their home in the Dominican Republic, and she talked fondly about her and her grandmother squatting on the ground to examine the grass and the insects. When prompted to provide a title for these memories, Mia offered "With Guidance, Young Girl Explores Life." In another memory, Mia remembered watching cows nursing and caring for their young while her father milked cows nearby. Her title for this memory was "Mom Delivers Nourishment and Health." Finally, Mia shared her memory of sitting on the sofa with her grandmother, watching a show called *People: A Musical Celebration* that told the story of a young girl who learns that differences among people and cultures make the world more interesting and exciting. The title for this final memory was "War Divides; Differences Unite." As Mia responded to each of the CCI prompts, Winslow recorded her responses on a whiteboard. Occasionally, Winslow paused to clarify points in Mia's narrative. Writing on the whiteboard allowed peer group members to focus on Mia and to listen intently and respectfully as she narrated aspects of her life experiences.

Although CCI questions and prompts seem to have little connection to matters of career on the surface, Winslow knew that client responses yield important clues to a person's identity and life aspirations. In addition, these microstories offer a glimpse into past experiences that inform a client's present situation. This leads to understanding how the client connects the combination of past experiences and current situations to the future. Understanding this connection is vital for discerning how clients make meaning and envision themselves in life and career (Savickas, 2013). The entire process requires helping clients construct their story and then deconstruct it by examining biases and mistaken ideas. After deconstruction, the counselor and client work together to reconstruct the story, and this helps to turn the career challenge into a possible solution. The themes and patterns that emerge form the basis for the co-construction of an edited narrative that provides the client with meaning and motivation to seek new likelihoods and resurrect initiatives that were stuck in the old narrative.

Mia's choice of role models reveals central components to her self-concept. As noted in several of her CCI responses, Mia's maternal grandmother played a prominent role in Mia's life. Mia viewed her grandmother as a gentle and kind woman who was concerned about all forms of life. She knew her grandmother worked hard and noted her "toughness" in running a household while simultaneously helping take care of the tobacco and dairy farm. Winslow speculated with Mia that her remembrances of her grandmother's affection toward Mia increased Mia's desire to have the same type of relationship with children. As Mia agreed that her grandmother had influenced her greatly in wanting to work with children, one of the group members commented, "Due to your parents' ongoing message to you, perhaps you saw teaching as the way to accomplish that goal."

Winslow invited input from other group members and wanted to know, in particular, what themes they could identify across Mia's story. One group member noted Mia's interest in science-oriented magazines and television shows. Another remembered Mia's earlier comment that she enjoyed these because of her curious nature and asked Mia, "I wonder to what extent you perceive that teaching children will satisfy your inquisitive mind." Mia murmured that she did not know at this point, and Winslow explored her work in the day care facility with her. She admitted that her current work did not allow her any avenue for "exploring or discovering."

Other group members observed the continuity of the theme by highlighting Mia's preferred elementary school subjects and offered that the combination of her preferred subjects lent itself toward her interest in people and making the world a better place and her interest in science. Winslow asked Mia, "I know your culture and family supported more traditional roles for women, such as teaching. Could it be that you have considered careers beyond teaching?" Mia agreed but stated she did not want to disappoint her parents by not going into teaching, a profession they had repeatedly told her was suitable for her. She confessed that, as a child, she dreamed of becoming a pediatrician. "I knew, though, that my family could never afford for me to pursue that type of education," Mia stated. Using a motto from Mia's youth, Winslow replied, "So, you have made do with what was available." Mia nodded.

One of the group members asked Mia to help him understand her other motto, asking if she knew what the colors of the rainbow represent. Another group member speculated there might be a connection to the diversity represented in the show Mia remembered watching with her grandmother. Mia admitted she had never thought much about it but commented that she had always been curious about cultures beyond her own and, in particular, how other cultures raised their children. Even though she did not know much about her home country, Mia said she believed culture was an important aspect to knowing "who one is."

As Winslow and Mia's peers continued to explore and reconstruct Mia's narrative, it became clear that Mia felt limited in her resources and by childhood messages, which had prevented her from pursuing her preferred career. Mia became animated as she talked about her desire to help children in medical situations, just as the kind nurse had helped her when she was a child. Even through her excitement, though, Mia continued to state that her family could not afford for Mia to gain the required education to become a doctor. A group member asked Mia, "Is there a related career that would be meaningful yet more affordable?" Immediately, Mia mentioned the nurse, again, who had cared for her when she was sick as a child. "I remember how gentle she was with me and how she would hold a cool cloth on my forehead. That felt so good, and I want to bring that type of comfort to others."

Together, Winslow, Mia, and her group member peers explored options based on themes that had emerged from Mia's narrative. One group member mentioned the possibility of Mia becoming a pediatric nurse, and Mia admitted that she had not considered that option. Another offered that he did not believe that becoming a nurse would be as expensive as becoming a doctor, and Winslow and Mia agreed that they would meet individually at a later time to explore the costs involved in pursuing a nursing degree and certification as a pediatric nurse practitioner.

With only a few minutes left, Winslow asked Mia to share her thoughts about the experience of being the focus of the session. She said she believed she had learned a lot about herself. She indicated she wanted to consider some things further, such as how to sustain her cultural identity while strengthening her emerging career identity. She admitted excitement about revisiting her academic major selection and constructing a different career trajectory. Mia finished by telling Winslow and her peers that, based on the identification of her life themes and their feedback about those themes, she felt more confident in her ability to move into her second year of college and to engage in educational pursuits that aligned more closely with her childhood dreams. See Table 8.1 for an application guide.

Conclusion

The Life Design Group represents a modality in which individuals can gain career traction while being fully supported by a trained career practitioner. In addition, such a group setting provides the added benefit of peer support, an important ingredient for ethnic minority first-generation students (Dennis, Phinney, & Chuateco, 2005). In Mia's case, she was able to recognize how early messages and memories influenced her to pursue a career that she was discovering was not as satisfying as she originally had thought. Furthermore, her experience in the group helped Mia to understand that she could dream and act beyond her limited thinking by modifying her dysfunctional career thoughts, honoring her cultural identity while embracing others, and pursuing a career in which she would find challenge and meaning.

Recommended Resources

Dockery, D. (2012). *School counselors' support for first-generation college students*. Retrieved from https://www.counseling.org/resources/library/vistas/vistas12/Article_61.pdf
First-year resources. (n.d.). Retrieved from http://www.sc.edu/fye/resources/fyr/index.html
Savickas, M., & Hartung, P. (n.d.). *Career Construction Interview worksheet*. Retrieved from http://www.vocopher.com/csi/cci.pdf
Williams, C. R., & Butler, S. K. (2010). *A new retention variable: Hope and first generation college students*. Retrieved from http://counselingoutfitters.com/vistas/vistas10/Article_11.pdf

References

Barclay, S. R., & Stoltz, K. B. (2016a). The Life Design Group: Career development through career construction counseling. *Journal of Student Affairs Research & Practice, 53*, 1–12.

Table 8.1
Practical Application Guide

Topic	Using Constructivist Group Career Counseling
General goals and purposes	1. Gain insight into the narrative of each group member 2. Magnify each group member's self-awareness of the sociocultural context that influences his or her career development process 3. Identify life and career themes with each group member that aid or hinder his or her individual career development process 4. Collaborate with group members, as a group and individually, to help them understand how they might utilize those themes to face and remedy their individual career concerns
Applicable modality	Group counseling
Applicable counselor settings	College/university career services, high school, private settings
Recommended time to complete	8–12 weeks (one week for each group member, plus two: the first session for an introduction/orientation and the last session for processing and closure)
Materials/equipment needed	Physical space (e.g., classroom), chairs, flip chart, whiteboard, and dry erase markers
Step-by-step outline of the process	*Week 1:* Group facilitator opens the group by providing an explanation of the group process and purpose. The group facilitator performs an icebreaker activity to help group members get to know one another and to begin building trust and cohesion. The group facilitator and group members work together to establish rules and guidelines for the group sessions. The group facilitator explains foundational rules pertaining to confidentiality, respect, and support. The group facilitator asks for a volunteer, who will be the focus of the next meeting and with whom the facilitator will conduct the Career Construction Interview (CCI). The group facilitator closes the group with a closing activity. *Week 2:* Group facilitator conducts CCI with the volunteer group member. The facilitator or a group member records CCI responses on a whiteboard or flip chart. The group facilitator and group members aid the group member volunteer in deconstructing, reconstructing, and co-constructing the narrative. *Weeks 3–7:* The CCI process continues on a rotation basis until all group members have been the focus of the group meeting. *Week 8:* The group facilitator uses this session to process the group experience with group members. Group facilitator conducts a closing activity and schedules individual meetings with group members, as needed, for further consultation and counseling.

Barclay, S. R., & Stoltz, K. B. (2016b). The Life Design Group: A case study assessment. *The Career Development Quarterly, 64,* 83–96.

Barclay, S. R., Stoltz, K. B., & Wolff, L. A. (2011). Career development through career construction counseling: A group method. In T. Fitch & J. Marshall (Eds.), *Group work and outreach plans for college counselors* (pp. 49–54). Alexandria, VA: American Counseling Association.

Barclay, S. R., & Wolff, L. A. (2012). Exploring the career construction interview for vocational personality assessment. *Journal of Vocational Behavior, 81,* 370–377. doi:10.1016/j.jvb.2012.09.004

Brott, P. E. (2004). Constructivist assessment in career counseling. *Journal of Career Development, 30,* 189–200. doi:10.1023/B:JOCD.0000015539.21158.53

Bullock-Yowell, E., Peterson, G. W., Wright, L. K., Reardon, R. C., & Mohn, R. S. (2011). The contribution of self-efficacy in assessing interests using the Self-Directed Search. *Journal of Counseling & Development, 89,* 470–478.

Clark, M. A., Severy, L., & Sawyer, S. A. (2004). Creating connections: Using a narrative approach in career group counseling with college students from diverse cultural backgrounds. *Journal of College Counseling, 7,* 24–31.

Dennis, J. M., Phinney, J. S., & Chuateco, L. I. (2005). The role of motivation, parental support, and peer support in the academic success of ethnic minority first-generation college students. *Journal of College Student Development, 46,* 223–236. doi:10.1353/csd.2005.0023

Engle, J., & Tinto, V. (2008). *Moving beyond access: College success for low-income, first-generation students.* Retrieved from http://www.pellinstitute.org/publications-Moving_Beyond_Access_2008.shtml

Garriott, P. O., Flores, L. Y., & Martens, M. P. (2013). Predicting the math/science career goals of low-income prospective first-generation college students. *Journal of Counseling Psychology, 60,* 200–209.

Grier-Reed, T. L., & Conkel-Ziebell, J. L. (2009). Orientation to self and career: Constructivist theory and practice in the classroom. *Learning Assistance Review, 14,* 23–36.

Grier-Reed, T., & Ganuza, Z. (2012). Using constructivist career development to improve career decision self-efficacy in TRiO students. *Journal of College Student Development, 53,* 464–471. doi:10.1353/csd.2012.0045

Grier-Reed, T. L., Skaar, N. R., & Conkel-Ziebell, J. L. (2009). Constructivist career development as a paradigm of empowerment for at-risk culturally diverse college students. *Journal of Career Development, 35,* 290–305. doi:10.1177/0894845308327275

Hooker, S., & Brand, B. (2010). College knowledge: A critical component of college and career readiness. *New Directions for Youth Development, 127,* 75–85. doi:10.1002/yd.364

Kilk, K. L. (1997). The relationship between dysfunctional career thoughts and choosing an academic major. *Dissertation Abstracts International: Section A. Humanities and Social Sciences, 58*(8), 3038.

Lam, P. C., Srivatsan, T., Doverspike, D., Vesalo, J., & Mawasha, P. R. (2005). A ten-year assessment of the pre-engineering program for under-represented, low income and/or first generation college students at the University of Akron. *Journal of STEM Education, 6,* 14–20.

Marcia, J. E. (1966). Development and validation of ego identity status. *Journal of Personality and Social Psychology, 5,* 551–558.

Marcia, J. E. (1980). Identity in adolescence. In J. Adelson (Ed.), *Handbook of adolescent psychology* (pp. 159–187). New York, NY: Wiley.

Mitcham, M., Greenidge, W., Bradham-Cousar, M., Figliozzi, J., & Thompson, M. A. (2012). Increasing career self-efficacy through group work with culturally and linguistically diverse students. *Journal of School Counseling, 10,* 1–26.

Olson, J. S. (2014). Opportunities, obstacles, and options: First-generation college graduates and social cognitive career theory. *Journal of Career Development, 41,* 199–217. doi:10.1177/0894845313486352

Orbe, M. P. (2004). Negotiating multiple identities within multiple frames: An analysis of first-generation college students. *Communication Education, 53,* 131–149. doi:10.10/03634520410001682401

Orbe, M. P. (2008). Theorizing multidimensional identity negotiation: Reflections on the lived experiences of first-generation college students. In M. Azmitia, M. Syed, & K. Radmacher (Eds.), *New directions for child and adolescent development: No. 120. The intersections of personal and social identities* (pp. 81–95). San Francisco, CA: Jossey-Bass. doi:10.1002/cd.217

Padgett, R. D., Johnson, M. P., & Pascarella, E. T. (2012). First-generation undergraduate students and the impacts of the first year of college: Additional evidence. *Journal of College Student Development, 53,* 243–266. doi:10.1353/csd.2012.0032

Patton, W. (2005). A postmodern approach to career education: What does it look like? *Perspectives in Education, 23,* 21–28.

Peabody, M., Hutchens, N., Lewis, W., & Deffendall, M. (2011). *First-generation college students at the University of Kentucky.* Lexington: University of Kentucky.

Purdie, J. R., & Rosser, V. J. (2011). Examining the academic performance and retention of first-year students in living-learning communities and first-year experience courses. *College Student Affairs Journal, 29,* 95–112.

Saunders, D. E., Peterson, G. W., Sampson, J. P., & Reardon, R. C. (2000). Relation of depression and dysfunctional career thinking to career indecision. *Journal of Vocational Behavior, 56,* 288–298.

Savickas, M. L. (1993). Career counseling in the postmodern era. *Journal of Cognitive Psychotherapy, 7,* 205–215.

Savickas, M. L. (2011). *Career counseling.* Washington, DC: American Psychological Association.

Savickas, M. L. (2013). Career construction theory and practice. In R. W. Lent & S. D. Brown (Eds.), *Career development and counseling: Putting theory and research to work* (2nd ed., pp. 147–183). Hoboken, NJ: Wiley.

U.S. Department of Education. (2014a). *Federal TRiO programs current-year low-income levels.* Retrieved from http://www2.ed.gov/about/offices/list/ope/trio/incomelevels.html

U.S. Department of Education. (2014b). *Federal TRiO programs.* Retrieved from http://www2.ed.gov/about/offices/list/ope/trio/index.html

Walpole, M. (2007). Economically and educationally challenged students in higher education: Access to outcomes. *ASHE-ERIC Higher Education Report, 33.* doi:10.1002/aehe.3303

Watts, A. G. (1996). *Careerquake: Policy supports for self-managed careers.* London, England: Demos.

Chapter 9

Early Recollections With a Paroled African American Male: A Career-Focused Group Approach

Kevin B. Stoltz

Rates of incarceration in the United States have doubled since 1994 (Bureau of Justice Statistics, 2013). According to Durose, Cooper, and Snyder (2014), recidivism statistics in 30 states indicate that three out of four offenders are arrested again within 5 years of their original release. With the increase in arrest rates and the high recidivism rates reported for offenders, counselors may prove to be an important resource in helping to reverse these disappointing cultural trends. One critical contribution that counselors can provide is service focused on career transition and development. As several researchers have pointed out (McWhirter, 2013; Morgan, 2013; Shivy et al., 2007; Varghese, 2013), career interventions for offenders are not well understood and are not commonly provided to offenders. Current programs often lack the centrality of career development and focus mainly on educational instruction and training (Shivy et al., 2007; Thompson & Cummings, 2010; Vernick & Reardon, 2001).

Barclay, Stoltz, and Wolff (2011) presented early recollections (ERs) as part of a group intervention focused on helping college students develop career identities. This intervention supports the use of ERs in both group and individual career counseling. In this chapter, I discuss the use of ERs in providing career counseling interventions to offenders using a group format. The use of ERs is presented as a way to assess and treat some of the risk factors of criminal behavior and recidivism. The use of ERs for group career counseling is demonstrated with examples from a case study.

Criminogenic Factors

Offenders high in prisonization (i.e., accepting the ways and culture of prison life) have lower career maturity and lack a job planning attitude, and Homant and Dean (1988) determined that securing employment for ex-offenders without improving their overall psychological adjustment does not lessen recidivism rates. *Recidivism* is defined as the return to incarceration due to criminal offenses after a previous release. Varghese and Cummings (2013) posited that stable employment is the greatest predictor of reduced recidivism, and they emphasized the importance of providing career development programs for ex-offenders. Present career interventions lack sufficient focus on offender attitudes; Varghese (2013) highlighted the necessity of understanding offender characteristics such as negative attitudes toward work. Without addressing these negative attitudes and thoughts (prisonization) concerning work, little improvement is expected in recidivism rates (Varghese, 2013; Vernick & Reardon, 2001).

Andrews, Bonta, and Hoge (1990) presented eight risk factors of criminal behavior and recidivism. These predictors include antisocial history, personality pattern, associates, thinking, family and marital relationships, school and work history, leisure interests, and substance use. According to Morgan (2013), no intervention in offender counseling can be successful without exploring these eight criminal risk factors. Morgan also noted that work attitudes are an important dimension in these risk factors.

Psychological interventions are regarded as important contributions to offender treatment models (McWhirter, 2013). One specific area of psychology and counseling that is emerging is the application of narrative approaches to career counseling (Savickas, 2011). Narrative approaches enable clients to conceptualize specific aspects of life and experience as *stories*. Career construction theory (Maree, 2010; Savickas, 2011) looks at early memories to help clients build career narratives. Counselors can use these early memories as an aid in therapeutic assessment and intervention when addressing some of the criminogenic risk factors (e.g., antisocial thinking, perceptions of family and marital relationships, thinking about work and work activities) while performing career work with offenders.

Consistent evidence has shown that offender treatment must be focused on criminogenic factors (Andrews et al., 1990). As noted earlier, eight factors are recognized as focal points for interventions with offenders. Andrews et al. (1990) posited a model of risk, need, responsivity (RNR) as an approach to addressing criminogenic factors in treatment. *Risk* concerns the assessment of the likelihood of recidivism so that treatments can be adjusted to the level of risk. Exposing offenders low in criminogenic factors to counseling interventions focused on these factors can have a deleterious effect (Andrews et al., 1990; Bonta & Andrews, 2007; Dowden & Andrews, 2000); therefore, appropriate assessment is imperative for treatment.

Need is the construct that focuses treatment on those that demonstrate the greatest levels of risk. Although counselors may perceive that the client has other issues (e.g., low self-esteem, depression, family discord), these are not considered criminogenic factors and should not be primary intervention targets (Andrews & Bonta, 2010; Andrews et al., 1990; Dowden & Andrews, 2000). According to Gendreau (1996), focusing on noncriminogenic factors may actually increase recidivism. However, employment opportunity and stability is an identified predictor of recidivism and is included as a criminogenic factor for primary treatment. Gendreau, Goggin, and Gray (1998) stated that career development often is not a focus in addressing criminogenic factors; however, research supports including career development as a necessary and important aspect of blending the RNR model with career interventions for offenders.

Finally, the *responsivity* construct brings attention to choosing interventions that will have the greatest effects on the criminogenic factors. This focus is on interventions that teach and train offenders, increase interpersonal skills, and help offenders learn to interact in positive ways.

The RNR model can be used as the framework for building and incorporating treatments designed to have a positive effect on criminogenic factors. One such treatment includes the use of ERs as a way of assessing risks such as negative attitudes and beliefs or private logic (Adler, 1932) that were generated from early childhood experiences. ERs represent latent personality attributes and indicate current thinking, attitudes, and behaviors (Ansbacher, 1979; Clark, 2002). In addition, ERs can be used to assess attitudes and beliefs about interpersonal relationships that may lead to delinquent and criminal behavior (Elliot, Fakouri, & Hafner, 1993; Rehman & Manzoor, 2003).

Researchers (Hafner, Fakouri, & Etzler, 1986; Kasler & Nevo, 2005; Watkins, 1984) have explored using ERs to assess career attributes in a way similar to the person and environment fit. However, today ERs are emerging as a way of assessing career identity in narrative approaches to career counseling. Savickas (1998) used ERs in a formal, semistructured interview focused on career counseling. Others (Stoltz, Wolff, & McClelland, 2011; Taber & Briddick, 2011) support the use of ERs beyond matching schemes. This emerging body of literature supports the use of ERs for identifying clients' strengths and career identity (Savickas, 2011).

The use of ERs in a group career counseling intervention for offenders integrates many concepts from the offender treatment literature. ERs represent aspects of the RNR model. By using ERs to focus on the assessment of offender thinking, perceptions, and antisocial personality patterns, counselors can target negative and antisocial cognitions, especially those centered on work and work relationships. Also, by building strong group cohesion, offenders can learn and rehearse new behaviors that translate into a wider and more empathic set of interpersonal skills.

Using ERs in Career Work

ERs are brief memories reported by clients that help counselors understand thinking patterns, behaviors, and ways of social interaction (Clark, 2002).

There are many ways of structuring the collection of ERs (Eckstein & Kern, 2009). Various techniques may be used when instructing the client to recall significant memories (not stories told to them, but actual memories of events). Most approaches limit memories to those before the age of 10 years old. However, newer approaches (Walton, 1998) posit that memories in adolescence and early adulthood also may be applicable. Asking the client to report the memory as if it were a video segment is helpful in organizing the data retrieved from the memory. Asking for the most salient moment in the memory and having the client report the predominant emotional content of the memory is effective during the assessment phase. Usually three to five memories are sufficient to construct patterns or themes in the client's cognitive, behavioral, and interpersonal dimensions. The themes become the focus of helping the client understand his or her thinking, behavioral, and attitudinal patterns. Alteration of those patterns that contain criminogenic factors is an appropriate counseling goal when working with offenders.

Before collecting ERs, the counselor strives to develop a positive working alliance with the client. Once the client shows signs of trust and involvement, the counselor explains that ERs assist in learning about thinking, behavioral, and attitudinal patterns developed early in the client's life. Because these patterns are part of development, clients often benefit from exploring and understanding the genesis of individualized thinking (private logic), behavioral patterns, and attitudinal patterns. This explanation lays the foundation for the client to understand the purpose for this technique.

To begin, ask the client to remember an event from early childhood, preferably before the age of 10 years old. This should be an actual memory of an event and not something told to the client. Once identified, invite the client to tell the story of the event, in this case to the group. Do not interrupt the client with questions or attempt to influence the telling of the story. Allowing the client to present the story from the actual memory without influence is optimal (Eckstein & Kern, 2009). The counselor follows the storyline and transcribes as much of the content as possible so that recalling the events and elements of the ER with high accuracy is possible. Once the client has finished the story, the counselor may ask the following questions: What is the predominant emotion that comes with this memory? What is the most important scene or picture in the ER story? What emotion is associated with this scene or frame? What is a caption or headline for the event? Again, the counselor tries to record these answers with high accuracy to avoid influencing the memory. Repeating this process, collecting the content of three to five memories, helps to develop consistency of themes across ERs.

Interpreting the content of ERs is a collaborative effort. The counselor does not provide an expert interpretation; rather, counselor and client engage in a reflective process together that includes the client's perspectives. Considering the completeness (storyline and outcome) and unity (causal links, timeline, context, emotions) of the ER event is important

(Singer & Bonalume, 2010). Complete stories that involve these elements indicate meaning making and relevance to the client's narrated identity (McAdams & McLean, 2013; Singer, 2004).

Reflecting on the ultimate goal of the client in the ER helps to define how the client views problems. Dreikurs (1968) theorized four goals of misbehavior for children: attention, power, revenge, and withdrawal. These goals are helpful in considering the adult client's goals as well, but Dreikurs was clear that adult goals are more complicated and may include complex relationships and context. Also, considering the client's social embedded-ness in the ER is important. Is the client alone or with others? Does gender or family place (birth order) influence the relationships in the ER?

From a career perspective, what skills, values, and interests are present in the ERs? Does the client show attention to the aesthetic elements of the context? This could indicate a strong interest in the visual arts and could be the seed for developing more articulated career interests. Does the client demonstrate strong attention to detail or organization? This could indicate traits better suited for conventional careers. This perspective is worthy of discussion and can help to give the client additional career trait information that may lead to further development and understanding of career and personal identity.

After taking time to reflect on the meaning of the content of the ERs, the counselor makes proposals to the client and asks for the client's perspec-tives (e.g., "Could it be that in your ER you are wanting to be recognized?" which may indicate a desire for attention). Proposals that invite the cli-ent to cointerpret and reflect are key elements of this process. The client participates in interpreting the ERs and explores the possibilities. This becomes a meaning-making endeavor by which the client gains insight and begins to understand why specific memories are important to self-understanding and as self-constructing devices. Ultimately, the purpose of collecting and cointerpreting ERs is to promote the strengths, skills, interests, goals, and identity of the client in more socially useful endeavors. The case of Al that follows illustrates this work with a young offender.

The Case of Al

Al is a member of an offenders group focused on exploring and planning for career transition into ex-offender status. Al is a 26-year-old African American male. His family includes his mother (currently incarcerated for drug abuse), his three sisters, and his estranged father. Often, Al and his sisters were cared for by his maternal grandmother. Al suffered beatings and abuse throughout his childhood from various adults and peers. He reported having a recalcitrant attitude in grade school and was suspended and expelled often. He dropped out of middle school and engaged in criminal activity to support himself.

During group screening interviews, Al met threshold requirements for criminogenic factors (e.g., antisocial history, thinking, and associates, and minimal family support), which qualified him for the career counseling group that includes these factors in treatment. Specifically, Al believed that he should be able to work in leadership positions and make a significant salary. A primary goal in his treatment was to revise this thinking and decrease his expectation of attaining high employment goals in a short time. He possessed no specific training and had an employment history of labor jobs in the construction industry. He never completed a general education development test or other specific training. Although Al did express many criminogenic factors, he also expressed a sincere hope to stop living this life. His older sister visited him regularly, and he knew she loved him and wanted a meaningful family relationship.

Application of ER to Address Criminogenic Career Factors

Al's early memories included themes of striving for power and recognition. In his first ER, Al stated:

Dialogue (Client ER 1)	Scene and Emotion
Al: I was about 7 and I was hanging out with some friends. We were playing basketball, and I wanted to be captain of the team. But one of the other guys, who was older, always claimed he was captain. So, this time, when we were playing, I tripped him and he fell and broke his arm. We stopped playing, but I remember being happy because I got him to stop pushing us around.	His most salient scene was his peer getting up from the ground and starting to cry. His emotion was anger, and he said he felt powerful in stopping him.

This is an excellent example of criminogenic thinking contained in an ER. Al reported having a goal (to be captain; that is, seeking power) and asking for his goal to be met. When the goal was not granted, he took measures to achieve his goal through violence. Upon achieving his power goal, he felt vindicated in overcoming his peer through the use of devious means.

The following excerpt is from the group counseling session in which counselor and client explored the possible unconscious goal expressed in the ER:

Dialogue (Group Session)	Possible Themes
Counselor: Al, I would like you to reflect on what you wanted to achieve by being captain.	
Al: I wanted to take a turn at calling the plays and leading the group . . . it just seemed fair for all of us to take a turn.	
Counselor: Did you achieve your goal?	Latent goals of power and
Al: Yes.	recognition
Counselor: But Al, in the memory you said you stopped playing, and you did not get to play in the role as captain.	Belongingness
Al: Well, I never thought of that. I just felt vindicated to stop him.	

During the group session, when Al shared this recollection, the counselor asked Al to reflect on what he wanted to achieve by being captain. Al shared that he wanted to take a turn at calling the plays and leading the group (latent goals of power and recognition). "It just seemed fair for all of us to take a turn." This statement showed his interest in belonging to a group ("all of us") and can be construed as positive social interest—that is, wanting to include everyone in the group. The counselor asked Al if he achieved his goal. Al said "yes." The counselor pointed out that he did not get to be captain and that the group did not get to play, which was his stated (manifest) goal. This appeared to be new information for Al as he admitted that he never thought of that; he just always felt vindicated. A fellow group member, nodding his head yes, also recalled his habit of thinking he achieved his goals through violence. Through this group process, the member was learning that he was not really achieving his goal. The counselor focused the group on this type of distorted and unprocessed thinking, asking for more examples. One group member shared that this type of thinking is what led to his incarceration. He said that he was seeking independence by stealing, but that act had caused him to lose the independence he had achieved before he was imprisoned. These examples demonstrate how criminogenic thinking can be identified through the use of ERs.

Al shared another ER concerning an interaction in his family when he was 4 years old. He recalled:

Dialogue (ER 2)	Scene and Emotion
Al: My mom's boyfriend and my mom were arguing. He slapped her, and I remember yelling at him to stop. He laughed, and I threw a toy at him. He hit me with his fists, and I began to cry while my mother screamed at him. He knocked her down to the floor and left. Counselor: It must have been frightening for you to see that.	His most salient scene was when he first saw the boyfriend hit his mother. He felt angry and wanted to stop him.

After reflecting the anger and fear that Al felt, the counselor pointed out that his goal was different from what occurred. He wanted the boyfriend to stop hitting his mother, but the scene ended with both he and his mother being hit by the boyfriend. Al responded:

Dialogue (Group Session)	Possible Themes
Al: I just could not stand by and watch that. Counselor: As you think about it now, are there other things you could have done? Maybe call for help or go get a neighbor? Al: I am not really sure, my first instinct is to take charge and face violence with violence.	

(Continued)

Dialogue (Group Session, continued)	*Possible Themes*
Another Group Member: Yes, that is my instinct too when I have seen that kind of thing, and it usually ends badly for me. I usually get arrested or go to court, which is not what I was intending to do when I reacted.	Latent goals of power
Counselor: Al, what was your intention in the memory?	
Al: To stop him from hurting my mother. It is just not right to hit a woman or child.	
Counselor: You are both saying that you attempt to stop violence and help the target of an attack. That really speaks to an altruistic aspect of your personalities. Could it be that both of you are saying that you do care about others and injustice? Your intentions seem to suggest a general ethic of care.	Belongingness and social interest

The ER in this segment served to open a conversation about immediate behaviors and their results. And the latent content helped the counselor begin to build altruism and empathy in the group members. The discussion centered on how to control immediate behaviors and reactions. For example, the counselor shared the psychological process of "Stop, Think, Act" with the group. The counselor commented that people often react to situations without thinking. These reactions reflect perceptions that may be linked to early experiences. By understanding how early experiences govern behaviors, individuals can learn to stop and think before acting.

Al's third recollection recounted an incident at school. He reported being in second grade and having an altercation with his teacher. He stated:

Dialogue (ER 3)	*Scene and Emotion*
Al: I was bored in class, and I started talking with my friend. The teacher called me out, and I got embarrassed and angry because she told me I never pay attention. I just did not like hearing that I never paid attention. I stood up and called her a liar and threw my books on the floor. She told me to go to the office, and I stormed out. I don't remember much else, just that.	His most salient scene was when he heard the teacher say "never." He became angry.

This ER recounts Al's experience with losing attention and becoming frustrated. When he hears that he never pays attention, he becomes explosive. In the memory, Al was attempting to gain recognition for being patient, but when he heard that he was not patient, he reacted with anger. Helping Al learn to work with his impatience and being able to recognize that he will not always be accepted is a focus of this ER.

Dialogue (Group Session)	*Possible Themes*

Another Group Member: That always gets
me going, when people say I never
do anything right. People are so
negative when you screw up. Once you
get the reputation, you get sentenced
to that *all the time* attitude.

Counselor: When you hear a blanket statement,
one that categorizes you negatively,
then both of you react with anger.
I wonder if you are both attempting
to fit in (goal) and gain some respect
(positive recognition), and when you hear
these absolute statements you figure that
you are being told you do not belong here
and never will.

Al: Yes, I used to try, and then I just gave up.
It is so much easier being around people
that think like you. Trying to fit in with   Attention and withdrawal
normal people just does not work.

Counselor: This is really an important statement.
What I am understanding is that you find
it easier to be with people who think like
you do rather than with people that may
have different experiences of you. There is
difficulty in hearing that you are not
meeting someone's expectations.

In this ER, Al is attempting to communicate that he wants to be accepted, and when he is not, he becomes violent. Focusing on his original goal of wanting to be a part of the group is an important point in interpreting this memory. Stressing this desire of wanting to be accepted and striving to belong is an important intervention in rebuilding this sense of social interest (Adler, 1932). Identifying this as a positive goal helps reinforce to the group members that they can strive to belong and practice belonging. This focus can lead to a discussion and rehearsal of prosocial behaviors and conflict resolution training.

Applying Narrative Themes to Career Counseling

Collectively, the themes from these recollections are applicable to many aspects of social functioning. The career aspect is the goal for this group, so I will discuss the implications of these themes with a career focus in mind. One of the first issues that came up was Al's admission that he seeks employment where he can have more power, as illustrated in the basketball game memory. He wants to contribute and have a voice. Al needs help learning how to temper his frustration when people do not want to hear him and to avoid the use of violence when he feels threatened or ignored. Accentuating that he wants to contribute is an important aspect of this memory and his way of approaching work. Helping Al learn from his story that he wants to contribute is an important positive aspect of Al's identity.

A focus in assisting Al in inventorying his skills and abilities is working with him so that he can know when he has something to contribute. Simply wanting to contribute is not enough; Al must begin to understand that he may need to learn things before he has valuable and marketable contributions. This will be a difficult area for Al. He wants to be in an important position, but he does not currently possess credible skills and training to market himself. In addition, he does not respond well to individuals who recognize his lack of skills (e.g., the teacher ER). Working with Al in controlling his reactions is an area for developing his career adaptability dimension of control (Savickas, 2011).

Helping Al restory the second ER from one of trauma to one of him caring for another person (his mother) contributes to building his altruism and empathy. From a career perspective, he can draw on this experience when exploring an employer's attitude toward him. Understanding that he is not owed a position, but may be given an opportunity, is an important attitude shift for Al. The content of the third recollection is relevant here as well. By being prepared for attitudes of judgment and doubts of being able to adjust, Al can practice avoiding displaying anger and resentment. He can learn and practice an empathic response to an employer and attempt to explain that he has learned to be more patient and open to accepting feedback. Also, he can practice accepting that people have different opinions of him, and that he does not need to lash out in anger when he feels threatened by those opinions. Rehearsal exercises in the group will help him to restory his ERs of rejection and violence and to portray his attitudes of wanting to promote fairness and altruism. This may improve his social responsibility and workplace relationships.

Two of Al's ERs tell a story of him wanting to be respected and accepted as having something to contribute (i.e., the basketball game and protecting his mother). Reminding Al that he wants to contribute is a way of building on a strength. Using this strength to build a career identity for Al is a primary way of using his story to augment his actions of concern for others (e.g., peers in the basketball memory, mother in the violent incident). This is similar to a social theme using Holland's coding. Helping Al search for and build a career plan that includes ways for him to help others (social advocacy) seems an appropriate use of this storied trait that brings meaning to Al's survival of the traumas he has experienced in life. Consistently reminding Al of his career goal will help to mitigate his frustration with being held to and judged by social standards and conventions.

Ultimately, the use of these ERs serves to inform the counselor and Al of his attitudes toward social responsibilities and tasks. The counselor's skill in understanding and storying the latent content and goals is crucial to the success of using early memories.

In summary, these early memories provide insights into Al's ways of thinking about the world and reacting to experiences. Once developed, the themes can be addressed from many theoretical approaches (e.g., cognitive behavior theory, existential theory, social cognitive career theory). Success and change can be measured by alterations in the memories and revisions to the stories of Al's life over time (Rehfuss, 2009). Keeping attuned to specific word choice, emotional expression, and self-regulation strategies will assist Al in preparing for life beyond incarceration. Table 9.1 provides an application guide to using this technique.

Conclusion

An assessment tool that focuses on the use of ERs can help offenders in a career transition group in a correctional institution. The goal of the assessment is to gauge the presence and severity of criminogenic attitudes possessed by the client. The criminogenic factors then become the focus of a therapeutic intervention. Helping the client to understand and identify his or her thinking patterns is the first step in building strategies to alter and change these early stories. Although it is applicable to many life roles, using this assessment with a career identity and adaptability focus can be especially helpful for offenders. By understanding their personal life story and how it interacts with the social responsibilities and expectations of work life, these young offenders are gaining strategies for success in life.

Recommended Resources

Carns, M. R., & Carns, A. W. (1994). The use of the Adlerian life-style guide and the four goals of misbehavior in supervision. *Individual Psychology, 50*, 341–348.

Chronister, K. M., & McWhirter, E. H. (2008). *OPTIONS.* Unpublished curriculum manual. Eugene, OR: University of Oregon. Retrieved from https://www.apa.org/education/ce/community-reentry.pdf

Duran, L., Plotkin, M., Potter, P., & Rosen, H. (2013). *Integrated reentry and employment strategies: Reducing recidivism and promoting job readiness.* Retrieved from https://www.bja.gov/publications/csg-reentry-and-employment.pdf

Harland, A. (Ed.). (1996). *Choosing correctional options that work: Defining the demand and evaluating the supply.* Thousand Oaks, CA: Sage. https://us.sagepub.com/en-us/nam/choosing-correctional-options-that-work/book4257

National Criminal Justice Reference Service. https://www.ncjrs.gov/viewall.html

References

Adler, A. (1932). *What life should mean to you.* London, England: Allen & Unwin.

Andrews, D. A., & Bonta, J. (2010). *The psychology of criminal conduct* (5th ed.). Cincinnati, OH: Anderson.

Table 9.1
Practical Application Guide

Topic	Using Early Recollections (ERs) in a Career-Focused Group Setting
General goals and purposes	1. To draw attention to relationships between offender early recollections and present thinking and behavior 2. To teach the offender how to understand personal needs (private logic) and develop new views toward criminal behavior and the work self
Applicable modality	Individual and group (group application requires establishing a therapeutic environment prior to using this application)
Applicable counselor settings	Correctional facility, parole reporting center, juvenile correctional facility
Recommended time to complete	Initial session (50 minutes per individual in group). Follow-up session (30 minutes per group member). Additional follow-up session (as needed).
Materials/equipment needed	Writing pad or paper, pen or pencil, whiteboard and dry erase markers
Step-by-step outline of the process	1. Prepare the client for talking about ERs by explaining the purpose (e.g., ERs help to identify established patterns of thinking, attitudes, and behavior.) Also, asking the client what may be helpful in the counseling process is important at this time if not covered earlier. 2. Ask the client to think of an early memory, preferably before the age of 10. (Ask the client to focus on a specific early memory of an event, not report on a story told to him or her.) 3. Have the client tell the entire memory as if the client were reporting a video segment. 4. Write the memory and underline key words or phrases. 5. Have the client report the most salient moment in the memory. 6. Have the client reflect the general emotional climate of the scene. 7. Reflect on the memory and the goal for which the client was striving. 8. Repeat Steps 1 through 7, collecting at least three ERs. 9. Attempt to relate the latent goals to the client's stated need for help or assistance. 10. Develop general themes for striving toward positive relationships. Also, include career identity and adaptability (strengths) in the themes. 11. Weave the themes (with a positive motive when present) into the client's story, and ask the client for feedback to co-construct an altered story. 12. Develop a future story with positive goals. 13. Integrate other applicable treatments.

Andrews, D. A., Bonta, J., & Hoge, R. D. (1990). Classification for effective rehabilitation: Rediscovering psychology. *Criminal Justice and Behavior, 19*, 19–52.

Ansbacher, H. L. (1979). Alder's place today in the psychology of memory. In H. A. Olson (Ed.), *Early recollections: Their use in diagnosis and psychotherapy*. Springfield, IL: Charles C Thomas.

Barclay, S. R., Stoltz, K. B., & Wolff, L. A. (2011). Career development through career construction counseling: A group method. In T. Fitch & J. Marshall (Eds.), *Group work and outreach plans for college counselors* (pp. 49–54). Alexandria, VA: American Counseling Association.

Bonta, J., & Andrews, D. A. (2007). *Risk-need-responsivity model for offender assessment and rehabilitation* (User Report 2007-06). Ottawa, Ontario, Canada: Public Safety Canada.

Bureau of Justice Statistics. (2013). *Federal justice statistics, 2010* (Index No. NCJ 239913). Washington, DC: Author.

Clark, A. J. (2002). *Early recollections: Theory and practice in counseling and psychotherapy*. New York, NY: Brunner-Routledge.

Dowden, C., & Andrews, D. A. (2000). Effective correctional treatment and violent reoffending: A meta-analysis. *Canadian Journal of Criminology, 42*, 449–467.

Dreikurs, R. (1968). *Psychology in the classroom: A manual for teachers* (2nd ed.). New York, NY: Harper & Row.

Durose, M. R., Cooper, A. D., & Snyder, H. N. (2014). *Recidivism of prisoners released in 30 states in 2005: Patterns from 2005 to 2010* (Research Report No. NCJ 244205). Retrieved from http://www.bjs.gov/index.cfm?ty=pbdetail&iid=4986

Eckstein, D., & Kern, R. M. (2009). *Psychological fingerprints: Lifestyle assessment and interventions* (6th ed.). Dubuque, IA: Kendall/Hunt.

Elliot, W. N., Fakouri, M. E., & Hafner, J. L. (1993). Early recollections of criminal offenders. *Journal of Individual Psychology, 49*, 68–75.

Gendreau, P. (1996). The principles of effective intervention with offenders. In A. T. Harland (Ed.), *Choosing correctional options that work: Defining the demand and evaluating the supply* (pp. 117–130). Thousand Oaks, CA: Sage.

Gendreau, P., Goggin, C., & Gray, G. (1998). Case need domain: Employment. *Forum on Corrections Research, 10*, 16–19.

Hafner, J. L., Fakouri, M. E., & Etzler, D. R. (1986). Early recollections of individuals preparing for careers in chemical, electrical, and mechanical engineering. *Journal of Individual Psychology, 42*, 360–366.

Homant, R. J., & Dean, D. G. (1988). The effect of prisonization and self esteem on inmates' career maturity. *Journal of Offender Counseling, Services & Rehabilitation, 12*, 19–40. doi:10.1300/J264v12n02_03

Kasler, J., & Nevo, O. (2005). Early recollections as predictors of study area choice. *Journal of Individual Psychology, 61*, 217–232.

Maree, J. G. (2010) Career-story interviewing using the three anecdotes technique. *Journal of Psychology in Africa, 20*, 369–380.

McAdams, D. P., & McLean, K. C. (2013). Narrative identity. *Current Directions in Psychological Science, 22*, 233–238.

McWhirter, E. H. (2013). Vocational psychology, offenders and ex-offenders, and social justice: A critical perspective. *Counseling Psychologist, 4,* 1040–1051.

Morgan, R. D. (2013). Vocational psychology in corrections: It is about time. *Counseling Psychologist, 4,* 1061–1071.

Rehfuss, M. C. (2009). The future career autobiography: A narrative measure of career intervention effectiveness. *The Career Development Quarterly, 58,* 82–90.

Rehman, G., & Manzoor, A. (2003). Early recollections of Pakistani criminal offenders: A validity study. *The Journal of Individual Psychology, 59,* 187–192.

Savickas, M. L. (1998). Career-style interview and counseling. In T. Sweeney (Ed.), *Adlerian counseling: A practical approach for a new decade* (3rd ed., pp. 289–320). Muncie, IN: Accelerated Development Press.

Savickas, M. L. (2011). *Career counseling. Theories of psychotherapy series.* Washington, DC: American Psychological Association.

Shivy, V. A., Wu, J., Moon, A. E., Mann, S. C., Holland J. G., & Eacho, C. (2007). Ex-offenders reentering the workforce. *Journal of Counseling Psychology, 54,* 466–473.

Singer, J. A. (2004). Narrative identity and meaning making across the adult lifespan: An introduction. *Journal of Personality, 72,* 437–459. doi:10.1111/j.0022-3506.2004.00268.x

Singer, J. A., & Bonalume, L. (2010). Autobiographical memory narratives in psychotherapy: A coding system applied to the case of Cynthia. *Pragmatic Case Studies in Psychotherapy, 6,* 134–188.

Stoltz, K. B., Wolff, L. A., & McClelland, S. S. (2011). Exploring lifestyle as a predictor of career adaptability using a predominantly African American rural sample. *Journal of Individual Psychology, 67,* 147–161.

Taber, B. J., & Briddick, W. C. (2011). Adlerian-based career counseling in an age of protean careers. *Journal of Individual Psychology, 67,* 107–121.

Thompson, M. N., & Cummings, D. L. (2010). Enhancing the career development of individuals who have criminal records. *The Career Development Quarterly, 58,* 209–218.

Varghese, F. P. (2013). Vocational interventions with offenders: Interdisciplinary research, theory, and integration. *Counseling Psychologist, 41,* 1011–1039.

Varghese, F. P., & Cummings, D. L. (2013). Introduction: Why apply vocational psychology to criminal justice populations? *Counseling Psychologist, 41,* 961–989. doi:10.1177/0011000012459363

Vernick, S. H., & Reardon, R. C. (2001). Career development programs in corrections. *Journal of Career Development, 27,* 265–277.

Walton, F. X. (1998). Use of the most memorable observation as a technique for understanding choice of parenting style. *The Journal of Individual Psychology, 54,* 487–494.

Watkins, E. C., Jr. (1984). Using early recollections in career counseling. *Vocational Guidance Quarterly, 4,* 271–276.

Chapter 10

The Storied Approach to Career Co-Construction With an Older Female Client

Pamelia E. Brott

Many of our models for career development are inadequate for understanding the needs of the 40.3 million adults over the age of 65 in the United States (Werner, 2011), with females continuing to outnumber males in the older population at every year of ages 65 to 100+ years. There is a growing interest in understanding this phase of life, and new concepts are being introduced (e.g., bridge employment, third chapter, encore careers, Life Reimagined) that are redefining later life stages as being both dynamic and productive.

In this chapter, I begin with a brief look at career counseling models from a development perspective and a diversity perspective. Next I examine the storied approach (Brott, 2001) as a constructivist's guiding framework as it relates to career counseling with older women. Co-construction relies on revealing the life story from an idiographic (i.e., individual) perspective. Instead of taking on the mantle of being old, the story unfolds in a rich texture of life experiences, wisdom, and lessons learned. Both life line and life roles techniques can help to illuminate and co-construct the client's life story and create active steps (Brott, 2004, 2005). Finally, I introduce a case study to illustrate using the storied approach with an older female client.

Developmental Perspective

The classic career development models of the 20th century, such as Super's (1980) life-span, life-space model, were predominantly based on White working males and reflected an age-related progression through a series of stages across social roles. This age-related progression was based on a more or less predictable movement from growth and exploration (childhood and adolescence), to establishment (young adult) and maintenance (middle adult), and then to decline (older adult), when an average life expectancy was 68.8 years (National Center for Health Statistics, 2015). Over the course of his lifetime, Super revised his developmental model to reflect an individual's ability to recycle through stages based on employment-related transitions (e.g., moving to a new location, changing employment either vertically or laterally) and to reconceptualize the later stage of development as a disengagement from working rather than a decline (Super, 1990).

As the 21st century began, revised definitions of retirement and later stages of life were introduced. Bridge employment (Ulrich & Brott, 2005), third chapter (Lawrence-Lightfoot, 2009), encore careers (Encore, 2014), and Life Reimagined (AARP, 2014) better capture the dynamic nature of increasing life expectancy (currently 78.7 years; National Center for Health Statistics, 2015) and the impact of the baby boomers within the workforce. These changes notwithstanding, the onset of an economic depression in 2007, which resulted when the housing bubble burst and unemployment skyrocketed to 10% nationally in 2009 (U.S. Bureau of Labor Statistics, 2015), led to an unpredictable career path for most U.S. citizens and had a crippling effect on older individuals whose retirement incomes were devastated (Mackenzie, 2008).

What exactly constitutes an "older" worker continues to lack an explicit and widely agreed-upon definition. For instance, AARP requires an individual to be at least 50 years of age for membership, the Age Discrimination in Employment Act of 1967 protects individuals 40 years or older, the Social Security Administration cites 67 as the normal retirement age (Social Security Administration, 2015), and the U.S. Census for labor force statistics uses 65 years and over (Werner, 2011). The 2010 U.S. Census reported over 40.3 million adults aged 65+, representing a 12.4% increase from the 2000 Census (Werner, 2011). From this older population, 6.7% made up the civilian labor force in 2010 compared to 4.3% in 2000. The employment participation of the older (65 years and over) female population in 2010 was 3 million (13.8% of the labor force), which is a 47% increase in employed older females since 2000. Clearly, the demographic of older females in the U.S. population represents a significant concern for career counselors. For the purposes of this chapter, older female adults will be defined as females aged 65+ years in the United States.

Diversity Perspectives

In counseling, diversity embraces many dimensions and acknowledges multiple identities that include age, gender, race, ethnicity, sexual preferences, class, power and privilege, and language (Hays, 2008). Various writers have helped counseling professionals recognize "this elusive concept called culture" (Stead, 2004, p. 391) and suggest that, from a social constructionist perspective, the term *narrative identity* captures the person's evolving life story, which provides meaning and purpose (McAdams & Olson, 2010). Narrative identity is a personalized interpretation of self in a social world (Savickas, 2011): It is the story of "me" and my interpretations of the world.

More than 35 years ago, Vontress (1980) brought attention to the challenges of counseling older individuals (≥50 years of age) from cultural minorities in the United States. He called for counselors to be open to the nuances of metalanguage through both verbal and nonverbal communication; to structure explicitly the counseling relationship so that clients understand the benefits of self-disclosure; to be prepared to address transference that may result from clients' life experiences of rejection, marginalization, and discrimination stemming from cultural differences (i.e., racial/ethnic, age); and to be aware of countertransference that may influence counselors' attitudes toward older minority group clients (Vontress, 1980). These concerns echo Kelly's (1955) personal constructs of subjective meaning making. Such considerations can be addressed by using an idiosyncratic, social constructivist counseling approach, particularly with older minority clients.

Generational cohorts have been of interest to social scientists from the perspectives of both social forces (i.e., sociohistorical) and collections of people born in a given time period (Lyons & Kuron, 2014). The social forces perspective emanates from the work of Karl Mannheim (1952), who saw early life experiences as a basis for experiencing life, which is the gestalt of one's social and historical context across a lifetime. Adults' attitudes and behaviors emerge from a collective memory of formative events in early life that become a generation's identity (Lyons & Kuron, 2014). In today's workforce, we refer to baby boomers or boomers (individuals born between 1940 and the mid-1960s), Generation X or Gen X-ers (those born between the early 1960s and the early 1980s), and either millennials or generation Y-ers (late 1970s to mid-1990s). The boomers grew up during the time of the Vietnam War, civil rights riots, the assassinations of Kennedy and King, protests and sit-ins, Woodstock, hippies, and the sexual revolution; they generally hold traditional values and a strong work ethic (Smola & Sutton, 2002).

Work values are evaluative standards an individual uses to assess the importance of preferences relating to work (Dose, 1997). Work ethic is one's beliefs and attitudes reflecting fundamental values of work and work-related activity (Meriac, Woehr, & Banister, 2010). Boomers feel strongly that work is one of the most important parts of a person's life, and a person's worth is how well he or she does a job (Smola & Sutton, 2002). Boomers' work ethic is based on working hard and overcoming every obstacle (Meriac et al., 2010).

The feminist movement of the 1960s brought attention to the need for career development models that embrace the unique experiences of women across life roles and life phases. O'Neil and Bilimoria (2005) identified three critical factors that make women's careers unique from men's: family responsibilities, relational emphasis, and underrepresentation at higher organizational levels. Their grounded theory supported the differences across three phases of a woman's career (idealistic achievement, pragmatic endurance, and reinventive contribution) where her advanced career (ages 46 to 60) is viewed as a time of "reinventive contribution" (p. 184). This phase reflects the values of the 1960s when she came of age by taking an activist stance on fairness and justice, by considering the impact of divorce or the death of a spouse on her life and career choices, and by embracing chances to make a difference. This phase of life provides opportunities to contribute meaningfully and is a time when success can be measured in terms of recognition, respect, and living an integrated life (O'Neil & Bilimoria, 2005). McMahon, Watson, and Bimrose (2012) synthesized from their research that the career adaptability of older women across three different countries (Australia, England, South Africa) is "deeply contextually embedded at many levels" (p. 767) as a recursive relational interplay of the individual, her social networks, and the sociopolitical system in which she lives.

Counseling older clients may be more about the client's perspective (i.e., first-person point of view, phenomenology) than the psychology of aging (i.e., theoretical, generalizability) that frequently leads to a loss/deficit model (Atkins & Loewenthal, 2004). It also may be about the counselor's perspective: putting aside one's own feelings and perceptions, questioning assumptions about aging, recognizing and confronting bias, and coming to terms with where the counselor fits in the age spectrum (Atkins & Loewenthal, 2004). The generational cohort concept, with particular attention to female perspectives, sheds light on how to uncover the source of meanings and the motivation in meeting needs.

Framework for Career Counseling With Older Female Clients

A career counseling framework applicable to older female clients is based on a collaborative process and acknowledges the importance of language. The counseling relationship is structured as a collaborative endeavor from which a working alliance will emanate, and the benefits of client self-disclosure are clearly articulated. Dialogue forms the basis of client–counselor interactions, and the language within this dialogue is paramount for understanding the "what" and "how" of the client's meanings. The client's language is filled with social and historical context from across the client's life course and conveys the narrative identity (i.e., "me and my interpretations"). The counselor's language is reflective and conveys a deepening understanding of the client's narrative identity. The counselor and client engage in a thoughtful discourse that explores the values and priorities comprising the subjective, meaning making, and personal world of the client. The counselor sets aside preconceived notions of what constitutes "older" and listens for the source of meanings and motivations.

Little is known about the antecedents of why (i.e., motivation) older females engage in career counseling. More is known about the antecedents that may influence retirement or staying at work for the older worker, namely wanting to continue to work, needing to continue to work, and embracing subjective well-being (Crowne, 2013). Recent career counseling models have included ecological (Betz, 2002; Cook, Heppner, & O'Brien, 2002) and constructivist (e.g., Brott, 2001; Savickas et al., 2009; Young & Collin, 2004) approaches. Drawing on Kelly's (1955) personal constructs, constructivism focuses on ways individuals view and interpret their lives and attend to a personal, meaning-making narrative that includes gender, age, and culture. The narrative counseling model uses the client's story as the guiding metaphor, which empowers the client to be an active agent in enacting future life chapters based on preferred ways of being (Brott, 2001).

Storytelling as a narrative approach to career counseling lends itself to clients reflecting on their thoughts, feelings, and experiences to illuminate the subjective meaning-making process of living a life. Clients are active participants in co-constructing their story with the counselor and in being intentional authors of past, present, and future chapters of the story (Brott, 2001). This is a collaborative process in which clients are experts in their lived lives, and the counselor is a reflective facilitator who assists in uncovering the "how" and "why" to assist clients in constructing the next steps in the life story. Qualitative assessments (e.g., life line, life roles circles, card sorts, goal map) are more amenable to a narrative, storytelling collaborative approach to career counseling. They provide information that aids in telling the client's story, identifying patterns, and uncovering meanings that can be woven into the narrative (Brott, 2004). Healy (1990) called for the reforming of career appraisals so that clients have a sense of agency (i.e., ownership) in the process: being in a collaborative role, engaging in self-observations, recognizing their interactions in context, and using aids to clarify and improve their choices and follow-through. This is an idiographic process; it is personal and distinct, with qualitative career assessments selected as aids for the client to explore meanings, themes, and preferences (Brott, 2015).

Constructivist Career Counseling With Older Female Clients

Career counseling with older female clients is best viewed as an idiographic process, with each client story being personal and distinct. It is a dynamic, interrelated process of *co-constructing, deconstructing, reconstructing,* and *constructing* (Brott, 2015). Qualitative assessment tools that best meet the needs of the client are selected in helping her to uncover, open up, unify, and actively engage in the next chapter of her story. Throughout this process, the most important tools are the collaborative venture of the client–counselor working alliance and language for finding meaning and purpose in the client's story.

The storied approach (Brott, 2001) lends itself to meeting the needs of older female clients by embracing personal subjective constructs such as age, gender, and racial/ethnic identity. This approach is an idiographic process of *co-constructing* (illuminating the past and present chapters of the story), *deconstructing* (opening up space in the story to enhance one's perspectives), *reconstructing* (weaving a unified storied identity), and *constructing* (authoring future chapters based on preferred ways of being). It engages the client and counselor in a collaborative, reflective relationship focusing on client agency. The case study of Valentina illustrates the *co-constructing* process with a focus on the collaborative relationship, language, qualitative assessment tools (i.e., life line, life roles circles), and the narrative identity.

The Case of Valentina

Valentina is a 65-year-old Latina who lives in a large mid-Atlantic town and was recently divorced from her childhood sweetheart after 46 years of marriage. She is the mother of six adult children and grandmother of 15 grandchildren, with a soon-to-be-born great-grandchild. All members of her family live within 1 hour's drive of her home. Valentina takes pride in the fact that "I have always been employed, even when I was raising my family" but she was recently notified that her current employer is downsizing. She can either relocate to another company location and continue her employment up to the age of 70 or take advantage of the company's retirement transition program with full retirement within 6 months. Her employer's human resources department offers career counseling through a local licensed practitioner, which Valentina has decided "can't hurt, and it may help me decide what I should do."

The counselor is a White female and is 10 years younger than her client. She has been using the storied approach (Brott, 2001) as an idiographic process (Brott, 2015) to *co-construct, deconstruct, reconstruct,* and *construct* the chapters of a client's story. Valentina presents in a respectful but guarded demeanor for the first session.

Dialogue	*Introducing the Process*
Counselor: How can I be of assistance to you?	Embracing the importance of language, the counselor is inviting Valentina into the process.
Valentina: Just tell me what to do because I am feeling like such a failure: My marriage failed, my employer doesn't want me anymore, and I just don't know what to do.	The counselor listens carefully to Valentina's language and hears her current frame of reference being about failure.
Counselor: Valentina, you are facing a number of challenges in your life and have taken a positive first step in taking control by seeking out counseling. There is so much emotion in facing these life challenges, but you have been successful in meeting so many life challenges already in your life. I cannot tell you what to do, but I can certainly help you figure out what to do. Ultimately, it is your choice what will be best for you.	Recognizing the importance of explicitly structuring the counseling relationship, honoring the client's lived experiences, and moving away from advice-giving and toward client agency, the counselor (a) reframes Valentina's response as challenges, (b) compliments her on taking a positive first step and being successful, and (c) places ownership (i.e., choice) with the client.

Co-Constructing

The purpose of co-constructing is to uncover the past and present chapters in the client story through a dialogue between the client and counselor from which a collaborative relationship (i.e., working alliance) is built. Qualitative tools are selected that will aid the client in telling her story through selected early memories so that the narrative identity emerges. Attention is paid to the language and emotional tone of these memories. The counselor, as a reflective facilitator, uses questions, probes, clarifying, and paraphrasing skills to reveal the client's subjective, meaning-making story.

Life Line

The counselor selects a life line (Brott, 2001, 2004) to be a visual representation of the chapters thus far in Valentina's story. The process begins with two or three early memories that stand out clearly and are personally remembered.

Dialogue	*Co-Constructing Process*
Counselor: Valentina, I want to better understand the current situation you find yourself in, and my questions will help me get to know you better. I want you to feel heard, so it is important for you to be open in expressing yourself. To help you tell your story, I am going to ask you to construct a life line on this large piece of paper because I want to remember what you are telling me about your memories. Would you be willing to try a life line?	The counselor places the paper in front of Valentina and allows her to select what she would like to write with (i.e., colored pencil, pen, marker).
Valentina: OK, but I'm not very good at writing.	As a reflective facilitator, the counselor listens to the client's language and is sensitive to her previous reference to failure and the current reference to herself as "I'm not very good."
Counselor: Then I think the life line will be helpful because you will just write down notes, words, and names.	The reframe (i.e., "helpful") focuses on notes, words, and names and away from the client's negative reference about writing.

The counselor asks Valentina to draw a line through the middle of the paper from the left edge to the right edge; dating the left edge with her birth date and the right edge with the current date. Then the counselor asks Valentina to place marks on the line indicating when she started kindergarten, graduated from high school, started work with her current employer, was married, and gave birth to each of her children.

Dialogue	*Co-Constructing Process*
Counselor: Valentina, I am beginning to see chapters in your life story. Can you see them?	The counselor introduces the narrative framework of chapters.

(Continued)

Dialogue (Continued)	*Co-Constructing Process*
Valentina: Gosh, I never thought about my life like that, but, yes, there are chapters: growing up, going to school, and having my own family. I did not realize how long I have been working for the same employer, and now they just want to let me go.	Valentina is able to "see" her life story and has given "titles" to these chapters.
Counselor: So, you can see how various parts of your life are intertwined, like your family and your work.	The counselor introduces how life is about family and work, and there is a relationship between these parts of one's life.
Valentina: Definitely.	
Counselor: Before we look at what is currently happening, I would like to go back and explore your earliest chapter with two or three of your earliest memories. Something you remember clearly. In other words, not something that you have been told, but what you distinctly remember. What would that be?	Co-constructing chapters in the client's life story is about revealing the story so that preferences, themes, and the meaning-making system of Valentina's life can be understood from her viewpoint. The importance of first-person details is emphasized (i.e., "what you distinctly remember").
Valentina: Oh, my favorite memory is when I was probably 4 or 5, when my whole family went on a picnic. Mommy was up really early in the morning packing everything up, and all of us kids had to stay out of the way so she could get everything ready. Daddy drove us to the park where he found a picnic table close to the water and under a tree. Mommy told all of us to go play while she fixed lunch. Daddy took us down to the water so we could play and let Mommy get everything ready.	The richness of this memory allows the counselor to learn more about Valentina's early life that may be reflective of her current personal identity. The memory holds the essence of what is important to her and can be explored to uncover what may be reoccurring themes; the only way to know is to ask Valentina.
Counselor: Valentina, would you just write down a few words anywhere on the paper within this chapter of your story that will help me remember what you have told me about this memory?	By asking the client to do the writing, the life line is her story. The words and phrases she chooses to write down should include people's names (e.g., Mommy, Daddy) as well as being a personal description of the memory.

(Continued)

Dialogue (Continued)	*Co-Constructing Process*
Counselor: Valentina, I am curious, is your family in the chapter called "My Own Family" similar to or different from the family you remember going on this picnic within the chapter "Growing Up"?	As themes begin to emerge, they can be explored for emotive responses and whether they are reflective of client values. In the case of Valentina, she sees how being organized and responsible, putting family first, and sharing the load are important values and can relate these values to other chapters in her life story (e.g., always having a job, taking care of her kids and grandkids, marriage is a partnership). The client's current situation can be explored to see if her emotion of failure may be linked not just to the job but also to her values and life roles.

Life Roles Circles

The life roles circles (Brott, 2004, 2005) help Valentina visualize how she can use her adaptability in writing the next chapter in her life story. The life roles circles activity uses ways in which we are relating, learning, pleasuring, working, and valuing in our life story. Relating embraces a variety of human interactions that include family, friends, and coworkers. Learning is all the ways we learn, whether it is about holding a job or living a life that includes formal schooling or on-the-job training, and life experiences. Pleasuring is about having fun and enjoying a life that includes hobbies, free time, and doing what you want to do. Working is how we make a living and how we contribute to our community. Valuing guides how we make our decisions across all life roles.

Dialogue	*Co-Constructing Process*
Counselor: Valentina, I am understanding your sense of failure from the perspective of what you value. You seem to be asking yourself, "How can I be responsible and take care of my family all by myself? What do I do if I have to move so far away?"	The counselor is clarifying with Valentina what was previously uncovered as her "sense of failure" from the viewpoint of her valuing life role (e.g., responsible, take care of family). This evaluative standard is how Valentina is assessing herself.
Valentina: Well, that sums it up. I really do feel like I am failing my kids and grandkids. And I now need to do all of it by myself. I can't retire, but I don't want to move so far away.	Valentina confirms the counselor's understanding and is feeling heard. Valentina articulates how her relating role (i.e., kids,

(Continued)

Dialogue (Continued)	*Co-Constructing Process*
	grandkids) and working role (i.e., retire, move away) are caught up in her feeling of failure (i.e., recurring theme).
Counselor: Let's take a look at these life roles you are struggling with and see if we can figure out some options. Only you will know what is best for you, but maybe I can help you look at options.	Possibly, Valentina may be feeling like she is failing because she cannot see options. The counselor sees an opportunity to collaborate with Valentina by identifying options that are a recursive relational interplay.
Valentina: Well, that's why I came to counseling.	The goal of counseling has shifted from "just tell me what to do" to options (i.e., opening up the story) based on her narrative identity.

Life roles for Valentina can be explored in the present tense and in the future tense. A piece of paper is folded in half and placed folded on the table in front of the client. The current date (i.e., present tense) is written at the top of the half sheet. Valentina is asked to draw five circles representing her life roles, with the size of the circle reflecting her current involvement in that life role and its position on the paper (i.e., circles overlapping or not) illustrating whether these life roles are interrelated or not. Once her current life roles are explored, the folded paper is flipped over, and the client selects a time in the future (i.e., future tense), writes the date at the top, and draws the five circles representing the involvement and interrelationship she would like to have across these five life roles. When the folded paper is opened up, the client can use the middle of the paper to jot notes about options and priorities for her life roles based on her narrative identity. Figure 10.1 displays Valentina's life roles qualitative assessment activity.

Dialogue	*Co-Constructing Process*
Counselor: Valentina, let's talk about your options for the next chapter in your life story. At the age of 65, what do you see as important to you in the next 5 years?	The counselor's focus is on the source of meanings and motivation in meeting needs based on Valentina's idiosyncratic perspective; Valentina's narrative identity.
Valentina: Well, I need to stay healthy, I want to spend time with my grandkids and my new great-grandbaby, and I don't want to worry about money.	Valentina clearly articulates her priorities based on her wants and needs. This is her preferred way of being.
Counselor: Tell me how that will be reflected across these five life roles.	The counselor is introducing reconstructing (i.e., weaving a *(Continued)*

Dialogue (Continued)	*Co-Constructing Process*
	unified storied identity) into the next chapter in the life story.
Valentina: I want my relating to be really BIG! But I need to work so I have money to take care of myself and do things for my grandkids.	The circles help Valentina to "see" what is important to her and where she will find her motivation for the next chapter in her life story.
Counselor: So, your valuing role of "family first" is being honored, and your working role will allow you to enjoy your relating role with family.	The counselor paraphrases what may be the narrative identity for Valentina.
Valentina: YES!	Valentina confirms.
Counselor: So, what is the first step you can take to make this happen?	The emphasis is on client action and ownership (i.e., client agency).

What is emerging from this discourse is the next chapter in Valentina's story. A new large sheet of paper is placed in front of her, a line is drawn through the middle of the page, and she is asked to place a mark on the

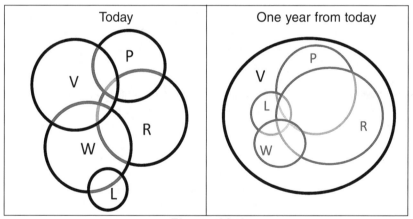

Figure 10.1
Life Roles Circles

Note. The life roles circles qualitative assessment tool for Valentina begins by folding a full sheet of paper in half. She constructs the display on the left representing her five life roles today. She flips the folded sheet over and constructs the display on the right using a future tense (i.e., 1 year from today). When the page is opened up as displayed above, the client and counselor process the life story, reflecting on the size of circles, relationships between and among the circles, and placement of the circles on the page. This leads to identifying her priorities and options, which will be her action steps for the next chapter in her life story (i.e., narrative identity). R = relating; L = learning; P = pleasuring; W = working; V = valuing.

future life line representing the next chapter in her life story. Valentina begins by writing down on the page her values and motivations for this next chapter, names of the people she wants in this chapter, and notes of the first steps she needs to take to enact this next chapter. A title is given to the chapter so she has a clear future direction. See Table 10.1 for an application guide.

Table 10.1
Practical Application Guide

Topic	The Storied Approach to Career Co-Construction
General goals and purposes	Using an idiographic process of co-construction, the client will 1. Experience a working alliance that is a collaborative, reflective process. 2. Engage in a discourse to uncover the subjective, meaning-making narrative identity (i.e., "me and my interpretations"). 3. Explore the past and present chapters of the life story to uncover themes, priorities, and values. 4. Conceptualize the life story through the life roles of relating, learning, pleasuring, working, and valuing. 5. Create the next chapter in the life story that embraces her values, motivations, and relationships. 6. Specify active steps to begin living life in the next chapter that is reflective of her narrative identity.
Applicable modality	Individual and small group (4 to 6 clients)
Applicable counselor settings	Agency, private practice, corporate/business
Recommended time to complete	*One-Session Format* (45 to 60 minutes) focusing on one or two early memories to uncover aspects of current narrative identity and select aspects that are her preferences for her next chapter *Three-to-Five Session Format* (45 to 60 minutes each session) allows for further development using the life line and life roles circles to uncover past and present chapters, life story through life roles, create next chapter with specific steps to begin living next chapter that is reflective of her narrative identity.
Materials/equipment needed	Large manila or newsprint paper 8-1/2 × 11 plain paper Colored pencils, pens, and markers
Step-by-step outline of the process	1. Set the parameters of a collaborative process (i.e., working alliance) as a dialogue and the importance of client self-disclosure. 2. Introduce the life line with past and present chapters. 3. Ask the client to identify an early memory. 4. Use probing, reflecting, clarifying, paraphrasing skills to uncover the narrative identity.

(Continued)

Table 10.1 *(Continued)*
Practical Application Guide

Topic	The Storied Approach to Career Co-Construction
Step-by-step outline of the process *(Continued)*	5. Listen to the client's language (e.g., idiosyncratic words and phrases) to reveal the historical context of her life experiences.
	6. Direct the client to write down notes on the life line within the chapter where the early memory occurred.
	7. Ask the client to identify a second early memory.
	8. Explore whether there are themes that have reoccurred in her life and in which chapters.
	9. Introduce life roles circles: relating, learning, pleasuring, working, valuing.
	10. Draw life roles circles based on current size of importance and relative position among all five life roles.
	11. Draw life roles circles based on future chapter.
	12. Identify first active steps to move from current to future life roles in her next chapter.
	13. Use another paper to draw the life line into the future and focus on the next chapter.
	14. Title the next chapter in her life story.
	15. Challenge the client if she defers to socially constructed norms (e.g., "Is this you?" or "Do you want this to be you?").

Conclusion

Providing older female clients with opportunities to create a narrative identity that is personal and empowering opens up their life stories and honors their perspectives. Counseling is about uncovering the story of past and present chapters so that preferences and patterns can be viewed as reflections of current (and future) motivations and needs. The life line and life roles circles are examples of qualitative assessments that can be used to assist in exploring the "how" and "why" of these motivations and needs through early memories, valuing clients' life experiences, and using language that conveys the subjective, meaning-making story of their lives. Emerging from this collaborative process is the next chapter of the story with first steps for clients' active agency.

Recommended Resources

AARP. (2016). *Life reimagined.* Retrieved from http://lifereimagined.aarp.org

Lawrence-Lightfoot, S. (2012). *The third chapter: Life between 50 and 75* [Video file]. Retrieved from https://www.youtube.com/watch?v=rIGgBLpzqrU

Schlossberg, N. K. (2015). *Transitions through life.* Retrieved from http://www.transitionsthroughlife.com

TransitionWorks. (2015). *Transition guide: A new way to think about change.* Retrieved from http://transitionguide.com

160 Procedures

References

AARP. (2014). *Getting to know Americans 50+*. Retrieved from http://www. aarp.org/content/dam/aarp/research/surveys_statistics/general/2014/ Getting-to-Know-Americans-Age-50-Plus-Demographics-AARP-res-gen.pdf

Atkins, D., & Loewenthal, D. (2004). The lived experience of psychotherapists working with older clients: An heuristic study. *British Journal of Guidance & Counselling, 32*, 493–509. doi:10.1080/03069880412331303295

Betz, N. E. (2002). Explicating an ecological approach to the career development of women. *The Career Development Quarterly, 50*, 335–338. doi:10.1002/j.2161-0045.2002.tb00581.x

Brott, P. E. (2001). The storied approach: A postmodern perspective for career counseling. *The Career Development Quarterly, 49*, 304–313. doi:10.1002/j.2161-0045.2001.tb00958.x

Brott, P. E. (2004). Constructivist assessment in career counseling. *Journal of Career Development, 30*, 189–200. doi:10.1023/B:JOCD.0000015539.21158.53

Brott, P. E. (2005). A constructivist look at life roles. *The Career Development Quarterly, 54*, 138–149. doi:10.1002/j.2161-0045.2005.tb00146.x

Brott, P. E. (2015). Qualitative career assessment processes. In M. McMahon & M. Watson (Eds.), *Career assessment: Qualitative approaches* (pp. 31–40). Rotterdam, The Netherlands: Sense.

Cook, E. P., Heppner, M. J., & O'Brien, K. M. (2002). Career development of women of color and White women: Assumptions, conceptualization, and interventions from an ecological perspective. *The Career Development Quarterly, 50*, 291–305. doi:10.1002/j.2161-0045.2002.tb00574.x

Crowne, K. A. (2013). Developing a better understanding of the older worker. *Journal of Applied Business and Economics 15*, 54–63.

Dose, J. (1997). Work values: An integrative framework and illustrative application to organizational socialization. *Journal of Occupational and Organizational Psychology 70*, 219–241. doi:10.1111/j.2044-8325.1997.tb00645.x

Encore. (2014). *Encore: Purpose and passion in your second act*. Retrieved from www.encore.org

Hays, P. A. (2008). *Addressing cultural complexities in practice: Assessment, diagnosis, and therapy* (2nd ed.). Washington, DC: American Psychological Association.

Healy, C. C. (1990). Reforming career appraisals to meet the needs of clients in the 1990s. *The Counseling Psychologist, 18*, 214–226. doi:10.1177/0011000090182004

Kelly, G. A. (1955). *The psychology of personal constructs*. New York, NY: Norton.

Lawrence-Lightfoot, S. (2009). *The third chapter: Passion, risk, and adventure in the 25 years after 50*. New York, NY: Sarah Crichton Books.

Lyons, S., & Kuron, L. (2014). Generational differences in the workplace: A review of the evidence and directions for future research. *Journal of Organizational Behavior, 35*, 139–157. doi:10.1002/job.1913

Mackenzie, S. (2008). *The impact of the financial crisis on older Americans.* Washington, DC: AARP Public Policy Institute. Retrieved from http://assets.aarp.org/rgcenter/econ/i19_crisis.pdf

Mannheim, K. (1952). *Essays on the sociology of knowledge.* London, England: Routeledge & Kegan Paul.

McAdams, D. P., & Olson, B. D. (2010). Personality development: Continuity and change over the life course. *Annual Review of Psychology, 61,* 517–542. doi:10.1146/annurev.psych.093008.100597

McMahon, M., Watson, M., & Bimrose, J. (2012). Career adaptability: A qualitative understanding from the stories of older women. *Journal of Vocational Behavior, 80,* 762–768. doi:10.1016/j.jvb.2012.01.016

Meriac, J. P., Woehr, D. J., & Banister, C. (2010). Generational differences in work ethic: An examination of measurement equivalence across three cohorts. *Journal of Business and Psychology, 25,* 315–324. doi:10.1007/sl0869-010-9164-7

National Center for Health Statistics. (2015). *National vital statistics reports.* Retrieved from http://www.cdc.gov/nchs

O'Neil, D. A., & Bilimoria, D. (2005). Women's career development phases. *Career Development International, 10,* 168–189. doi:10.1108/13620430510598300

Savickas, M. L. (2011). *Career counseling.* Washington, DC: American Psychological Association.

Savickas, M. L., Nota, L., Rossier, J., Dauwalder, J., Duarte, M. E., Guichard, J., & van Vienen, A. E. M. (2009). Life designing: A paradigm for career construction in the 21st century. *Journal of Vocational Behavior, 75,* 239–250. doi:10.1016/j.jvb.2009.04.004

Smola, K. W., & Sutton, C. D. (2002). Generational differences: Revisiting generational work values for the new millennium. *Journal of Organizational Behavior, 23,* 363–382. doi:10.1002/job.14

Social Security Administration. (2015). *Normal retirement age.* Retrieved from http://www.ssa.gov/oact/progdata/nra.html

Stead, G. B. (2004). Culture and career psychology: A social constructionist perspective. *Journal of Vocational Behavior, 64,* 389–406. doi:10.1016/j.jvb.2003.12.006

Super, D. E. (1980). A life-span, life-space approach to career development. *Journal of Vocational Behavior, 16,* 282–298. doi:10.1016/0001-8791(80)90056-1

Super, D. E. (1990). A life-span, life-space approach to career development. In D. Brown & L. Brooks (Eds.), *Career choice and development: Applying contemporary theories to practice* (2nd ed., pp. 197–261). San Francisco, CA: Jossey-Bass.

Ulrich, L. B., & Brott, P. E. (2005). Older workers and bridge employment: Redefining retirement. *Journal of Employment Counseling, 42,* 159–170. doi:10.1002/j.2161-1920.2005.tb01087.x

U.S. Bureau of Labor Statistics. (2015). *U.S. labor force statistics from the current population survey.* Retrieved from http://data.bls.gov/timeseries/LNS14000000

Vontress, C. E. (1980). Problems in counseling older minorities. *Counseling and Values, 24,* 118–126. doi:10.1002/j.2161-007X.1980.tb01079.x

Werner, C. A. (2011). *The older population: 2010.* Retrieved from http://www.census.gov/prod/cen2010/briefs/c2010br-09.pdf

Young, R. A., & Collin, A. (2004). Introduction: Constructivism and social constructionism in the career field. *Journal of Vocational Behavior, 64,* 373–388. doi:10.1016/j.jvb.2003.12.005

Chapter 11

Using the Genogram for Career Assessment and Intervention With an Economically Disadvantaged Client

Donna M. Gibson and Julia V. Taylor

Economically disadvantaged individuals are those who earn a total income in relation to the size of their families that does not exceed 70% of the *Lower Living Standard Income Level* (U.S. Department of Labor, 2014). Based on census information, approximately 51 million individuals are living below the poverty line. Many of these individuals qualify to receive public assistance and food stamp benefits, but often these benefits do not move them above the poverty line. Despite misperceptions that individuals living in poverty either are lazy or do not want to work, 80% of low-income children in rural and urban poverty areas have at least one working parent (Churilla, 2008; Pressley & Sifford, 2012). Hence, it cannot be assumed that economically disadvantaged families are not working. In addition, they can and do influence career decision making in their children and other family members.

In this chapter, the career genogram is introduced as a postmodern tool for working with clients who are considered economically disadvantaged. Because the career genogram is "the most commonly recognized and frequently administered qualitative instrument for gathering information about the influence of family in career decision-making" (Chope, 2005, p. 406), it is appropriate to focus its use on how the culture of poverty and family expectations affects a person's attitudes and decision making about careers. To illustrate how the career genogram can be used with this population, we explore and apply it to the case of an economically disadvantaged client.

Family Systems and Career Considerations

Genograms are a graphic representation of family structure and dynamics, typically across three generations (McGoldrick, Gerson, & Petry, 2008). Serving for both assessment and intervention purposes, genograms were historically used by counselors working with couples and families. Specifically, they were developed from Bowen's intergenerational family systems theory (Kerr & Bowen, 1988), and they allow for an exploration of intergenerational family experiences, behaviors, and patterns (Malott & Magnuson, 2004).

Within the genogram, parents, siblings, grandparents, uncles, aunts, and significant individuals who may not be related biologically to the client are documented with the use of symbols, graphic connecting lines, dates (i.e., birthdates, dates of death, and dissolved marriages and relationships), and descriptive words (McGoldrick et al., 2008). For example, males are depicted with the shape of a square and females with the shape of a circle. Connecting lines between these shapes denote marriages and committed relationships. One slash mark across these connecting lines indicates a separation in the relationship, and two slash marks across those lines indicates a more permanent separation such as divorce.

Family System Resources

To put the family genogram into context, constructing ecomaps of the community resources and agencies involved with families may be necessary (Marchetti-Mercer & Cleaver, 2000). This information is also obtained from the client, and connecting lines may illustrate the flow of energy between these entities and the family system. For example, a local church or synagogue may provide spiritual and financial support to a family, so the genogram would have an arrow from this graphic representation to the genogram.

Because the genogram is co-constructed between the client and the counselor, it represents a constructivist approach to assessment and intervention within the counseling relationship. Historical, cultural, and multicultural factors affecting the client can be accounted for in the genogram. For instance, clients who were raised by single parents or by grandparents can create a genogram that represents this structure accurately. When creating and processing the genogram with clients, there may be a tendency to focus on behaviors and relationships that hinder the client in obtaining goals. It is essential to include both the individual's strengths and supports and the supports for the entire family that build resilience for coping with difficult circumstances (Taylor, Clement, & Ledet, 2013).

Although originally used in family counseling, the genogram currently is used with individual clients for a variety of reasons. The career genogram includes a diagram of the client's family members, their occupations, hobbies and interests, and training and educational experiences; this information helps in exploring the client's role models within the family system. The main purpose of the genogram process is to explore the family's influence on the client's career decision making. However, multicultural factors and the interaction of these factors with career-related factors also can be explored in counseling.

Economically Disadvantaged Individuals and Families

One significant cultural and contextual factor that affects the client's career decision making is economic status. Although there is a wide range of economic circumstances and influences for individuals, this chapter focuses on those who are economically disadvantaged and those experiencing poverty. Viewed through a constructivist lens, "economically disadvantaged" can be defined in many different ways; however, it is best viewed through the lens of the person's own experiences and perceptions. Pressley and Sifford (2012) reported that "poverty is typically defined by income or to what extent fundamental needs (i.e., food, water, clothing, shelter) and access to critical services (i.e., health care, education) are available" (p. 36). It is a persistent myth that only nonworking individuals meet the criteria for poverty, as many working families are below the poverty level and are considered *working poor*.

In the United States, meritocracy—the perception that all individuals have opportunities to achieve the American dream if they work hard enough (Levine, 2006)—is a questionable philosophy when economic factors are considered. Public assistance benefits rarely move families above the poverty line, and more than half of the families eligible for public assistance fail to enroll in public assistance programs because of the stigma of receiving benefits (Bean & Mattingly, 2011; McConnell & Ohls, 2002). These factors contribute to perpetual unemployment as well as to low educational achievement. Although there are increasing opportunities for first-generation college students to attend college, students from impoverished families are at risk for higher rates of anxiety and depression (Barratt, 2011). This may be related to the self-imposed pressure to do well for the "family" and the challenges of working to supplement financial aid and commuting to school. Cementing these emotions is the additional layer of feelings of isolation, embarrassment, and not belonging that are consistent with being a first-generation college student. The few first-generation college students who complete degrees typically do not return to their family homes because of a lack of job opportunities. Therefore, the community and environments of their families of origin go unchanged, and economic disadvantage continues.

The working poor have few if any opportunities to implement their interests, values, and abilities in their work lives (Blustein, 2008; Fouad & Brown, 2000; Navarro, Flores, & Worthington, 2007; Sachs, 2005). In essence, the chances for an individual to implement his or her self-concept or vocational identity may be nonexistent due to a lack of freedom of choice, access to education and training, or opportunities for self-expression in the work environment (Blustein, Coutinho, Murphy, Backus, & Catraio, 2011). Hence, traditional career choice and development approaches to career counseling may not be applicable with this population where *work* includes efforts of labor to care for families and *career* is a privileged subset of work in which vocational identity and self-concept are integral factors. Career counseling with economically disadvantaged clients should include exploration of the client's resources and barriers early in the counseling process, assistance in accessing resources, enhancement of clients' work-based and academic skills, facilitation of empowerment, and an examination of how "internalizations of social barriers affect the ways in which individuals experience themselves in relation to the world of work" (Blustein et al., 2011, p. 225).

A Constructivist Lens on the Use of Career Genograms

Due to these possible internalizations—the taking of ownership of the social barriers that have led to or maintained a status of being economically disadvantaged—externalizing problems identified in the construction of a genogram can promote new understandings of the context of those problems (Sexton & Cheney, 2001). Identifying possible resources and strengths in the genogram can give clients the impetus for changes related to vocational identity and empower them to seek opportunities they did not perceive prior to constructing and processing the genogram.

There are some additional considerations for using the genogram with economically disadvantaged clients. First, clients may have limited information about career interests, values, attitudes, or roles of their family members if there have been limited work or educational opportunities and experiences. The counselor may want to construct the genogram with several family members present to explore these factors and how they influence the client. Second, the client may be defensive about his or her economic circumstances. The counselor needs to examine his or her own biases and assumptions about individuals who are in poverty or are economically disadvantaged when constructing questions to guide the genogram process. Third, the client may present with resistance to new ideas constructed from the genogram information. For example, issues related to power and hierarchy in family relationships and gender roles may play a significant part in the client's vocational identity or self-concept. In a genogram, these hierarchies may become obvious as words and descriptors are written on the diagram. Counselors need to be aware that adequate time should be provided for the client to absorb and process this information. Finally, counselors need to monitor clients for possible anxiety, depression, and other mental health issues that may be contributing to unemployment. Appropriate assessment and intervention should be incorporated into the counseling relationship. The case study that follows illustrates use of the genogram in career counseling with an economically disadvantaged client.

The Case of Marisa

Marisa is 26 and lives in Jackson, Mississippi, with her three children, ages 4, 6, and 8. She met her husband, Brad, while she was in high school, and they married when she was 18 years old, shortly after finding out that she was pregnant with their first child. Marisa never graduated from high school. Brad went to work with Marisa's father at a local steel manufacturing plant. Brad earned enough to pay rent and utilities for their small apartment, but they also received some government assistance for food. They could not afford child care, so Marisa stayed at home to take care of the children.

After their youngest child was born, Brad and Marisa began having marital problems. Because of his short temper, Brad would easily become overwhelmed and frustrated with the children. Brad expected the house to be clean and dinner to be cooked when he got home from work. When this didn't happen, he often became enraged and withdrew from his family by staying out all night. Marisa became depressed and withdrew from her friends and family.

Brad was recently laid off from the steel manufacturing plant, and he has sought work in neighboring towns. The tension has increased significantly in the home with Marisa and Brad arguing incessantly. During an argument one evening, Brad left the home. He has not been seen in a month, and the rumor in the community is that he has left town.

Because of financial circumstances, Marisa and her children are living with her parents temporarily. Her mother and father have been married for 34 years and have a marriage similar to Marisa and Brad's. Her mother and father married young, and her mother never worked. Her father was unengaged with Marisa and her sisters but provided financially for the family. Marisa's father also blames her for Brad leaving town and putting the family in desperate financial circumstances. He has demanded that she and her family find a place to live within the next month.

Marisa is receiving government assistance for food but not for living expenses. She is seeking full-time employment, but other than a job at a local diner in high school she has never been employed. She is concerned that she will not be able to provide for her family because of her lack of education, employment experience, and resources.

Based on the information in Marisa's story, several issues complicate this client's needs. This is not unique in career counseling and indicates a need for counselors to be knowledgeable of a wide range of resources that can be offered to clients. The career genogram is a useful resource, as it offers a way to assess not only the needs of clients but the human resources available to them. This section illustrates the use of a career genogram with Marisa, an economically disadvantaged client, and includes introducing the genogram, co-constructing the genogram, implementing the genogram as part of career awareness and decision making, assessing cultural considerations, and building on the client's strengths.

Introducing the Career Genogram

Marisa's main goal of obtaining full-time employment is a focus that should be kept in mind when explaining the purpose of creating a career genogram. The counselor can also explain how many career-related decisions are influenced by family views and economic circumstances (Chope,

2005). By examining work-related and educational patterns in her family, Marisa may be able to recognize her personal work-related interests and future career goals. The counselor should also explain to Marisa that they will explore the roles, behaviors, and attitudes of family members and how they could possibly influence her decision making about work and educational opportunities. Marisa will need to know that the counselor will be asking a lot of questions about her family, including information about her parents and grandparents. The process of creating the actual genogram may consist of several counseling sessions, with modifications to the genogram being made in future sessions if needed. Thus, this process can be an important aspect of rapport and trust building in the relationship. For Marisa, who may believe that community resources such as counseling cannot be relied upon, building trust may take additional time and could be met with resistance initially. Being mindful of this, the counselor should be direct in communicating with Marisa and be consistent in providing follow-up to their sessions.

Before the actual construction of the genogram diagram, Chope (2005) suggested creating a chart of the information for each generation of the client's family members on both parents' side of the family, including grandparents, aunts and uncles, cousins, parents/stepparents, and siblings. Although different types of information can be collected for genograms, collection of information should be tailored for the specific counseling purpose. In Marisa's case, the purpose is for career counseling. Basic information for the career genogram can include names, ages, deaths, significant illnesses (including mental health issues), educational levels, and work/career roles. Once this information is collected, the foundation of the career genogram can be constructed. The counselor needs to explain the symbols used (i.e., circles, squares) and the meaning of the lines connecting the symbols (i.e., relationships). This should be an interactive process with Marisa as she provides input on the types of relationships among the family members. Figure 11.1 depicts Marisa's career genogram and should be referred to in the next section regarding implementation of the genogram in career counseling.

Implementing the Career Genogram Process With Marisa

Although Marisa presents with a typical nuclear family, currently she is separated from her husband (as depicted by the single slash mark in the line connecting their symbols in the genogram). Nonnuclear families also can be depicted using similar symbols and lines, but these relationships may require additional comments on the genogram. Genograms can be constructed using a number of creative methods. In addition to the traditional use of symbols and lines, genograms can be drawn with different colors and symbols, shapes, and connections (Gibson, 2005). Pictures of the family can be drawn or pasted into a pictorial depiction of a genogram. The key to these creative symbols and connective lines needs to be clearly communicated between client and counselor for processing to be successful. In this case study, a traditional genogram format was

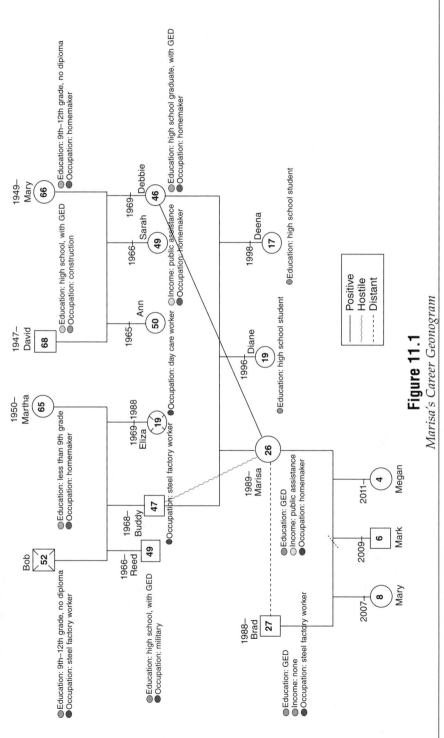

Figure 11.1

Marisa's Career Geonogram

Note. GED = general educational diploma.

used with symbols and connecting lines typical of standard genogram formats. Figure 11.1 was created using an online genogram software program that can be used to create both genograms and ecomaps (www. genogramanalytics.com/).

Once the basic information about family members, occupations, and educational levels is collected with Marisa, the counselor diagrams the three generations of adult family members and Marisa's nuclear family with her estranged husband and three children. Marisa is asked to examine the genogram and make corrections as necessary, and the counselor then asks her the following open-ended questions to elicit more information about the influence of Marisa's family on her occupational and educational decision making:

- What are the educational patterns depicted in your family?
- What work or occupational patterns are represented in your family?
- Which educational pattern do you identify with the most? Share more about that.
- Which work or occupational pattern do you identify with the most? Share more about that.
- Of all your family members, whom do you identify with the most? Share more about that.
- Who, in the family, has had the most influence on your educational choices? Share more about that.
- Who, in the family, has had the most influence on your occupational choices? Share more about that.
- What values are/were most important to your family?

Examining Marisa's Genogram
As depicted in the conversation with Marisa that follows, the roles of men and women emerged and led to additional questions about traditional and changing expectations:

Counselor: Marisa, based on what you have reported so far, it looks like your family has always lived and worked in this area. What do you recognize as the work patterns of either the men or the women?
Marisa: Now that I look at it, it looks like most of the women only work at home, except my sister, and that is only recent.
Counselor: What do you think about that?
Marisa: Well, that's the way it always happened. Someone had to cook, clean, and take of the children. We didn't have anyone to take care of the children to go work somewhere else.
Counselor: Do you think this was the expectation for the females in your family—to stay at home and take care of home and family?
Marisa: I guess so . . . but there were not a lot of other options. Sometimes my sisters and I would talk about doing other things when we were in high school, but we didn't know how we could do them. Mama and Daddy would talk about us getting married and starting our own families, so I guess we were expected to do that. But now with the mill closing, it looks like even the men are going to need to learn some new skills.

Marisa's responses to these questions presented a picture of family in which the roles of women were to support the male breadwinners. All of the family members depicted in the genogram had lived in the same community all of their lives, and many of the males worked at the local steel factory. The steel factory was the biggest employer in the community but recently had begun to decline in business. The majority of employees were male and earned minimum wage. With few other work opportunities available, education was less valued, and neither male nor female family members pursued further education or training after high school.

With the decline in the steel factory business, other businesses that employ both male and female workers equally have moved into the community. However, the steel factory workers who have been laid off need additional training and at least a general educational diploma to be hired. Female workers interested in these opportunities also need to meet educational and training requirements. When asked about these opportunities, Marisa reported the following:

Counselor: What do these new businesses mean for you and your family?
Marisa: I hope some of my family can get a job.
Counselor: Would that include you, as well?
Marisa: I guess so. I don't think I have the skills needed to work these new jobs, but maybe I could take care of the workers' children.
Counselor: I know that you have your own children to take care of, but do you enjoy being around children most of the day?
Marisa: I truly do. I'm already getting a little sad about my youngest one going to kindergarten next year. I love seeing their faces light up when they learn something new.
Counselor: It sounds like you would do a great job providing this service.

Although Marisa wasn't interested in the new jobs that were typical for the new companies and businesses in the area, she was interested in providing child care to those who needed it. This was consistent with her description of Aunt Ann as the family member she identifies with most for both educational and occupational aspirations. Marisa reported enjoying her children and her nieces and nephews (not depicted in Figure 11.1). When asked if she would want to be employed as a child care worker, she reported that she would want to do that but is concerned that her lack of education and training will prevent this from occurring. Financially, she is not able to reconcile how she can afford to work and take care of her own children. Marisa also reports feeling "in limbo" in her relationship with her estranged husband.

Cultural Considerations in Marisa's Assessment
In taking a constructivist approach to working through Marisa's concerns with her, it is important for the counselor to help Marisa process these concerns in a cultural context:

Counselor: How do you think the economy in this community has contributed to your occupational/educational aspirations?

Marisa: I think because I grew up within a community that had a harder economy, it made me and my family believe there was no use to think about other options like more training and education. Basically, you work where you live. Everyone did it, so I did too!

Counselor: That's very understandable, but it looks like the opportunities in your community are changing. Although the role of the women in your family as the person taking care of home and family hasn't changed, the steel mill closure has made changes for several of the men in the family. With the men not working or leaving the community to take another job, what has this meant for you and the other women who have been at home?

Marisa: It has been more stressful, and the kids know this too! We need more help getting food, and we had to ask the local community center for help with presents for the children during the holidays. A lot of us [women] have talked about getting jobs outside of the home, but we didn't know who would take care of the kids or what to do about transportation to the jobs.

Counselor: These sound like legitimate concerns, but ones that several of you have thought about due to these changing circumstances. Would you consider working in a child care job, like your aunt, if some of these concerns could be addressed?

Marisa: Yes, I think I would like that, and it would help our family at the same time.

The counselor asked Marisa several questions to explore how she assessed the effect of the economic circumstances of the community on her family, as well as her readiness to explore work options and address challenges with those options. Through the process of discussing Marisa's responses to these questions, the counselor is able to externalize what Marisa reported as her issues to those that were occurring for many of the women in her family (and community) over several generations. This normalized Marisa's prior decisions about education and work. Marisa recognized that her aunt Ann had observed some of the changes in the economy 2 years ago and had attended a special training program to prepare her to work in child care. In essence, her aunt Ann had become the exception to the pattern of homemaker with minimum education or occupational training and could be considered a resource if Marisa wanted to pursue the same type of training.

Additional resources for Marisa included her parents, who were allowing her and her children to stay in their home until Marisa could achieve some level of stability. Although her father was perceived as being angry with Marisa, processing the genogram, the roles of males in the family, and the changing economics in the community allowed Marisa to realize that her father may be frustrated and worried about his family. This could be true for Marisa's husband also. This could not be confirmed without their reports, but it provided Marisa with alternative perceptions about her situation and how these perceptions can influence her decision making. Marisa's mother was reported to be a positive resource, as she volunteered to take care of Marisa's children while Marisa was in counseling sessions and pursuing employment opportunities. Because the steel factory was in the process of limiting its business, the factory owners were offering career services for employees and employee partners. These included career counseling, additional education, and training opportunities. This was the main reason Marisa received career counseling at this time.

Finally, Marisa's strengths were reflected to her as important resources. Despite being left by her husband to provide for her children, Marisa demonstrated resilience in pursuing career counseling and applying for public assistance. In her family, only Marisa's aunt Sarah received public assistance, which represented failure based on her family's transmitted values. In essence, her family had internalized the use of public assistance as embarrassing and had transmitted that stigmatizing message throughout the generations. When seeking these resources was reframed by the counselor as a strength and part of her resilience, Marisa reported that she had never perceived public assistance as anything but something shameful. With her desire to seek additional training to become a child care worker and also to apply for and receive public assistance, she was breaking several family behavior patterns. To do this took a lot of strength and resilience, characteristics that the counselor credited to Marisa (Bimrose & Hearne, 2012).

Through the genogram process, the counselor was able to explore Marisa's educational and occupational family patterns, behaviors, and roles. These were put in the cultural/economic context of the community in which Marisa's family lived and was planning to stay. By externalizing these problems, the counselor helped Marisa develop new perceptions of her issues and goals for the future, and by recognizing her strengths and the resources available to her, Marisa was able to develop a sense of self as a worker and provider for her family. See Table 11.1 for an application guide.

Conclusion

Although traditional career theory has provided counselors with a greater understanding of the role of "self" in career goal setting and decision making, those approaches do not integrate multicultural contexts adequately. For clients who are economically disadvantaged, the privilege of developing a "career self" is often not experienced. Therefore, counselors need a mechanism with which to assess and explore the systemic and cultural influences on decisions related to work and education to provide appropriate career counseling. The career genogram is one tool that integrates clients' perceptions about those influences into career counseling that matches their needs.

Table 11.1
Practical Application Guide

Topic	Using the Genogram for Career Assessment and Intervention
General goals and purposes	1. Obtain information on the career and educational influences of those whom client considers family/support. 2. Explore connection between familial career/educational history to client's current career/educational issues. 3. Explore systemic/cultural influence to presenting career issue. 4. Explore systemic/cultural influence to resolving presenting career issue.
Applicable modality	Individual, dyadic, family, small-group, and large-group/classroom counseling
Applicable counselor settings	Couples/family, school, college and student development, career, mental health and community agency, private practice
Recommended time to complete	If genogram is completed outside of session, then fewer counseling sessions will be warranted. Typically, two to three sessions are needed to create and discuss genogram in counseling. It also can be revisited in subsequent counseling sessions.
Materials/equipment needed	Paper, pencil, pen, crayons. Computer versions are available, and pictures from magazines and client can be utilized.
Step-by-step outline of the process	1. Explain purpose and process of genogram with client. 2. Gather information about education, occupations, roles of family members across at least three generations. This should be a time for rapport building. 3. Co-construct actual diagram of the genogram with client. 4. Ask and discuss process questions with client. 5. Externalize client's career issues in cultural and economic contexts, as applicable. 6. Examine exceptions, in family, that can promote alternative thinking and perceptions about current situation. 7. Review client strengths and available human and physical resources to aid in decision making and goal attainment. 8. Follow up with client on goal achievement and resource needs.

Utilizing the career genogram as a constructivist counseling approach encourages clients to be the authors of their own stories. Issues related to clients' circumstances and choices can be acknowledged, and problems can be externalized so that clients can create solutions without being mired in shame, guilt, anger, or frustration. The genogram also provides a blueprint for examining family patterns, exceptions to those patterns, and resources that can be used in career goal setting and decision making within the context of economic challenges.

Recommended Resources

Beauregard, T. A. (2007). Family influences on the career life cycle. In M. Ozbilgin & A. Malach-Pines (Eds.), *Career choice in management and entrepreneurship: A research companion* (pp. 101–126). Cheltenham, England: Edward Elgar. Retrieved from http://eprints.lse.ac.uk/3320/1/Family_influences_on_the_career_life_cycle_%28LSERO%29.pdf

Benefits.gov. (n.d.). *Your path to government benefits.* Retrieved from http://www.benefits.gov

Family, Career and Community Leaders of America, Inc. (2014). *Career family tree worksheet.* Retrieved from http://breitlinks.com/careers/career_pdfs/familytreews.pdf

GenogramAnalytics [Online computer software]. Retrieved from http://www.genogramanalytics.com/

Johnson, C. (2010). *Using the family tree of careers: Branching out with others!* Retrieved from http://www.ncda.org/aws/NCDA/pt/sd/news_article/37317/_PARENT/layout_details_cc/false

References

Barratt, W. (2011). *Social class on campus: Theories and manifestations.* Sterling, VA: Stylus.

Bean, J. A., & Mattingly, M. J. (2011). *More than one in ten American households relies on supplemental nutrition assistance program benefits* (Issue Brief No. 20). Durham, NH: The Carsey Institute.

Bimrose, J., & Hearne, L. (2012). Resilience and career adaptability: Qualitative studies of adult career counseling. *Journal of Vocational Behavior, 81,* 338–344. doi:10.1016/j.jvb.2012.08.002

Blustein, D. L. (2008). The role of work in psychological health and well-being: A conceptual, historical, and public policy perspective. *American Psychologist, 63,* 228–240. doi:10.1037/0003-066X.63.4.228

Blustein, D. L., Coutinho, M. T. N., Murphy, K. A., Backus, F., & Catraio, C. (2011). Self and social class in career theory and practice. In P. J. Hartung & L. M. Subich (Eds.), *Developing self in work and career: Concepts, cases, and contexts* (pp. 213–229). Washington, DC: American Psychological Association. doi:10.1037/12348-013

Chope, R. C. (2005). Qualitatively assessing family influence in career decision making. *Journal of Career Assessment, 13,* 395–414. doi:10.1016/j.jvb.2012.08.002

Churilla, A. (2008, Summer). *Urban and rural children experience similar rates of low-income and poverty* (Issue Brief No. 2). Retrieved from http://www.carseyinstitute.unh.edu/IB_UrbanRuralChildren08.pdf

Fouad, N. A., & Brown, M. T. (2000). The role of race and class in development: Implications for counseling psychology. In S. D. Brown & R. W. Lent (Eds.), *Handbook of counseling psychology* (3rd ed., pp. 379–408). New York, NY: Routledge.

Gibson, D. M. (2005). The use of genograms in career counseling with elementary, middle, and high school students. *The Career Development Quarterly, 53,* 353–363. doi:10.1016/j.jvb.2012.08.002

Kerr, M. E., & Bowen, M. (1988). *Family evaluation: An approach based on Bowen theory.* New York, NY: Norton.

Levine, R. (Ed.). (2006). *Social class and stratification: Classic statements and theoretical debates* (2nd ed.). Lanham, MD: Rowman & Littlefield.

Malott, K. M., & Magnuson, S. (2004). Using genograms to facilitate undergraduate students' career development: A group model. *The Career Development Quarterly, 53,* 178–187.

Marchetti-Mercer, M. C., & Cleaver, G. (2000). Genograms and family sculpting: An aid to cross-cultural understanding in the training of psychology students in South Africa. *The Counseling Psychologist, 28,* 61–80.

McConnell, S., & Ohls, J. (2002). Food stamps in rural America: Special issues and common themes. In B. A. Weber, G. J. Duncan, & L. A. Whitener (Eds.), *Rural dimensions of welfare reform* (pp. 413–432). Kalamazoo, MI: Upjohn Institute.

McGoldrick, M., Gerson, R., & Petry, S. (2008). *Genograms: Assessment and intervention* (3rd ed.). New York, NY: Norton & Norton.

Navarro, R. L., Flores, L. Y., & Worthington, R. L. (2007). Mexican American middle school students' goal intentions in mathematics and science: A test of social cognitive career theory. *Journal of Counseling Psychology, 54,* 320–335. doi:10.1087/0022-0167.54.3.320

Pressley, C., & Sifford, A. (2012). Poverty: Urban and rural. In D. C. Sturm & D. M. Gibson (Eds.), *Social class and the helping professions: A clinician's guide to navigating the landscape of class in America* (pp. 35–50). New York, NY: Routledge.

Sachs, J. D. (2005). *The end of poverty.* New York, NY: Penguin Press.

Sexton, E., & Cheney, C. O. (2001, Fall). The use of genograms with students with emotional and behavioral disorders. *Beyond Behavior,* 27–29.

Taylor, E. R., Clement, M., & Ledet, G. (2013). Postmodern and alternative approaches in genogram use with children and adolescents. *Journal of Creativity in Mental Health, 8,* 278–292.

U.S. Department of Labor. (2014). *Updated data for persons defined as economically disadvantaged youth and adults.* Retrieved from http://www.doleta.gov/budget/disadvantagedYouthAdults.cfm

Using Life Role Analysis for Career Assessment and Intervention With a Transgender Client

Varunee Faii Sangganjanavanich and Jessica A. Headley

As society becomes increasingly diverse, so too does the world of work. In recognition of these cultural shifts, multiculturalism and diversity have been widely accepted as an integral part of career development for the past two decades. Professional and ethical standards require career development researchers and practitioners to understand multicultural and diversity issues and to utilize culturally infused approaches in their work with clients from diverse backgrounds. In the career development literature, more and more attention has been paid to marginalized populations in need of counseling services, including sexual minorities such as transgender individuals.

Transgender individuals are underrepresented in the career development literature, particularly in career assessment. Despite the growing demand to deliver comprehensive career services to this population, career practitioners are ill prepared (Dispenza, Watson, Chung, & Brack, 2012; Pepper & Lorah, 2008; Sangganjanavanich & Headley, 2013). To provide effective services, it is necessary for career practitioners to understand the lived experiences of transgender clients and to be knowledgeable of affirmative assessment practices that address this aim. Traditional standardized career assessments may not be applicable to transgender individuals because of gender biases and stereotypes. Qualitative career assessments provide an opportunity for transgender individuals to express their unique career development needs and help to situate their lived experiences within a complex sociopolitical context. As an affirmative, qualitative assessment, Life Role Analysis is an ideal tool for counseling transgender clients who present with issues related to career development.

In this chapter, we describe career developmental needs pertaining to transgender individuals. We also discuss complexities in career development that transgender individuals experience and current career development practice for these individuals within a sociopolitical context. Multicultural considerations in working with transgender clients also are considered. The case study illustrates how Life Role Analysis can be implemented with a transgender client.

Life Role Analysis

From the 1940s to the 1990s career counseling assessment relied heavily on traditional, standardized approaches that focused on human traits, interests, or development (Sharf, 2010). Although standardized approaches have several benefits, they often lack attention to individuality. Results of these approaches rely heavily on an individual's comparison to a norm group instead of on meaning derived from personal experiences situated in a particular sociopolitical and cultural context. Influenced by a postmodern framework, constructivist career development approaches emerged in response to the unique needs of individuals from diverse backgrounds in the ever-changing world of work. Constructivist approaches introduce a new paradigm to the field of career development, addressing the issues of subjectivity and complexity within one's career development rather than determining one's definite career path. Constructivist career theorists (e.g., Brott, 2004, 2005; Peavy, 1997; Savickas, 1997) have embraced the idea of interconnectedness among one's life roles, belief system, and culture in conceptualizing career development across the life span. Constructivist interventions used during the assessment process help individuals unfold their life stories as they are connected to their career development and work toward constructing, or narrating, a meaningful and desirable chapter for the future. An individual's perceptions of events and relationships situated in the past and present are central to this process. Unlike with traditional approaches, the client is treated as an expert and assumes an active role in career counseling.

Life Role Analysis is one of several postmodern career assessments and interventions based on the influence of early works by theorists from various approaches (e.g., Adlerian therapy, reality therapy, and existential philosophy) who stressed the importance, and arguably the necessity, of engaging in various life roles in order to experience personal and relational wellness (for a further discussion, see Brott, 2005). In the field of career development, theorists such as Donald Super have paid particular attention to how life roles influence one's career interests, experiences, and trajectory in the world of work. Nine roles identified in Super's (1990) conceptual model of life roles across the life span, referred to as the *life rainbow*, include child, student, leisurite, citizen, worker, spouse, homemaker, parent, and pensioner (see Sharf, 2010, for further details). An individual may engage in multiple roles at the same time or transition from one role to another depending on personal and environmental influences.

Life Role Analysis acknowledges the complex and dynamic nature of life roles and empowers clients to examine and reexamine how life roles in various domains (e.g., family, community, and work) influence their career development (Brott, 2005) and personal wellness. Constructivist approaches to career counseling are well suited to incorporating life roles in the client's formulation of a subjective narrative frame of reference (Brott, 2005). With increased meaning comes an opportunity for individuals to actively create a narrative for the future that enriches their personal and career development. The creation of a future narrative involves an understanding of how various life roles are interconnected and, importantly, how these connections can be strengthened to promote wellness. One technique to uncover these connections, as discussed by Gysbers (2006), is to work with a client to visually represent the dynamics and influences of life roles, life settings, and life events using the following steps:

- Draw three separate circles to represent different developmental periods in the past, present, and future (e.g., 10 years ago, today, and next year).
- Within these circles, the client indicates the salience of life roles held at the time by drawing circles that may touch, overlap, or be separated by space (to represent relationship dynamics), with larger circles indicating more role salience.
- Depending on the presenting issue, it may be more beneficial for a client to focus on one or two developmental periods.

An additional technique, discussed by Brott (2005), is to identify the costs and benefits of messages received, and often internalized, from parental figures and the broader culture (e.g., family, community, and media) about various life roles and to rework oppressive messages to positively influence the client's preferred future narrative. Each future narrative is unique: Some individuals may desire to work on balancing various life roles (e.g., parent and worker); others may desire to open up, reduce, or close opportunities for engagement in roles.

Career Concerns and Needs of Transgender Individuals

Transgender individuals face challenges in multiple life areas, including career development (Sangganjanavanich, 2009). In the world of work, gender incongruence and discomfort can be linked to one's unique career concerns and needs on levels ranging from individual (e.g., gender identification), to interpersonal (e.g., rejection from coworkers), to organizational (e.g., employment discrimination based on gender expression). For example, a common issue faced by transgender employees is experiencing the use of incorrect pronouns (e.g., "she" instead of "he") in daily interactions and documentation by coworkers and supervisors. This situation may lead to confusion, anger, and fear, not only for transgender employees but also for other individuals in the work environment, which may complicate interpersonal relationships among them. According to Barclay and Scott (2006), when individuals have gender expression that is different from cultural norms, they are likely to experience social marginalization and ostracism. This, in turn, may create a larger scale impact on the organizational operation, affecting overall productivity (O'Neil, McWhirter, & Cerezo, 2008), policy development, and practice related to gender expression antidiscrimination (Transgender Law Center, 2012).

In addition to the aforementioned challenges, transgender individuals often are unable to access career development services that address their unique needs. Not only do career practitioners lack understanding of and preparedness for dealing with transgender issues (Pepper & Lorah, 2008; Sangganjanavanich & Headley, 2013), but traditional career services relying on standardized assessments present several dilemmas, including issues related to gender norming, gender stereotypes, and systematic oppression. Postmodern career assessments can be used to address these complex issues because they provide an opportunity for the client and the practitioner to explore how cultural factors influence the client's career development and trajectory.

Culture and Narrative With Transgender Individuals Through Life Role Analysis

Viewing the individual's life through a constructivist and holistic lens, Life Role Analysis can be effectively utilized when working with transgender individuals who present with career issues. In conjunction with exploring and honoring the relationship between one's identity and one's career aspirations within various life roles, this approach stresses the importance of understanding the ways in which sociopolitical and cultural contexts influence an individual's career narrative. Accordingly, the career counselor's role is not to make assumptions but to assume an inquisitive stance and provide a space for individuals to share their unique stories (Brott, 2004). Through active collaboration, the counselor embraces an individual's story and helps her or him to identify themes that are constructed, deconstructed, and reconstructed throughout the assessment process.

As previously noted, transgender individuals present unique career concerns that too often are not adequately addressed through standardized assessments and traditional career development approaches. Life Role Analysis appears, for many reasons, to be an ideal career assessment and intervention when working with transgender individuals. First, like other qualitative career assessments, Life Role Analysis allows flexibility and fluidity in terms of individual characteristics and takes individuality and uniqueness into account when considering career developmental needs. Second, it permits transgender individuals to consider and examine the role of sociopolitical and cultural contexts that influence their career development. Lastly, clients assume an active role in the counseling process and have an opportunity to explore life and career complexities without value judgments from the counselor. To enhance understanding of how to implement Life Role Analysis with transgender clients, we present a case study of a transgender individual and discuss the case study in detail.

The Case of Sharon

Sharon is a middle-aged African American sales manager at an electronics store. She is a transgender woman who came out to her family and close friends, but not at the workplace. After a year of examining her gender transition options, she decided to come out at work a month ago. Reactions from the administration, coworkers, and employees were rather unpleasant. First, she found out that her name was removed from next year's promotion list within her company. Second, she received anonymous threatening notes on her desk almost every day when arriving at work. Third, she was asked to meet with the human resource director to "transition" to a new position where she would be taking orders from online customers.

For the past 3 weeks, Sharon has been working in her new position. She reported that she is unhappy with her new responsibilities and misses "the way things were" in her old position prior to coming out. In addition to thinking about finding new employment, Sharon also is contemplating changing her career. However, she is concerned that being a transgender woman will prevent her from obtaining new employment or being able to pursue further education and training. In particular, she fears losing the stable income and financial security that currently support her ex-spouse and two children. Sharon stated that she is seeking career counseling services to help her make good decisions for her professional future that will help her become more satisfied at work and improve her relationships with others.

Introducing Life Role Analysis to Clients

Prior to introducing Life Role Analysis to the client, it is important to help the client navigate issues surrounding gender transition (e.g., providing mental health referrals, role playing conducting a conversation with supervisors and coworkers, dealing with workplace discrimination). For instance, the career counselor can discuss Sharon's concerns related to workplace discrimination and its impact on her overall quality of life. The career counselor also can provide resources concerning workplace discrimination (see Recommended Resources). This may help address immediate concerns regarding gender transition in the workplace before utilizing Life Role Analysis as a career intervention.

As with other career assessments and interventions, it is important that the counselor assess Sharon's suitability and readiness for Life Role Analysis. Individuals who show a willingness to openly discuss concerns related to their career development, and are able to engage in a deeper discussion of how these concerns affect their lives, are good candidates for Life Role Analysis. Some clients are eager to engage in this assessment and intervention, but others may feel skeptical about the process or may find it challenging to analyze the ways in which their multiple life roles directly and indirectly influence their career development. To proactively address these issues, the counselor should demystify the purpose and process of Life Role Analysis and provide a safe and affirming space for clients to ask questions and express any concerns prior to implementation.

Implementation of Life Role Analysis

Following introduction of Life Role Analysis and Sharon's consent to use this approach, the counselor's next task is to invite Sharon to share her story. As previously discussed, numerous techniques can be utilized to achieve this goal. Drawing from the work of Gysbers (2006), we demonstrate the utility of a visual method that allows for client exploration, meaning making, and change:

- With the intention of visually representing the importance of life roles and their connections, the counselor invites the client to draw three circles on a blank paper to represent the past, present, and future. This step can be tailored to the unique needs of the client; for example, the counselor might ask the client to draw two circles (e.g., present and future) as appropriate to the presenting career concerns.
- Next, the counselor prompts the client to think about what life roles are important to him or her by providing a list of roles or asking the client a question.
- With those roles in mind, the client is asked to draw smaller circles for each of his or her roles within the larger circles.

Three considerations for the client are worth noting: (a) The bigger the circle, the more salient the role; (b) roles can overlap and touch to represent relationships; and (c) roles can change over time. When addressing these considerations, it is important for the counselor to encourage the client to use creativity when representing his or her life roles and their connections. Providing a client with the space to fully express his or her story is a crucial aspect of implementing a constructivist assessment and intervention. The following exchange between Sharon and the counselor occurred after Sharon finished drawing her visual representation of Life Role Analysis (see Figure 12.1):

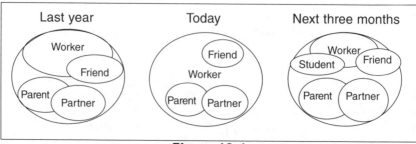

Figure 12.1

Life Role Analysis

Counselor: Tell me about your role analysis, based on your drawing.

Sharon: In the first circle [last year], I drew circles for parent, partner, friend, and worker. Being a worker was a really big part of my life, and most of my friends were from my department. Also, my ex-spouse and children were (and still are) big parts of my life. I was happy with the way things were.

Once the drawing is complete, the counselor inquires about the importance of Sharon's life roles and their connections. At this point, the following question can be asked: "How do you see the interconnectedness among these roles?" This part of the process allows Sharon to use her own words to describe the meaning and dynamics of roles, struggles and distress related to specific roles, and satisfactions and benefits related to specific roles.

Counselor: I notice overlaps between the role of worker and friend, and parent and partner. It seems that these roles are interconnected.

Sharon: Yes, that was the case. And the circles for parent and partner are the same size because I believe that my roles as a parent and partner are equally important to me. Currently, my worker role is much bigger. It is the entire circle! I am experiencing so many struggles as a result of coming out at work. I kind of expected to face some of these struggles. I just didn't know the extent to which these struggles would impact my life. I feel as though my feeling so consumed at work makes me emotionally unavailable for other parts of my life.

Throughout the storytelling process, the counselor may utilize questions that are specifically focused on career (e.g., "How do you think the poor relationship with your ex-spouse and children influences your satisfaction at work?") and how one's identity as a worker is related to personal well-being (e.g., "How have your struggles at work, like poor relationships with coworkers and institutional discrimination, affected your well-being?"). It is important to note that career and personal wellness are interrelated, as demonstrated below:

Counselor: I noticed that you added a student role in your circle for the future. And your other roles seem to change. I would really like to hear more about how you see your role as a worker and student relating to your relationships with family and friends.

Sharon: Becoming a student gives me an opportunity to prepare for a new job. If I am working toward change, I believe that I will be happier as I will be focusing on my future career goals and because of that, I can focus more on my relationships. My friend circle still overlaps with my worker circle, but not as much. It has been hard to lose some of my friendship here at work, but I am looking forward to meeting new people.

The counselor's next task is to facilitate Sharon's career-exploring and decision-making processes. In addition to providing space for Sharon to discuss the importance of life roles and their connections, Life Role Analysis can be used to set goals. To facilitate changes, it is important to note that the counselor should assist the client in setting realistic and attainable goals (e.g., time frame, means, resources) when contemplating the third circle (the future). The following dialogue between Sharon and the counselor is an example of how to help clients comprehend their goals:

> *Counselor:* Let's talk about your future roles for a bit. Do you have any career or personal goals in mind?
>
> *Sharon:* Yes, I need to identify steps to apply for a training program. I know I have to be done with the program before even thinking about applying for a job. I would also like to reconnect with my ex-spouse and children and to make sure I can become a part of their lives again.
>
> *Counselor:* I am curious how much you know about applying for and completing the training program.
>
> *Sharon:* I picked up a packet the other day and read through it. It told me the application process and things I would need. It also said I could complete the program within 6 months if I went full time.
>
> *Counselor:* How realistic a goal is it for you to complete the program within that time frame? And what are resources involved to complete the program?

The counselor can utilize Sharon's visual representation, and subsequent analysis, to spark additional opportunities for exploration and meaning making (e.g., examining the role of culture and how it shapes life roles and interactions with others). In addition, the visualization can be used to assess Sharon's progress throughout the counseling process (e.g., comparing the visualization to treatment goals). As Sharon unpacks her story from session to session, it is important to provide opportunities to update the visual representation that captures emerging desires and functioning in existing roles, or in new ones. See Table 12.1 for an application guide.

Conclusion

Life Role Analysis presents many advantages when working with transgender clients. Caution should be exercised when implementing this assessment and intervention. It is important that career practitioners create a safe and nonjudgmental therapeutic environment in which transgender individuals may fully explore different life roles within their context without feeling judged. Career practitioners need to be aware of the potential costs and benefits of using Life Role Analysis to provide effective services to transgender clients. Benefits of utilizing qualitative assessments include challenging passivity and empowering clients to assume an active role in counseling; fostering a cooperative and intimate therapeutic relationship that allows for mutuality and openness; emphasizing a more integrative, holistic, and developmental approach to conceptualizing and addressing client issues; and integrating adaptable and flexible techniques that meet

Table 12.1
Practical Application Guide

Topic	*Using Life Role Analysis for* *Career Assessment and Intervention*
General goals and purposes	1. Promote one's understanding of the relationship between personal wellness and career distress. 2. Explore the ways in which multiple identities and sociocultural and political context influence one's personal and career development. 3. Identify life and career themes that emerge during the analysis. 4. Describe how the emergent themes can be used to address one's career distress.
Applicable modality	Individual, dyadic, triadic, and group counseling
Applicable counselor settings	College/university career services, community agency, school, private practice
Recommended time to complete	Two to three sessions for individual counseling. More time is needed for other modalities.
Materials/equipment needed	Flip chart/poster-size paper, different color markers/crayons, adhesive tape, pictures (if applicable)
Step-by-step outline of the process	1. Introduce Life Role Analysis. 2. Invite client to create a visual representation of life roles using large circles to represent different time periods (e.g., past, present, future). 3. Prompt client to think about the importance of her or his life roles. 4. Allow client to utilize her or his creativity to visually represent her or his life roles using smaller circles (that are drawn inside the large circles from Step 2). 5. Inquire about life roles and their connections, with a particular focus on career development and personal wellness. 6. Facilitate client's career exploration and decision-making process. 7. Revisit and revise client's visual representation throughout the counseling process as needed.

the unique needs of the client (Goldman, 2011; Okacha, 1998). Despite these benefits, it has been noted that some clients and counselors may find the approach to be time consuming, labor intensive, and lacking in scientific rigor compared to standardized tools, and these concerns should be kept in mind (Goldman, 2011; Okacha, 1998).

It has been argued that utilizing qualitative assessments requires a counselor to be a multiculturally competent practitioner. Goldman (2011) explained that observational and interpretational skills are the basis for conceptualizing and addressing client issues. Competencies for working with transgender clients can be further developed by adhering to professional competencies and standards set forth by the profession (e.g., American Counseling Association, 2010; World Professional Association for Transgender Health, 2011), reviewing the extant literature, seeking consultation and supervision, and taking advantage of training and professional development opportunities. Although the central focus of this approach is on the client's unique life experiences, it is essential for career practitioners to have a solid foundation from which to contextualize the client's experiences.

Recommended Resources

Carroll, L., Gilroy, P. J., & Ryan, J. (2002). Counseling transgendered, transsexual, and gender-variant clients. *Journal of Counseling & Development, 80,* 131–139.

Chavez-Korell, S., & Johnson, L. T. (2010). Informing counselor training and competent counseling services through transgender narratives and the transgender community. *Journal of LBGT Issues in Counseling, 4,* 202–213.

National Center for Transgender Equality. (2014). *Employment discrimination and transgender people.* Retrieved from http://www.transequality.org/sites/default/files/docs/kyr/EmploymentKnowYourRights_July2014.pdf

Savickas, M. L. (1995). Constructivist counseling for career indecision. *The Career Development Quarterly, 43,* 363–373.

Savickas, M. L. (1997). Constructivist career counseling: Models and methods. In R. Neimeyer & G. Neimeyer (Eds.), *Advances in personal construct psychology* (Vol. 4, pp. 149–182). Greenwich, CT: JAI Press.

Transgender Law Center. (2013). *Model transgender employment policy: Negotiating for inclusive workplaces.* Retrieved from http://transgenderlawcenter.org/wp-content/uploads/2013/12/model-workplace-employment-policy-Updated.pdf

Transgender Law Center. (2015). *Workplace discrimination against lesbian, gay, bisexual, and transgender Americans.* Retrieved from http://transgenderlawcenter.org/wp-content/uploads/2015/03/TLC-testimony-USCCR-March-2015.pdf

References

American Counseling Association. (2010). American Counseling Association competencies for counseling with transgender clients. *Journal of LGBT Issues in Counseling, 4,* 135–159. doi:10.1080/15538605.2010.524839

Barclay, J. M., & Scott, L. J. (2006). Transsexuals and workplace diversity: A case of "change" management. *Personnel Review, 35,* 487–502. doi:10.1108/00483480610670625

Brott, P. E. (2004). Constructivist assessment in career counseling. *Journal of Career Development, 30,* 189–200.

Brott, P. E. (2005). A constructivist look at life roles. *The Career Development Quarterly, 54,* 138–149.

Dispenza, F., Watson, L. B., Chung, B., & Brack, G. (2012). Experience of career-related discrimination for female-to-male transgender persons: A qualitative study. *The Career Development Quarterly, 60,* 65–81.

Goldman, L. (2011). Qualitative assessment: An approach for counselors. *Journal of Counseling & Development, 60,* 616–621.

Gysbers, N. C. (2006). Using qualitative career assessments in career counseling with adults. *International Journal for Educational and Vocational Guidance, 6,* 95–108.

O'Neil, M. E., McWhirter, E. H., & Cerezo, A. (2008). Transgender identities and gender variance in vocational psychology: Recommendations for practice, social advocacy, and research. *Journal of Career Development, 34,* 286–308. doi:10.1177/0894845307311251

Okacha, A. A. G. (1998). Using qualitative appraisal strategies in career counseling. *Journal of Employment Counseling, 35,* 151–160.

Peavy, R. V. (1997). A constructive framework for career counseling. In T. L. Sexton & B. L. Griffin (Eds.), *Constructivist thinking in counseling practice, research, and training* (pp. 122–140). New York, NY: Teachers College.

Pepper, S. M., & Lorah, P. (2008). Career issues and workplace considerations for the transsexual community: Bridging a gap of knowledge for career counselors and mental health care providers. *The Career Development Quarterly, 56,* 330–343.

Sangganjanavanich, V. F. (2009). Career development practitioners as advocates for transgender individuals: Understanding gender transition. *Journal of Employment Counseling, 46,* 128–135. doi:10.1002/j.2161-1920.2009.tb00075.x

Sangganjanavanich, V. F., & Headley, J. A. (2013). Facilitating career development concerns of gender transitioning individuals: Professional standards and competencies. *The Career Development Quarterly, 61,* 354–366. doi:10.1002/j.2161-0045.2013.00061.x

Savickas, M. L. (1997). Constructivist career counseling: Models and methods. In R. Neimeyer & G. Neimeyer (Eds.), *Advances in personal construct psychology* (Vol. 4, pp. 149–182). Greenwich, CT: JAI Press.

Sharf, R. S. (2010). *Applying career development theory to counseling* (5th ed.). Belmont, CA: Brooks/Cole, Cengage Learning.

Super, D. E. (1990). A life-span, life-space approach to career development. In D. Brown & L. Brooks (Eds.), *Career choice and development* (2nd ed., pp. 197–261). San Francisco, CA: Jossey-Bass.

Transgender Law Center. (2012). *Groundbreaking! Federal agency rules transgender employees protected by sex discrimination law.* Retrieved from http://transgenderlawcenter.org/ cms/blogs/552-24

World Professional Association for Transgender Health. (2011). *Standards of care for the health of transsexual, transgender, and gender nonconforming people* (7th version). Retrieved from http://www.wpath.org/documents/Standards%20of%20Care% 20V7%20-%202011%20WPATH.pdf

Chapter 13

Using Personal Construct Psychology: Constructing a Career With an Asian American Client

Jennifer M. Taylor

In this chapter, I explore personal construct psychology (PCP) as an individualized approach to meeting the career exploration needs of Chen, an Asian American female client. Following a brief explanation of the theoretical underpinnings of PCP relevant to career counseling within multicultural contexts, I focus on a PCP intervention: repertory grids or reptests. Then I take a trip to our career counseling session with Chen and examine the use of PCP with Chen as our case study. Finally, I explore the benefits of PCP in career counseling and discuss practical and critical multicultural considerations when using PCP.

PCP was conceptualized 60 years ago as a comprehensive theory of personality development. It is a theory that has withstood the test of time and retains contemporary appeal. PCP has been expanded to many other domains, including business, education, and marketing. PCP is grounded in the notion that each individual has a personal worldview that helps create his or her reality. This worldview is made up of a multitude of constructs (perceptions) that help us identify ways in which some things are similar to, but distinct from, others (Bannister & Mair, 1968). A construct is a personally chosen word or phrase that describes the essence of a chosen term. These constructs are created as internal theories of reality and as tools that help people understand and interpret their experiences and the world in which they live.

The tenets of the theory are grounded in the notion that each person is an "incipient scientist" who creates constructs or hypotheses about the world around him or her in an effort to improve his or her capability of predicting the future (Kelly, 1955). For example, a counselor might view some clients as enmeshed with their families, and other clients may be viewed as avoidant with their families (Fukuyama & Neimeyer, 1985). These worldviews will influence the counselor's predictions about, and course of treatment for, the client.

Outside of the counseling session, consistent with the scientific method, we test our constructs in our everyday life and, if necessary, constructs are revised over time as new information is obtained. Furthermore, constructs are bipolar—there are two ends to each dimension—and not just conceptual; they represent dimensions of meaning and themes in people's lives.

To understand constructs and how individuals make sense of experiences, we must understand their dimensions of meaning. For example, to one person the construct "mother" may describe a range from nurturing to inattentive, whereas to another person "mother" might describe a range from responsible to irresponsible or authoritative to democratic. Constructs are personal, and the dimensions of meaning differ for each individual.

Within the career counseling context, PCP offers an individualized approach to investigating meanings people place on particular career paths and to exploring underlying values and interests. In relation to career counseling, a client may be confident or unsure about career paths, and this will influence the client's approach to decision making (Neimeyer, 1992). Kelly (1955) noted that a client's career choice "has far-reaching implications to one's approach to life; implications including much more than the assigned workaday duties and the size of the paycheck" (p. 747). In an effort to explore the personal meanings that clients place on career paths and how such constructs relate to their approach to life, repertory grids can be particularly useful.

What Are Repertory Grid Tests?

Although Role Construct Repertory Tests, or reptests, were not specifically designed for use in career counseling, Kelly (1955) alluded to the use of reptests for career choice exploration in his book. A reptest can be used as a technique for uncovering specific constructs. Kelly noted that a "vocational construct system" (p. 740) for the world of work is composed of bipolar constructs interconnected through a matrix of meaning (e.g., fast paced vs. slow paced, creative vs. conventional, high paying vs. low paying, and independent vs. team-oriented; Neimeyer, Marmarosh, Prichard, Leso, & Moore, 1992).

Reptests permit users to sort binary constructs into categories through a matrix grid format. In the simplest sense, a reptest is a decision matrix that involves several chosen components (e.g., careers) that are rated (or ranked) in relation to a variety of bipolar constructs (Neimeyer, 1989). This matrix can be used to explore salient interests, values, and skills within a wide variety of career paths. It is in exploring these contrasts that clients can gain greater clarity of their vocational values and interests in support of choosing a career. Reptests can be used to invite our clients to reflect on ways in which particular career paths, for example, share similarities and differences with other career paths.

The reptest involves two basic stages: (a) uncovering underlying constructs that are meaningful to the client and (b) discovering which career path honors the most salient constructs for the client. Within those two stages, attending to the cultural influences of constructs is vital, and understanding our own cultural biases and assumptions as counselors is equally important.

Attending to the Impact of Culture in a Reptest

Each client is a member of multiple cultural groups and may ascribe to different cultural groups to varying degrees. For example, a client may identify as an African American, atheist, gay, able-bodied male, but the client may most closely identify as an African American and, thus, the African American culture would be most salient to that client. Some clients may be more or less acculturated than others, so some components of their cultural identity may not influence their career decision making to the same extent as do other components of their cultural identity. The cultures to which clients most strongly identify play an important role in understanding their values. Reptests can be used to honor and explore workplace values consistent with, or discriminant from, the cultures to which our clients ascribe. Thus, in addition to their usefulness when exploring different career paths, reptests also can be used to help clients explore similarities and differences between values highly regarded in cultures ranging in personal relevance for the client.

As an example, reptests have been utilized to help counselors explore their knowledge and awareness of clients from diverse cultural groups (Fukuyama & Neimeyer, 1985). Utilizing the Cultural Attitudes Repertory Technique, counselors are invited to consider clients whom they have worked with from various cultural groups (the cultural groups are listed on the top row of the reptest). Counselors are then asked to consider how two of the groups are similar to each other but different from a third group during counseling. Those responses or constructs (e.g., individualistic vs. collectivistic) are included on the right side of the grid. After descriptive sets are formed, counselors are invited to rank the importance of each construct in cross-cultural counseling. Next, counselors place a positive or negative sign next to the bipolar constructs, indicating their general values or preferences in counseling. Finally, counselors place a corresponding positive or negative sign next to each of the grids that correspond with each of the cultural groups and constructs. The total number of pluses from each column (cultural group) is then divided by the total number of bipolar constructs to create a positivity percentage (Neimeyer & Neimeyer, 1981).

In addition, the reptest can be used to explore a client's perceived supports and barriers among different career paths while keeping the client's cultural identifications in mind. To use the reptest to examine salient cultural values, start by exploring the cultures with which your client identifies (e.g., gender, sexual orientation, socioeconomic status [SES], ethnic group, able bodied, religious/spiritual orientation). Through an extensive literature review, Wong and Yuen (2012) found these common values in the Taiwanese culture: (a) economic gains; (b) personal growth; (c) work/life balance, leisure, health, and convenience of work location; (d) opportunities for advancement; (e) positive work environment; (f) harmony at work and in personal life, and job security; (g) autonomy; (h) altruism; and (i) a sense of accomplishment/high self-esteem (see also Leuty & Hansen, 2011). Chen, the client in the case study, identifies as Taiwanese, but not all of these values may be true for Chen. To illustrate the influence of culture, we visit Chen, who describes herself as bisexual, female, high SES, Taiwanese, American, Christian.

The Case of Chen

Chen, a 20-year-old bisexual Taiwanese female undergraduate student, walks into my office for her first career counseling session and shares that she has been struggling to decide on a career path. She feels pressure from her parents to pursue a degree in law, but there is something about that path that just doesn't feel right to her. "I feel stuck . . . and I need your help," she tells me. I need a theory that helps Chen share her story and explore her sense of self as well as make sense of her interests, values, and skills and the influence that her culture has played in her career decision.

To help Chen uncover her interests, values, and skills, I use a reptest. Reptests can be conducted in a number of ways. The simplest way to conduct a reptest is to ask the client to consider ways in which the careers that the client is considering are similar to or different from each other. In the following example, I break down the general reptest into three more focused career tools, comparing and contrasting career paths based on Chen's interests, skills, and values.

Step 1: Define Salient Career Constructs

The reptest starts with a grid (see Table 13.1 and Table 13.2) and can be constructed using a pencil and paper or using a computer program, such as *WebGrid 5, FLEXIGRID*, or *EnquireWithin* (www.EnquireWithin.co.nz). For the purposes of this exercise, the reptest is demonstrated in a manner similar to a pencil and paper test.

Chen notes that she has considered pursuing an occupation as a lawyer, a professor, and an accountant, but she has also considered pursuing a career path that would not require formal education. Although she expresses concerns about what others would think about her dropping out of school, she shares that she has a love for animals and organic food and has considered farming as well. Given the diversity of her career interests, I begin by selecting two occupations and asking her, "In relation to your interests, do you see lawyer and professor as more similar or more different from each other?" Chen states that she sees them as "more similar." Now I ask

Chen, "In what ways are lawyer and professor similar to each other and different from either an accountant or a farmer?" Chen responds, "Well, a lawyer and a professor work inside, whereas a farmer works outside." Chen's first bipolar construct on this grid will be "works inside" versus "works outside." The two components of the bipolar construct are then placed on the first row of the last two columns in the grid in Table 13.1.

This process is then repeated, and Chen is prompted to continue comparing and contrasting four selected career paths until she has reached a threshold of comparisons that she feels has adequately described how the career paths compare and contrast with each other. Reptests can be composed of varying numbers of constructs, from just a few to hundreds of constructs. Weiner and Craighead (2010) noted that studies suggest that there tend to be diminishing returns after 15 to 20 constructs have been created.

If your client is having trouble deciding how two careers are similar to each other but different from a third, it is often helpful to provide prompts and encouragement. Landfield (1971) recommended that you urge your client to say anything that comes to his or her mind, without worrying about whether or not the responses are repetitive. If your client is struggling to come up with constructs, it may be helpful to remind your client that many people find the reptest to be challenging, particularly because it is something new. Other experts recommend prompting your client with something like, "I think I understand what you are saying, but just to be sure, please tell me again what you are thinking" or "Please tell me again how X and Y are similar to one another but different from Z" (Fransella, Bell, & Bannister, 2003). Typically, when clients are asked to repeat the two ends of a bipolar construct, they add greater specificity and preciseness to their constructs.

Step 2: Explore Preferences for Career Constructs

Once a list of constructs has been developed, I ask Chen, "When you consider working inside versus working outside, which option sounds more

Table 13.1
Repertory Grid Examining Interests

Lawyer	Professor	Accountant	Farmer		
–	–	–	+	+ Works outside	– Works inside
–	–	–	+	+ Works in a rural town	– Works in a big city
+	+	–	+	+ Set my own hours	– Work "regular" hours/clock in
–	–	–	+	+ Works in solitude	– Works with many people
–	–	–	+	+ Requires little formal education	– Requires a lot of formal education
1/4	1/4	0/5	5/0		

appealing to you?" (Note that I could explore Chen's skill preferences by asking, "When you consider a job that requires 'hands-on' skills versus one that does not require 'hands-on' skills, which would you prefer?" I could also explore Chen's value preferences by asking, "When you consider a job that is stable versus seasonal, which would you prefer?") The construct component that Chen prefers will be noted with a plus sign next to it (e.g., working outside), and the construct component Chen does not prefer will be given a minus sign (e.g., working inside). I then go down the list of constructs, asking Chen which of the two ends of the bipolar construct she would prefer, noting her responses with a positive or negative sign.

Step 3: Examine Each Career Path as Fulfilling Each Positive or Negative Construct

Next, Chen is asked to note which of the professions on the first row of the grid involve working inside (with a negative sign in the cell that corresponds with the occupation and the construct) or outside (with a positive sign in the corresponding cell). The same process is practiced with the other constructs: For example, Chen is asked to place a positive sign next to the career paths that involve working in a big city versus a rural town.

Alternatively, Chen could be asked to place a rating or ranking next to each of the career options (in relation to their fulfillment of a particular construct). The most common rating system involves a 5- or 7-point scale, but the scales can range from as little as 2 points (either the positive side of the construct "fits" for the career or it does not) or as many as 100 points or more.

For example (utilizing a 7-point Likert scale), Chen could be prompted, "Consider a rating scale, with +3 denoting a very positive rating of the fulfillment of your interests (or skills or values) and −3 denoting a very negative rating of the fulfillment of your interests (or skills or values). When you think about a career as a lawyer, professor, accountant, or farmer, do you think each career path would allow you to work outside very often (which would be reflected in a score of +3), inside very often (−3) or somewhere in between those two values?" Each answer is listed in the corresponding cell. If Chen stated, "I think a lawyer would work inside an office often but may be called to meet with people or investigate a scene outside of the office sometimes," Chen might give the cell that corresponds with the first column and the first construct row a "−2." The sign is negative because Chen has noted that she prefers working outside rather than inside.

One final alternative way to compare and contrast career options involves asking Chen to *rank*, rather than rate, each career path in relation to its fulfillment of various bipolar constructs. For example, Chen may be asked, "When considering careers that involve working outside versus working inside, please indicate which career involves working outside the most (with a score of 4) and working outside the least (or working inside the most; with a score of 1)." No matter which of these three processes is conducted (assigning a positive or negative sign, assigning a rating point value, or assigning a ranking score), the process is then repeated until all of the cells are filled in with either a positive or negative sign (or with a number ranking or number rating and sign). If rankings are chosen, they can be designated in two ways: (a) Each bipolar construct can be compared with the other bipolar constructs and ranked by the importance the client places on them, or (b) each career path can be ranked in relation to its fulfillment of each bipolar construct (in comparison to other careers on that same construct).

Step 4: Analyze the Results

An (optional) final stage involves formally scoring the instrument. The reptest can be scored in many ways, including both quantitatively and qualitatively. From a quantitative perspective, in the simplest sense, the positive and negative signs can be totaled under each column to uncover the alignment of each career path with the fulfillment of relevant constructs. The positive scores in each column also can be divided by the total number of constructs to create a positivity percentage for each career path. Alternatively, Landfield's (1983) Reptest Scoring Program and other computer scoring systems (including SPSS) can be used to score a reptest.

In exploring Chen's results, farming, for example, yields five positive ratings and no negative ratings with regard to Chen's interest areas (see Table 13.1), whereas accounting provides no positive ratings and five negative ratings with regard to her interest areas. It is important to remember that Chen's viewpoints are based on her own constructions about the world of work, her understanding of the skills required for various jobs, and her perceptions of the values provided by each career path. Although Chen's perceptions about careers may not necessarily represent reality, utilizing constructivism in career counseling is beneficial because it provides a window into the client's way of understanding the world and allows us to see the world through the client's lens (Neimeyer, 1992).

In fact, reptests can provide many insights for the client and the counselor. The counselor can use reptests as a means to facilitate Chen's reflection on her interests and values. For example, after completing the reptest, the client may be asked to look at the occupations with the highest ratings and those with the lowest ratings, and several reflective questions may be posed. Is Chen surprised by any of the results? In what ways does the reptest confirm, validate, or contradict career paths she was considering or career paths she had previously discounted?

In addition, using reptests, I can explore Chen's workplace preferences. For example, if I were to conduct the reptest by exploring her values, I might find that the downsides that Chen sees to becoming a farmer are that it would require seasonal work, may be disregarded by society, may involve a lower income, and may involve some level of risk. Interestingly, in looking at her values through the reptest, I may find that Chen has some ambivalence toward all of the careers she is considering, seeing both positive and negative components to each career field. Although Chen's interests and skills align with the farming field, some of her values are not consistent with the values she believes a farming career would provide. In addition, Chen may have ambivalence toward each of the careers from the perspective of their salience with her values. I might find that all of the career paths explored have some positive and negative ratings for the values constructs. If this is the case, Chen's values reptest could indicate several career decision-making challenges, including doubt or confusion regarding her salient values, or it may indicate that she finds each career included in the reptest satisfying to her values system. In this case, the client may benefit from exploring which values, among those listed in the reptest, are most important to her and focusing on careers allowing her to fulfill and engage with those relevant values.

Aside from formally scoring the reptest and analyzing the scores, from a qualitative perspective, counselors can also gain information about clients by uncovering patterns in the clients' responses. For example, by scanning the last two rows of the reptest, I can uncover Chen's preferences. This reptest might show that Chen prefers careers that allow her to set her own hours and careers requiring little formal education (despite the fact that she is in college and feels pressure from her parents to continue her schooling!). If I scan Chen's responses from top to bottom, I can explore her viewpoints on different career choices. Even through a quick scan of the positive and negative values assigned to various career paths, it is easy to note that Chen seems to view a career in farming as more positive and as more interesting than a career in law, teaching, or accounting. If there is a considerable amount of variability in your client's responses, this may indicate that your client more strongly prefers one career path over others (see Table 13.1). If, however, all of the scores are relatively similar, this may suggest that the client is indecisive, with an undifferentiated approach to decision making. As noted previously, if your client is indecisive, a number of next steps can be taken. If the career interest reptest yields no differentiation, consider adding a career values reptest or a career skills reptest, as you may find differentiation among various careers through additional testing. If no differentiation is found among various career paths, it may be useful to begin by processing the source of the client's indecisiveness with him or her. If, for example, the client does not know enough about the career paths to determine how certain careers are similar to or different from each other, the client may be encouraged to learn more about various career paths first through online or media sources (e.g., the Occupational Outlook Handbook, www.myplan.com), through shadowing others, or through conducting interviews with people in career paths of interest.

You can also look for patterns in the frequency of scale usage. If Chen utilizes many of the scalar options to classify the constructs, this suggests flexibility in her thought process. If Chen only uses a few of the scalar options (e.g., rates all careers with a +3 or −3, with no variability of responses in between), this might indicate some rigidity in her thought process, which could be something useful to explore further with her. If there is a high proportion of ratings with zero in the grid, this may indicate that

Chen is not able to define many careers using either polar dimension of the construct. In this case, it may be useful to process with Chen what she feels she knows or does not know about various career paths and, thus, encourage her to explore the career paths further.

Finally, values are embedded within the bipolar constructs. Because of this, it is important to explore with your client the ways in which his or her values align or conflict with his or her cultural background. Utilizing another reptest, Chen's cultural identities (e.g., Asian culture, American culture, women's culture, bisexual culture, Christian culture, high-SES culture) would be placed on the first row of the reptest. Then, I would ask Chen, "In what ways are the American culture and the high-SES culture similar to each other but different from the others?" Chen might say, "The American and high-SES cultures value independence, whereas the others value teamwork." I would then ask Chen if she values independence or teamwork more (and place a "+" in the cells corresponding with the cultures that she believes embody that value and a "–" in the cells corresponding with cultures that embody the alternative value). If you choose to ask your client to rank order the constructs by order of importance, you can also uncover which value constructs are most salient to your client. In the case of Chen, I might ask her, "Which constructs align with your values as a Taiwanese individual? Which conflict?" In looking at Chen's reptest, her most salient workplace value might involve independence, a value she believes is consistent with the American culture and the high-SES culture. Chen may feel conflicted about her parents' wishes for her career path and her own wishes because of the tension between the values embedded in traditional Taiwanese culture (e.g., teamwork) and the values embedded in American culture (e.g., independence).

Utilizing the Reptest to Explore Supports and Barriers

I have compared and contrasted career paths based on Chen's interests, skills, and values. The last demonstration of the reptest involves using the tool to explore Chen's perceived supports and barriers as they relate to each career path she is considering. As in the previous reptests, a grid system is employed. Each profession is placed on the top row of the reptest. Chen is asked, "In what way do you feel supported in two of the career paths but not in a third?" (Note that a similar question could be asked in relation to her perceived career barriers.) Chen responds, "My parents are supportive of me becoming a lawyer or a professor, but they are not supportive of me becoming a farmer." Chen's perceived supports for various career paths (e.g., parental emotional support, denoted with a positive sign) and barriers (e.g., no parental emotional support, denoted with a negative sign) are then organized into two columns on the far right side of the grid in Table 13.2.

The final step involves asking Chen to consider under which side of the bipolar construct (positive or negative) each career path falls. Her response is then indicated with a positive or negative sign in each cell corresponding with the appropriate career path and construct. Chen may

Table 13.2

Repertory Grid Examining Perceived Supports (+) and Barriers (−)

Lawyer	Professor	Accountant	Farmer		
−	−	−	+	+ Do not need money to fund training	− Need money to fund training
+	+	+	−	+ Parents support this field	− Parents do not support this field
−	−	−	+	+ Lives in a rural area (near farmland)	− Does not live near a university
−	−	+	−	+ Experience in the career path	− Little experience in the career path
1/3	1/3	2/2	2/2		

believe that as a bisexual woman, for example, she would not be accepted in a traditionally male-dominated career path, and she may have foreclosed that career path as an option. This could lead to an interesting discussion with Chen about perceived discrimination, concerns about microaggression in workplace environments, and gender-role constructs. Thus, this reptest can be a useful tool to understand the ways in which our clients feel supported or obstructed in relation to pursuing various career paths. See Table 13.3 for an application guide.

Conclusion

In this chapter I have explored the use of reptests, a constructivist career counseling tool used to compare and contrast careers by interests, skills, and values. PCP shines in terms of its usefulness with diverse populations. Because the client is viewed as the "scientist," is the one who guides the session, and is given space to tell his or her story without the mental health professional interpreting the story for him or her, PCP has great appeal when working in multicultural contexts. PCP and reptests provide a certain sense of structure in the session while still fostering creativity and flexibility with the client.

Reptests are particularly well suited for use in career counseling contexts because they provide space for clients to explore workplace preferences that are uniquely salient for them. It is important to keep in mind that the value of the reptest rests in exploring the client's constructs, not our own, so we must be careful not to influence our clients by injecting our own constructs in their systems. When clients are struggling to make a career decision, utilizing PCP and reptests offers us an opportunity to view the world through the clients' lenses and offers our clients an opportunity to explore their salient interests, skills, and values in personally meaningful ways.

Table 13.3

Practical Application Guide

Topic	Utilizing Personal Construct Psychology
General goals and purposes	To help clients explore their values, interests, skills, and cultural and familial influences
Applicable modality	Individual clients, group career counseling, couples counseling, family counseling
	(*Note.* If you want to conduct reptests with more than one client, you could have clients complete the reptests separately and compare them, or you could complete the reptests simultaneously, with each client's response on one area of the grid.)
Applicable counselor settings	High school, college/university, agency, private practice, organization, group practice
Recommended time to complete	Allow 1 hour to complete and process the repertory grid in the session together; may be completed in one session, but it could be useful to readminister the repertory grid at a later point in career counseling.
Materials/equipment needed	Drawing paper, pen/pencil; if you would like to analyze the reptest results statistically, scoring software may be helpful (e.g., CIRCUMGRIDS [Chambers & Grice, 1986], G-PACK [Bell, 1987], FLEXIGRID [email: Finn.Tschudi@psykologi.uio.no], or Rep5 [http://repgrid.com/])
Step-by-step outline of the process	*Step 1:* Define salient career constructs.
	Step 2: Explore preferences for career constructs.
	Step 3: Examine each career path as fulfilling each positive or negative construct.
	Step 4: Analyze the results.

Recommended Resources

Carlson, J. (Director). (2004). *Constructivist therapy* [Motion picture on DVD]. USA: American Psychological Association.

Carlson, J. (Director). (2008). *Constructivist therapy over time* [Motion picture on DVD]. USA: American Psychological Association.

Centre for Personal Construct Psychology. (2009). *What is personal construct psychology?* Retrieved from http://www.centrepcp.co.uk/whatis.htm

Constructivist Psychology Network. (2015). *Constructivist psychology network.* Retrieved from http://www.constructivistpsych.org/

Grier-Reed, T., & Ganuza, Z. M. (2011). Constructivism and career decision self-efficacy for Asian Americans and African Americans. *Journal of Counseling & Development, 89*, 200–205.

A manual for the repertory grid. (n.d.). Retrieved from http://www.terapiacognitiva.net/record/pag/contents.htm

Neimeyer, G. J. (Ed.). (1992). *Constructivist assessment: A casebook.* Newbury Park, CA: Sage.

Savickas, M. L. (1997). Constructivist career counseling: Models and methods. *Advances in Personal Construct Psychology, 4*, 149–182.

Scheer, J. (2010). *The psychology of personal constructs: The PCP portal*. Retrieved from http://www.pcp-net.de/info/centre.html

References

Bannister, D., & Mair, J. M. M. (1968). *The evaluation of personal constructs*. London, England: Academic Press.

Bell, R. C. (1987). *G-Pack—Version 3.0: A computer program for the elicitation and analysis of repertory grids*. Unpublished manual, University of Melbourne, Melbourne.

Chambers, W. V., & Grice, J. W. (1986). Circumgrids: A repertory grid package for personal computers. *Behavior Research Methods, Instruments and Computers, 18*, 468.

Fransella, F., Bell, R., & Bannister, D. (2003). *A manual for repertory grid technique* (2nd ed.). Chichester, UK: Wiley.

Fukuyama, M. A., & Neimeyer, G. J. (1985). Using the Cultural Attitudes Repertory Technique (CART) in a cross-cultural counseling workshop. *Journal of Counseling & Development, 63*, 304–305.

Kelly, G. A. (1955). *The psychology of personal constructs* (Vols. 1–2). New York, NY: W. W. Norton.

Landfield, A. W. (1971). *Personal construct systems in psychotherapy*. Chicago, IL: Rand McNally.

Landfield, A. W. (1983). *Reptest scoring program*. Unpublished manuscript, University of Nebraska–Lincoln, Lincoln, NE.

Leuty, M. E., & Hansen, J. I. C. (2011). Evidence of construct validity for work values. *Journal of Vocational Behavior, 79*, 379–390.

Neimeyer, G. J. (1989). Personal construct systems in vocational development and information-processing. *Journal of Career Development, 16*, 83–96.

Neimeyer, G. J. (1992). Personal constructs in career counseling and development. *Journal of Career Development, 18*, 164–173.

Neimeyer, G. J., Marmarosh, C., Prichard, S., Leso, J. F., & Moore, M. (1992). The role of construct type in vocational differentiation: Use of elicited versus provided dimensions. *Journal of Counseling Psychology, 39*, 121–128.

Neimeyer, G. J., & Neimeyer, R. A. (1981). Functional similarity and interpersonal attraction. *Journal of Research in Personality, 15*, 427–435.

Weiner, I. B., & Craighead, W. E. (2010). Repertory grid methods. In *The Corsini encyclopedia of psychology* (Vol. 4, pp. 1453–1454). Hoboken, NJ: Wiley.

Wong, S. W., & Yuen, M. (2012). Work values of university students in Chinese mainland, Taiwan, and Hong Kong. *International Journal for the Advancement of Counseling, 34*, 269–285.

Chapter 14

Tools to Connect: Using Career Card Sorts With a Latina Client

Cassandra A. Storlie and Janice A. Byrd

With the steady increase in diversity in the United States, Latinos/as have become the largest minority group, making up approximately 17% of the total population (U.S. Census Bureau, 2013). The increasing numbers of Latinos/as in the United States have further inspired counselors to center counseling services to match the collectivistic needs of this population (Arredondo, Gallardo-Cooper, Delgado-Romero, & Zapata, 2014). Counselors face unique challenges in supporting the career needs of Latino/a clients and are called to extend career assessments and interventions beyond traditional methods of career counseling. Card sorts have been widely used by counselors to facilitate purposeful career exploration through client narratives (Parker, 2006). Narrative methods, considered to be constructivist approaches, guide culturally sensitive career counseling with individuals by integrating a holistic conceptualization of the client (Brott, 2001). Constructivist assessments, such as card sorts, are used to facilitate the exploration of the client's story and to provide opportunities for critical reflection so clients may better understand how they make meaning through work and career (Brott, 2001; Hoskins, 1995).

Values card sorts, in particular, provide counselors with a postmodern, constructivist assessment tool to use with individuals from a variety of cultures. Moreover, values card sorts can act as a vehicle in propelling clients to self-examine their career development in the context of their personal, social, environmental, professional, family, and cultural values. Clients have an opportunity to thoroughly examine their values, facilitating insight into their aptness for certain types of work or related activities.

In this chapter, we provide background information on the use of card sorts in career counseling and salient career development issues affecting the Latino/a community and illustrate the use of a values card sort in working with a Latina first-generation college student.

Constructivist Frameworks

Counseling recommendations for Latinos/as have included an emphasis on having a constructivist understanding of the cultural context of Latinos/as, being flexible in the counseling process, choosing culturally appropriate assessment instruments, and providing Latinos/as with a variety of career information (Fouad, 1995). Within a constructivist framework, the narrative career approach is emerging in career counseling (Parker, 2006; Savickas, 1993, 2012). Narratives enable clients to use their unique personal experiences to create a story with which the counselor may move the client forward. The client serves as the author of her or his career story, and the counselor functions as coauthor (Cochran, 1997; Parker, 2006). Within the storied approach articulated by Brott (2001), clients construct their own stories to generate knowledge and meaning in three interwoven phases: (a) co-construction, (b) deconstruction, and (c) construction. To initiate the deep exploration necessary for the three phases, the counselor often uses constructivist assessments to help facilitate an active examination of the client's story. These assessments collect qualitative experiences to construct the client's narrative in his or her own voice and include the following methods: autobiographies, card sorts, journaling, conceptual mapping, genograms, and life lines. Card sorts are a postmodern career assessment that uncovers how meaning is embedded within a client's world of work and how decisions on career choice fit in a client's life design (Savickas, 2012).

Card Sorts

One of the "most common forms of constructivist assessments" (Parker, 2006), card sorts enable clients to make meaning of an experience that is unique to them and their current career development journey. Constructivist and narrative career assessments allow for the fluidity of the lived experience to help inform career decision making in the context of significant facets of one's life. Typical card sorts allow for restriction on specific labels that provide a foundation based on interests or values (Parker, 2006). Yet the use of an experiential exercise within a career counseling session facilitates kinesthetic or "hands-on" learning that, in turn, provides a stronger sense of meaning making for the client. Brott (2004) discussed the significance of narrative methods in providing the stories of individuals who may not readily be heard. Although card sorts have limited empirical support, counselors and researchers should take note that they facilitate exploration of the best practices within marginalized populations.

Various types of card sorts are used by counselors, including values card sorts, interest card sorts, occupational choice card sorts, motivated skills card sorts, vocational card sorts, transferable skill card sorts, and retirement activities (Brott, 2004; Knowdell, 2003; Parker, 2006). Most card sorts are grounded in theories of classification and demonstrate effectiveness in career exploration. Administration of each of these various sorts is quite similar, and only the type of card sort (i.e., values, interests, etc.) dictates the content and characterization of labels on each card. Cards sorts have high face validity and serve as a catalyst for in-depth discussion (Knowdell, 2003). Moreover, they are considered nonthreatening, flexible, energizing, and nearly effortless (Knowdell, 2003).

Values Card Sorts

When administering a values card sort, the counselor produces a stack of approximately 50 cards (less may be used), with each card labeled with a specific value, such as "Integrity" or "Honesty." Next, the counselor reads a script that advises the client to sort the stack of cards into five piles based on personal preference using the following categories: *least important, not very important, neither important nor unimportant, somewhat important*, and *most important*. The use of a Likert scale helps the client identify personal preferences. In addition, the stack of cards often includes a few blank cards for the client to write in values that may not be represented in the original stack of cards, which provides additional autonomy. Generally, the client is instructed not to exceed a certain number of cards in each pile (e.g., 10 per pile). This forces the client to carefully consider the importance of the card item in his or her world (Parker, 2006).

Throughout this exploratory process, the client examines the values identified on the cards and reflects on the personal meaning and the roles these values play in the client's career development. Values card sorts provide an avenue for further accentuation of the importance of the client's story and the ways that different values influence the meaning of career fit and life design. Life design is a paradigm that can be adapted for individuals in diverse cultural settings and that allows clients to author their own career by activating, stimulating, and developing personal resources. McAdams (2013) noted that clients should be encouraged to be agents of their present and future by being authors of their life narratives. This allows clients to actively design, rather than be passively shaped by, their life (Nota & Rossier, 2014). The administration of a values card sort can occur individually or in a group format in which clients select specific values that hold meaning and discuss the salience of these implications. If the card sort is conducted in a group setting, it is important that clients listen attentively to one another without interrupting when personal stories are being shared. Whether working individually or in a group, the counselor guides the client in the process of creating his or her narrative based on what is revealed while reflecting on the values labeled on the cards (Parker, 2006).

Values and Worldview

Values card sorts empower clients by engaging them in critical self-reflection without altering their worldview, and they help clients embrace a proactive and attentive position about their work life. Counselors must be aware of how they either empower or disempower any client through their counseling approaches, always being mindful that cross-cultural challenges can arise (Sue & Sue, 2013). Using values card sorts to generate narratives helps counselors learn more about the worldview of the client, allows the client to make his or her own meaning, and decreases the possibility of the counselor imposing his or her own cultural beliefs on the client (Hoskins, 1995). When working with ethnic and cultural minority clients, it is essential for counselors to utilize career assessments that have been deemed culturally sensitive. Narrative career counseling approaches embrace all elements of self, including multiple life roles such as family member, student, worker, and community member. This approach attends to multicultural concerns that are often not addressed by traditional career counseling techniques (Niles & Hartung, 2000).

As a narrative assessment tool, card sorts focus on the influence of the environment, culture, and family in the client's life (Thomas & Gibbons, 2009). DeVaney and Hughey (2000) noted that clients from diverse backgrounds share many developmental issues, but their unique ethnic identity greatly influences psychosocial and career development. Generally, ethnic minority clients are strongly influenced by their families and may have traditions, rules, and customs that directly affect their career path. Some minority clients perceive their career paths to be predetermined, and as a result they do not feel supported if they choose a career not considered valuable by the family (Clark, Severy, & Sawyer, 2004; DeVaney & Hughey, 2000).

Cultural Values and Latinos/as

Traditional career counseling approaches often neglect collectivistic values held by ethnic minority groups, such as Latinos/as. Among the Latino/a community, collectivistic values frequently supersede the values of American society (Arredondo et al., 2014; Storlie & Jach, 2012). As a result, family unity and additional collectivistic characteristics play a pivotal role in individual decisions for Latinos/as (Santiago-Rivera, Arredondo, & Gallardo-Cooper, 2002; Sue & Sue, 2013). Ignoring such differences during the career counseling process neglects the unique career and cultural issues experienced by and embedded in the life designs of Latinos/as. Therefore, postmodern interventions that provide opportunities to integrate cultural values and help clients choose a best fit career are recommended for Latinos/as. Making use of culturally sensitive career counseling approaches with Latinos/as enables them to author their story both as an individual and from a collectivist perspective. Specifically, using values card sorts with Latino/a clients provides an opportunity to sort through values and identify how these values may influence individual career choices. We illustrate this approach in the case study that follows.

The Case of Linda

Linda is a first-year Latina college student at a large midwestern university. She is fluent in Spanish, but English is her first language. She maintained a 4.0 grade point average in high school and is the youngest in her family. Linda's parents are from Mexico and own a small family restaurant. They are supportive of Linda's college pursuit and hope she will get a college degree in business and come back to help run the restaurant for generations to come. Linda's family has made multiple financial sacrifices to help pay her college tuition, including putting a lien on their home last fall. Linda goes to the college career center to meet with a counselor. She is very concerned about the financial burden her family is taking on to support her college journey, and she is struggling with her introductory business classes in her first semester at the university. Moreover, she has an increased sense of responsibility to help her family because, with her in college, they are short one worker at the family restaurant.

Linda is having difficulty differentiating between her values and life roles as a student and as a daughter. She values her family and the business they have built from the ground up, but Linda longs to become an elementary school teacher and fears she will never pursue her dream if she doesn't speak up and make some difficult decisions now. She worries that her parents will disapprove if she switches her major to education, and she is also concerned that her siblings will be upset with her for not coming back to help with the restaurant.

Card sorts allow clients to construct their own meaning, remain true to their individual values, and explore career-related issues from a bias-free perspective (Flores & Spanierman, 1998; Parker, 2006). To enhance objectivity when working with the career needs of Latinos/as, we recommend that counselors evaluate their own levels of cultural competency and reflect on their own cultural, social, and educational background and how it may influence their understanding of their clients' cultures and career development. Postmodern, constructivist assessments, such as values card sorts, allow clients to explore their individual values without the imposition of counselor bias.

Assisting Linda in coauthoring her story through the use of a values cards sort can underscore how her values influence her life choices and can provide insight into a career choice that will be a good fit for her life design. The counselor chooses a values card sort over other types of card sorts (e.g., interest, occupational) in this scenario because Linda is struggling with exploring how her unique values are affecting her decision making. This exploration of values serves as a basis for creating life goals that can help guide career choice and influence work life (Pope, Flores, & Rottinghaus, 2014). Prior to administering a values card sort with Linda, it is essential that the counselor understand the cultural and social elements that are likely to be influencing her current career problem.

Cultural Considerations in Linda's Career Assessment

The career counseling literature has focused on addressing the cultural context of personal variables. However, values are contextual, and the intersection of environmental variables across cultural groups needs to be incorporated in postmodern, culturally sensitive career counseling approaches. Latino/a college students often experience life role conflicts in which they feel culturally obligated to conform to the expectations of their families while residing in an academic setting that promotes individual choice (Arredondo et al., 2014). In Linda's situation, her roles as a student, daughter, and future business partner in her family's restaurant create a context of conflicting values and life roles. Her struggle to meet her parents' expectations, supported by her collectivist worldview, is in opposition to her individual desire to become an elementary school teacher. This value contradiction is likely to create confusion and frustration, and it is an important issue to assess prior to and during the administration of a values card sort with Linda.

In addition, the family unit strongly shapes Latino/a students' perception of education (Henry, Plunkett, & Sands, 2011), and this circumscribes their concept of future career possibilities. Latino/a students view parental support as essential (Henry et al., 2011), which may be particularly difficult for Linda in light of her desire to be an elementary school teacher and her parents' desire for her to run their family restaurant. The pressure to be submissive to authority figures, intergenerational conflicts, and the stress of being consistent in family role expectations may create feelings of isolation or dysfunctional coping among Latinos/as (Sue & Sue, 2013). Quite often the family will financially and emotionally support a student's choice to attend college, but the importance placed on familial responsibilities may create stress in the transition to college life for a Latina first-generation student (Sy & Romero, 2008). Longitudinal research has shown that familial support is a contributing factor to better grades among Latino/a students (Azmitia, Cooper, & Brown, 2009; Henry et al., 2011), so Linda's career choice conflict may be adding to her current struggle in her business classes. Further assessment of why Linda is struggling academically is warranted to get a clear understanding of the career problem.

Social Considerations in Linda's Career Assessment

The psychosocial needs of the Latino/a population may be overlooked by some career service providers (Santiago-Rivera et al., 2002). Socially, Latinos/as have been victims of discrimination in the workplace (Arredondo et al., 2014), with approximately 6 out of 10 (61%) saying that discrimination is a "major problem" and prevents them from succeeding (Lopez, Morin, & Taylor, 2010). Linda's experience with discrimination or microaggressions in her classes and on the college campus may also affect her choice of academic major and career choice. "Latino youth describe discrimination based on English fluency, immigration concerns, negative stereotypes, poverty, and skin color" (Edwards & Romero, 2008, p. 26). Throughout the career assessment, it is essential for the counselor to grasp the lived experience of being a Latina college student and assess for incidences of discrimination that may be affecting adjustment to college. Higher rates of discrimination and oppression have been found to lead to mental health issues such as depression (Edwards & Romero,

2008) and anxiety (Sue & Sue, 2013), which discourage a healthy career development trajectory. Telzer and Garcia (2009) found that Latina college women have a poorer self-perception, lower self-esteem, and a decreased sense of personal attractiveness compared to peers with a lighter skin color. These issues may have an impact on the mental health, socialization, and ethnic identity development of Latina women (Telzer & Garcia, 2009) and their future career paths.

Additional Considerations in Linda's Career Assessment

Latinas frequently have numerous obligations to their family, work, and school while attending college (Sy, 2006). These life roles, such as daughter, sister, cousin, student, and employee, are influenced by cultural values and affect the career decision making of Latinas in college. Placing familial roles before other roles is not uncommon for Latina college students (Sy & Romero, 2008). Narrative approaches, such as values card sorts, allow student and counselor to explore life role salience and to "assess the relative importance of the work role in the context of other life roles." This approach helps counselors to better understand the "values that individuals seek or hope to find in various life roles" (Nevill & Super, 1986, p. 3).

Generational concerns should also be considered because Linda is a first-generation U.S. citizen. She may feel more strongly compelled to abide by more traditional family norms because her parents are immigrants. Likewise, because work and family have been intertwined for Linda with the family restaurant, it may be exceedingly difficult to assess how to differentiate the value of her individual career needs, the value of her family desires, and the needs of the family restaurant, particularly when her parents are sacrificing their finances and resources to support Linda's college education.

The Values Card Sort as a Culturally Sensitive Intervention

During the administration of the values card sort with Linda, it is important for the counselor to be culturally sensitive when observing Linda's verbal and nonverbal reactions while classifying the values she finds most important. In addition, the counselor will take special note of values that may be difficult for her to classify (e.g., Linda spends a long time deliberating over whether "Loyalty" is *somewhat important* or *most important*). Once all the values cards are classified based on the aforementioned Likert scale, the counselor can help Linda author her "story" by examining how she makes meaning of these values in her life, what elements influenced her to classify the values in the manner in which she did, and what values she had the most difficulty classifying. The counselor may integrate the storied approach described by Brott (2001) during this intervention because it can guide clients to uncover their present narrative and build a future narrative based on their desires.

In Phase 1, co-construction, client and counselor work together to explore the client's past and present to unearth pivotal experiences, people, and preferred language:

Dialogue	Phase
Counselor: Linda, reflect on some experiences that have been most meaningful to you, particularly as you are dealing with this current dilemma.	Values are a part of the self-exploration process and help to guide career decisions. During co-construction, Linda is prompted to reflect on past experiences that may help inform her future career decisions. With the help of the counselor, Linda can explore her values to make meaning of past experiences and their relation to her career decision making.
Linda: Well, mostly it's been my family and especially my parents. They have done everything for me, including risking losing their home just so I can go to college. They have always been there to support me through the thick and the thin . . . which is why I feel so torn.	

In Phase 2, deconstruction, client and counselor analyze themes from the previous stage to make connections in Linda's story:

Dialogue	Phase
Counselor: Linda, last time we met we centered on your values of loyalty and dedication. I am curious about the connections you have made with these values to your possible career as an elementary school teacher.	In Phase 2, the goal is to collaboratively work with Linda to explore how her values connect with a future career. In this case, analyzing prior themes can help determine alignment of her values to her potential career choice. Through deconstruction, Linda can reflect on her work values and identify the reasons she is not doing well in her current business class.
Linda: Actually, I have thought a lot about this since we last talked. I think my loyalty to my own career and to wanting to be a teacher is complicated . . . for example, I think that is why I am failing my business class right now. My heart just isn't in it, and the more I try and study for my business class, the worse I feel. I don't want to let anyone down. And I definitely don't want to let myself down, including my future goals.	

In Phase 3, construction, the client creates future chapters of her story by reflecting on patterns identified in previous phases:

Dialogue	Phase
Linda: Now that we have met several times, I think I know what I need to do. Although it is going to be painful for me and will be painful for my family, I have to come clean about my desire to have a future career as an elementary	In the final stage, Linda is able to construct her future story by purposeful reflection. She is able to make a decision after discovering her core values. *(Continued)*

Dialogue (Continued)	*Phase*
school teacher. I love my family, but I will have to find a different way to be loyal to them so I can become more congruent with my goals. I am dedicated to working with kids. I have been around kids all my life, and I want to make a difference in their lives. . . . I want to be a good role model and show them that they can be anything they want to be in this world.	She notes that some values conflict with each other but ultimately makes a decision based on the values she feels are most important and true to her.

Here Linda identifies themes and patterns she wishes to develop or eliminate within her career development trajectory. These themes and patterns may directly align with Linda's most important values and can be further processed and understood in session. By more deeply exploring the meaning of these values and the manner in which Linda prioritized and classified them, invaluable information can be gathered that will assist her during the career development process. For example, this knowledge can directly inform future steps in the client–counselor relationship, such as the administration of additional career assessments, potential job searches, academic preparation and course selection, and job location. As a postmodern intervention, the values card sort helps the counselor capture Linda's current construction of her life and helps Linda reconstruct her story to align with her career preference.

As the counselor addresses these different values while processing this intervention with Linda, what it means to be female and from the Latina culture must be taken into consideration. Linda may understand the value of work and career from a collectivistic perspective in alignment with her cultural background. The counselor will want to adapt this intervention to address the values that Linda deem as most important and explore the role these values play in her life narrative. Values that gravitate toward the *most important* category tend to have a strong influence on career satisfaction and decision making. An investigation into how different careers (e.g., business or education) best match Linda's values will be critical in helping her.

With the unique challenges facing Latinos/as in the world of work (Arredondo et al., 2014), counselors may encounter difficulty in providing effective career development services. Values card sorts are used to support clients in the process of generating and exploring their personal narratives and illuminate meaning making in the development of career plans and occupational trajectories. As the meaning maker, a client's interpretation of his or her life story complements and enhances other career assessments, leading to purposeful decision making in choosing a career. Constructivist and narrative career counseling approaches utilize a holistic perspective that encourages clients to explore how their self-organizing principles influence the way they view the world and make life decisions

(Hoskins, 1995). The use of a values card sort in career counseling guides clients in the intentional process of individual and subjective exploration within a therapeutic and collaborative counseling relationship. See Table 14.1 for an application guide.

Conclusion

Latinos/as will be an increasingly large part of the population making career decisions in future years (Gushue, Clarke, Pantzer, & Scanlan, 2006). Counselors must adapt and improve their practices by infusing postmodern approaches when working with Latinos/as on career issues.

Table 14.1
Practical Application Guide

Topic	Values Card Sorts
General goals and purposes	Clients will explore their values to clarify and set priorities for what is important to find meaning and satisfaction in life work
Applicable modality	All clients seeking career services
Applicable counselor settings	May be conducted in an individual or group setting
Recommended time to complete	Approximately 1 hour, with follow-up sessions to process the use of this intervention
Materials/equipment needed	Cards representing various values and pictures
Step-by-step outline of the process	1. Introduce the goal of values card sorts. 2. Provide instructions on how to classify 50 values cards according to how important the value is in the client's career satisfaction by rating each card in one of the following categories: • Least Important • Not Very Important • Neither Important nor Unimportant • Somewhat Important • Most Important The client is limited to having only 10 cards in each category. 3. Instruct the client to define his or her top five values and supply an example of how the client knows that value is being satisfactorily met. 4. Instruct the client to rate how each of the top five values is currently being met using a 5-point rating scale. 5. Explore what influenced the client to classify the values in his or her chosen category. 6. Explore the values that presented the most difficulty in classifying.

Enrollment of Latinos/as aged 18 to 24 years in all colleges, including those enrolled in community colleges and 4-year institutions, now exceeds 2 million students (Fry & Lopez, 2012). With approximately 41% of Latinos/as aged 20 and over not graduating from high school and only 10% of Latino/a high school dropouts completing a general educational diploma (Fry, 2010), using culturally sensitive postmodern counseling theories and approaches such as values card sorts is strongly recommended when addressing their unique cultural, social, and familial barriers to the world of work (Storlie & Jach, 2012). We encourage career professionals to engage in professional development training centered on culturally sensitive techniques that enhance the understanding of an individual's worldview, identity development, and contribution to society through work (Sue, Arredondo, & McDavis, 1992; Vespia, Fitzpatrick, Fouad, Kantamneni, & Chen, 2010).

Recommended Resources

Knowdell, D. (2015). *Career values card sort—Online version.* Retrieved from https://www.careerplanner.com/Shop/Knowdell-CareerValuesCards.cfm

Savickas, M. L. (2009, June). *The role of values in careers: Meaning and mattering in life design.* Opening address for the 9th Biennial Conference of the Society for Vocational Psychology, St. Louis, MO. Video retrieved from http://www.vocopher.org/Values/values.html

Savickas, M. L., & Hartung, P. (2012). *Career construction interview.* Retrieved from http://www.vocopher.com/CSI/CCI.pdf

References

Arredondo, P., Gallardo-Cooper, M., Delgado-Romero, E. A., & Zapata, A. L. (2014). *Culturally responsive counseling with Latinas/os.* Alexandria, VA: American Counseling Association.

Azmitia, M., Cooper, C. R., & Brown, J. R. (2009). Support and guidance from families, friends, and teachers in Latino early adolescents' math pathways. *Journal of Early Adolescence, 29,* 142–169. doi:10.1177/0272431608324476

Brott, P. E. (2001). The storied approach: A postmodern perspective for career counseling. *The Career Development Quarterly, 49,* 304–313.

Brott, P. E. (2004). Constructivist assessment in career counseling. *Journal of Career Development, 30,* 189–200.

Clark, M. A., Severy, L., & Sawyer, S. A. (2004). Creating connections: Using a narrative approach in career group counseling with college students from diverse cultural backgrounds. *Journal of College Counseling, 7,* 24–31.

Cochran, L. (1997). *Career counseling: A narrative approach.* Thousand Oaks, CA: Sage.

DeVaney, S. B., & Hughey, A. W. (2000). Career development of ethnic minority students. In D. A. Luzzo (Ed.), *Career counseling of college students: An empirical guide to strategies that work* (pp. 233–252). Washington, DC: American Psychological Association.

Edwards, L. M., & Romero, A. J. (2008). Coping with discrimination among Mexican descent adolescents. *Hispanic Journal of Behavioral Sciences, 30,* 24–39. doi:10.1177/0739986307311431

Flores, L. Y., & Spanierman, L. B. (1998). An examination of a culturally sensitive university career center: Outreach, services, and evaluation. *Journal of Career Development, 25,* 111–122.

Fouad, N. (1995). Career behavior of Hispanics: Assessment and career intervention. In F. L. Leong (Ed.), *Career development and vocation behavior of racial and ethnic minorities* (pp. 165–187). Mahwah, NJ: Erlbaum.

Fry, R. (2010). *Hispanics, high school dropouts and the GED.* Retrieved from http://www.pewhispanic.org/2010/05/13/hispanics-high-school-dropouts-and-the-ged/

Fry, R., & Lopez, M. H. (2012). *Hispanic student enrollments reach new highs in 2011: Now largest minority group on four-year college campuses.* Retrieved from www.pewhispanic.org/2012/08/20/hispanic-student-enrollments-reach-new-highs-in-2011/

Gushue, G. V., Clarke, C. P., Pantzer, K. M., & Scanlan, K. R. (2006). Self-efficacy, perceptions of barriers, vocational identity, and the career exploration behavior of Latino/a high school students. *The Career Development Quarterly, 54,* 307–317.

Henry, C. S., Plunkett, S. W., & Sands, T. (2011). Family structure, parental involvement, and academic motivation in Latino adolescents. *Journal of Divorce and Remarriage, 52,* 370–390. doi:10.1080/10502556.2011.592414

Hoskins, M. (1995). *Constructivist approaches for career counselors.* Unpublished manuscript, ERIC Clearinghouse.

Knowdell, R. (2003). Card sort career assessment tools. *Career Planning and Adult Development Journal, 19,* 150–160.

Lopez, M. H., Morin, R., & Taylor, P. (2010). *Illegal immigration backlash worries, divides Latinos.* Retrieved from http://www.pewhispanic.org/2010/10/28/illegal-immigration-backlash-worries-divides-latinos/

McAdams, D. P. (2013). The psychological self as actor, agent, and author. *Perspectives on Psychological Science, 8,* 272–295.

Nevill, D. D., & Super, D. E. (1986). *The Salience Inventory: Theory, application and research* (Research ed.). Palo Alto, CA: Consulting Psychologists Press.

Niles, S. G., & Hartung, P. W. (2000). Emerging career theories. In D. A. Luzzo (Ed.), *Career counseling of college students: An empirical guide to strategies that work* (pp. 23–41). Washington, DC: American Psychological Association.

Nota, L., & Rossier, J. (Eds.). (2014). *Handbook of the life design paradigm: From practice to theory, from theory to practice.* Göttingen, Germany: Hogrefe.

Parker, H. L. P. (2006). Card sorts: Constructivist assessment tools. In M. McMahon & W. Patton (Eds.), *Career counselling: Constructivist approaches* (pp. 176–186). New York, NY: Routledge.

Pope, M., Flores, L. Y., & Rottinghaus, P. J. (2014). *The role of values in careers.* Charlotte, NC: Information Age.

Santiago-Rivera, A. L., Arredondo, P., & Gallardo-Cooper, M. (2002). *Counseling Latinos and la familia: Multicultural aspects of counseling and psychotherapy.* Thousand Oaks, CA: Sage.

Savickas, M. L. (1993). Career counseling in the postmodern era. *Journal of Cognitive Psychotherapy, 7*, 205–215.

Savickas, M. L. (2012). Life design: A paradigm for career intervention in the 21st century. *Journal of Counseling & Development, 90*, 13–19.

Storlie, C. A., & Jach, E. A. (2012). Social justice collaboration in schools: A model for working with undocumented Latino students. *Journal for Social Action in Counseling and Psychology, 4*, 99–116.

Sue, D. W., Arredondo, P., & McDavis, R. J. (1992). Multicultural counseling competencies and standards: A call to the profession. *Journal of Counseling & Development, 70*, 477–486.

Sue, D. W., & Sue, D. (2013). *Counseling the culturally diverse: Theory and practice* (6th ed.). New York, NY: Wiley.

Sy, S. R. (2006). Family and work influences on the transition to college among Latina adolescents. *Hispanic Journal of Behavioral Development, 28*, 368–386.

Sy, S. R., & Romero, J. (2008). Family responsibilities among Latina college students from immigrant families. *Journal of Hispanic Higher Education, 7*, 212–227.

Telzer, E. H., & Garcia, H. A. (2009). Skin color and self-perceptions of immigrant and U.S. born Latinas: The moderating role of racial socialization and ethnic identity. *Hispanic Journal of Behavioral Sciences, 31*, 357–374. doi:10.1177/0739986309336913

Thomas, D. A., & Gibbons, M. M. (2009). Narrative theory: A career counseling approach for adolescents of divorce. *Professional School Counseling, 12*, 223–229.

U.S. Census Bureau. (2013). *American community survey 2005–2009.* Retrieved from http://www.census.gov/acs/www/

Vespia, K. M., Fitzpatrick, M. E., Fouad, N. A., Kantamneni, N., & Chen, Y.-L. (2010). Multicultural career counseling: A national survey of competencies and practices. *The Career Development Quarterly, 59*, 54–71. doi:10.1002/j.2161-0045.2010.tb00130.x

Possible Selves Mapping With a Mexican American Prospective First-Generation College Student

Rebecca E. Michel

A high school diploma is no longer enough for most people to secure the career or lifestyle they imagine. The value of a postsecondary education is well accepted, and significant efforts have been made to support students who further their training past high school. For example, the White House "Reach Higher" (2014) initiative aimed to motivate every student to complete some level of postsecondary education, whether in a professional training program, community college, or university. By exposing students to college and career opportunities, offering lower cost educational options, and creating a college-going culture, more students are expected to gain access to postsecondary education. However, whether these students will be prepared to meet the challenges of college and career remains unclear.

Many students enroll in postsecondary education to reach their career goals. However, only 3 out of 5 undergraduate students will earn their bachelor's degree within 6 years (U.S. Department of Education, 2014), and racial and ethnic minorities who are first in their family to attend college graduate at even lower rates (Chen & Carroll, 2005). As an example of this, fewer than 1 in 10 Mexican Americans have obtained a bachelor's degree by the time they are 25 years of age or older (Motel & Patten, 2012). These first-generation college students (FGCSs) often lack familial role models and find themselves academically, financially, and emotionally unprepared for postsecondary education. Intentional interventions for these students must begin well before their first college class.

Prospective first-generation college students (PFGCSs) are middle and high school students whose parents lack education beyond high school

(Gibbons & Borders, 2010). To help these young adults transition into postsecondary education and the world of work, comprehensive school counseling programs have been designed to develop "career ready" students (Gysbers, 2013). Ideally, these students will be prepared to make career and educational choices and to navigate various life roles and events. Professional counselors can work with PFGCSs to provide them with strategies to successfully prepare them for postsecondary education and their transition into the working world. Following high school, these individuals might decide to enter the workforce; enlist in the military; or enroll in a certificate program, apprenticeship, technical school, community college, college, or university. Special consideration must be given to working with diverse student populations, including individuals from ethnic and racial minorities and those who identify as lesbian, gay, bisexual, or transgender. Postmodern career counseling approaches that include interventions to help students envision "possible selves" can be particularly meaningful with diverse PFGCSs. *Possible selves* are "the ideal selves that we would very much like to become. They are also the selves we could become and the selves we are afraid of becoming" (Markus & Nurius, 1986, p. 954).

In this chapter, I describe Possible Selves Mapping, a qualitative assessment tool that helps clients develop their own identity and improve their career decision-making skills. I explain the multicultural and contextual factors and describe the benefits of using this assessment tool with PFGCSs. I then illustrate the use of this mapping tool in the case study that follows.

Possible Selves Mapping

Shepard and Marshall (1999) developed Possible Selves Mapping, a qualitative assessment tool that can be used with PFGCSs to help them develop their identity and improve their decision making. Based on the work of Markus and Nurius (1986), this assessment encourages clients to expand their self-concept by thinking about who they *could* become, who they *hope* to become, and who they *fear* they might become in the future. This postmodern approach acknowledges each individual's subjective experience as the person constructs his or her own perspectives and realities. It can be enlightening for people to consider the different possible selves they could become depending on their circumstances, decisions, and behaviors (Markus & Nurius, 1986). This process illuminates how the decisions made today can influence the person you can become tomorrow.

Within career counseling, this assessment asks individuals to consider several variations of who they might become in the future. In considering their future selves, individuals clearly envision themselves in different careers. Adolescents and young adults are generally able to identify many possible selves (Cross & Markus, 1991) because educational and career possible selves are most prevalent during this developmental stage of life (Dunkel, 2000). As they imagine themselves in the future, clients evaluate how interesting and achievable possible careers would be based on their expected knowledge, skills, and abilities. Careers identified as both interesting and achievable are explored further with a counselor.

Once potential occupations of interest are identified, individuals brainstorm several possible steps required to reach each career goal. For example, one possible path for a high school student planning to become a middle school teacher is to (a) earn passing grades in high school, (b) graduate high school, (c) enroll and earn an associate's degree at a local community college, (d) transfer to a 4-year university majoring in education, (e) join campus extracurricular activities designed for education majors, (f) receive mentoring from a middle school teacher, (g) complete educational tests and field placements, (h) graduate, (i) network with middle school teachers and administrators, and (j) secure a position as a middle school teacher. Visualizing the steps required to become a middle school teacher can put students on a successful path to reaching their career goals. Even if their path takes some unexpected turns along the way (e.g., retaking a class, transferring schools, changing majors), it can be comforting to use a process like this to map out a possible career path.

Multicultural and Contextual Factors

Vocational exploration varies across cultures, and constructivist assessments may be useful for individuals seeking to make meaning of their unique experiences (Neimeyer, 1992). Researchers have explored the concept of possible selves with individuals in various cultures (Meara, Day, Chalk, & Phelps, 1995; Oyserman, Gant, & Ager, 1995; Perry & Vance, 2010; Yowell, 2002), and the Possible Selves Mapping assessment tool has been utilized with rural adolescents (Shepard & Marshall, 1999) and with adults (Shepard & Quressette, 2010). However, additional research is needed to examine the impact of Possible Selves Mapping with diverse populations (e.g., individuals living in an urban setting, racially and ethnically diverse adolescents, PFGCSs).

Similar to other postmodern career assessments, Possible Selves Mapping invites individuals to be the expert on their own experiences. In a focused, yet flexible dialogue, counselors urge clients to share stories about their abilities, values, and interests with the aim of empowering them to discover their own life possibilities (McMahon & Patton, 2002). This process allows counselors to recognize and appreciate the unique multicultural and contextual factors influencing individuals' career stories. When counselors reflect this information to clients, clients gain greater insight into their own hopes and fears, which can help them create a more meaningful career story.

Possible Selves Mapping With PFGCSs

PFGCSs tend to be members of racial or ethnic minority groups, to come from low-income families, to perceive less support from family and friends, and to feel less academically prepared for college (Ishitani, 2003; Lohfink & Paulsen, 2005). Developmentally, these adolescents are striving to construct a meaningful identity (Erikson, 1968), and they welcome the opportunity to explore ideas about their future career and educational pursuits (Flum & Bluestein, 2000). They tend to make career choices based on their learning experiences; self-efficacy; and outcome expectations, interests, and goals (Lent, Brown, & Hackett, 1994). Their college decisions are based on family expectations, K–12 schooling, institutions of higher education, and state and federal policies (Perna, 2000). At this life stage, their career and educational plans are notably influenced by the expectations of their parents, teachers, and mentors; this is especially true among racial minorities such as Mexican American students (Fisher & Padmawidjaja, 1999; Flores & Obasi, 2005; Ginorio & Huston, 2001). Despite greater societal emphasis on attending college, PFGCSs may be unsure about enrolling in postsecondary education. Counselors can use Possible Selves Mapping to help these students envision possibilities and consider career options.

Historically FGCSs have struggled with retention and academic success during college (Chen & Carroll, 2005). FGCSs may be academically and socially unprepared to assimilate into the college environment and may experience "impostor phenomenon," in which they feel they do not belong at college (Davis, 2010, p. 48). Feeling like an outsider can cause these students to feel disconnected from other students, faculty members, and the college community. A career counselor could use Possible Selves Mapping to help these students consider the steps required to become more academically and socially prepared for postsecondary education and to balance the multiple roles in their lives.

Many FGCSs enroll in postsecondary education while also working to earn income. It can be difficult to balance the demands of college classes with being engaged in the workforce. FGCSs must develop a clear understanding of the purpose of both roles (i.e., college student and wage earner) to prioritize time spent on each activity. These individuals might feel compelled to work additional hours to earn money rather than invest time in academics or get involved on campus (Majer, 2009). FGCSs may not appreciate how extracurricular involvement may benefit them now or in the future. However, extracurricular activities can enhance peer connections, well-being, professional development, and retention (Booth, Travis, Borzumato-Gainey, & Degges-White, 2014). It can be helpful for FGCSs to envision possible selves in various roles in college and in the world of work.

Support from parents helps build confidence in one's ability to overcome educational and career barriers (Turner, Alliman-Brissett, Lapan, Udipi, & Ergun, 2003), especially among racial and ethnic minorities (Constantine, Wallace, & Kindaichi, 2005) and FGCSs (Dennis, Phinney, & Chuateco, 2005). However, FGCSs are typically unable to rely on their parents for suggestions to help them navigate the college culture (Torres & Hernandez, 2009), which can cause feelings of resentment and lead to a strained parent–child relationship (Zavadil & Kooyman, 2014). Without insight from parents or a clear plan to overcome barriers, these FGCSs may be overwhelmed by the challenges faced during postsecondary education.

Some difficulties may be alleviated if these students can clearly envision themselves being successful in college prior to setting foot on campus. A case example is provided next to illustrate how a counselor can utilize Possible Selves Mapping with a Mexican American PFGCS.

The Case of Javier

Javier, an 18-year-old Mexican American high school senior, has come to counseling for assistance with career decision making. As his parents' oldest son, he feels pressure to earn money for his family, and he is currently employed at a local grocery store. Javier would eventually like to leave his job to look for work in a more progressive company that recognizes and accepts his bisexual orientation. Javier is on track to graduate from high school, but he is unsure about his postgraduation plans. His teachers and school counselor have encouraged him to enroll in a community college or university because he has taken high school classes that have prepared him for college, earned a 3.6 grade point average, and scored above average on the SAT. Javier's teachers have informed him that postsecondary education could set him up to earn more money for his family in the future. Javier's parents did not attend college, but he believes they might support a decision to enroll in college if they understood the potential financial payoff. Unfortunately, at this time Javier is unsure about the type of career he would like to pursue. He would like to choose a career he will excel in and enjoy, but he has limited knowledge of the types of occupations available to him. He is looking for a professional counselor to help him explore more about himself and determine his next steps after graduation.

Utilizing Possible Selves Mapping

In the first session with Javier, the counselor begins by asking him what he is hoping to gain from their conversation. This question allows Javier to provide his expectations for the counseling sessions in his own words, claim his role as expert, and begin to shape the dialogue (Javier replies, "I would like to determine what to do after high school because right now I'm not really sure."). The counselor states that many high school students are unsure about their career and educational pursuits. Individuals have many options after high school with regard to their career goals, including enrolling in additional education or entering the workforce. Family, educational, and societal expectations often affect the choices students make. Meeting with a counselor at this stage of life can help students identify career interests and gain skills to create self-defined plans for the future.

In an effort to honor Javier's lived experiences, the counselor asks questions throughout the sessions to help him visualize his educational and career path and to construct a personally meaningful career story. Thinking about current life roles helps him brainstorm the various life roles (i.e., possible selves) he would like to have in the future. Javier shares more about himself and describes his meaningful life roles: second-generation Mexican American, oldest male in a family of five, high school student, athlete, identifies as bisexual, active member of a progressive religious community, employed at a local grocery store, and bilingual. Rapport is built by providing a safe space for Javier to share his current worldview and important life roles.

The counselor explains the concept of possible selves, including hoped-for and feared careers, lifestyles, and relationships. Each person might have several ideas about what type of career, lifestyle, and relationships he or she could have in the future. The counselor explains that each person may envision him- or herself in a variety of different occupations. For example, someone might imagine him- or herself as a painter, a teacher, a professional athlete, or in another career. All of these ideas could be useful to consider when making career-related decisions. The counselor explains that they will be using the Possible Selves Mapping Exercise (Shepard, 2010; Shepard & Marshall, 1999) to guide the remainder of Javier's counseling session. This assessment includes a series of questions about Javier's career and life goals. Javier is encouraged to provide comprehensive answers during the assessment to develop meaningful intervention outcomes later in the session. He records his responses on a Possible Selves Map, which he and the counselor will explore together later in the counseling process.

Javier is invited to relax and to think about "what you hope to become" (positive projections) and "what you fear, dread, or don't want for yourself" (negative projections) in the future (Shepard & Marshall, 1999, p. 41). He lists several positive and negative projections of possible selves on a sheet of paper. Next, Javier ranks the list of possible selves in order of importance. He places a star next to the possible self he feels most able to achieve and rates his *capability* regarding becoming that possible self on a 7-point Likert-type scale (1 = *not at all capable* to 7 = *completely capable*). Javier then evaluates his *ability* to achieve or prevent each possible self.

The counselor asks Javier, "How likely is it that this possible self will happen?" Javier then rates the likelihood using a 7-point Likert-type scale (1 = *not at all likely to happen* to 7 = *completely likely to happen*). Finally, Javier reflects on actions that could bring about or prevent the possible selves from emerging. The counselor explains that information gathered from this assessment will guide interventions in the next phase of counseling, which may be a continuation of the current counseling session or may occur in a separate counseling session.

During the intervention phase, the counselor explores Javier's possible selves in greater detail. All of Javier's possible selves are seen as meaningful, and further examination could lead to greater self-concept and identity development. Latino students may be more likely to change their postsecondary plans when family responsibilities and educational goals conflict (Ginorio & Huston, 2001). To explore the messages Javier has received about his career and educational possibilities, the counselor may engage in critical consciousness by encouraging Javier to deconstruct the meaning beneath each hoped-for and feared possible self. By naming the familial, educational, and societal messages he has received about each possible career, Javier can gain insight into why some careers are seen as more desirable than others. This may lead Javier to add or remove possible selves from his original list and make more self-authorized career decisions.

Next, Javier brainstorms the skills, knowledge, and abilities required for each of the possible careers. If Javier is unsure about the tasks required for a career, the counselor teaches him how to access career-related information (e.g., O*NET, Occupational Outlook Handbook). After gaining a clear understanding of the tasks required for each career, the counselor helps Javier evaluate each career by asking these questions based on social cognitive career theory (Lent et al., 1994):

- Do you have interests aligned with that career? (This question identifies interests.)
- How much confidence do you have that you would be able to complete the tasks required for that career? (This question evaluates self-efficacy.)
- Do you believe you will experience positive outcomes if you pursue that career? (This question assesses outcome expectations.)
- What obstacles do you see in trying to reach your career goals? (This question clarifies barriers.)
- What supports do you have in trying to reach your career goals? (This question illuminates supports.)

In answering these questions, Javier eliminates possible careers from his list (a) if they do not align with interests, (b) if he does not believe he could successfully complete the required tasks, or (c) if he identifies too many barriers to reaching the career goal.

Exploring Javier's Cultural Background

Javier's cultural background as a Mexican American man will likely influence his interests, self-efficacy, and perceived educational and career barriers. It is important for the counselor to discuss Javier's current level of acculturation into the Anglo culture and how this may be influencing his career interests (Flores, Robitschek, Celebi, Anderson, & Hoang, 2010), educational aspirations (Flores, Navarro, & DeWitz, 2008), and career decision-making self-efficacy (Flores, Ojeda, Huang, Gee, & Lee, 2006). The counselor also asks Javier questions to determine his level of college self-efficacy, which has been shown to predict educational goals and performance (Garriott & Flores, 2013). The counselor also discusses any additional career-related concerns Javier may be having.

Javier is asked to clearly state all the barriers he expects to encounter in a career or postsecondary educational environment. Some Mexican American students might question whether they have the ability, support from friends, confidence to succeed, and talent to fit in at college. In general, Mexican American high school students have not received adequate academic preparation to prepare them for college (Gándara & Contreras, 2009). Thus, they may believe they lack the appropriate study skills, motivation, and career decision making required to be successful in a postsecondary environment (McWhirter, Torres, Salgado, & Valdez, 2007). Some Mexican American students believe they will experience more postsecondary barriers than Caucasian students (McWhirter et al., 2007), which also influences their educational and career plans and goals (Ojeda & Flores, 2008). Mexican American students are likely to encounter numerous challenges during college, but a positive self-concept, encouragement from family and friends, and a supportive transition into a postsecondary institution can help these students achieve success (Sheffield, 2011). By discussing the anticipated barriers as well as strategies to overcome each barrier, Javier will become more empowered to make college and career decisions.

As a bisexual man, Javier also may encounter college and career-related barriers specific to his sexual orientation. During high school, rather than focusing on his career development like many of his heterosexual peers, Javier may have focused his attention on exploring his sexuality, leading to his current vocational indecision (Schmidt & Nilsson, 2006). It is common for adolescents to experience this bottleneck, in which they put off career development because they are focused on their sexual identity development (Hetherington, 1991). It is important for the counselor to utilize a theoretical approach that encourages Javier to explore how cultural factors, including his ethnic background and sexual orientation, have affected his career development.

Once Javier chooses an occupation that is achievable based on his interests, skills, knowledge, and abilities, he establishes a specific plan to reach his career goals. This plan will guide Javier's career decision making after high school, whether he decides to join the workforce full time, apply to a community college or university, or take a different path entirely. If Javier decides to continue in the workforce, he may question whether he will be accepted as a bisexual man in his chosen occupation. It is possible that he will still experience discomfort within his work setting and have difficulty networking to move into another position. Thus, he could face career dissatisfaction and sexual orientation discrimination with regard to pay and promotions (Keeton Parnell, Lease, & Green, 2012). Gay and bisexual men earn less income than heterosexual men regardless of education and occupation (Black, Makar, Sanders, & Taylor, 2003). This can be especially troubling because Javier and his parents expect him to earn more money to support the family. Thus, Javier may consider enrolling in a training program or postsecondary education in an effort to increase his earning potential.

If Javier decides to enter community college, college, or a university, he will be the first member of his immediate family to do so. In general, FGCSs lack role models who can guide them through the transition to postsecondary education. If his social support system is lacking, this will likely influence his career indecision and affect his adjustment to college (Schmidt, Miles, & Welsh, 2011). As a bisexual male, he might also experience harassment, fear for his safety, and a lack of confidence (Rankin, 2003). Thus, it is important for the counselor to connect Javier with mentors who can assist him with the transition to college. To identify possible mentors, Javier could complete a career genogram (Prosek, 2013) in which he identifies occupations held by his family members. Although his parents did not attend college, it is possible that other family members have postsecondary training and education.

It may also be helpful to expand Javier's network beyond his family. Working with his school counselor, Javier can obtain contact information for alumni from his high school who are enrolled in college or working in specific careers of interest and who could provide valuable guidance as mentors. Javier can conduct informational interviews with these alumni to determine strategies for college and career success. They will be able provide him with insight into balancing work and school as well as getting involved on campus. He also can connect with individuals within his religious community who may serve as mentors. Ideally, by the time Javier leaves for college, he will have multiple strategies to help him be academically and socially prepared for college life. Javier is empowered by knowing that even if his career intentions change along the way, he can use Possible Selves Mapping to create a new path with specific steps to achieve his goals. See Table 15.1 for an application guide.

Conclusion

Possible Selves Mapping is a postmodern career model that can be used with culturally diverse adolescents to enhance self-concept and identify development. This approach can help PFGCSs consider their options, prepare academically and socially for college, and determine strategies to overcome barriers. Through curious questioning, counselors guide individuals to make self-authorized career decisions and create manageable plans for achieving their career goals. This helps to develop career-ready students and set them on a path to discovering purpose, meaning, and career satisfaction.

Recommended Resources

Bureau of Labor Statistics. (2015). *Occupational outlook handbook.* Retrieved from http://www.bls.gov/ooh/
Career One Stop. (2015). *What's my next move guide.* Retrieved from http://www.careeronestop.org/whats-my-next-move.aspx/
Michel, R. E. (2013). Possible selves mapping. In C. Wood & D. Hays (Eds.), *A counselor's guide to career assessment instruments* (6th ed., pp. 503–507). Broken Arrow, OK: National Career Development Association.
My Next Move. (2015). *What do you want to do for a living?* Retrieved from www.mynextmove.org
O*NET. (2015). *Build your future with O*NET online.* Retrieved from https://www.onetonline.org/

Table 15.1

Practical Application Guide

Topic	Possible Selves Mapping
General goals and purposes	1. Consider career goals, fears, and self-concepts to engage in meaningful career planning. 2. Construct, rank, and evaluate hoped-for and feared possible selves. 3. Identify potential occupations to pursue or avoid. 4. Determine the steps required to reach one's career goals.
Applicable modality	Individual, couples, family, group, classroom lesson
Applicable counselor settings	School, career, college and student development, mental health/community agency, private practice
Recommended time to complete	The assessment takes approximately 20 to 30 minutes to complete, depending on the number of possible selves an individual constructs.
Materials/equipment needed	Paper and pen/pencil
Step-by-step outline of the process	1. Introduce Possible Selves Mapping and provide developmentally appropriate examples. 2. Invite the client to relax and think about "what you hope to become" (positive projections) and "what you fear, dread, or don't want for yourself" (negative projections). 3. Prompt the client to rank these possible selves in order of importance and place a star next to the possible self the client feels most able to achieve. 4. Ask the client to rate the capability he or she has to become that possible self (1 = *not at all capable* to 7 = *completely capable*) and ability to achieve or prevent each possible self (1 = *not at all likely to happen* to 7 = *completely likely to happen*). 5. Assist the client in brainstorming actions required to bring about or prevent the possible selves from emerging. 6. Allow the client to deconstruct the meaning of each possible self and add or remove possible selves from the list. 7. Prompt the client to identify careers of interest based on possible selves and brainstorm the skills, knowledge, and abilities required for each possible career. 8. Ask follow-up questions to access client interests, self-efficacy, outcome expectations, barriers, and supports for each possible career. 9. Allow the client to establish steps to cope with unplanned events and barriers when making career decisions and achieving career goals. 10. Revisit the Possible Selves Map throughout the counseling process as necessary.

Shepard, B. (2005). Embedded selves: Co-constructing a relationally based career workshop for rural girls. *Canadian Journal of Counselling, 39*, 231–244.

References

Black, D. A., Makar, H. R., Sanders, S. G., & Taylor, L. J. (2003). The earnings effects of sexual orientation. *Industrial & Labor Relations Review, 56*, 449–469. doi:10.2307/3590918

Booth, N. R., Travis, S. P., Borzumato-Gainey, C., & Degges-White, S. (2014). Social involvement: Helping students find their place in campus life. In S. Degges-White & C. Borzumato-Gainey (Eds.), *College student mental health counseling* (pp. 69–80). New York, NY: Springer.

Chen, X., & Carroll, C. D. (2005). *First-generation students in postsecondary education: A look at their college transcripts* (NCES 2005-171). Washington, DC: U.S. Department of Education, National Center for Education Statistics.

Constantine, M. G., Wallace, B. C., & Kindaichi, M. M. (2005). Examining contextual factors in the career decision status of African American adolescents. *Journal of Career Assessment, 13*, 307–319. doi:10.1177/1069072705274960

Cross, S., & Markus, H. (1991). Possible selves across the life span. *Human Development, 34*, 230–255. doi:10.1159/000277058

Davis, J. (2010). *The first-generation student experience: Implications for campus practice and strategies for improving persistence and success.* Sterling, VA: Stylus.

Dennis, J. M., Phinney, J. S., & Chuateco, L. I. (2005). The role of motivation, parental support, and peer support in academic success of ethnic minority first-generation college students. *Journal of College Student Development, 46*, 223–236. doi:10.1353/csd.2005.0023

Dunkel, C. (2000). Possible selves as a mechanism for identity exploration. *Journal of Adolescence, 23*, 519–529. doi:10.1006/jado.2000.0340

Erikson, E. H. (1968). *Identity: Youth and crisis.* New York, NY: Norton.

Fisher, T. A., & Padmawidjaja, I. (1999). Parental influences on career development perceived by African American and Mexican American college students. *Journal of Multicultural Counseling and Development, 27*, 136–152. doi:10.1002/j.2161-1912.1999.tb00220.x

Flores, L. Y., Navarro, R. L., & DeWitz, S. J. (2008). Mexican American high school students' postsecondary educational goals: Applying social cognitive career theory. *Journal of Career Assessment, 16*, 489–501. doi:10.1177/1069072708318905

Flores, L. Y., & Obasi, E. M. (2005). Mentor's influence on Mexican American students' career and educational development. *Journal of Multicultural Counseling and Development, 33*, 146–164. doi:10.1002/j.2161-1912.2005.tb00013.x

Flores, L. Y., Ojeda, L., Huang, Y., Gee, D., & Lee, S. (2006). The relation of acculturation, problem solving appraisal, and career decision-making self-efficacy to Mexican American high school students' educational goals. *Journal of Counseling Psychology, 53*, 260–266. doi:10.1037/0022-0167.53.2.260

Flores, L. Y., Robitschek, C., Celebi, E., Anderson, C., & Hoang, U. (2010). Social cognitive influences on Mexican Americans' career choices across Holland's themes. *Journal of Vocational Behavior, 76,* 198–210. doi:10.1016/j.jvb.2009.11.002

Flum, H., & Bluestein, D. L. (2000). Reinvigorating the study of vocational exploration: A framework for research. *Journal of Vocational Behavior, 56,* 380–404. doi:10.1006/jvbe.2000.1721

Gándara, P., & Contreras, F. (2009). *The Latino education crisis: The consequences of failed school policies.* Cambridge, MA: Harvard University Press.

Garriott, P. O., & Flores, L. Y. (2013). The role of social cognitive factors in Mexican American students' educational goals and performance: A longitudinal analysis. *Journal of Latina/o Psychology, 1,* 85–94. doi:10.1006/jvbe.2000.1721

Gibbons, M. M., & Borders, L. D. (2010). Prospective first-generation college students: A social-cognitive perspective. *The Career Development Quarterly, 58,* 194–208. doi: 10.1002/j.2161-0045.2010.tb00186.x

Ginorio, A., & Huston, M. (2001). *¡Sí se puede! Yes, we can!: Latinas in school.* Washington, DC: American Association of University Women Educational Foundation.

Gysbers, N. C. (2013). Career-ready students: A goal of comprehensive school counseling programs. *The Career Development Quarterly, 61,* 283–288. doi:10.1002/j.2161-0045.2013.00057.x

Hetherington, C. (1991). Life planning and career counseling with gay and lesbian students. In N. J. Evans & V. A. Wall (Eds.), *Beyond tolerance: Gays, lesbians, and bisexuals on campus* (pp. 131–145). Alexandria, VA: American College Personnel Association.

Ishitani, T. T. (2003). A longitudinal approach to assessing attrition behavior among first-generation students: Time-varying effects of pre-college characteristics. *Research in Higher Education, 44,* 433–449. doi:10.1023/A:1024284932709

Keeton Parnell, M., Lease, H., & Green, M. L. (2012). Perceived career barriers for gay, lesbian, and bisexual individuals. *Journal of Career Development, 39,* 248–268. doi:10.1177/0894845310386730

Lent, R. W., Brown, S. D., & Hackett, G. (1994). Toward a unifying social cognitive theory of career and academic interest, choice, and performance. *Journal of Vocational Behavior, 45,* 79–122. doi:10.1006/jvbe.1994.1027

Lohfink, M. M., & Paulsen, M. B. (2005). Comparing the determinants of persistence for first-generation and continuing-generation students. *Journal of College Student Development, 46,* 409–428. doi:10.1353/csd.2005.0040

Majer, J. (2009). Self-efficacy and academic stress among ethnically diverse first-generation community college students. *Journal of Diversity in Higher Education, 2,* 243–250. doi:10.1037/a0017852

Markus, H., & Nurius, P. (1986). Possible selves. *American Psychologist, 41,* 954–969. doi:10.1037/0003-066X.41.9.954

McMahon, M., & Patton, W. (2002). Using qualitative assessment in career counseling. *International Journal of Vocational and Educational Guidance, 51,* 51–60.

McWhirter, E. H., Torres, D. M., Salgado, S., & Valdez, M. (2007). Perceived barriers and postsecondary plans in Mexican American and White adolescents. *Journal of Career Assessment, 15*, 119–138. doi:10.1177/1069072706294537

Meara, N. M., Day, J. D., Chalk, L. M., & Phelps, R. E. (1995). Possible selves: Applications for career counseling. *Journal of Career Assessment, 3*, 259–277. doi:10.1177/106907279500300402

Motel, S., & Patten, E. (2012). *Hispanic of Mexican origin, 2010.* Washington, DC: Pew Hispanic Center.

Neimeyer, G. J. (1992). Personal constructs in career counseling and development. *Journal of Career Development, 18*, 163–173. doi:10.1177/089484539201800301

Ojeda, L., & Flores, L. Y. (2008). The influence of generation level, parents' educational level, and perceived barriers on the educational aspirations and expectations of Mexican heritage high school students. *The Career Development Quarterly, 57*, 84–95. doi:10.1002/j.2161-0045.2008.tb00168.x

Oyserman, D., Gant, L., & Ager, J. (1995). A socially contextualized model of African American identity: Possible selves and school persistence. *Journal of Personality and Social Psychology, 69*, 1216–1232.

Perna, L. W. (2000). Differences in the decision to attend college among African Americans, Hispanics, and Whites. *The Journal of Higher Education, 71*, 117–141. doi:10.2307/2649245

Perry, J. C., & Vance, K. S. (2010). Possible selves among urban youths of color: An exploration of peer beliefs and gender differences. *The Career Development Quarterly, 58*, 257–269.

Prosek, E. A. (2013). Career genogram. In C. Wood & D. Hays (Eds.), *A counselor's guide to career assessment instruments* (6th ed., pp. 459–464). Broken Arrow, OK: National Career Development Association.

Rankin, S. R. (2003). *Campus climate for gay, lesbian, bisexual, and transgender people: A national perspective.* New York, NY: National Gay and Lesbian Task Force Policy Institute.

Reach Higher. (2014). Retrieved from https://www.whitehouse.gov/reach-higher.

Schmidt, C. K., Miles, J. R., & Welsh, A. C. (2011). Perceived discrimination and social support: The influences on career development and college adjustment of LGBT college students. *Journal of Career Development, 38*, 293–309. doi:10.1177/0894845310372615

Schmidt, C. K., & Nilsson, J. E. (2006). The effects of simultaneous developmental processes: Factors relating to the career development of lesbian, gay, and bisexual youth. *The Career Development Quarterly, 55*, 22–37. doi:10.1002/j.2161-0045.2006.tb00002.x

Sheffield, M. L. (2011). *Stories of success: First generation Mexican-American college graduates* (Doctoral dissertation). Retrieved from http://hdl.handle.net/2286/R.A.56948

Shepard, B. (2010). *Future bound: A lifeworks expedition workshop for rural youth.* Retrieved from pathstothefuture.com/pdf/Future_Bound-Blythe_Shepard.pdf

Shepard, B., & Marshall, A. (1999). Possible selves mapping: Life-career exploration with young adolescents. *Canadian Journal of Counselling, 33*, 37–54.

Shepard, B., & Quressette, S. (2010). *Possible selves mapping intervention: Rural women and beyond.* Retrieved from http://counselingoutfitters. com/vistas/vistas10/Article_51.pdf

Torres, V., & Hernandez, E. (2009). Influence of an identified advisor/mentor on urban Latino students' college experience. *Journal of College Student Retention Research, Theory, & Practice, 11*, 141–160. doi:10.2190/CS.11.1.h

Turner, S. L., Alliman-Brissett, A., Lapan, R. T., Udipi, S., & Ergun, D. (2003). The career-related parent support scale. *Measurement and Evaluation in Counseling and Development, 56*, 44–55.

U.S. Department of Education. (2014). Institutional retention and graduation rates for undergraduate students. In *The condition of education 2014* (NCES 2014-083) (pp. 194–197). Washington, DC: National Center for Education Statistics.

Yowell, C. M. (2002). Dreams of the future: The pursuit of education and career possible selves among ninth grade Latino youth. *Applied Developmental Science, 6*, 62–72. doi:10.1207/S1532480XADS0602_2

Zavadil, A., & Kooyman, L. (2014). Understanding diverse populations on the college campus. In S. Degges-White & C. Borzumato-Gainey (Eds.), *College student mental health counseling* (pp. 51–68). New York, NY: Springer.

Chapter 16

The Life Design Genogram: Self-Construction With an Italian Female Transitioning to the World of Work

Annamaria Di Fabio

Career counseling interventions that use story to help clients give meaning to their personal and professional lives have emerged in the 21st century (Hartung, 2013; Maree, 2007). In this approach, life design counselors help clients construct their own stories (Guichard, 2013; Savickas, 2005, 2011; Savickas et al., 2009). The life design counselor helps clients construct, deconstruct, co-construct, and reconstruct their own stories to highlight the life themes that bring cohesion to their lives and give direction for continuing to live them (Savickas, 2011). Through this process, clients construct their own subjective career, giving meaning and direction to their own stories during the career and life transitions they encounter (Savickas, 2011).

All of this is reflected in the success formula of Savickas's *My Career Story* (2011), which emphasizes the importance of self-discovery and the use of one's values and life purposes in creating a professional and life path that satisfies purpose and meaning for the person. This parallels the overall focus of narrative, which is how to understand and enhance the power of the individual's story (Savickas, 2005). This is a significant move away from a traditional objective observation of the individual and toward subjective engagement with the person (Rehfuss, 2009). In the narrative perspective, it is important to assess and highlight changes in life and occupational self-narratives (Rehfuss & Di Fabio, 2012), which provides an expanded, fuller, or clearer conceptualization of the self (Savickas, 2010). Through telling biographical stories about different life experiences and future desires, individuals unify themselves and give meaning to their lives as they design their future selves (Guichard, 2013; Savickas, 2011). Tying an individual's career to his or her authentic self (Di Fabio, 2014a) and having a purposeful awareness of self identity is pivotal for success in the 21st century. The awareness of plural identities (Guichard, 2013) takes into account one's own system of subjective identity forms and also the aspired subjective identity form (SIF). SIF refers to the main role that the individual wishes to achieve in the construction of the future chapter of his or her life, and it is important for continually promoting the development of one's resources and increasing one's authenticity (Guichard, 2004). The reflexivity process fosters authenticity and enhances awareness about self-presentation strategies. Paulhus (1984, 1986) made a clear distinction between impression management, which is a conscious bias in favor of self, and self-deception, which is an unconscious distortion of self. Telling stories anchored to the Life Design Genogram serves to check the authentic self against family messages, and we can help clients recognize elements useful to disempower the processes by which they deceive themselves in their life projects (Di Fabio, 2014a).

At its foundation, narrative is intrinsically qualitative, and the Life Design Genogram is an effective assessment and intervention that allows individuals to tell their stories to themselves and to the counselor. This engages clients in a reflective co-construction that helps them to recognize the storied self that permeates the past and the present and provides direction for the future (Savickas, 1997). In writing the next chapter of one's life, it is not only about the process of deciding but also about becoming something more and different (Savickas, 2011). The Life Design Genogram was developed based on both career construction theory (Savickas, 2005, 2011) and life construction theory (Guichard, 2013). These theories enable clients to build future selves based on authentic intentionality.

In this chapter, I describe the Life Design Genogram and present a case study of Angela, a woman from southern Italy who recently graduated with a degree in law from the University of Florence. She has requested career counseling to assist her with decisions related to transitioning from the university to the world of work.

The Career Genogram

The genogram has traditionally been used in family therapy (Bowen, 1978) to help family members reflect on intergenerational family influences. It has been adapted for use in career interventions (McGoldrick & Gerson, 1985) and focuses on occupational choice (Dagley, 1984; Gysbers & Moore, 1987; Isaacson & Brown, 1997; Okiishi, 1987). In career interventions, the genogram initially was considered a common form of qualitative career assessment that gave a proactive role to the client (McMahon, 2008; Patton, 2007). This view has been expanded and is now being used as a postmodern, qualitative technique to help clients tell their stories during the career intervention (Gysbers, Heppner, & Johnston, 2009). Using the career genogram allows people to connect their past to their present and to design their future (e.g., Alderfer, 2004).

The Career Construction Genogram (Di Fabio, 2012) was developed on the foundation of the Strengthened Career Genogram (Di Fabio, 2010) and represents a postmodern career tool to empower individuals from a narrative perspective. In this framework, the genogram is seen as both a career assessment and a useful intervention when working with individuals' life stories that help them become more self-aware. In career counseling, clients often want to construct a new story and need help clarifying that the self is a unique story and not simply a list of traits (Savickas, 2005).

The Life Design Genogram

The Life Design Genogram highlights the subjectivity and complexity of relationships from the past and the present, which is essential in designing the future. Using the Life Design Genogram, clients construct meaning and purpose through narrative rather than from a state and trait assessment (Savickas, 2005, 2011). The Life Design Genogram combines the Career Construction Genogram (Di Fabio, 2012) and the Life Genogram (Di Fabio, 2014a). This perspective also draws on the theory of social construction aligning with Savickas et al.'s (2009) life design theory because it views the self not as a process of individual construction but as a co-construction through a collaboration with the social group and the community. The Life Design Genogram (Di Fabio, 2014a) draws on the self-construction theory of Guichard (2009), which conceptualizes individuals as being plural in nature, meaning that the individual's identity is a dynamic system consisting of differing SIFs. In addition, it pulls from Guichard's (2013) subsequent and more complete life construction theory, which highlights the belief that individuals in postmodern societies unify themselves by connecting their different life experiences to make sense and meaning of their lives. Thus, the Life Design Genogram guides individuals to unify themselves through connecting their different life experiences expressed in their narratives of the past and the present to provide direction for the future. The tool enables individuals to act with intention while constructing future stories that are based on a more authentic perspective of the self (Di Fabio, 2014b).

The Life Design Genogram uses an enhanced reflection method, which includes a thorough reflection and detailed articulation of each member of the family. This is accomplished by first focusing on career with the Career Construction Genogram and then focusing on life with the Life Genogram. The enriched reflection method for both genograms includes these four reflection activities:

- Reflecting on the dreams and aspirations of each person who appears in the genogram (jewel case)
- Reflecting on both self-ascribed qualities and qualities attributed to the person by others (mirror)
- Reflecting on the messages handed down explicitly to new generations (letter)
- Reflecting on the personal motto of each member in the genogram (parchment)

After following this process for each family member, clients identify the work and life mottos of each guiding line (the father line and the mother line) and then produce their own authentic work and life mottos. Next, clients are invited to reflect on their own work and life mottos, confirming or distancing themselves from the work and life mottos of the guiding lines in the construction of their own future. Savickas (2011) highlighted that the motto becomes the best advice that individuals can give themselves for constructing their future career and life. Through dialogue with the counselor, clients begin to design a future that is in harmony with their personal formula for success (Savickas, 2011).

The Case of Angela

The case study describes the process and usefulness of the Life Design Genogram in facilitating Angela's ability to identify the work and life perspectives handed down to her by her guiding lines (i.e., motto of the father line and motto of the mother line). In addition, it clarifies how she constructed and expanded her work and life mottos based on her own personal meaning, inspiring the construction of her own professional and personal path and structuring the next chapter of her life story. The case study describes and tries to answer two questions:

- How does the Life Design Genogram apply to the case of a young Italian woman from southern Italy graduating with a law major, and transitioning from the university to the world of work?
- How does the Life Design Genogram help this young woman reflect on work and life perspectives handed down to her from her guiding lines?

Client Background

Angela has just graduated from law school at a large city university in Italy. She is visiting the United States and staying with friends she met at the university. One of her friends suggested that she participate in career counseling from a local career practitioner to assist her as she transitions from the university to the world of work.

Angela is 26 years old and comes from a small town in Sicily where her entire family still lives. Overall, the labor market in Italy is character-ized by instability and economic constriction, with little job creation. This is even worse in the southern regions of Italy. In addition, the southern regions of Italy are known to have stronger prejudices against women working, so it is even more difficult for a woman to successfully obtain meaningful work in her field of interest. Angela desires to use her law training to work in the field of international relations. Ideally she would like to obtain a position with the World Bank Group in the United States or with a similar type of international organization in Europe. A conflict arises as her family wants her to return to Sicily, where she may have the opportunity to complete a law internship with a firm that employs her aunt. Her family suggests this career placement because this particular firm allows women to work minimal hours a day, enabling Angela to have more time for a future husband and children. She is currently single.

The Client's Career Concern

Angela requested the Life Design counseling intervention because she is uncertain about what to do with her training in law after graduation. Angela struggles with the expectations of her family of origin that she come back home and complete her law internship in the law firm of her aunt. To establish herself, Angela feels that it is necessary to do what she desires, which is to work in an international organization. However, she does not know if she will be able to manage the conflict with her family due to their expectations for her.

Steps in the Life Design Genogram

The qualitative assessment using the Life Design Genogram was carried out over five 1-hour sessions. This intervention aims to increase and promote the awareness of the authentic self (Di Fabio, 2014a), moving away from strategies of self-presentation such as impression management and self-deception (Paulhus, 1984, 1986). There are two goals: the first is to facilitate full awareness of one's own authentic meanings according to the personal success formula of Savickas (2011), and the second is to increase awareness of one's own SIFs (Guichard, 2010) and of one's core SIF (Guichard, 2013)—that is, a SIF within which the person wants to achieve "self-actualization." As an assessment tool, the Life Design Genogram collects useful information that enables individuals to recognize the complexity of the messages they have received on work and life from their family and also highlights the individuals' unique intervention needs. The Life Design Genogram as an intervention helps the individual to consciously build a new motto of a future career and life for the next chapter of her life. This part of the Life Design Genogram as intervention is titled "From my genogram toward my future."

The qualitative assessment of the Life Design Genogram gathers valuable information. It allows the client to express her needs while enabling the counselor to recognize the unique needs of diverse clients settled in their life story. The qualitative intervention through the Life Design Genogram facilitates adaptability and intentionality (Savickas, 2011), using guided metareflections (Maree, 2013) in the dialogical perspective of "To make oneself Self" (Guichard, 2004). This kind of intervention supports the client in making sense of her life while building future stories based on authentic intentionality and facilitates the passage from intention to action (Savickas, 2013).

In retrieving the overall framework of one's life story from the extended roots of the family, the client has the opportunity to deal with the complexity of the relational and contextual influences in which her life story is embedded. Equipped with this information, the client can examine and reexamine the influences, so that her future narrative can become more personal and more authentic. The assessment part of the Life Design Genogram facilitates the identification of themes and entails a careful and effective process to construct, deconstruct, co-construct, and reconstruct the story of the client. This helps the client to clarify life themes that bring cohesion to her life and that can give direction for continuing to live it (Savickas, 2011). Also, the Life Design Genogram begins the process of uncovering the complex scenario of the client's life story, permits the specific needs of each client to emerge, and prepares the ground for a more effective process of reflexivity, which is required by the intervention. Therefore, the Life Design Genogram is an exploratory phase of the intervention.

When beginning the administration of the Life Design Genogram, the counselor includes an explanation of the purpose of the two instruments and instructs the client in how to build both the Career Construction Genogram and the Life Construction Genogram. The participant is asked to respond with detailed reflection (described at the beginning of this chapter) on each member of the family. In particular, the client is asked to focus on career with the first genogram and on life with the second genogram, identifying the work mottos and then the life mottos from both the father's and mother's lines. After this step, the participant is asked to reflect in depth, thinking carefully about the findings before providing her own work motto and her own life motto. The participant is also asked to reflect on whether her personal mottos on work and life are either consistent with or divergent from her two family lines. In addition, the client will explore which line she feels she most resembles, how they may differ, and how they can evolve beyond these lines. At the end of the genogram, the participant is asked to answer this question: "What will you take away from the Life Design Genogram that is particularly helpful for you to remember?" After the client has reflected on the work done, the client notes the following: (a) What was the most impressive thing I learned from my Life Design Genogram? and (b) What was the thing that most impressed me in relation to my professional and personal life until now, and in relation to my future professional and personal life?

After the Life Design Genogram assessment, the intervention continues with the part of the genogram titled "From my genogram toward my future." This part includes the exercise "Me and the Future." In this exercise, the participant is asked to answer one question each related to the four dimensions of career adaptability: concern, control, curiosity, and confidence (Savickas, 2001; Savickas & Porfeli, 2012). The first question relating to concern is "How much concern do I have for myself in the future? Why?" This is followed by the participant completing the following sentence: "With respect to the future, I am . . . ," choosing from a list of adjectives such as "anticipating," "predicting," and so forth. The second question relates to control and asks "How much do I feel in control of my future? Why?" The participant then indicates all of the characteristics that describe her by completing the following sentence: "With respect to the future, I am . . . ," choosing from a list of adjectives such as "autonomous," "responsible," and so forth. The third question relates to curiosity: "How much curiosity do I have related to building my future? Why?" The participant indicates all of the characteristics that describe her by completing the following sentence: "With respect to the future, I am ... ," choosing from a list of adjectives such as "investigative," "inquiring," and so forth. The fourth question relates to confidence and asks "How much confidence do I have in building my future? Why?" The participant indicates all of the characteristics that describe her by completing the following sentence: "With respect to the future, I am ... ," choosing from a list of adjectives such as "productive" or "capable."

This work is followed by exercises of metareflection (Maree, 2013) and dialogical counseling based on "To make oneself Self" (Guichard, 2004). The participant reflects on the meaning of new discoveries and traces her future authentic intentionality. The process facilitates passage from intention to action. At the end of this intervention, two questions are administered: (a) "What specific thing do I take away for me, which is very important for me to remember?" and (b) "Why is this very important for me to remember in constructing my future purposeful self?" These two questions allow the participant to reflect on and select the most useful new discoveries to use in constructing an authentic new intentionality and writing the next chapter of her life.

Application of the Life Design Genogram

The first assessment used with Angela was the Life Design Genogram. The counselor explained how to create a genogram. Angela's questions about the process were answered until she understood enough to start drawing her Life Design Genogram (see Figure 16.1).

The analysis of Angela's Life Design Genogram revealed several mottos. The first to emerge were the work and life mottos of her parental lines. The work motto from the father's line was "Choose a prestigious type of work." The work motto from the mother's line was "It is not important for a woman to work." The life motto from the father's line was "Appearances are more important than who you are." The life motto from the mother's line was "Family is the most important thing."

The counselor interacted with Angela to facilitate reflection and increase awareness about the value and meaning of the family's life and work mottos. The counselor asked Angela, "What is your personal work motto and what is your life motto?" Angela answered, "My personal work motto is 'My work is a part of myself,' and my personal life motto is 'The most important thing for me is not appearances but to be real.'" Then the counselor asked Angela, "What will you take away from the Life Design Genogram that is particularly helpful for you to remember?" Angela elaborated and described how her mottos were very different from the mottos of her parents. With respect to her work motto, Angela particularly highlighted "My work motto is different from my maternal line because for me work is an essential part of myself." She needed to express herself completely through work, and she did not want to renounce her work to

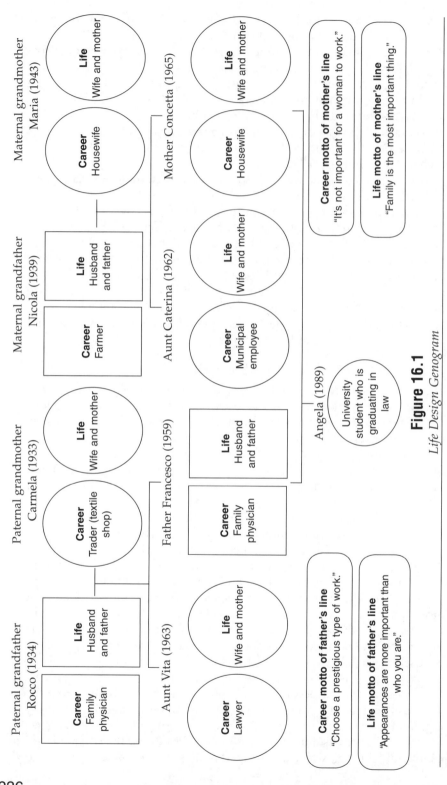

Figure 16.1
Life Design Genogram

Note. A square represents a male individual and a circle represents a female individual. An additional key to individuals follows on the next pages.

Paternal grandfather, Rocco (1934)

Career	*Life*
Family physician	Husband and father
Jewel case: Surgeon	Jewel case: He did what he wished
Mirror: *Intelligent with a sense of practical*; reliable and competent	Mirror: *Committed and careful*; faithful and generous
Letter: "It is important to make a prestigious job and that it will be recognized by society."	Letter: "It's important to keep up appearances."
Parchment: "The work is important if other people recognize it is important."	Parchment: "In life it is important how other people see you."

Paternal grandmother, Carmela (1933)

Career	*Life*
Trader (textile shop)	Wife and mother
Jewel case: Having a textile factory	Jewel case: She did what she wished
Mirror: *Determined, intrapreneurial, hard worker*	Mirror: *Determined, self-confident, faithful, careful*
Letter: "Prestige and money are really important."	Letter: "Do what you want but always try to keep up appearances."
Parchment: "A prestigious job for society is a source of satisfaction."	Parchment: "In life it is important only to keep up appearances."

Maternal grandfather, Nicola (1939)

Career	*Life*
Farmer	Husband and father
Jewel case: He always thought to be a farmer and to carry on the family business	Jewel case: He did what he wished
Mirror: *Meticulous, hard worker*, passion for the job	Mirror: *Faithful to family values, serious*, dedicated to family
Letter: "Work for your family."	Letter: "The family must always come in first place."
Parchment: "Work and family."	Parchment: "Family and work."

Figure 16.1 *(Continued)*
Life Design Genogram

Note. A square represents a male individual and a circle represents a female individual. Jewel case = career life dreams and aspirations; Mirror = self-ascribed personal qualities listed first in italics with personal qualities attributed to the person by others to follow; Letter = messages about work transmitted to new/future generations; Parchment = the personal motto on work/life of each member of the genogram.

Maternal grandmother, Maria (1943)

Career	Life
Housewife	Wife and mother
Jewel case: Seamstress	Jewel case: She did what she wished
Mirror: *Patient, precise,* meticulous, tenacious	Mirror: *Patient, serious,* attentive to the needs of her family
Letter: "For a woman it isn't important to work but to take care of the family."	Letter: "For a woman the most important thing is to deal with the family."
Parchment: "The best job is what you do for your family."	Parchment: "Family first of all."

Aunt, Vita (1963)

Career	Life
Lawyer	Wife and mother
Jewel case: She would like to dedicate more to career	Jewel case: She did what she wished
Mirror: *Determined, fierce, competitive,* competent, prepared	Mirror: *Determined, ambitious,* attentive mother but also hard worker
Letter: "You must be very determined to get what you want."	Letter: "Try always to get what you want by all means."
Parchment: "The prestige of the job is everything to a person."	Parchment: "The reputation is everything."

Father, Francesco (1959)

Career	Life
Family physician	Husband and father
Jewel case: To be a researcher in medicine	Jewel case: He would like to engage more in social events
Mirror: *Passionate about research, investigative,* creative, competent, qualified	Mirror: *Sensitive, attentive to others,* unselfish
Letter: "Try to do your job well because people judge you."	Letter: "In life it is important the image that you give outside."
Parchment: "Work is a way to get money and prestige."	Parchment: "In life it is important to give a good image of ourselves."

Figure 16.1 (Continued)
Life Design Genogram

Note. A square represents a male individual and a circle represents a female individual. Jewel case = career life dreams and aspirations; Mirror = self-ascribed personal qualities listed first in italics with personal qualities attributed to the person by others to follow; Letter = messages about work transmitted to new/future generations; Parchment = the personal motto on work/life of each member of the genogram.

Aunt, Caterina (1962)

Career	Life
Municipal employee	Wife and mother
Jewel case: She did what she wished	Jewel case: She did what she wished
Mirror: *Meticulous, precise,* serene, reliable	Mirror: *Quiet, serene,* realized
Letter: "Make a job that allows you to have space for the family."	Letter: "In life, always keep in mind that you have a family."
Parchment: "The family comes before work."	Parchment: "The family is the center of life."

Mother, Concetta (1965)

Career	Life
Housewife	Wife and mother
Jewel case: Teacher	Jewel case: She would like to work and not to be only the housewife
Mirror: *patient, generous, extrovert, sociable, gentle*	Mirror: *Patient, generous with her family,* attentive to the needs of her family
Letter: "It's important to work but also to take care of his family."	Letter: "The family is important but you have to understand what you want to do to really realize."
Parchment: "The family first of all also before the personal and professional realization."	Parchment: "However the family is the most important thing."

Figure 16.1 *(Continued)*
Life Design Genogram

Note. A square represents a male individual and a circle represents a female individual. Jewel case = career life dreams and aspirations; Mirror = self-ascribed personal qualities listed first in italics with personal qualities attributed to the person by others to follow; Letter = messages about work transmitted to new/future generations; Parchment = the personal motto on work/life of each member of the genogram.

take care of a family even if she would like to become a wife and a mother in the future. She said it was also different from her father's line because "it's not important for me to have a prestigious job, but it is essential that I can express myself through my job." Angela's work motto especially expressed the importance of work to the construction of her authentic self and identity. On the basis of these elements, Angela gained a greater awareness of what she would like to do and how her desire to work in international relations would enable her to express herself through work and place her in a very prestigious environment.

With regard to her life motto, Angela noted that again her mottos did not agree with either of her parental life mottos. She particularly highlighted that her life motto was the opposite of her father's life motto. For Angela, it was fundamental to live a life that permited her to express herself completely through both her work and her personal life. She would like to try to construct her own life and not follow the life that her family desired and expected of her. At the present moment, it was essential for Angela to realize that her occupational daydream was to work in an international organization. Angela needs to leave her family to build her own independent life. Leaving would allow her to continue to grow and fully realize her potential. Through broadening her horizons in the international arena she would be able to emerge from the constraints of a monocultural reality that for her was unsustainable. In addition, Angela reflected that she also desired to distance herself from the life motto of her maternal line. She considered it to be very important to focus on professional achievement at this time. In the future, she would not neglect the family that she would like to build and balance with work. At the present, however, she felt that work must be her primary focus, as it was essential to help her realize and construct herself.

The exercise "Me and the Future" permitted Angela to reflect on the career adaptability resources she could use in facing the challenge of her future. Regarding the first question about *concern*, Angela answered, "I have a lot of apprehension about my future because I'm really interested in constructing my life. I think the choices I make today can influence my future. The terms that describe me and my future are *involved* and *anticipating*."

Concerning the second question about *control*, she answered: "I think I can control my future. I'm positive about my future, and I would like to construct my life independently of others. The terms that describe me are *positive attitude* and *autonomous*."

With regard to the third question about *curiosity*, she answered, "I'm curious about my future because I want to know which path I will follow to begin working in an international context, and I'm gathering information. The terms that describe me are *investigative* and *inquiring*."

In relation to the fourth question about *confidence*, she answered, "I have confidence to build my future because I'm competent and can overcome obstacles. The terms that describe me are *capable* and *resilient*."

Regarding the last two questions, Angela reported what she would take away from the exercise that was particularly helpful for her to remember. She wanted to choose work that would allow her to completely realize herself and she needed it to be in an international context. This was particularly helpful for her to remember because she has never forgotten the importance of having work that was significant for her, and was right now she wanted to realize her dream of working in international relations in the United States.

The Life Design Genogram helped Angela gain greater self-awareness of what was vitally important to her professionally; that is, work for her is critical to her identity (Guichard, 2005). Nevertheless, she did not want to forget the eventual importance of family. This reflection allowed Angela to get in touch with her authentic self (Di Fabio, 2014a), enabling her to reflect on strategies of impression management and self-deception (Paulhus, 1984, 1986).

The Life Design Genogram also allowed Angela to express her unique needs based on the overview of her storied family constellation and to regain possession of her life through delineating the most authentic meaning for her: the discovery, defining what was true success for her in accordance with her personal success formula (Savickas, 2011). After reflecting on her personal work motto, Angela was confronted with her core SIF, which expressed the need for self-actualization. She desired work in an international organization, particularly in the United States, and decided to begin to look for information about possible positions with an international organization in the United States such as the World Bank Group. In addition, she had a secondary SIF consistent with the System of SIFs (Guichard, 2010), which was her desire for a future family consistent with her personal life motto and the life motto of her mother's line. However, at this point in her life, Angela's main aspired SIF was working in an international organization, and she was committed to realizing this. See Table 16.1 for an application guide.

Conclusion

Using the Life Design Genogram as an assessment and intervention in the case study highlighted the value of narrative processes in self-construction, which is in line with the reflections of Savickas (2005, 2010) and Guichard (2005, 2009). The Life Design Genogram focuses on the career and life mottos of both parental lines to increase clients' own level of awareness, enabling individuals to authentically produce their own career and life mottos, leading to a new chapter in their professional and personal life.

Recommended Resources

Busacca, L. A. (2007). Career construction theory: A practitioner's primer. *Career Planning and Adult Development Journal, 23,* 57–67.
Chope, R. (2006). Assessing family influence in career decision making. *VISTAS Online, 40,* 183–186. Retrieved from http://www.counseling. org/resources/library/vistas/vistas06/vistas06.40.pdf
McGoldrick, M., & Gerson, R. (1985). *Genograms in family assessment.* New York, NY: W. W. Norton.
Remley, T. P., Jr., Bacchini, E., & Krieg, P. (2010). Counseling in Italy. *Journal of Counseling & Development, 88,* 28–32. Retrieved from http://www. ircep.org/doc/ItalyACAJCD_88_01_Win10article07.pdf

References

Alderfer, C. (2004). A family therapist's reaction to the influences of the family of origin on career development: A review and analysis. *The Counseling Psychologist, 32,* 569–577.
Bowen, M. (1978). *Family therapy in clinical practice.* New York, NY: Aronson.

Table 16.1

Practical Application Guide

Topic	Using the Life Design Genogram
General goals and purposes	1. Recognize the complexity of the messages collected by the client on work and life by her or his family. 2. Help the client to build her or his new motto of future career and life for the next chapter of his or her life. 3. Promote awareness of the authentic self, taking distance from self-presentation strategies. 4. Facilitate awareness of one's own authentic meanings and identity. 5. Facilitate the passage from intention to action through a clearer future purposeful self.
Applicable modality	Both individual counseling and group counseling using the power of the audience (Di Fabio, 2013; Di Fabio & Maree, 2012)
Applicable counselor settings	This is not traditional group counseling. The intervention is divided into time periods during which participants complete the exercises in written form and periods during which they interact individually with the counselor while the other participants form an audience. Members of the group are participants in individual counseling with the counselor but also as the audience, listening to other participants without intervening directly. College/university career services, employment centers, private practice
Recommended time to complete	Five sessions (1 hour per session) for individual counseling Three sessions (8 hours per session) for group counseling (group not more than 15 people)
Materials/equipment needed	Sheets with the instructions for the Life Design Genogram; the "Me and the Future" exercises; exercises of metareflection White papers for drawing the genogram and writing reflective thoughts and narrative
Step-by-step outline of the process	1. Introduce and explain the Life Design Genogram. 2. Invite the client to draw her or his Life Design Genogram. 3. Facilitate the client going in depth, thinking carefully about the findings and then producing her or his own work motto and life motto. 4. Facilitate the client's reflection on whether these personal mottos on work and on life are in line with or divergent from each of the two family lines. 5. Facilitate the client's reflection on career adaptability through the exercise "Me and the Future." 6. Facilitate the client's reflection on the authentic meaning of new discoveries and metaphorically trace "the North Star" of his or her future authentic intentionality through exercises of metareflection, preparing the client for action.

Dagley, J. (1984). *A vocational genogram.* Unpublished manuscript, University of Georgia, Athens, GA.

Di Fabio, A. (2010). Life designing in 21st century: Using a new, strengthened career genogram. *Journal of Psychology in Africa, 20,* 381–384.

Di Fabio, A. (2012). Evaluation of the effectiveness of the New Career Construction Genogram. *Cypriot Journal of Educational Sciences, 7,* 287–297.

Di Fabio, A. (2013). Applying career construction in group-based contexts with adults. In A. Di Fabio & J. G. Maree (Eds.), *Psychology of career counseling: New challenges for a new era. Festschrift in honour of Mark Savickas* (pp. 83–99). New York, NY: Nova Science.

Di Fabio, A. (2014a). "Constructing my future purposeful life": A new life construction intervention. In A. Di Fabio & J.-L. Bernaud (Eds.), *The construction of identity in the 21st century: A festschrift for Jean Guichard* (pp. 219–239). New York, NY: Nova Science.

Di Fabio, A. (2014b). The new purposeful identitarian awareness for the twenty-first century: Valorize themselves in the life construction from youth to adulthood and late adulthood. In A. Di Fabio & J.-L. Bernaud (Eds.), *The construction of the identity in 21st century: A festschrift for Jean Guichard.* New York, NY: Nova Science.

Di Fabio, A., & Maree, J. G. (2012). Group-based life design counseling in an Italian context. *Journal of Vocational Behavior, 80,* 100–107.

Guichard, J. (2004). Se faire soi. *L'Orientation Scolaire et Professionnelle, 33,* 499–534.

Guichard, J. (2005). Life-long self-construction. *International Journal for Educational and Vocational Guidance, 5,* 111–124.

Guichard, J. (2009). Self-constructing. *Journal of Vocational Behavior, 75,* 251–258.

Guichard, J. (2010, March). *Les théories de la construction des parcours professionnels et de la construction de soi: Deux approches de la construction de la vie individuelle.* Paper presented at Colloque International INETOP, Paris, France.

Guichard, J. (2013, September). *Which paradigm for career and life designing interventions contributing to the development of a fairer world during the 21st century.* Lecture presented at the IAEVG International Conference, Montpellier, France.

Gysbers, N. C., Heppner, M. J., & Johnston, J. A. (2009). *Career counseling: Contexts, processes, and techniques.* Alexandria, VA: American Counseling Association.

Gysbers, N. C, & Moore, E. J. (1987). *Career counseling: Skills and techniques for practitioners.* Englewood Cliffs, NJ: Prentice Hall.

Hartung, P. J. (2013). Career as story: Making the narrative turn. In W. B. Walsh, M. L. Savickas, & P. J. Hartung (Eds.), *Handbook of vocational psychology* (4th ed., pp. 33–52). New York, NY: Routledge.

Isaacson, L. E., & Brown, D. (1997). *Career information, career counseling, and career development* (6th ed.). Needham Heights, MA: Allyn & Bacon.

Maree, J. G. (Ed.). (2007). *Shaping the story: A guide to facilitating narrative career counseling.* Pretoria, South Africa: Van Schaik.

Maree, J. G. (2013). *Counselling for career construction: Connecting life themes to construct life portraits. Turning pain into hope.* Rotterdam, The Netherlands: Sense.

McGoldrick, M., & Gerson, R. (1985). *Genograms in family assessment.* New York, NY: W. W. Norton.

McMahon, M. (2008). Quality career assessment: A higher profile in the 21st century? In J. A. Athanasou & R. Esbroeck (Eds.), *International handbook of career guidance* (pp. 587–601). Dordrecht, The Netherlands: Springer.

Okiishi, R. W. (1987). The genogram as a tool in career counseling. *Journal of Counseling & Development, 66,* 139–143.

Patton, W. (2007). Theoretical underpinnings and practical application of constructivist approaches to career counselling. In K. Maree (Ed.), *Shaping the story: A guide to facilitating narrative career counselling* (pp. 121–133). Pretoria, South Africa: Van Schaik.

Paulhus, D. L. (1984). Two component models of socially desirable responding. *Journal of Personality and Social Psychology, 46,* 598–609.

Paulhus, D. L. (1986). Self-deception and impression management in test responses. In A. Angleitner & J. S. Wiggins (Eds.), *Personality assessment via questionnaire* (pp. 143–165). New York, NY: Springer Verlag.

Rehfuss, M. C. (2009). The future career autobiography: A narrative measure of career intervention effectiveness. *The Career Development Quarterly, 58,* 82–90.

Rehfuss, M., & Di Fabio, A. (2012). Validating the future career autobiography as a measure of narrative change. *Journal of Career Assessment, 20,* 452–462.

Savickas, M. L. (1997). Career adaptability: An integrative construct for life-span, life-space theory. *The Career Development Quarterly, 45,* 247–259.

Savickas, M. L. (2001). Toward a comprehensive theory of career development: Disposition, concerns and narratives. In F. T. L. Leong & A. Barak (Eds.), *Contemporary models in vocational psychology: A volume in honor of Samuel H. Osipow* (pp. 295–320). Mahwah, NJ: Erlbaum.

Savickas, M. L. (2005). The theory and practice of career construction. In S. D. Brown & R. W. Lent (Eds.), *Career development and counseling: Putting theory and research to work* (pp. 42–70). Hoboken, NJ: Wiley.

Savickas, M. L. (2010, July). *Life designing: Framework and introduction.* Paper presented at the 27th International Congress of Applied Psychology, Melbourne, Australia.

Savickas, M. L. (Ed.). (2011). *Career counseling.* Washington, DC: American Psychological Association.

Savickas, M. L. (2013, September). *Life designing. What is it?* Invited keynote at the IAEVG International Conference, Montpellier, France.

Savickas, M. L., Nota, L., Rossier, J., Dauwalder, J.-P., Duarte, M. E., Guichard, J., & Van Vianen, A. E. M. (2009). Life designing: A paradigm for career construction in the 21st century. *Journal of Vocational Behavior, 75,* 239–250.

Savickas, M. L., & Porfeli, E. J. (2012). Career Adapt-Abilities Scale: Construction, reliability, and measurement equivalence across 13 countries. *Journal of Vocational Behavior, 80,* 661–673.

Chapter 17

Relational Cultural Career Assessment: The Case of an Indian Immigrant First-Year College Student

Sneha Pitre and Donna Schultheiss

Relational cultural career assessment provides a holistic approach for gathering information to inform career counseling interventions. Contemporary conceptualizations of work and relational life (e.g., Blustein, 2011; Richardson, 2012; Schultheiss, 2007), together with the emergence of constructivist and social constructionist perspectives in the career field (Young & Collin, 2004), have cultivated an environment in which qualitative career assessment has come to be identified as acceptable practice (Whiston & Rahardja, 2005). This movement has also been fostered in part by career practitioners seeking assessment approaches that are closer to the course of everyday work with clients than traditional means of career assessment (Young & Collin, 2004). By providing a complex framework for understanding how relationships and the intersection of other identities (e.g., race, class, culture, gender, and sexuality) are experienced in the career domain, a relational cultural paradigm provides a viable conceptual foundation for a holistic assessment of individuals' working lives. Qualitative relational cultural career assessment expands the nexus of work and relationships by embracing a more inclusive conceptualization of the work and relationship space. This approach emphasizes the centrality of culture and other forms of diversity as a central part of relationship and acknowledges a broad definition of work, which includes unpaid work (Schultheiss, 2007).

Situated within a social constructionist paradigm, the primary objective of qualitative relational cultural career assessment is to construct an in-depth understanding of the role of relationships in clients' lives and careers. Counselors facilitate an exploration of how clients' relational and work worlds intersect to gain a rich understanding of how clients connect and interact with others and how these connections are interdependent with their work lives (Schultheiss, 2005). The synthesis of qualitative relational cultural assessment with more traditional career practices presents an opportunity for a comprehensive approach that is highly synchronized with daily life experience. This approach recognizes and supports the value of relational connection as an opportunity to enrich both work and relational life (cf. Schultheiss, 2003, 2005, 2007). In this chapter, the evolution of theoretical advances leading to relational cultural career assessment is described and illustrated with a case example of an Indian immigrant first-year college student.

Relational Career Assessment

A fundamental goal of constructivist and social constructionist career assessment is to help clients learn how to make sense of life experiences over time, and how to make connections between these experiences and various systems of influence, such as the family and other interpersonal relationships (Peavy, 1996). This process points to the need for understanding and exploration of career decision making in a relational cultural framework in which an individual's sociocultural factors are highlighted and evaluated. For more than a decade, there have been calls to attend to the relational context when considering career development and work life (e.g., Blustein, 2001; Schultheiss, 2003). Schultheiss suggested that relational perspectives emphasize relationship as a critical component of developmental progress, emotional health, and interpersonal life. Relational theory provides a framework that emphasizes the value of considering relationships in one's understandings of career and work life. Thus, relational perspectives enrich traditional understandings of career by acknowledging the potential adaptive function of interpersonal connection in approaching career tasks and validating real-life career experiences. In addition, they offer the opportunity to increase awareness of one's relational needs and provide a means of connecting important areas of one's life, love, and work (Jordan, 1991).

Relational career assessment is a relatively new approach to understanding career and work life. Although few qualitative relational assessments have been introduced directly into the practice literature (e.g., Ponterotto, Rivera, & Sueyoshi, 2000; Schultheiss, 2003), there is a growing qualitative research base on which implications for assessment practice have been based (Stead et al., 2012). The Relationships and Career Interview (Schultheiss, 2003, 2005) emerged from qualitative research (Schultheiss, Kress, Manzi, & Glasscock, 2001; Schultheiss, Palma, Predragovich, & Glasscock, 2002) as a means of assessing clients' perceptions of their relationships and the impact of these relationships on career progress. The semistructured interview begins by encouraging clients to discuss how their relationships have been influential in their career development and decision making. The counselor guides the client to consider specific influential aspects of relationships, including those that are facilitative or growth oriented and those that are neutral, negative, or conflictual. Clients are asked to call to mind a particularly difficult career decision they have had to make to facilitate a close examination of relational processes and to validate relational experiences associated with past decisions. Throughout the assessment, the counselor helps the client identify recurrent relational themes and recognize work as a potent source of social connectedness or alienation that affects life functioning.

The difference between relational career assessment and relational cultural career assessment is that in relational cultural assessment the cultural context and intersectional identities are central to relational experience and meaning. Relational cultural career assessment, described next, emerged from the Relationships and Career Interview (Schultheiss, 2003) by integrating contemporary relational and feminist theory in assessment practices (Schultheiss, 2013a, 2013b).

Relational Cultural Career Assessment

Relational cultural career assessment is based on the relational cultural paradigm for vocational psychology (Schultheiss, 2007). This paradigm emphasizes the significance of culture as a relational process; that is, relationships are thought to both represent and reproduce culture (Jordan & Walker, 2004). The essence of this paradigm suggests that the nexus of work, relationships, and culture provides a means of understanding and mattering to others. Mattering provides individuals with a sense of social meaning and relatedness, thereby contributing to a sense of belonging (Schultheiss, 2013a). Another essential component of this paradigm is that work is understood to include both paid and unpaid work. It includes caregiving, volunteer work, and other work that one does for others and for the community. The cultural aspects of relationships relate to the impact of race, class, and other identities and associated aspects of inequality and privilege (Collins, 1991; Crenshaw, 1994). These identities intersect and are viewed as social processes rather than being viewed primarily as characteristics of individuals. Intersectionality refers to the assertion that one cannot understand any one of these identities in isolation; they must instead be considered in combination (Cole, 2009).

Consistent with social constructionism (cf. Burr, 1995; Gergen, 1999), the focus of relational cultural career assessment is on social processes and on understanding that one's worldview is continuously influenced by dynamic historical and cultural processes and practices. This approach is sensitive to the complexities of 21st-century work and the needs of people with diverse intersecting identities. This perspective assumes that what transpires in relationships is key to the facilitation or hindrance of career progress, competence and self-worth, and the experience of fulfilling and satisfying work lives (cf. Schultheiss, 2003, 2013a).

In relational cultural career assessment, practitioners inquire about clients' self-understandings and identities that are socially constructed within relationships, as well as clients' perceptions of how relational cultural experiences influence the career development and work domain. This is accomplished by asking open-ended questions and exploring recurring themes from therapeutic material. Relational cultural career narratives frequently concern themes such as belongingness; isolation and alienation at work; multiple intersecting life roles and identities; inclusive definitions of work; multidimensional aspects of social support (e.g., emotional, social, instrumental, tangible; Cutrona, 1996); and the consistency, availability, and reliability of others as a secure emotional base. The assessment relies on a semistructured interview that demands an active role for clients in a collaborative and cooperative process with the counselor. The goal is to work with clients' self-perceptions and personal meanings to assist them in developing insight and navigating work and relational life. Counselors help clients learn how to make sense of life experiences and the role of various systems of influence that impact career development and work over time, such as the family and other interpersonal relationships.

Drawing on the research of Kacar-Khamush (2015), counselors begin the semistructured interview by acknowledging that everyone has different aspects of themselves, or identities (e.g., gender, race, ethnicity, religion, sexual orientation), that make them unique and that these identities are experienced in relationships in various ways with different people. Clients are then encouraged to talk about their relational cultural experiences associated with their intersecting identities and to explore how these experiences relate to their career development and work life. For example, counselors might ask, "As a South Asian woman, how have your experiences with others impacted your career development and decision-making process?" Client narratives are likely to reflect complex, ambiguous, dynamic, and contradicting relational cultural experiences across persons, contexts, and time. Counselors are urged to listen for themes associated with the relational cultural experiences that come to bear on career and work progress and outcomes. Previous research suggests that common themes may include privilege, success, pride, coping, and resiliency, as well as challenge, disadvantage, conflict, disruption, fear, uncertainty, unpredictability, oppression, and discrimination (Schultheiss, 2013b). An exploration of the degree to which the relational cultural career experience is characterized as a space of embeddedness and belonging or alienation and disconnection can be informative in formulating an understanding of the nexus of clients' relational cultural experiences and work lives (cf. Blustein, Schultheiss, & Flum, 2004; Kacar-Khamush, 2012).

Clients are then guided to discuss how their relationships with important people in their lives have been influential in their career development and decision-making process and to assess their confidence and comfort level in relying on others for support, advice, or information. Through guided exploration, the range of influence is explored—from positive and facilitative relationships to those that are negative and reveal vulnerable shortcomings in the availability and accessibility of positive influences in the individual's life (Schultheiss, 2003). Further drawing on the Relationships and Career Interview, clients are encouraged to discuss how they have made career decisions in the past, and they are asked to call to mind a specific difficult career decision. This process provides clients with the opportunity to closely evaluate their relational influences by focusing on a particularly challenging experience. A case example is provided next to illustrate this assessment method.

The Case of Pooja

Pooja is a 19-year-old, single woman whose family immigrated from India to the United States when she was 12 years old. She is a freshman at a large public urban university and has made an appointment at the university counseling center to seek help with the transition from high school to college, with deciding on a college major, and with family distress due to her career concerns. She has specifically indicated that she needs help in choosing a major that aligns with both her interests and those of her family. Her family values higher education and would like Pooja to pursue a degree in a field that is both practical and marketable, such as engineering, business, medicine, or teaching. Her good grades in high school and college suggest that she is a hardworking student who enjoys learning. Because family contact and connection is important for Pooja, she chose to attend a university close to home so that she could live with her parents and her 27-year-old sister, Shruti.

During her first counseling session, Pooja reported that she likes to read English literature and has earned many awards for her writing in both high school and college. The academic advisor recognized her interests and abilities in writing and encouraged her to write a monthly column for the college newspaper. Pooja has written articles on several topics, including religion, multicultural issues, college stressors, and the transition from college to working life. In session, she reported that her older sister often provides her with career-related information and emotional support with issues concerning interpersonal relationships, college stress, and acculturation. Her older sister earned a master's degree in business administration from the same urban university that Pooja attends, and her sister now works in a marketing firm at a job that she enjoys. Pooja often talks with her sister about possible college majors and future job opportunities. She enjoys discussing her personal experiences with her sister and her sister's friends because it has helped her to improve her self-confidence and her acculturation to the United States. Pooja has mentioned that she ultimately wants to be productive like her sister and to have a job that she enjoys.

In India, Pooja's mother earned a bachelor's degree in banking and finance and was employed as an assistant bank manager. When Pooja was 12 years old, Pooja's mother supported her husband's decision to move the family to the United States for better work opportunities. For the past

7 years, she has raised her two daughters and not worked outside of the home. Pooja's father earned a master's degree in software engineering in India, and he now works as a software engineer in the United States. He is the sole wage earner for the family and makes all major decisions in the home, such as those concerning finances, his daughters' education, and implementation of family values and discipline.

Pooja disclosed that her parents value education and have always emphasized the science, technology, engineering, and mathematics (STEM) fields as career options for both Pooja and Shruti. Although she does not have a strong interest in the STEM fields and would like to explore other options, she does not want to upset her parents and would like to make a decision that is acceptable to all. Pooja talked about her cultural values and those of her family. Although she has some extended family in the United States, most of her relatives live in India. She reported that she comes from a very close-knit family, values her Indian heritage, and makes decisions that are strongly driven by family approval and support. She would not like to disappoint her parents, and she indicated that it is important for her to be able to manage the demands of work and family both now and in the future. She wants to choose a major that will allow her flexibility and the opportunity to be creative.

The relational cultural assessment reveals how relational cultural experiences have contributed to Pooja's striving to progress effectively in the career domain. Pooja stated that she is close to her parents, respects and values her relationship with them, and seeks support and guidance from them in many situations. Based on her cultural values and those of her family, she is likely to make decisions based on information and guidance from her primary support system, which consists of her parents and her older sister. Although Pooja receives some career information from her sister and her sister's friends, her main sources of support and guidance are her parents. Her deference to the wishes of her parents, together with her desire to be a respectful and obedient daughter, may affect her career-related decisions. Her parents have a limited view of college majors and may provide her with information and support for options only in the fields of science and technology. However, Pooja seems uninterested in pursuing a career in STEM-related fields. Because of the limited choices provided and discussed by her parents, Pooja is likely to consider a constricted range of majors and possess limited information and knowledge about careers in her field of interest. In Indian culture, parental support and approval of a daughter's aspirations and plans for a professional career are likely to contribute to girls' positive self-image, self-confidence, and self-fulfillment (Maslak & Singhal, 2008). These factors could all be contributing to her decision-making difficulties.

It is important to understand the cultural background of the client to engage in effective career assessment. The counselor and client interaction can be enhanced by the counselor's attention to multicultural issues. Multicultural competencies (Arredondo et al., 1996) are essential to creating a therapeutic environment in which clients perceive that they and their narratives are understood and accepted. This requires that counselors possess awareness of their own personal cultural beliefs and the ways in which their beliefs may influence their interpretation of clients' experiences (Toporek & Flamer, 2009). A culturally sensitive assessment will integrate culturally relevant information about Pooja with the counselor's efforts to understand Pooja's cultural, personal, and career realities. Identifying similarities and differences in the career development of White Americans and Asian Americans can help counselors design culturally relevant career services (Leong, 1991, 1993).

Counselors must be sensitive, knowledgeable, and prepared to competently assist a diverse clientele by addressing needs beyond those directly related to ethnicity. In Pooja's case, this means discussing not just her identity as a person of Asian descent but also her identity as a woman of color, an immigrant, a college student, and any other relevant aspects of her identity (Hackett & Lonborg, 1993). Identifying gender-role stereotypes, such as the expectations placed on women in the male-dominated Indian society, is important in understanding a client like Pooja's career development and decision making. This might include examining the purpose and meaning of education for women as well as expectations for household responsibilities in the context of her culture. Women of Indian descent may be caught between the traditional expectations of Indian society (which typically require women to remain in the home) and their own aspirations (which may include employment outside the home). This can create complexities and conflicts in the lives of the women and in their interpersonal relationships (Maslak & Singhal, 2008) because women are often expected to accommodate their careers to fit their families (Karambayya & Reilly, 1992).

Relational assessment can facilitate Pooja's exploration of her important relationships with others, such as her parents, sister, and those who influenced her success with school and writing. The counselor can actively encourage Pooja to examine the roles of these relationships in her career development and decision making. Through engagement and exploration, both Pooja and her counselor can gain a deeper understanding of how Pooja reacts to others and how her relationships and intersecting identities are interdependent with her career and work world. A discussion about her relationship with her mother and father, and the implications of her decision-making style within those relationships and her sociocultural context, will lead to greater self-exploration and self-knowledge. Pooja could be supported to discuss and clarify the importance of family expectations (Fouad et al., 2008), work and family attributes and roles, and the implications of these aspects of her relational cultural experiences.

Pooja may be caught between the tradition of her cultural heritage and the values of a predominantly individualistic Western culture (Leong, 1991; Tang, Fouad, & Smith, 1999). Assessment will help her explore the nature of support offered by each parent. Although Pooja's mother may be emotionally supportive, the degree to which she provides various other dimensions of support (such as esteem support and tangible assistance) is unclear and will need to be examined.

Pooja's increased awareness of her relationships will enhance her understanding of the influence of those relationships on her career development and decision making and highlight how she negotiates her relationships with her family and her own needs and goals. She may be encouraged to seek relational support from her parents, sister, advisor, and others. Pooja's counselor can use specific strategies from the Relationships and Career Interview to encourage Pooja to think about her past decisions, paying particular attention to the involvement of others, such as her parents, sisters, extended family, and advisor (Schultheiss, 2005). She can be encouraged to describe and discuss a difficult career decision and the role her relationships played in her decision-making process. The counselor can assist Pooja in assessing her satisfaction with her decisions and the strategies used, including her involvement with and reliance on others, and the extent and quality of the information gathered.

Pooja's parents are likely to have a thoughtful influence on the intellectual, social, and emotional components of their children's lives. Pooja may not be aware of the degree to which her parents exert influence on her career decision-making process. The assessment process can focus on exploring and identifying her parents' role and their guidance in her everyday life to increase her self-awareness (Chope, 2005). Asian American parents are likely to provide strong guidance about career (Leong, 1991) and to exert influence on their children's choices and aspirations, preferably hoping for career choices to be practical and marketable. Research (e.g., Fouad et al., 2008) suggests that family, culture, external factors, career goals, role models, work values, and personal characteristics are also domains of influence on the career choices of Asian Americans. Therefore, Pooja may be confronted with choosing a career that is acceptable to her and her parents, which can result in increased difficulties making career decisions. Pooja can be encouraged to engage in a sensitive meaning-making process to understand her cultural and familial values as they relate to her relational cultural context (Schultheiss, 2003).

Acculturation factors and generational status also play very important roles in Pooja's thoughts, behavior, and feelings about her career choice. Asian Americans also may choose from a limited range of occupations because they are likely to be affected by existing stereotypes and assumptions that they excel in technically related occupations and achieve high levels of education (Tang et al., 1999). Research suggests that those who are more acculturated are more likely to choose less stereotypical occupations compared to those who are less acculturated (e.g., Tang et al., 1999). In the assessment process, the counselor must also attend to the sociostructural factors that will affect Pooja, such as discrimination (Fouad et al., 2008). Exploration of experiences of discrimination will inform a richer understanding of Pooja's situation.

Southeast Asians are often reserved about discussing their problems because of fear of familial rejection. This is likely to affect Pooja's interpersonal communication and career choice (Mathews, 2000). Sharing a problem with an outsider is likely to be viewed as bringing shame on one's family, and family problems are often kept in the family. Many Southeast Asian parents take complete financial responsibility for their children until they complete their studies, find a job, or are married. High levels of academic success are valued, and children's success is very important because it reflects on the parents. This presents another important issue to address in the assessment phase. See Table 17.1 for an application guide.

Conclusion

In summary, relational cultural career assessment provides an evaluation tool to better assist clients in understanding the impact of relational cultural experiences on career development and work outcomes. Relational cultural practices are the products of interactions and negotia-

Table 17.1
Practical Application Guide

Topic	Relational Cultural Career Assessment
General goals and purposes	1. To provide an in-depth exploration and examination of the role of relationships in one's life and career 2. Qualitative assessment of the client's perceptions of his or her relationships on career exploration and decision making 3. Explore quality of relationships 4. Process past career decisions, critical incidents 5. Gain a complete view of the client's relational cultural experiences 6. Assist the client in identifying and accessing available relational resources
Applicable modality	Individual
Applicable counselor settings	University counseling center, high school, community agency, private practice
Recommended time to complete	Three to four sessions of 1 hour each minimum
Materials/equipment needed	None
Step-by-step outline of the process	1. Inquire about the client's identities that are socially constructed within relationships. 2. Inquire about the client's perceptions of how relational cultural experiences are influential in the career domain. 3. Explore recurring themes in therapeutic material. 4. Help the client learn the role of systems of influence (e.g., family) on career choices. 5. Clarify how important people have been influential in career. 6. Discuss past career decisions, including a difficult decision.

tions between people and groups, and these experiences are central to understanding and intervening in people's enactments of careers (Schultheiss, 2013b; Schultheiss, Kacar-Khamush, et al., 2011; Schultheiss, Watts, Sterland, & O'Neill, 2011). As illustrated in the case of Pooja, perspectival material from one's own life is uniquely relevant to career and life planning and choices. The synthesis of knowledge and the personal understanding of the interdependence of work and relational life provide important information that can augment traditional means of career assessment, including objective scores of interests, personality, aptitude, and other traits.

Recommended Resources

Baker Miller, J. (1986). *What do we mean by relationships?* Retrieved from http://www.jbmti.org/images/pdf/22sc.pdf

Jean Baker Miller Training Institute at the Wellesley Centers for Women. (2016). Retrieved from http://www.jbmti.org/

McMahon, M., Patton, W., & Watson, M. (2003). Developing qualitative career assessment processes. *The Career Development Quarterly, 51*, 194–202.

Schultheiss, D. E. P. (2003). A relational approach to career counseling: Theoretical integration and practical application. *Journal of Counseling & Development, 81*, 301–310.

References

Arredondo, P., Toporek, R., Brown, S. P., Jones, J., Locke, D. C., Sanchez, J., & Stadler, H. (1996). Operationalization of the multicultural counseling competencies. *Journal of Multicultural Counseling and Development, 24*, 42–78. doi:10.1002/j.2161-1912.1996.tb00288.x

Blustein, D. L. (2001). The interface of work and relationships: Critical knowledge for 21st century psychology. *The Counseling Psychologist, 29*, 179–192. doi:10.1177/0011000001292001

Blustein, D. L. (2011). A relational theory of working. *Journal of Vocational Behavior, 79*, 1–17. doi:10.1016/j.jvb.2010.10.004

Blustein, D. L., Schultheiss, D. E. P., & Flum, H. (2004). Toward a relational perspective of the psychology of careers and working: A social constructionist analysis. *Journal of Vocational Behavior, 64*, 423–440. doi:10.1016/j.jvb.2003.12.008

Burr, V. (1995). *An introduction to social constructionism.* London, England: Routledge.

Chope, R. C. (2005). Qualitatively assessing family influence in career decision making. *Journal of Career Assessment, 13*, 395–414. doi:10.1177/1069072705277913

Cole, E. R. (2009). Intersectionality and research in psychology. *American Psychologist, 64*, 17–180. doi:10.1037/a0014564

Collins, P. H. (1991). *Black feminist thought: Knowledge, consciousness, and empowerment.* New York, NY: Routledge.

Crenshaw, K. W. (1994). Mapping the margins: Intersectionality, identity politics, and violence against women of color. In M. A. Fineman & R. Mykitiuk (Eds.), *The public nature of private violence* (pp. 93–118). New York, NY: Routledge.

Cutrona, C. E. (1996). *Social support in couples: Marriage as a resource in times of stress.* Thousand Oaks, CA: Sage. doi:10.4135/9781483327563

Fouad, N. A., Kantamneni, N., Smothers, M. K., Chen, Y. L., Fitzpatrick, M., & Terry, S. (2008). Asian American career development: A qualitative analysis. *Journal of Vocational Behavior, 72,* 43–59. doi:10.1016/j.jvb.2007.10.002

Gergen, K. J. (1999). *An invitation to social construction.* London, England: Sage.

Hackett, G., & Lonborg, S. D. (1993). Career assessment for women: Trends and issues. *Journal of Career Assessment, 1,* 197–216. doi:10.1177/106907279300100301

Jordan, J. V. (1991). The meaning of mutuality. In J. V. Jordan, A. G. Kaplan, J. B. Miller, I. P. Stiver, & J. L. Surrey (Eds.), *Women's growth in connection* (pp. 81–96). New York, NY: Guilford Press.

Jordan, J. V., & Walker, M. (2004). Introduction. In J. V. Jordan, M. Walker, & L. M. Hartling (Eds.), *The complexity of connection: Writings from the Stone Center's Jean Baker Miller Training Institute* (pp. 1–8). New York, NY: Guilford Press.

Kacar-Khamush, B. (2012, August). *Understanding careers from a relational perspective: Experiences of Muslim female international students.* Student poster presented at the annual meeting of the American Psychological Association, Orlando, FL.

Kacar-Khamush, B. (2015). *Social identity experiences of Muslim female international students in education and career settings.* Doctoral dissertation, Cleveland State University, Cleveland, OH.

Karambayya, R., & Reilly, A. H. (1992). Dual earner couples: Attitudes and actions in restructuring work for family. *Journal of Organizational Behavior, 13,* 585–601. doi:10.1002/job.4030130605

Leong, F. T. (1991). Career development attributes and occupational values of Asian American and White American college students. *The Career Development Quarterly, 39,* 221–230. doi:10.1002/j.2161-0045.1991.tb00394.x

Leong, F. T. (1993). The career counseling process with racial-ethnic minorities: The case of Asian Americans. *The Career Development Quarterly, 42,* 26–40. doi:10.1002/j.2161-0045.1993.tb00242.x

Maslak, M. A., & Singhal, G. (2008). The identity of educated women in India: Confluence or divergence? *Gender and Education, 20,* 481–493. doi:10.1080/09540250701829961

Mathews, R. (2000). Cultural patterns of South Asian and Southeast Asian Americans. *Intervention in School and Clinic, 36,* 101–104. doi:10.1177/105345120003600205

Peavy, V. (1996). Constructivist career counselling and assessment. *Guidance and Counselling, 11,* 8–14.

Ponterotto, J. G., Rivera, L., & Sueyoshi, L. A. (2000). The career-in-culture interview: A semi-structured protocol for the cross-cultural intake interview. *The Career Development Quarterly, 49*, 85–96. doi:10.1002/j.2161-0045.2000.tb00753.x

Richardson, M. S. (2012). Counseling for work and relationship. *The Counseling Psychologist, 40*, 190–242. doi:10.1177/0011000011406452

Schultheiss, D. E. P. (2003). A relational approach to career counseling: Theoretical integration and practical application. *Journal of Counseling & Development, 81*, 301–310. doi:10.1002/j.1556-6678.2003.tb00257.x

Schultheiss, D. E. P. (2005). Qualitative relational career assessment: A constructivist paradigm. *Journal of Career Assessment, 13*, 381–394. doi:10.1177/1069072705277912

Schultheiss, D. E. P. (2007). The emergence of a relational cultural paradigm for vocational psychology. *International Journal for Educational and Vocational Guidance, 7*, 191–201. doi:10.1007/s10775-007-9123-7

Schultheiss, D. E. P. (2013a). A relational and cultural paradigm as a theoretical backdrop for considering women's work. In W. Patton (Ed.), *Conceptualising women's working lives: Moving the boundaries of our discourse* (pp. 51–62). The Netherlands: Sense Publishers. doi:10.1007/978-94-6209-209-9_3

Schultheiss, D. E. (2013b, July). *Intersectionality and relationships: The challenges and resiliency of Turkish immigrants.* Presentation at the annual meeting of the American Psychological Association, Honolulu, HI.

Schultheiss, D., Kacar-Khamush, B. K., Conrad, J. B., Wallace, E., Bransteter, I., Michalos, S., . . . & Graham, S. (2011, September). *Work and family integration: Turkish immigrants in the United States.* Presentation at the International Conference: Vocational Designing and Career Counseling: Challenges and New Horizons, Padova, Italy.

Schultheiss, D. E. P., Kress, H. M., Manzi, A. J., & Glasscock, J. M. J. (2001). Relational influences in career development: A qualitative inquiry. *The Counseling Psychologist, 29*, 216–241. doi:10.1177/0011000001292003

Schultheiss, D. E. P., Palma, T. V., Predragovich, K. S., & Glasscock, J. M. J. (2002). Relational influences on career paths: Siblings in context. *Journal of Counseling Psychology, 49*, 302–310. doi:10.1037/0022-0167.49.3.302

Schultheiss, D., Watts, J., Sterland, L., & O'Neill, M. (2011). Career, migration and the life CV: A relational cultural analysis. *Journal of Vocational Behavior, 78*, 334–341.

Stead, G. B., Perry, J. C., Munka, L. M., Bonnett, H. R., Shiban, A. P., & Care, E. (2012). Qualitative research in career development: Content analysis from 1990–2009. *International Journal of Educational and Vocational Guidance, 12*, 105–122. doi:10.1007/s10775-011-9196-1

Tang, M., Fouad, N. A., & Smith, P. L. (1999). Asian Americans' career choices: A path model to examine factors influencing their career choices. *Journal of Vocational Behavior, 54*, 142–157. doi:10.1006/jvbe.1998.1651

Toporek, R. L., & Flamer, C. (2009). The résumé's secret identity: A tool for narrative exploration in multicultural career counseling. *Journal of Employment Counseling, 46*, 4–17. doi:10.1002/j.2161-1920.2009.tb00061.x

Whiston, S. C., & Rahardja, D. (2005). Qualitative career assessment: An overview and analysis. *Journal of Career Assessment, 13,* 371–380. doi:10.1177/1069072705277910

Young, R. A., & Collin, A. (2004). Introduction: Constructivism and social constructionism in the career field. *Journal of Vocational Behavior, 64,* 373–388. doi:10.1016/j.jvb.2003.12.005

Chapter 18

Solution-Focused Career Counseling With a Male Military Veteran

Seth C. W. Hayden and Mark B. Scholl

The current landscape of military service presents unique elements in personal and professional development for military service members. Military engagements abroad at various stages of conflict create an unpredictable landscape in which to consider short- and long-term personal and professional goals. Counselors tasked with supporting military service members in their career development appear ideally positioned to positively influence this population's transition to civilian employment. To effectively assist with the career development of military service members, it is essential to utilize approaches that integrate the context of the military. Solution-focused career counseling (SFCC) provides a framework in which to address career development concerns of military service members and veterans that accounts for the unique experience of this population.

In this chapter, we explore the characteristics of this population, the rationale as well as the foundational elements of SFCC, and the application of this approach. A case study is provided to further illustrate the use of SFCC when working with military service members and veterans. Relevant resources pertaining to this topic are listed at the end of the chapter.

Distinct Experience of Military Veterans

Culture of the Military

Military members operate within a unique context involving impactful lived experiences specific to their way of life. Military service members exist in a distinct subset of society in a culture governed by rules, traditions, values, and laws (Coll et al., as cited in Rausch, 2014). The environment of the military plays a large role in constructing the organization of meaning, perspective, and information for service members (Rausch, 2014). This context often provides support related to this unique experience, offering significant benefits to military service members related to challenges that may potentially arise. The amount and nature of the time spent in the military are important considerations related to the experience of veterans (Black, Westwood, & Sorsdal, 2007).

The defined structure, a prominent aspect of military life, may be antithetical to the individualistic, materialistic, litigious culture that constitutes several aspects of North American society (Black et al., 2007). One analogy is that of a one-way door to a different view of the world. Once you go in, you can never return to the perspective from which you came (Black et al., 2007). Connected to, but distinct from, these challenges is the career development of military veterans.

Career Development Needs of Military Members

It is important to note that most military veterans reintegrate into society without a diagnosable or debilitating condition (Bonar & Domenici, 2011). There are instances, however, in which military veterans may experience difficulty in their transition back into civilian life. Apart from difficulties with adjustment related to differing contexts (Buzzetta & Rowe, 2012), military veterans may return with significant physical and psychological injuries (Marchione, 2012; Tanielian & Jaycox, 2008).

Because of these and other associated aspects of military service that veterans experience, career development is often significantly affected. Though seemingly improving in a general sense, veterans of the recent engagements in Afghanistan and Iraq still struggle to find employment compared with their peers in the general population (Bureau of Labor Statistics, 2014). Some concerns are related to translating military experience to civilian employment, and other concerns focus on the career development needs of individuals with postcombat injuries such as posttraumatic stress disorder and traumatic brain injury (Hayden, Green, & Dorsett, 2013; Hayden, Ledwith, Dong, & Buzzetta, 2014). In addition, specific skills such as résumé preparation, interviewing, networking, and negotiating a job offer have been identified as key areas for counselors to focus on when addressing the developmental needs of military veterans (Clemens & Milsom, 2008; Hayden et al., 2014).

Strategies to effectively address these concerns have been the subject of an ongoing discussion within the profession of counseling. Several models have been proposed as being potentially useful in addressing these concerns (Bullock, Braud, Andrews, & Phillips, 2009; Clemens & Milsom, 2008; Phillips, Braud, Andrews, & Bullock, 2007). In addition to previous approaches to addressing the career development needs of military veterans, approaches that integrate the contextual elements of military experience into the provision of career services need to be considered. A solution-focused approach to career development assistance effectively accounts for this aspect of military veterans' experience.

Postmodern Perspective

The postmodern perspective views human knowing as an active process of subjective meaning making on the part of the individual. Constructivism, a related and recently developed counseling perspective, posits that individuals create meaning in their own lives. An important distinction can be made between nihilistic and neopragmatic postmodernism. According to Woodward (2002), in nihilistic postmodernism, because values are necessarily relativistic, humanity's highest ideals are devalued, rendering them and human life meaningless. However, postmodernists have offered a useful response to nihilistic postmodernism. Similar to existentialists, postmodernists assert that humans have the freedom and the capacity to choose what to believe, how to behave, and what values to hold. By making these choices, humans add meaning to their lives. Along the same lines, Rorty (1979) integrated pragmatism with postmodernist thought. This integration is referred to as *neopragmatism* (Hansen, 2014; Polkinghorne, 1992; Rorty, 1999). Of relevance to career counseling practice, beliefs, values, and behaviors that enhance life's meaning meet the criterion of usefulness, and solution-focused counseling is grounded in neopragmatic postmodernism. The postmodern perspective and related counseling approaches have exerted a powerful influence on counseling and psychotherapy practices (Corey, 2017; Hansen, 2014; Murdock, 2013).

Solution-Focused Approach

Several important aspects of the military service member's experiences are particularly relevant to the use of a postmodern solution-focused approach. First of all, the military service member is typically undergoing a significant life transition from the military to the civilian way of life. During this transition, the individual's identity also is undergoing a significant transformation from a military identity to a civilian identity. A foundational assumption underlying the postmodern perspective, and social constructionism, is that the self is multiple and that a single stable self is a modernist myth. Individuals have multiple selves (e.g., parent, worker, military service member, citizen), and these selves are continually being modified through the changing perceptions, roles, and life contexts of individuals (Gergen, 1999; Hansen, 2014; Peavy, 1998). Finally, an approach that is solution focused, rather than problem focused, decreases the potential deleterious effects of posttraumatic stress-related symptoms that might otherwise impede progress toward career-related goals.

The self may be viewed as a project that is perpetually being constructed by the individual (Peavy, 1998). A self that is *thicker,* or more complex, is more capable of fluidly adapting to the changing contextual demands faced by a military veteran adapting to a civilian way of life. Solution-focused counseling can assist an individual in envisioning and articulating a thicker, more adaptive self-identity. Along the same lines, Savickas (2005) noted that constructivist and social constructivist approaches, such as SFCC, promote *career adaptability*, which is "an individual's readiness and resources for coping with current and imminent vocational development tasks, occupational transitions, and personal traumas" (p. 51). A number of other researchers also recommend applying solution-focused methods to the career counseling and development process (see Burwell & Chen, 2006; Miller, 2004a, 2004b, 2006; Scholl & Cascone, 2010).

Several important implications for career counseling practice logically follow from the postmodern and solution-focused perspective. First, consistent with social constructivism, the counselor's role in SFCC is collaborative and egalitarian. Although the counselor may be directive in terms of facilitating a given technique such as guided imagery or using the miracle question, the counselor is more egalitarian in terms of facilitating the client's articulation of a personally meaningful solution. The client is perceived and acknowledged as the expert on what constitutes a meaningful solution. Second, the client is encouraged to envision the preferred future reality, counseling outcomes, and self-identity. As a part of the process, the counselor may facilitate processes of reauthoring and envisioning that emphasize the client's imagination or creative ability, and these can be facilitated intentionally through processes of *deconstructing* and *reconstructing* the client's current perceptions of reality. Finally, a solution-focused approach should incorporate goal development and action planning to address the criticism that solution-focused approaches too often fail to include action elements (Reid, 2006). These action elements can facilitate a smoother life transition and implementation of the military service member's envisioned career identity.

To illustrate the implementation of a solution-focused approach in addressing the career development needs of veterans, we have provided a case study, which follows. The case study is not designed to be overly prescriptive or confining, as it is important to adapt interventions to the specific career concerns of a military veteran in need. The case study comprises an amalgam of our clinical experiences and does not specifically describe the experience of a single client. It is recognized that there is significant diversity in both the characteristics of the counselor and the military veteran as well as the manner in which assistance can be provided. The case study connects the frequently indicated areas of career concerns of this population with the solution-focused approach. This is a general description of how solution-focused counseling may be applied to work with a military veteran, but the approach must be modified to match the personality and needs of individual clients.

The Case of Dan

Dan is a veteran who served in the U.S. Army for the past 15 years and whose primary function was that of an infantryman. Dan joined the Army upon graduation from high school with the thought of eventually supplementing his college education. The events of 9/11 dramatically altered Dan's level of engagement in the military, and he has experienced three deployments, one to Afghanistan and two to Iraq. Each deployment involved significant combat experience.

Dan has accumulated college credits through a local community college by taking both standard lecture and online classes. Initially Dan was interested in engineering, but he is unsure whether this is still the path he desires. He has come to the counselor, Teanca, with the presenting concern of finding an area of study and, by extension, a professional field that he finds "meaningful."

Dan initially presents as being somewhat emotionally withdrawn, providing only minimal two- to three-word responses to open-ended questions. He is married and has two young children (aged 4 and 7 years). Addressing his lack of certainty related to career options is examined through the lens of a solution-focused approach.

Early Phase

The counselor's belief in Dan's ability to generate his own solutions, as well as her recognition of his having operated within the structured environment of the military, underpinned her decision to use a SFCC approach. Teanca begins the process of working to shift the nature of Dan's attention from a problem orientation to a solution-focused perspective. A key element of the initial phase of counseling is to identify Dan as a person as opposed to a collection of problems. Teanca asks Dan questions such as these: "What do you do?" "How far have you come?" "How do you spend your day?" (Ratner, George, & Iveson, 2012). By not immediately jumping into the presenting concern, the focus of attention is on Dan rather than on the problem. Furthermore, Teanca moves the conversation to a desired outcome related to their efforts. In this aspect of the interaction, Dan is viewed as the expert in his creation of a meaningful solution (Reid, 2006). Dan indicates that he "would like to find a career that fits my interests." Though this statement is somewhat vague, Teanca honors Dan's capability to articulate his goals.

The use of questions in a solution-focused approach is intended to distinguish a problem orientation from solution-building conversations (Richmond, Jordan, Bischof, & Sauer, 2014). Teanca initially focused on shifting attention from what has not been working for Dan to things that have been successful for him in relation to goal attainment. A solution-building strategy she implemented to assist in the process is to discuss *instances of success* (Ratner et al., 2012). She urged him, "Tell me about a time in your life when you were able to define and accomplish a goal." Dan pondered this question for a moment and shared the following: "With my unit during a deployment. I am unable to get into specifics, but we were presented with a task in which we were required to support another unit who was engaged with the enemy. They were in a remote area, which was very difficult to get to, so we had to really work together to define our objective and come up with a plan to accomplish the mission. In the end, we were able to offer support with no casualties in either unit." Teanca affirmed Dan's ability to identify this success as well as his willingness to share this success story in the context of counseling.

Teanca proceeded by inquiring about the manner in which this experience translates to Dan's current career goal. She asked, "How do you see this experience as being applicable to our current goal of finding an occupation that matches your interests?" Dan was puzzled by this question and took several minutes to respond. He then indicated, "I guess it is useful in that we had to take stock of our assets and obstacles and work together to accomplish the mission. We also had to ask each other for help several times as it was impossible to get the job done without assistance from my fellow unit members." Teanca emphasized Dan's ability to be able identify the lessons learned from this experience and determined that it might be useful to keep these in mind as they proceed with the goal of finding an occupation that fits his interests.

With this discussion, Teanca was able to move the focus to highlighting Dan's ability to identify and accomplish a previous goal that has pertinence to the current career goal. With a collaborative relationship established, it was time to move to developing a meaningful solution to his concern. The middle phase discussion further explores this process of creation of personal meaning associated with his career goals.

Middle Phase

SFCC is constructivist in that clients create meaning with aspects of their lives and careers that are important to them to develop meaningful career goals (Miller, 2006). Miller observed that these goals reflect clients' positive views of their interests, abilities, values, and resources. At the heart of the matter is the view of the client as actively constructing meaning. It is important, consequently, for the counselor to assist the military veteran in building his or her own career plans and in formulating a personally meaningful career identity (O'Connell, 1998). SFCC entails a process of constructing, deconstructing, and reconstructing the client's preferred identity. This process involves both intrapersonal reflection and interpersonal interactions between the counselor and the client (Miller, 2006).

With regard to constructing a preferred identity and future goals, solution-focused counseling is founded on the belief that clients have the natural ability to construct meaning. Counselors use special prompts and questions (e.g., the miracle question) to facilitate the client's meaning-making process. At the same, it is important to recognize that clients vary in their levels of readiness for the construction process and in the degree to which they need "orienting" before they are ready to engage in the solution-focused counseling process (Neimeyer & Bridges, 2003).

One informal approach for assessing a client's readiness to engage in solution-focused counseling, recommended by Gelatt (1991), involves asking the client to read a list of four metaphors—roller coaster, colossal dice game, mighty river, and great ocean—and decide which one best matches the client's belief regarding his or her influence over the future (Kaufman,

1976). These metaphors entail an increasing sense of personal agency with regard to shaping one's personal future, and a greater sense of personal agency may also be taken as indicating a greater degree of readiness for constructing personal meaning. Teanca presents the four metaphors and encourages Dan to develop an original metaphor, if possible.

On an intrapersonal level, Dan considers the four choices but then chooses and shares his personal metaphor of a "wilderness survivor" traversing rugged terrain with many peaks and valleys. Based on his specialized knowledge, he asserts that he is able to anticipate the challenges associated with different types of terrain. He can climb a tall tree or stand on high ground to scan the land in all directions and plan his route, taking factors such as degree of risk, climate, and available resources into account.

Representative of the interpersonal level of meaning making, Teanca highlights aspects of Dan's metaphor that support his belief in his own personal agency in shaping his future. She points out that whereas his "wilderness survivor" metaphor emphasizes his surviving alone, the career development process necessarily will involve interpersonal relationships with faculty, advisors, and peers. This process is known as *contrasting*. She extends Dan's metaphor to include processes (e.g., faculty and advisors in academia are likened to indigenous people serving as survival guides in a wilderness setting) by which he might similarly select an appropriate career path. This process is known as *dilating* (Neimeyer & Bridges, 2003).

Having found that Dan appears to be ready for a solution-focused approach, Teanca asks Dan to complete an exercise in which he first identifies three preferred possible future selves that are highly relevant to his occupational hopes. In the second part of the exercise, Dan rank orders the three possible selves from most to least preferred. Dan describes his most preferred possible self as the owner of his own contracting business. By identifying his most preferred possible self, he is constructing an occupational identity that represents a meaningful goal to attain. Possible selves are cognitive, behavioral, and affective in nature and include expectations of what an individual will become in the future (Markus & Nurius, 1986; Robinson, Davis, & Meara, 2003). Possible selves are useful for assisting clients in focusing on their vision of the future that includes concrete details (Robinson et al., 2003).

Teanca next assists Dan in deconstructing his most preferred possible self. She gives Dan a transferrable skills inventory and instructs him to identify two categories of skills he believes to be highly relevant to his possible self: skills he currently possesses and new skills he envisions himself using as a part of his future identity as a contractor. For each skill Dan endorses as highly relevant, whether he possesses the skill now or someday will posses it, he is instructed to provide a brief story or example of a time he has used or would use the skill. Consistent with solution-focused counseling, Dan creates stories illustrating his use of skills he does not yet possess but will plausibly use in his imagined future role as a contractor. Deconstructing the contractor role in this way allows Dan to more systematically consider how well his chosen future self fits with the skills he prefers to use. The deconstruction process also includes a similar activity involving clarification of values. At one point Dan states that customer satisfaction is one of his highest values. Teanca comments that this sounds significant and asks for elaboration, a counselor response known as *nuancing*. She uses dilating statements to call attention to wider implications of Dan's stated values, and at one point uses contrasting to call attention to a potential conflict between two of Dan's higher values—namely, *customer satisfaction* and *economic wealth*. Through the use of nuancing, dilating, and contrasting, Teanca ensures that Dan is actively deconstructing his most preferred possible occupational self. After analyzing this construct through a thorough process of deconstruction, Dan is in a better position to understand how committed he is to the role of a contractor.

Later Phase

As previously mentioned, Reid (2006) observed that solution-focused counseling does not include action elements as part of the treatment plan. To address this potential limitation, the counselor works with Dan to co-construct an action plan and related intermediate goals. The action plan forms a bridge between Dan's current and future identities (Scholl & Cascone, 2010).

Early steps in Dan's action plan include shadowing a contractor for a day to gather some firsthand observations of the nature of the occupational role. In addition to this, Dan completes an informational interview in which he asks a contractor questions about the nature of his occupational role, including, "What do you like most about your occupation?" and "What do you like least?" Completion of these early tasks decreases the likelihood that Dan will unnecessarily expend significant time and energy preparing for the occupational role only to find that the role is not sufficiently rewarding. Furthermore, Dan's participation in these activities serves to enhance his *career adaptability* (Savickas, 2005), or readiness for the challenging school-to-work transition.

Career adaptability encompasses "an individual's readiness and resources for coping with current and imminent vocational developmental tasks, occupational transitions, and personal traumas" (Savickas, 2005, p. 51). Career adaptability includes four attitudes: curiosity, concern, confidence, and control. These four attitudes are all useful for coping with career transitions. Career *curiosity* refers to an inquiring and exploratory attitude with regard to understanding how the individual's identity fits into an occupation in the world of work. Career *concern* means that an individual has a future orientation and feels invested in planning for the future. Career *confidence* relates to an individual's anticipation of positive outcomes as a result of his or her intentional efforts. Career *control* indicates that the individual feels capable of and responsible for constructing his or her career. As Dan's curiosity, concern, confidence, and control increase, his attitudes and ability to mobilize the resources required for successfully transitioning from school to work are enhanced (Savickas, 2005). For example, Dan's willingness to participate in the informational interviewing and shadowing activities demonstrates a high level of career curiosity. Dan reports that as a result of completing these activities he feels an enhanced sense of confidence that the role of contractor is an appropriate one for him to pursue. The discussion of intermediate action steps with the counselor enhances Dan's concern regarding completing these steps and also enhances his sense of control or personal agency in his career development.

Dan demonstrated his capability in identifying his goals and developing a plan related to goal attainment. He also engaged in abstract exercises such as describing his personal metaphor and engaging in future-oriented thinking. Not all clients who are military veterans can effectively engage in the cognitively complex tasks outlined in this case study. Issues such as traumatic brain injury or posttraumatic stress disorder may impede swift progress through the application of this approach. Continual monitoring by the counselor related to the affective and cognitive engagement of clients is a necessary component when assisting military veterans in their career development. To ensure a positive outcome, the counselor must adapt to the needs of the client. See Table 18.1 for an application guide.

Table 18.1
Practical Application Guide

Topic	Solution-Focused Approach to Career Counseling
General goals and purposes	1. Clients construct or envision personally meaningful goals based on positive images of their own competence, achievements, resources, strengths, and successes 2. The counselor encourages clients to work on building solutions at two different levels: macro level (e.g., hoped-for selves, description of ideal position) and micro level (e.g., values, transferrable skills) 3. Application of solution-focused therapy within context of career counseling 4. Develop tangible solutions and associated steps to resolve career choice based on desired outcomes of the client
Applicable modality	Individual and group counseling
Applicable counselor settings	College/university career services, community agency, private practice, military and veterans service delivery center
Recommended time to complete	Five to six sessions for individual counseling and roughly the same number for group counseling. Solution-focused counseling tends to be brief in terms of number of sessions.
Materials/equipment needed	Individual learning plans, whiteboard, erasable markers, notepads, pencils
Step-by-step outline of the process	1. Shift from problem orientation to solution focus. 2. Identify solution to career concern. 3. Construct personal identity. 4. Deconstruct personal identity. 5. Reconstruct personal identity. 6. Develop action plan.

Conclusion

SFCC can be useful in working with a military population because of its structural similarity to the goal-oriented and task-focused culture of the military. This approach also honors the unique experience of military veterans by encouraging clients to educate the counselor about their experience as well as their desired outcome for the process. In transitioning from the military to the civilian world of work, a military veteran may experience a loss of identity, role, purpose, and mission. This approach offers an opportunity for the client to recover from these losses by constructing a new preferred future identity, role, purpose, and mission. Focusing on the solution and considering the metaphor of a new mission can resonate with members of this population. Additionally, military veterans engaged in SFCC are taking responsibility for their choices regarding progress toward a meaningful solution. SFCC is strongly aligned with the culture that military veterans are familiar with, thus providing a useful framework for career assistance.

For military veterans, focusing on strengths relevant to articulating a preferred personal identity and career future can promote a positive and optimistic approach to conceptualizing their career development. SFCC offers a theoretically grounded, culturally responsive approach to assisting a population in need of competent career assistance.

Recommended Resources

Hall, L. K. (2011). The importance of understanding military culture. *Social Work in Health Care, 50,* 4–18.

O*NET. (n.d.). *Military crosswalk search.* Retrieved from https://www.onetonline.org/crosswalk/MOC/

Simpson, A., & Armstrong, S. (2009). From the military to the civilian work force: Addressing veteran career development concerns. *Career Planning & Adult Development Journal, 25,* 177–187.

Stein-McCormick, C., Osborn, D. O., Hayden, S. C. W., & Hoose, D. V. (2013). *Career counseling with veterans* (Monograph). Broken Arrow, OK: The National Career Development Association.

U.S. Chamber of Commerce Foundation. (n.d.). *Hiring our heroes.* Retrieved from https://www.uschamberfoundation.org/hiring-our-heroes

U.S. Department of Veterans Affairs/Department of Defense. (n.d.). *Veterans employment center.* Retrieved from https://www.ebenefits.va.gov/ebenefits/jobs

Weiss, E. L., Coll, J. E., Gerbauer, J., & Smiley, K. (2010). The military genogram: A solution-focused approach for resiliency building in service members and their families. *The Family Journal, 14,* 395–406.

References

Black, T., Westwood, M. J., & Sorsdal, M. N. (2007). From the front line to the front of the class: Counseling students who are military veterans. In J. A. Lippincott & R. B. Lippincott (Eds.), *Special populations in college counseling: A handbook for mental health professionals* (pp. 3–20). Alexandria, VA: American Counseling Association.

Bonar, T. C., & Domenici, P. L. (2011). Counseling and connecting with the military undergraduate: The intersection of military service and university life. *Journal of College Student Psychotherapy, 25,* 204–219. doi:10.1080/87568225.2011.581925

Bullock, E. E., Braud, J., Andrews, L., & Phillips, J. (2009). Career concerns of unemployed U.S. war veterans: Suggestions from a cognitive information processing approach. *Journal of Employment Counseling, 46,* 171–181.

Bureau of Labor Statistics. (2014). *2014–2015 Occupational outlook handbook.* Retrieved from http://www.bls.gov/ooh/

Burwell, R., & Chen, C. P. (2006). Applying the principles and techniques of solution-focused therapy to career counseling. *Counseling Psychology Quarterly, 19,* 189–203.

Buzzetta, M., & Rowe, S. (2012, November). Today's veterans: Using cognitive information processing (CIP) approach to build upon their career dreams. *Career Convergence: Web Magazine.* Retrieved from http://www.ncda.org

Clemens, E. V., & Milsom, A. S. (2008). Enlisted service members' transition into the civilian world of work: A cognitive information processing approach. *The Career Development Quarterly, 56,* 246–256.

Corey, G. (2017). *Theory and practice of counseling and psychotherapy* (10th ed.). Belmont, CA: Brooks/Cole.

Gelatt, H. B. (1991). *Creative decision making using positive uncertainty.* Los Altos, CA: Crisp.

Gergen, K. (1999). *An invitation to social construction.* Thousand Oaks, CA: Sage.

Hansen, J. T. (2014). *Philosophical issues in counseling and psychotherapy: Encounters with four questions about knowing, effectiveness, and truth.* Lanham, MD: Rowman & Littlefield.

Hayden, S., Green, L., & Dorsett, K. (2013). *Perseverance and progress: Career counseling for military personnel with traumatic brain injury.* Retrieved from http://counselingoutfitters.com/vistas/VISTAS_Home.htm

Hayden, S. C. W., Ledwith, K., Dong, S., & Buzzetta, M. (2014). Assessing the career-development needs of student veterans: A proposal for career interventions. *The Professional Counselor 4,* 129–138.

Kaufman, D. (1976). *Teaching the future.* Palm Springs, CA: ETC.

Marchione, M. (2012, May). *Almost half of new vets seek disability.* Retrieved from http://bigstory.ap.org/

Markus, H., & Nurius, P. (1986). Possible selves. *American Psychologist, 41,* 954–969.

Miller, J. H. (2004a). Extending the use of constructivist approaches in career guidance and counselling: Solution-focused strategies. *Australian Journal of Career Development, 13,* 50–58.

Miller, J. H. (2004b). Building a solution-focused strategy into career counselling. *New Zealand Journal of Counselling, 25,* 18–30.

Miller, J. H. (2006). Using a solution-building approach in career counselling. In M. McMahon & W. Patton (Eds.), *Career counselling: Constructivist approaches* (pp. 123–136). London, England: Routledge.

Murdock, N. (2013). *Theories of counseling and psychotherapy: A case approach* (3rd ed.). Upper Saddle River, NJ: Merrill.

Neimeyer, R. A., & Bridges, S. K. (2003). Postmodern approaches to psychotherapy. In A. S. Gurman & S. B. Messer (Eds.), *Essential psychotherapies: Theory and practice* (2nd ed., pp. 272–316). New York, NY: Guilford Press.

O'Connell, B. (1998). *Solution-focused therapy.* London, England: Sage.

Peavy, R. V. (1998). *SocioDynamic counselling: A constructivist perspective.* Victoria, Canada: Trafford.

Phillips, J., Braud, J., Andrews, L., & Bullock, E. (2007, November). Bridging the gap from job to career in U.S. veterans. *Career Convergence: Web Magazine.* Retrieved from www.ncda.org

Polkinghorne, D. (1992). Postmodern epistemology of practice. In S. Kvale (Ed.), *Psychology and postmodernism* (pp. 146–165). Thousand Oaks, CA: Sage.

Ratner, H., George, E., & Iveson, C. (2012). *Solution-focused brief therapy: 100 key points and techniques.* New York, NY: Routledge.

Rausch, M. A. (2014). Contextual career counseling for transitioning military veterans. *Journal of Employment Counseling 51,* 89–96.

Reid, H. L. (2006). Usefulness and truthfulness: Outlining the limitations and upholding the benefits of constructivist approaches for career counseling. In M. McMahon & W. Patton (Eds.), *Career counselling: Constructivist approaches* (pp. 30–41). New York, NY: Routledge.

Richmond, C. J., Jordan, S. S., Bischof, G. H., & Sauer, E. M. (2014). Effects of solution-focused versus problem-focused intake questions on pre-treatment change. *Journal of Systemic Therapies, 33,* 33–47. doi:10.1521/jsyt.2014.33.1.33

Robinson, B. S., Davis, K. L., & Meara, N. M. (2003). Motivational attributes of occupational possible selves for low-income rural women. *Journal of Counseling Psychology, 50,* 156–164.

Rorty, R. (1979). *Philosophy and the mirror of nature.* Princeton, NJ: Princeton University Press.

Rorty, R. (1999). *Philosophy and social hope.* New York, NY: Penguin Putnam.

Savickas, M. L. (2005). The theory and practice of career construction. In S. D. Brown & R. W. Lent (Eds.), *Career development and counseling: Putting theory and research to work* (pp. 42–70). Hoboken, NJ: Wiley.

Scholl, M. B., & Cascone, J. (2010). The constructivist resume: Promoting the career adaptability of graduate students in counseling programs. *The Career Development Quarterly, 59,* 180–191.

Tanielian, T., & Jaycox, L. H. (Eds.). (2008). *Invisible wounds of war: Psychological and cognitive injuries, their consequences, and services to assist recovery.* Santa Monica, CA: RAND.

Woodward, A. (2002). Nihilism and the postmodern in Vattino's Nietzsche. *Minerva: An Internet Journal of Philosophy, 6,* 51–67.

Chapter 19

Using the One Life Tools Narrative Framework: From Clarification to Intentional Exploration With an East Asian Female

Mark Franklin and Rich Feller

Postmodern career interventions call for reexamination of the nature, structure, and practice of career counseling. Career interventions that move clients to further and more purposefully design their work and life roles are increasingly augmenting mechanistic and static approaches. Constructivist and narrative approaches (Savickas, 2012) that account for clients' personality and their socially derived meanings rely on highly engaged processes and tools. The One Life Tools/CareerCycles (OLTCC) framework and practices for career counseling (see Recommended Resources), and tools such as the "Who You Are Matters!" game (Franklin, Feller, & Yanar, 2014) prove useful to diverse groups by integrating key elements of optimistic emotions in positive psychology (Fredrickson, 2001), creating psychological capital (Luthans, Youssef, & Avolio, 2007) and multicultural competency (Lee, 2012), facilitating and clarifying career and life stories, and initiating intentional exploration.

In this chapter, we explain the OLTCC framework and illustrate the use of face-to-face and digital interactions with a client named Angela to clarify and transform her career and life stories into inspired action. With her self-clarification comes a greater sense of possibility and motivation to engage in intentional exploration.

Changes in Careers Call for New Clarification Processes

Most people spend the majority of their waking hours doing something they consider to be a job, a career, or a calling, and career counseling has long been identified with one's job and engagement with paid work. The National Career Development Association (1997) defines *career counseling* as "the process of assisting individuals in the development of a life-career with focus on the definition of the worker role and how that role interacts with other life roles" (p. 1). Swanson (1995) saw it as an "ongoing, face-to-face interaction between a counselor and client in which the focus is on work or career-related concerns" (p. 245). The importance of placing career issues within the broader context of individual development is enhanced by Franklin's (2014) definition of career: "The full expression of who you are and how you want to be in the world. And it keeps on expanding as it naturally goes through cycles of stability and change" (p. 456).

Dramatic changes in the employee–employer relationship, in work options, and in the learning, earning, and opportunity structures, which have occurred in response to technological innovation and globalization, make courageous career choices on the part of workers necessary (Feller & Whichard, 2005). Helping clients integrate life roles while designing a purposeful life requires a more holistic, diverse, and strengths-based conceptualization of career development (Gysbers, Heppner, & Johnston, 2014).

With a "proliferation of career counseling approaches underpinned by postmodern and constructivist philosophies" (McMahon, Watson, Chetty, & Hoelson, 2012, p. 127), theories of vocational personalities and work environments continue to hold value. This integration of efforts calls for examination and stimulation of "new ways of gathering client information as career counseling unfolds" (Gysbers et al., 2014, p. 3).

Narrative assessment offers an opportunity to fully engage clients by honoring their past and by building the psychological capital (Luthans, Youssef, et al., 2007) necessary to navigate a life characterized by transitions. When clients go through the career and life clarification process (Zikic & Franklin, 2010), they generate hope, optimism, confidence, and resilience (Luthans, Avolio, Avery, & Norman, 2007), as well as curiosity and exploration (Kashdan, Rose, & Fincham, 2004), with evidence for this claim coming from a recent outcome study (Franklin, Yanar, & Feller, 2015). Collectively, this psychological capital (Luthans, Avolio, et al., 2007) ultimately leads to greater clarity and satisfaction with career and life choices. Angela's case study illustrates the use of the OLTCC narrative *method of practice* (a term drawn from the *Canadian Standards and Guidelines for Career Development Practitioners*, 2012) with an Asian female client.

The Case of Angela

Background Information

The CareerCycles practice has been used with clients from more than 180 countries of origin, throughout the life span, from early to late career. Clients have been diverse in religious beliefs and first languages and have come from all points on the spectrum of gender identity and sexual orientation. In selecting "Angela" (her name and personal details have been changed) for this case study, we necessarily focus only on aspects of diversity that have an impact on career development and management practice.

When Angela came for career counseling, she was a later career professional in her early 50s. She had professional career experiences largely in the financial services sector, with additional stints in media and education. Angela and her husband had immigrated to the United States in their 20s, having left their East Asian country of origin for better opportunities. Angela completed a multisession career counseling program.

Career Concern

Having reached a senior role at the financial institution where she worked, a change in leadership led to an amicable parting accompanied by a severance package that provided time to allow Angela to reimagine her career and life. She came to career counseling saying, "I have many plans, but no PLAN. What should I do next? I have a few ideas—should I choose one of them, or something new? And how will I make any plan actually happen?" Like many clients in transition, Angela experienced both positive and negative emotions. Although her work of the past few years had left her drained and bored, and the transition in which she found herself was worrisome, the prospect of change and the freedom it promised felt good. Asked to locate herself on a scale of 1 to 10, where 10 is feeling great about her career and life situation and 1 represents complete despair, Angela gave herself a 6 and said, "Freedom feels good!"

In the first session, Angela identified many possibilities for the next steps in her career and life. Among these were jobs with organizations that "do good" (such as an international agency or university), self-employment (such as a career in executive coaching), as well as some volunteer and lifelong learning possibilities.

Generating Optimism and Hope in the First Session

Clients like Angela begin their career counseling and career education process by speaking to a counseling service manager in an interactive intake interview. The counseling service manager listens to the client's questions and concerns, then probes and draws the client out, usually in a phone conversation lasting 15 minutes. Clients often do not know what to expect when contacting a career counselor or career professional (we use these terms interchangeably), and there are many services provided by career professionals, so it is important to ensure the clients' questions are aligned with the appropriate services. The client service manager makes an initial judgment call about this alignment, provides an overview of the OLTCC narrative model, introduces the career professional who will work with the client, schedules a first session, and provides details of the conversation to the career counselor.

In the first session, the career professional answers any questions the client has, and then explains the intentions of the session: (a) It will be useful in and of itself even if the client only attends this single session; (b) all details will be kept confidential; (c) the career professional will take notes during session that will be sent to the client or be made available in his or her online account; and (d) at the end of session, the career professional will take a few minutes to explain possible next steps in terms of programs and team member match.

Next, the career professional uses a *First Session Note Page* (italics indicate OLTCC tools) to guide three initial interventions and to collect data for the initial part of the session. For the first of these interventions, the client is prompted to formulate a career question. Angela's response (shown above) began with "I have many plans . . .". Second, the client is asked to name all the career and life possibilities that are "on your radar screen." Angela is curious about a job in an organization that does good, for example, the United Nations, a university, or a government department. She is also interested in a leadership position in a local nonprofit or a growing startup. She also has been considering taking a coaching certificate course and becoming an executive coach. Rounding out the list is a volunteer position in a youth program.

In her career and life, Angela desires variety and new experiences, to be productive, to see projects through to completion, and to do good for the world by having a positive impact on people's lives and sharing wisdom. These initial desires most often come from "flipping" complaints and dislikes, which is the third intervention. For example, Angela disliked the long hours and heavy responsibilities of her previous leadership position. The flipside of these easily articulated dislikes is "a sense of freedom."

At this stage, roughly 15 minutes into the session, the career professional reframes the conversation by introducing the "becoming empowered and proactive" model. The career counselor says, "Let me take just a few minutes to step back and reframe what you've told me so far so that we can move forward. I would like to start with this model. Please have a look as I walk you through it briefly." Clients respond well to using the term *roadmap* when describing this model, metaphorically illustrating the career management process as a journey using a map on which the client can locate herself, then follow along a mapped course.

Using notes from the handwritten *First Session Note Page*, the career counselor works with Angela to refine her career question and then writes it into the *Questions & Notes* page of her online account. Much of the OLTCC framework, including *Questions & Notes*, is implemented within a suite of online tools to allow for scalability and blended delivery. The career counselor creates a client account before meeting with the client and accesses the client's account during the first session, after which the client can access it on her own. After the *Questions & Notes*, Angela is introduced to the online *Career Sketch*, which is a helpful and holistic tool used to gather and organize all the elements of her situation. The "Desires" element of the *Career Sketch* was introduced as "what you want and what's important to you," and the career counselor added the items identified thus far. The "Possibilities" that Angela had named were also added, as were the "Thoughts & Feelings" that she'd shared.

To shift the client's affect toward the positive and better utilize resources, restating Desires can be very helpful. In Angela's case, as her initial Desires were added, the career professional asked, "Wouldn't it be great if you had variety and something new, and if your next step helped you be productive and see projects through to completion, and to feel that you're doing good for the world by making a positive impact and sharing wisdom?" Using the phrase "wouldn't it be great . . ." was inspired by Hicks and Hicks (2004). When Angela heard these Desires restated in such positive and personal terms, she immediately began nodding her head "yes." As a result of taking this approach, her affect was nudged toward the positive, thus invoking Fredrickson's (2001) "broaden and build" phenomenon. In career counseling terms, *broadens* refers to the number of career possibilities a client can see, and *builds* refers to internal resources such as hope and confidence for the upcoming intentional exploration.

Now that the client is familiar with the *Career Sketch*, the career professional can ask for a story or experience to add to the clarity emerging in the *Career Sketch*, to refine existing career possibilities, and to generate new ones. The client is given the following prompt: "I'd like to show you how this narrative process works. Please choose a story or experience you feel good about. It can be from work, volunteer, or personal experience. What comes to mind?"

Angela identifies a story about an opportunity she had to research and report on women in business for a local television station. Once a story is identified, the career professional asks a series of open-ended questions to "thicken" the story, a concept drawn from narrative therapy (White, 2007). One question might be "What did you like about this story?" Angela says she liked the diversity of topics and the sharing of wisdom, and these are added to her *Career Sketch* as Desires. When asked what skills and knowledge she drew on or developed, Angela lists researching, facilitating learning, reporting, creating stories, interviewing, and writing. All of these are added to Angela's *Career Sketch* as Strengths. She also mentions that she has been a good writer since childhood. When asked what personal qualities this story illustrates, Angela replies, "I'm very curious," and this is added to the *Career Sketch* under Personal Qualities.

Once confirmed with the client, all elements emerging from the story are added to the *Career Sketch*. As the content in the *Career Sketch* grows and clarification begins, the client becomes familiar with how this narrative approach works. At the end of each story, the career professional and the client can collaboratively identify new career Possibilities emerging from the story and its related Strengths, Personal Qualities, and other elements. The career professional might say something like this:

What career and life possibilities emerge for you from this story? As you and I both answer that question, let us "set the bar" at your curiosity. If you are curious about a possibility even if you know nothing about it, let us add it to your list. If you are not curious, it falls below the bar and we will discard it. Nevertheless, let us ask "Why not?" and in so doing we will identify desires that we may not have taken into account. For example, if I say, "How about being a long distance truck driver," and you say, "Not interested," then I'll ask why not, and you might say, "Because it's too isolating." Then we will know about another of your Desires, which will be the opposite of too isolating, maybe something like "I want to work closely with people." Ready to play?

In this manner, in Angela's case, three promising Possibilities are identified that she agrees to add to the list: reporting for a newcomer television station, management consulting through her network of executives, and instructor at an executive education center.

Once one of Angela's stories has been explored, it adds substantive material to her *Career Sketch*. Angela's East Asian cultural background and her immigration journey did emerge as relevant parts of her story in later sessions, but in the first session Angela acknowledged it (*Career Sketch* elements) in the form of language skills and the ability to connect with a wider multicultural audience in the television reporting experience. In later sessions, Angela and the career professional analyzed more of her career stories, and they illustrated both the challenges and the advantages of her immigrant status. In one story, she smartly leveraged her cultural background and language skills to win a position with the North American branch of an East Asian organization.

Because this case study is drawn from a fee-for-service career management practice, the end of the first session is the time to propose a program for a number of follow-up sessions to work through the processes of career and life clarification and intentional exploration. If referring the client to another career professional, this is the point at which to do so. In postsecondary education and agency settings where many OLTCC-trained career professionals work, there is no discussion of fees; however, clients are provided with an overview of the process using the roadmap, and trainees routinely report an increase in the number of second sessions. In Angela's case, she did agree to proceed with a program. Even if the client chooses not to proceed, the individual leaves this initial session having generated several new and promising possibilities and having clarified key Strengths, Desires, and other elements. After these initial sessions, clients usually report feeling more optimistic and hopeful.

Implementation of the "Becoming Empowered and Proactive" Program

At the end of the first session, Angela is given the task of constructing a timeline of her life. She is asked to add stories to an interactive time line in the categories of early years, education, and career and life. Each of these story categories is associated with a particular suite of narrative questions. These questions and the interactive timeline are embedded in an *Online Storyteller* tool (another OLTCC tool), which interactively asks the user questions and allows short responses to be input. This material is displayed in a way that is similar to the texting feature on most smartphones. Using the *Online Storyteller* tool, Angela responds interactively to questions about each story, and these items are automatically added to her *Career Sketch*.

The next two sessions are dedicated to working collaboratively to review Angela's expanding *Career Sketch*; to analyze additional stories; and to make sense of the collected Strengths, Desires and other elements identified from the stories. It is during these sessions that the influence of Angela's home country experiences emerges.

During the cultural revolution in China, her family had been forced to move from the city to the countryside. Education was a strong value held by her parents, and as a capable young woman, Angela aspired to go to university. Despite her parents' emphasis on studying science and engineering, Angela was influenced by her sister and chose to study education and English instead. Having English language skills in particular later gave her the confidence to move to North America with her husband. In these sessions, Angela acknowledges the influence of the experiences of these early years—her parents' struggles and her supportive siblings—all leading her to want to succeed in career and life according to traditional measures of success, such as position and income. Indeed, these influences drove Angela's career in her adopted country, leading her away from teaching and into business, first in human resources then in finance, following additional training and a business degree. However, after experiencing career success, the influence of her upbringing in a collectivist society led to a renewed desire to do good in the world. Angela also explains that years earlier she had completed another strengths survey that had placed Fairness/Equity/Justice among her top character strengths, which she attributed to her upbringing. Adding external assessment results to one's *Career Sketch*, such as Angela's character strengths, illustrates how assessment results may be integrated into the OLTCC framework and tools.

Getting Feedback is another intervention suggested to Angela, and she is receptive to doing it. In this career and life clarification experience, Angela approaches three trusted allies to receive structured feedback using a list of questions sent via email, with follow-up phone calls to receive feedback. In the third session, Angela and the career professional analyze the feedback and add it to her *Career Sketch*. Samples of what emerged from *Getting Feedback* include work with like-minded people (Desire); strategic planning and decision making (Strength); fair and just, possesses humility (Personal Quality); gets things done (Personal Quality); could be more succinct when communicating (Personal Quality); public speaking (Possibility).

Toward the end of the third session, Angela's *Career Sketch* contains more than 50 items across the seven elements (Desires, Strengths, and so on) and 20 career and life Possibilities. Angela is asked to prioritize these Possibilities (high, medium, low) according to her interest in exploring them further. She is then asked to generate her unique *Career Statement*, incorporating the most important and relevant items in her *Career Sketch* and including the high-priority Possibilities. An abridged form of Angela's *Career Statement* follows:

Here's what I want and what's important to me (Desires): I want to keep myself busy and productive; my plan is to do different things, have variety and "something new," and make a difference with people who appreciate my contribution. I want to do good for the world by making a positive impact. In all of this, I want to maintain a sense of freedom.

Here's what I want to do or use (Strengths): Facilitating learning, and strategic planning and decision making

Here's the kind of person I am and how others describe me (Personal Qualities): I'm very curious, and I get things done!

Here's what I bring with me (Assets): Financial services leadership experience, immigration experience, TV reporting experience

Here are my emerging interests (Natural Interest): Supporting youth

I'm mindful of how these people have influenced or continue to influence my career and life choices (Other People): Parents said, "Get an education!"; husband said, "Let's move from here to North America."

These are the Possibilities I'm most curious about:

- Coaching certification program
- Organization that does good (e.g., United Nations, university)
- Executive coach
- Volunteer at a youth program
- Management consulting

When Angela reads her *Career Statement* aloud in the fourth session, she is energized and excited. The career counselor listens carefully, affirms, and helps to assure her that she can indeed bring this *Career Statement* to life. By personalizing the content of her *Career Sketch* and then reading it aloud, Angela increases her sense of ownership of the resulting *Career Statement*. This is a rich, memorable, and important moment in the career counseling process, one that many clients remark on later, and in Angela's case, it will give her hope and optimism for moving forward. The career counselor then introduces Intentional Exploration as a process to help Angela explore the five Possibilities she had named in her *Career Statement*.

In session, the career counselor adds Angela's Possibilities to the *Exploration Plan*, another online tool within the OLTCC framework. Then, one by one, client and career professional begin to expand the Possibilities collaboratively by identifying clues, naming inspired actions, and listing possible requirements. For example, one of Angela's priority Possibilities is management consulting through her network of executives. When asked for clues she has been noticing about this Possibility, Angela says she has been speaking to her friend Linda who has a company executive in her network who is seeking someone to help them with a "culture diagnosis." Angela feels excited about working with that company to learn about its needs and conduct a consulting engagement. This clue is added to Angela's *Exploration Plan*, providing both a spark for action and a reminder for later, once the exploration is under way. Emphasizing the importance of clues, and asking clients to actively watch for clues aligned with their *Career Statement*, increases the likelihood of clients harnessing happenstance (Mitchell, Levin, & Krumboltz, 1999). Bloch (2005) introduced telling future stories that demonstrate the "strange links between events, links they describe as 'just luck' or coincidence" (p. 198) as a key part of her chaos theory of careers.

With clues identified and the associated good feelings that these clues engender, Angela is asked, "What do you want to do to explore this Possibility further?" This deceptively simple question can yield a number of inspired action steps the client is willing to do. It is deceptively simple because much of the career counseling process to this point is designed to make the inspired action so easy and so irresistible that the client will actually do it. Inspired action can naturally and easily follow close attention to clues linked to clients' stories. And indeed, an outcome study of this method of practice (Franklin et al., 2015) showed that clients experienced significantly increased levels of curiosity and exploration (Kashdan et al., 2009), leading to their inspired actions. For this Possibility, Angela wants to take the inspired actions of getting back into a conversation with her friend Linda and strategizing on a consulting practice using another OLTCC intervention focused on entrepreneurship. In a follow-up meeting, the career counselor checks with Angela about each of these actions. This kind of follow-up shifts the career professional's role from counseling to coaching. The results of inspired actions are assigned to a color-coded status, confirming whether the action was done, not done, how valuable it was, and possible next steps.

Inspired action can take many forms, including crafting experiments as clients go through a career change process. Ibarra (2003) referred to the notion of working identity and said that the biggest mistake people make when trying to change careers (and thus their working identity) is to delay taking the first step until they have settled on a destination.

The *Exploration Plan* is first written in Angela's fourth session, but a career professional can spend any number of sessions supporting clients through their Intentional Exploration. This number of sessions will depend on the organizational context and possibly the client's budget in the case of a fee-for-service practice.

Angela remains fairly optimistic and active during her Intentional Exploration. Many clients do experience emotional swings during this process, and to inoculate them against the emotional valleys, an intervention focusing on clients' thoughts and feelings is used, resulting in a positive thought constructed collaboratively. Angela's positive thought—"I am marketable, I am doing something I like and enjoy in my career and life. I am productive!"—when mentally rehearsed, can act as a touchstone for changing thinking habits and associated affect.

Guided by her *Exploration Plan* and career counselor, Angela engages in a productive Intentional Exploration, watching for clues and taking inspired actions for each of her priority Possibilities. In so doing, she is increasing her fund of self-knowledge and gaining clarity around her likes and dislikes in a process entirely aligned with "occupational engagement" as described by Krieshok, Black, and McKay (2009). Through this process, Angela eventually connected with an organization that provides support to organizational leaders. A volunteer position led to a remunerated position at a related organization where Angela is presently giving her gifts, sharing her strengths, and living her *Career Statement*. See Table 19.1 for an application guide.

Conclusion

The cultural context is critical to serving diverse groups as they complete a lifetime of transitions. The OLTCC framework and face-to-face and digital tools offer a fresh, innovative set of principles and practices for multicultural career counseling. Its potential to provide clarity and confidence to clients is increasingly evident with research as career counselors/professionals are trained in its approach.

Table 19.1
Practical Application Guide

Topic	OLTCC Framework
General goals and purpose	1. Explain the OLTCC framework to suggest an approach that will enhance clarification and intentional exploration. 2. Highlight face-to-face and digital tools used in the system. 3. Review the key elements of the "Who You Are Matters!" game.
Applicable modality	Individual, workshops, large group sessions
Applicable counselor settings	Private practice, college orientation sessions, career centers, community agencies, school and organizational settings
Recommended time to complete	Two to five sessions to complete in individual settings. Fewer sessions required when using Online Storyteller; 2 to 3 hours to complete game in workshop or other settings.
Materials/equipment needed	Handouts, Career Sketch and Career Statement and Exploration Plan, and for groups "Who You Are Matters!" game; Online Storyteller for blended delivery
Step-by-step outline of the process	A graphical model depicting the clarification and exploration processes guides the method and is shown to the client as a roadmap of the OLTCC experience.

Note. OLTCC = One Life Tools/CareerCycles framework from clarification to intentional exploration for diverse groups.

Recommended Resources

Feller, R., & Franklin, M. (2015). *Information on the Who You Are Matters! game, and Online Storyteller.* Retrieved from http://www.onelifetools.com

Franklin, M. (2015). *Information on the CareerCycles narrative, evidence-based method of practice and related training.* Retrieved from http://careercycles.com/career-counsellor-training

Franklin, M. (2015). *Career buzz* [Radio podcasts featuring hundreds of career stories illustrating the OLTCC processes] Retrieved from http://careercycles.com/radio

One Life Tools/Career Cycles (OLTCC) framework and model. Retrieved from http://http://onelifetools.com/

References

Bloch, D. P. (2005). Complexity, chaos, and nonlinear dynamics: A new perspective on career development theory. *The Career Development Quarterly*, *53*, 194–207.

Canadian standards and guidelines for career development practitioners. (2012). Retrieved from http://career-dev-guidelines.org/career_dev/

Feller, R., & Whichard, J. (2005). *Knowledge nomads and the nervously employed: Workplace change and courageous career choices.* Austin, TX: Pro-Ed.

Franklin, M. (2014). CareerCycles: A holistic and narrative method of practice. In B. C. Shepard & P. S. Mani (Eds.), *Career development practice in Canada: Perspectives, principles, and professionalism* (pp. 441–463). Toronto, Ontario, Canada: CERIC.

Franklin, M., Feller, R., & Yanar, B. (2014). Narrative assessment tools for career and life clarification and intentional exploration: Lily's case study. *Career Planning and Adult Development Journal*, *30*, 85–98.

Franklin, M., Yanar, B., & Feller, R. (2015). Narrative method of practice increases curiosity and exploration, psychological capital, and personal growth leading to career clarity: A retrospective outcome study. *Canadian Journal of Career Development*, *14*, 12–23.

Fredrickson, B. L. (2001). The role of positive emotions in positive psychology: The broaden-and-build theory of positive emotions. *American Psychologist*, *56*, 218–226.

Gysbers, N. C., Heppner, M. J., & Johnston, J. A. (2014). *Career counseling: Holism, diversity, and strengths* (4th ed.). Alexandria, VA: American Counseling Association.

Hicks, E., & Hicks, J. (2004). *Ask and it is given.* Carlsbad, CA: Hay House.

Ibarra, H. (2003). *Working identity: Unconventional strategies for reinventing your career.* Boston, MA: Harvard Business School Press.

Kashdan, T. B., Gallagher, M. W., Silvia, P. J., Winterstein, B. P., Breen, W. E., Terhar, D., & Steger, M. F. (2009). The Curiosity and Exploration Inventory-II: Development, factor structure, and initial psychometrics. *Journal of Research in Personality*, *43*, 987–998.

Kashdan, T. B., Rose, P., & Fincham, F. D. (2004). Curiosity and exploration: Facilitating positive subjective experiences and personal growth opportunities. *Journal of Personality Assessment, 82,* 291–305.

Krieshok, T. S., Black, M. D., & McKay, R. A. (2009). Career decision making: The limits of rationality and the abundance of non-conscious processes. *Journal of Vocational Behavior, 75,* 275–290.

Lee, C. C. (2012). A conceptual framework for culturally competent career counseling practice. *Career Planning and Adult Development Journal, 28,* 7–14.

Luthans, F., Avolio, B. J., Avey, J. B., & Norman, S. M. (2007). Positive psychological capital: Measurement and relationship with performance and satisfaction. *Personnel Psychology 60,* 541–572.

Luthans, F., Youssef, C., & Avolio, B. (2007). *Psychological capital: Developing the human competitive edge.* New York, NY: Oxford University Press.

McMahon, M., Watson, M., Chetty, C., & Hoelson, C. N. (2012). Examining process constructs of narrative career counselling: An exploratory case study. *British Journal of Guidance & Counselling, 40,* 127–141.

Mitchell, K. E., Levin, A. S., & Krumboltz, J. D. (1999). Planned happenstance: Constructing unexpected career opportunities. *Journal of Counseling & Development, 77,* 115–124.

National Career Development Association. (1997). *Career counseling competencies.* Columbus, OH: Author.

Savickas, M. L. (2012). Life design: A paradigm for career intervention in the 21st century. *Journal of Counseling & Development, 90,* 13–19.

Swanson, J. L. (1995). The process and outcome of career counseling. In W. B. Walsh & S. H. Osipow (Eds.), *Handbook of vocational psychology* (2nd ed., pp. 217–259). Hillsdale, NJ: Erlbaum.

White, M. (2007). *Maps of narrative practice.* New York, NY: Norton.

Zikic, J., & Franklin, M. (2010). Enriching careers and lives: Introducing a positive, holistic, and narrative career counseling method that bridges theory and practice. *Journal of Employment Counseling, 47,* 180–189.

Chapter 20

From the Systems Theory Framework to My System of Career Influences: Integrating Theory and Practice With a Black South African Male

Mary McMahon, Wendy Patton, and Mark Watson

Career counseling has a history of commitment to assisting individuals with career decisions and transitions so that they may have more rewarding and meaningful lives. Founded on Parsons's (1909) tripartite model, which emphasizes a process of matching individual traits with the factors inherent in particular occupations, career theory and career counseling have been developed in the limited context of Western middle-class settings primarily in the United States. Toward the latter part of the 20th century, increasing awareness of the growing diversity of society as well as the expansion of career counseling into new countries and cultures resulted in calls for innovative theoretical formulations and practices to accommodate the multicultural societies within which career counseling is practiced.

In this chapter, we describe one response to the challenges facing career theory and career counseling through the first comprehensive application in the field of systems theory. In particular, we describe the metatheoretical systems theory framework (STF; McMahon & Patton, 1995; Patton & McMahon, 2014) of career development and its practical application, the My System of Career Influences (MSCI) qualitative career assessment instrument (McMahon, Patton, & Watson, 2005a, 2005b, in press a, in press b; McMahon, Watson, & Patton, 2013a, 2013b). First, we briefly describe the philosophical underpinnings of career theory and then discuss the theoretical foundations of systems theory prior to outlining the STF and subsequently the MSCI. Second, we present an application of the MSCI with the hypothetical case study of a Black South African adult male.

Philosophical Underpinnings of Career Theory

Career development theory has been influenced by the logical positivist worldview for most of its relatively brief history, a worldview that is reflected in the trait and factor theories. Such theories value rationality and objectivity over subjectivity and knowledge that lacks objective value (Brown, 2002). Logical positivists believe that individuals can be studied separately from their contexts and that behavior is observable, measurable, and linear (Brown, 2002).

For a couple of decades now, the influence of the constructivist worldview (Patton, 2008), which emphasizes the individual in context perspective, has been growing. Individuals think about and reflect on their interactions within their contexts, and in doing so, they construct their own reality. In this view, reality is constructed from the inside out, and subjectivity is valued. Similarly, systems theory recognizes that individuals self-organize through complex and dynamic processes of learning and knowing through which they construct their own reality (Patton, 2008). Systems theory views individuals as open systems, constantly interacting with their environment, seeking stability through ongoing change. Human systems interact interdependently with other systems (e.g., family, workplace) and, through these interactions, self-perpetuate and evolve.

Assumptions of Systems Theories

Several key features of systems theory informed the conceptualization of the STF (Patton & McMahon, 2014). These features are briefly described below:

- Systems may be open or closed. Closed systems do not relate to or interact with their surrounding contexts. By contrast, open systems constantly interact with their contexts in complex, multifaceted relationships. The STF portrays an open system.
- Open systems are both wholes and parts; that is, they are entities in their own right as well as being interdependent subsystems of larger systems. Systems theory is holistic, as reflected in the STF.
- Patterns develop in the relationships and interactions that occur within and between systems.
- Acausality recognizes the complex multiplicity of relationships that exist within systems, and it precludes explanations based on isolated, reductionist, and simple causal linear relationships.
- Recursiveness is the process of ongoing, nonlinear, multidirectional interaction within and between systems.
- Discontinuous change emphasizes that systems experience constant change ranging from small and almost indiscernible perturbations to sudden and more overt changes.
- Abduction is a form of reasoning based on patterns, relationships, and lateral thinking rather than on linear, cause-and-effect logic.
- Story is a mechanism by which the relationships and patterns in systems are accounted for and made meaningful.

The STF

The STF (McMahon & Patton, 1995; Patton & McMahon, 2014) is the first metatheoretical framework of career development based on systems theory. See Figure 20.1. As such, the STF was not designed as a theory of career development. Functioning instead as a metatheory, the STF can have positioned within it concepts of career development described in the plethora of career theories.

The STF is composed of several key interrelated systems, including the individual system, the social system, and the environmental-societal

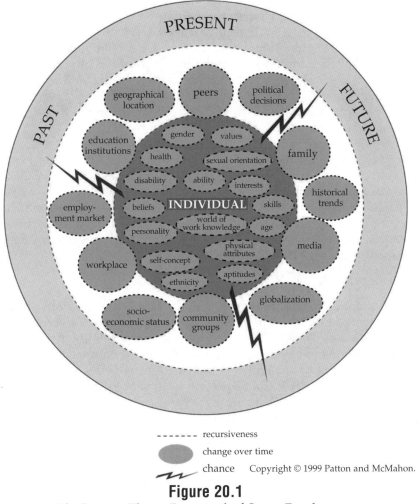

Figure 20.1

The Systems Theory Framework of Career Development

From *Career Development and Systems Theory: A New Relationship*, p.164, by W. Patton and M. McMahon, 1999, Pacific Grove, CA: Brooks/Cole. Copyright 1999 by W. Patton and M. McMahon. Reprinted with permission.

system (see Figure 20.1). The processes between these systems are demonstrated by the recursive nature of interaction within and between these systems, change over time, and chance. The individual system is composed of several intrapersonal content influences that include gender, age, self-concept, health, ability, disability, physical attributes, beliefs, personality, interests, values, aptitudes, skills, world of work knowledge, sexual orientation, and ethnicity. Influences representing the social system include peers, family, media, community groups, workplace, and education institutions. Environmental-societal system influences include political decisions, historical trends, globalization, socioeconomic status, employment market, and geographical location. Process influences include chance, change over time, and recursiveness (i.e., the interaction within and between influences). Through the combination of content and process influences, the STF portrays career development as a dynamic interplay between individuals and their systems of influence. With the individual as the central focus, constructing his or her own meaning of career, existing theories may be applied as relevant to each individual to account for specific influences. Indeed, in the telling of career stories, individuals construct their own STFs as reflected in the MSCI qualitative career assessment process.

The STF has been applied to career counseling diagrammatically through its representation as a therapeutic system (Patton & McMahon, 2014, Figure 20.2) to provide a map of career counseling (McMahon & Patton, 2006), and through the narrative career counseling approach, storytelling, which is based on the STF core constructs of connectedness, meaning making, agency, learning, and reflection (McMahon, 2005; McMahon & Patton, 2006; McMahon & Watson, 2012a, 2012b, 2013; McMahon, Watson, Chetty, & Hoelson, 2012a, 2012b; Patton & McMahon, 2006).

The MSCI Reflection Activity

The STF stimulated the development of the MSCI. This qualitative career assessment process assists individuals in reflecting on their career development influences. The MSCI was developed and tested through a rigorous process (McMahon, Watson, & Patton, 2005) based on suggestions for the development of qualitative career assessment processes (McMahon, Patton, & Watson, 2003). An adolescent version of the MSCI (McMahon, Patton et al., 2005a, 2005b, in press a, in press b) was initially published, followed by an adult version (McMahon et al., 2013a, 2013b), published in response to requests from practitioners.

The MSCI is a qualitative career assessment process that is guided by constructivist principles (McMahon & Patton, 2006). The subsystems of the STF provide the core structure of the MSCI, which enables individuals to construct their own system of career influences through a guided reflection process. Individuals construct their own MSCI subsystem by subsystem in the same sequential way that the STF is constructed (see Patton & McMahon, 2014, for a description of the process).

The following description of the MSCI is applicable to both the adolescent and adult versions, as the structure of each is similar. The MSCI

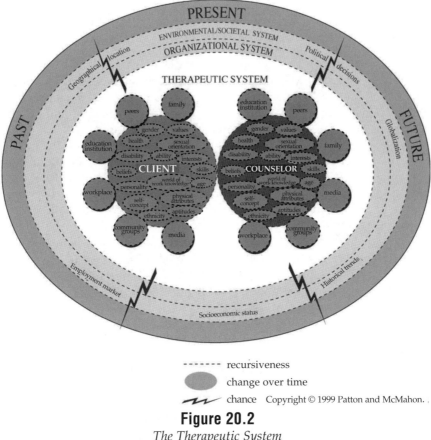

------- recursiveness

change over time

chance   Copyright © 1999 Patton and McMahon. .

Figure 20.2
The Therapeutic System

From *Career Development and Systems: Theory: A New Relationship*, p. 268 , by W. Patton and M. McMahon, 1999, Pacific Grove, CA: Brooks/Cole. Copyright 1999 by W. Patton and M. McMahon. Reprinted with permission.

is completed by individuals using a booklet that guides them through a structured reflection on their current career development and its influences. The booklet provides brief information, instructions and examples, and places where reflections can be recorded. Beginning with a page titled *My Present Career Situation*, individuals reflect on their occupational aspirations, work experience, life roles, previous decision making, and available support networks. Individuals then work through a series of pages titled *Thinking about who I am*, *Thinking about the people around me*, and *Thinking about society and the environment* on which they identify and prioritize their influences. The next page, *Thinking about my past, present, and future*, invites individuals to reflect on past career influences, present circumstances, and anticipated future lifestyle. Each of these pages contains a brief introduction about the title of the page, a diagram of the relevant system of the STF, example influences from which participants choose, and instructions about selecting and prioritizing influences. Subsequently, individuals are guided by instructions on a page titled *Representing My System of Career Influences* to collate the influences from the previous pages on a diagram titled *My System of Career Influences*.

The next page of the booklet, titled *Reflecting on My System of Career Influences,* provides a series of open-ended questions that guide individuals to reflect on their MSCI diagram and to elicit meaning and learning. The MSCI diagram and individuals' responses to the questions provide the stimulus for individuals to tell their story to peers in class and group situations or to career counselors in one-on-one settings. *My Action Plan* is a page on which individuals may plan their next steps with the guidance of open-ended questions. Because career development is a fluid and lifelong process, the MSCI booklet includes pages where individuals can revisit their reflection at a later date, complete a second MSCI diagram, and reflect on the changes that have occurred in their system of influences since the completion of the first diagram.

The MSCI *Facilitator's Guide* (McMahon et al., 2005b, 2013a; in press b) reviews constructivist assessment, overviews the theory base of the MSCI, and provides (a) a guide for using the MSCI with individuals as well as with groups (e.g., in classroom settings), (b) case studies and learning activities, and (c) a detailed description of the development and trialing process. A strength of the MSCI is its lengthy and rigorous trialing and development process in real-life settings in more than one country. The adolescent version was trialed in both Australia and South Africa, and the adult version was trialed by career counselors in Australia, South Africa, and England with a range of clients in settings including large public sector and private organizations. Reflecting its trialing in diverse settings, a recent review by Henfield (2013) concluded the following:

> In general, the purpose of the MSCI is to help individuals learn more about themselves and how multiple factors—sometimes outside of their control—influence career decisions; the assessment seems to do quite well in this regard. If more specific direction is needed . . . the onus seems to be on the facilitator as MSCI is intended to be a tool used to foster the relationship between counselor and client, which is in line with qualitative tradition. Further, the instrument seems to have the potential to be effective with diverse populations. (pp. 501–502)

A strength of the STF is its potential for multicultural application (Arthur & McMahon, 2005), and this is reflected through the use of the MSCI in diverse settings with diverse client groups (e.g., McMahon & Watson, 2013; McMahon, Watson, Foxcroft, & Dullabh, 2008; Yim, Wong, & Yuen, 2015). Furthermore, it has been translated into a number of languages, including Chinese, Dutch, German, French, and Italian. The MSCI enables individuals to consider their career decision making in the context of many personal, social, and environmental-societal influences. The following hypothetical case study illustrates the experience of an African client completing the MSCI in a group setting.

The Case of Andile

Although this case is hypothetical, it nevertheless synthesizes the experiences of career counselors working with Black South African adults in university environments (see, for example, McMahon et al., 2012a, 2012b). Andile is a 30-year-old Black South African university student in his final year of studying for a degree in electrical engineering. He has enrolled for a workshop conducted by the student counseling unit of his university that focuses on the transition from university life to working life. He did not initially meet the requirements for his degree course, and consequently he has been on an extended degree course that is available to older adult students. The degree Andile enrolled for includes a compulsory internship placement.

Andile has become less sure of his commitment to a career as an electrical engineer as he has gotten closer to completing his qualification, which has involved a further year of study because he needed to repeat several modules. In addition, Andile, along with most of his final year class, has been placed in a rural setting for his internship placement, which has put further stress on Andile. He has been married for 2 years, and his wife, Boniswe, holds a permanent position in a local motor manufacturing company. Boniswe has stated that she is opposed to moving from their present urban life, and Andile would be unhappy spending a lengthy time away from her, particularly as Boniswe is pregnant. In addition, Andile's parents have expressed the more traditional African cultural perspective that they expect him, as the eldest in the family, to be available to support them when needed.

Andile is confused about his present career direction, particularly because of the discrepancy between the lifestyle it will create and the lifestyle he and his wife would like to live. Andile has shared this introductory story with his fellow workshop participants, all of whom are in their final year of study.

We illustrate the application of the adult version of the MSCI in group settings here, but it should be noted that both forms may be used in one-on-one career counseling contexts or in group settings. Patton and McMahon (2014) advocated the use of experiential learning theory (A. Y. Kolb & Kolb, 2009; D. A. Kolb, 1984) in practical applications of the STF. Thus, in a group setting such as that in which Andile is participating, experiential learning theory involves a holistic learning process based on the experience of the participants and reflection on that experience through which new knowledge is created.

The focus of the workshop Andile enrolled in is on the transition from university, and the career counselor facilitating the workshop believes that the MSCI might assist participants to contextualize the decisions they are making as they prepare to leave university. The career counselor first gave each participant an MSCI workbook and explained that the reflection process guided by the workbook would take two sessions. Early research on the MSCI process (McMahon et al., 2008) revealed that individuals may need to learn how to think systemically prior to completing the MSCI booklet. Consequently, the first step in conducting group processes using the MSCI is to prepare participants to think systemically. To facilitate this, case studies about three individuals are provided in the *Facilitator's Guide* that tell stories about the systemic influences on career decision making.

In the first session, the career counselor facilitating Andile's workshop read the case study of Tom to the group and posed questions to them that illustrated systemic thinking. For example, the case study revealed that Tom needed to consider personal influences such as his skills and talents, his family circumstances, and the availability of work and learning opportunities both locally and in a large city for himself, his wife, and his family. As the workshop participants discussed Tom's case, Andile began to realize that career decision making is contextually located. He remarked that "no wonder it's so hard with all these people in my life to consider."

Andile's comment illustrates that his career development is taking place in a Black South African culture that values the concept of *ubuntu*. The word *ubuntu* means roughly that a person is a person because of other people (Watson, McMahon, Mkhize, Schweitzer, & Mpofu, 2011), and it challenges Westernized career theories and practices that focus on self-definition and self-identity. From an ubuntu perspective, systems of influence are viewed as being collectivist rather than individualist. McMahon et al. (2013a) specifically emphasized that the MSCI reflection process may not necessarily sequentially begin with individual influences and that facilitators should "ask individuals where they would prefer to start and in what order they wish to proceed" (p. 31).

Following the case study activity, workshop participants completed the page titled *My Present Career Situation* on which they wrote responses to a series of 10 open-ended questions related to their past and present career decisions, work experiences, life roles, advice they had received, and the most and least satisfying aspects of their previous work experiences. The purpose of this page is to enable individuals to begin a reflection process. For example, in response to questions about his previous work experience, Andile listed a wide variety of occupations in which he had worked for a short time. Typical of his cultural background, he wrote, "My family wanted me to go to university and to study for a profession. I am the first person in my family to do this."

The career counselor next explained to the group that they would complete three pages in the next section: *Thinking about who I am* (which asked them to consider their individual influences, such as personality and interests), *Thinking about the people around me* (which required them to think about their social influences, such as family), and then *Thinking about society and the environment* (which asked them to think about environmental-societal influences, such as geographic location, financial factors, and the availability of jobs). Consistent with the *Facilitator's Guide*, the career counselor told participants that they could begin with any page but that they needed to complete all three pages.

After a little thought, Andile turned to the page titled *Thinking about society and the environment* because of his present concern about his internship placement. The MSCI provides examples of possible influences, and it instructs individuals to mark examples that may apply to their particular career situation, to add other influences that are not listed, and to asterisk those that are most important to them. Andile selected his local area first and asterisked it as a major influence on him. He specifically added the location of his internship placement and wrote in large print how far away it was from the township where he and his family lived. Mindful of this distance and the potential separation from his family, particularly his wife, he turned to the page *Thinking about the people around me* and immediately added his wife's name in large print. He also asterisked his family as an important influence and specifically wrote the names of his parents. As an expectant father, he selected the influence "my children" and indicated that he wanted them to grow up in his close and supportive extended family. As he considered his future children and the opportunities he wanted them to have, he realized that he wanted to remain in the city where his township was located. He knew that the standard of education was considerably poorer in rural areas than in urban ones.

Having completed 4 years at university, Andile was realizing that he was experiencing increasing dissatisfaction with his course and with engineering as a possible future career. As Andile completed the MSCI booklet, his systems of influence emphasized the importance of his environmental-societal and social systems. For example, leaving his community to work in a rural setting for his internship placement had motivated Andile to participate in the workshop. Moreover, although mindful that his family had encouraged him to study in this field because of its prestige and potential contribution in the township where his family lived, he had begun to realize that he did not really enjoy engineering. Thus, when Andile turned to the page titled *Thinking about who I am*, he immediately ticked the influence of "culture" and "a value I hold" and asterisked them as important. He specifically underlined "helping people" as a value. On this page, other examples of influences included "my personality," "my gender," and "my interests," but none of these were selected by Andile. This may indicate the Black African cultural concept of *umuntu*, which emphasizes "developing as an individual who is always oriented toward other individuals" (Watson et al., 2011, p. 284). Andile attributed his dissatisfaction to his family circumstances rather than to his interests or his personality.

By the time the career counselor asked the group to complete the next page, *Thinking about my past, present, and future* and *Thinking about chance events*, Andile had already begun to realize the relationship between his current dissatisfaction and uncertainty about his internship placement and his future family life following his completion of university study. Beside the example of "the lifestyle I anticipate," Andile wrote, "Becoming a father and being a parent." He also considered the example of the influence "I want to combine family and work" and wrote "responsibility to my family." In the Black African culture, *family* has a broader definition, and it is expected that Andile will provide for his parents. Thus Andile was considering his responsibilities to his wife and future child as well as to his parents. On this page, Andile wrote, "BIG RESPONSIBILITIES." He also wrote notes related to "having a good income that can support my family" and "I don't want my children to struggle like I have." As he thought about his situation, he slowly wrote the words "My family's support got me to where I am. Somehow I must repay them."

In the second session, the career counselor explained to the group that the next step in the MSCI reflection process was to collate the influences recorded so far in their MSCI booklets into one page of the booklet titled *My System of Career Influences*. In explaining this step of the reflection process, the career counselor advised the group to consider all influences identified in the previous pages as well as their placement in the diagram in terms of their importance and relationship to each other. Furthermore, the career counselor explained that the group members could use colors or shapes in preparing their MSCI diagram. As the group composed their diagrams, the career counselor noticed a reflective silence in the room. In completing his diagram, Andile realized that his name was written in small print and that many of the influences he had identified were written in larger print and that he had colored some influences in for emphasis. He had also drawn three smiley faces (representing himself, Boniswe, and his future child) very close to where he had written his name.

When all of the diagrams were completed, the career counselor asked the group to consider their diagrams and answer the reflection questions on the page titled *Reflecting on My System of Career Influences*. These open-ended questions prompted the group members to consider topics such as what stands out most for you, what surprised you, what influences are least important for you, what would you like to change, what should stay the same, what were you not previously aware of, and what has been confirmed for you?

After the workshop participants had completed this process, the career counselor asked them to work with one or two other workshop participants and discuss their systems of influence diagrams and their reflections, reminding them that they did not have to talk about anything they didn't want to and that what they did talk about was to remain confidential. Subsequent to this small group activity, the career counselor invited discussion about the MSCI reflection process from the workshop participants. In the final step of the process, the career counselor explained the page *My Action Plan*, which encouraged participants to consider who they would talk to about the MSCI diagram, the action steps they might take, what information they may need and where they could obtain it, and what other resources they could use. Andile's answers to these questions indicated the importance of his family and community. He wrote that he would talk to Boniswe and his parents and to a neighbor who had also been to university. Finally, Andile wrote that after talking to his family he would consider seeing the career counselor to talk about his MSCI diagram and his internship placement dilemma. The career counselor invited the workshop participants to share their ideas about possible actions with the whole group and commented that if they heard useful ideas they could add these to their own action plan. In concluding the MSCI activity, the career counselor explained that workshop participants who would like to further explore their MSCI diagrams and action plans could make appointments for one-on-one career counseling. See Table 20.1 for an application guide.

Conclusion

In this chapter, we described the MSCI qualitative career assessment instrument, a practical application of the STF of career development. We

Table 20.1
Practical Application Guide

Topic	My System of Career Influences (MSCI) Reflection Process
General goals and purposes	1. Teach systemic thinking 2. Identify personal, social, and environmental-societal influences on career decision making 3. Reflect on the context of career decision making 4. Develop an action plan
Applicable modality	Individual and group counseling
Applicable counselor settings	*Adult version:* university, community college, private practice, organizational settings *Adolescent version:* school, private practice
Recommended time to complete	*Option 1:* Client completes MSCI as homework; one career counseling session (either individual or group) *Option 2:* Three career counseling sessions (either individual or group) *Option 3:* Multiple sessions that embed the one- or three-session process into a more comprehensive career learning process
Materials/equipment needed	Facilitator's Guide; copy of case study (contained in Facilitator's Guide); whiteboard or flip chart The MSCI (adult version) workbook; pens, pencils, colored markers
Step-by-step outline of the process	1. Read the case study to the group prior to a discussion of the systemic influences on career development (example questions for facilitating a discussion are contained in the Facilitator's Guide). 2. Begin the personalized MSCI reflection process by completing the page titled *My present career situation.* 3. Complete the remainder of the MSCI, page by page, culminating in the construction of a personalized MSCI diagram. 4. Complete the page titled *Reflecting on My System of Career Influences.* 5. Reflective conversation between group members who share stories about their MSCI diagrams. 6. Prepare an action plan.

provided an overview of the STF and, in particular, the MSCI, describing its purpose, structure, and potential use both individually and in group settings. The STF encourages an "individual in context" approach to career counseling and career assessment that depicts the complexity and dynamic nature of career development (McMahon, Watson, & Patton, 2014). A strength of the STF is its application as a metatheoretical base for multicultural career counseling.

A striking feature of the STF throughout its 20-year history is its utility in career counseling and qualitative career assessment in a range of international settings. The practical and user-friendly processes of the STF that accommodate cultural diversity (such as that shown by the example of the MSCI qualitative career reflection process) provide evidence of the rigor with which it has been developed across diverse cultural contexts. In addition, the translation of the MSCI into a number of languages attests to its growing international influence and the resultant emerging evidence base that supports its efficacy. Further research will cement both the STF and MSCI as an innovative instrument responsive to the diverse needs of individuals seeking career counseling and assessment in the 21st century.

Recommended Resources

McMahon, M., & Patton, W. (2002). Using qualitative assessment in career counselling. *International Journal of Educational and Vocational Guidance, 2*, 51–66. Retrieved from http://www.choixdecarriere.com/pdf/6573/Mcmahon_Patto%282002%29.pdf

Patton, W., & McMahon, M. (2006). The systems theory framework of career development and career counselling: Connecting theory and practice. *International Journal for the Advancement of Counselling, 28*, 153–166. Retrieved from http://eprints.qut.edu.au/2621/1/2621_1.pdf?iframe=true&width=80%&height=80%

References

Arthur, N., & McMahon, M. (2005). Multicultural career counseling: Theoretical applications of the systems theory framework. *The Career Development Quarterly, 53*, 208–222.

Brown, D. (2002). Introduction to theories of career development and choice. In D. Brown & Associates (Eds.), *Career choice and development* (4th ed., pp. 3–23). San Francisco, CA: Jossey-Bass.

Henfield, M. S. (2013). My System of Career Influences. In C. Wood & D. G. Hays (Eds.), *A counselor's guide to career assessment instruments* (6th ed., pp. 499–502). Broken Arrow, OK: National Career Development Association.

Kolb, A. Y., & Kolb, D. A. (2009). The learning way: Metacognitive aspects of experiential learning. *Simulation and Gaming, 40*, 297–327.

Kolb, D. A. (1984). *Experiential learning*. Englewood Cliffs, NJ: Prentice Hall.

McMahon, M. (2005). Career counselling: Applying the systems theory framework of career development. *Journal of Employment Counseling, 42*, 29–38.

McMahon, M., & Patton, W. (1995). Development of a systems theory framework of career development. *Australian Journal of Career Development, 4,* 15–20.

McMahon, M., & Patton, W. (2006). The systems theory framework: A conceptual and practical map for career counselling. In M. McMahon & W. Patton (Eds.), *Career counselling: Constructivist approaches* (pp. 94–109). London, England: Routledge.

McMahon, M., Patton, W., & Watson, M. (2003). Developing qualitative career assessment processes. *The Career Development Quarterly, 51,* 194–202.

McMahon, M., Patton, W., & Watson, M. (2005a). *My System of Career Influences.* Camberwell, Australia: ACER.

McMahon, M., Patton, W., & Watson, M. (2005b). *My System of Career Influences (MSCI). Facilitator's guide.* Camberwell, Australia: ACER.

McMahon, M., Patton, W., & Watson, M. (in press a). *My System of Career Influences (MSCI). Facilitator's guide* (2nd ed.). Brisbane, Australia: Australian Academic Press.

McMahon, M., Patton, W., & Watson, M. (in press b). *My System of Career Influences* (2nd ed.). Brisbane, Australia: Australian Academic Press.

McMahon, M., & Watson, M. (2012a). Story crafting: Strategies for facilitating narrative career counselling. *International Journal for Educational and Vocational Guidance, 12,* 21–224.

McMahon, M., & Watson, M. (2012b). Telling stories of career assessment. *Journal of Career Assessment, 20,* 440–451.

McMahon, M., & Watson, M. (2013). Story telling: Crafting identities. *British Journal of Guidance and Counselling, 41,* 277–286.

McMahon, M., Watson, M., Chetty, C., & Hoelson, C. (2012a). Examining process constructs of narrative career counselling: An exploratory case study. *British Journal of Guidance and Counselling, 40,* 127–141.

McMahon, M., Watson, M., Chetty, C., & Hoelson, C. (2012b). Story telling career assessment and career counselling: A higher education case study. *South African Journal of Higher Education, 26,* 729–741.

McMahon, M., Watson, M., Foxcroft, C., & Dullabh, A. (2008). South African adolescents' career development through the lens of the systems theory framework: An exploratory study. *Journal of Psychology in Africa, 18,* 531–538.

McMahon, M., Watson, M., & Patton, W. (2005). Developing a qualitative career assessment process: The My System of Career Influences reflection activity. *Journal of Career Assessment, 13,* 476–490.

McMahon, M., Watson, M., & Patton, W. (2013a). *My System of Career Influences (MSCI): Adult version. Facilitator's guide.* Brisbane, Australia: Australian Academic Press.

McMahon, M., Watson, M., & Patton, W. (2013b). *My System of Career Influences (adult version): Participant workbook.* Brisbane, Australia: Australian Academic Press.

McMahon, M., Watson, M., & Patton, W. (2014). Context-resonant systems perspectives in career theory. In G. Arulmani, A. Bakshi, F. Leong, & T. Watts (Eds.), *Handbook of career development: International perspectives* (pp. 29–42). New York, NY: Springer.

Parsons, F. (1909). *Choosing a vocation.* Boston, MA: Houghton Mifflin.

Patton, W. (2008). Recent developments in career theories: The influence of constructivism and convergence. In J. A. Athanasou & R. Van Esbroeck (Eds.), *International handbook of career guidance* (pp. 133–156). Dordrecht, The Netherlands: Springer.

Patton, W., & McMahon, M. (1999). *Career development and systems theory: A new relationship.* Pacific Grove, CA: Brooks/Cole.

Patton, W., & McMahon, M. (2006). The systems theory framework of career development and counseling: Connecting theory and practice. *International Journal for the Advancement of Counselling, 28,* 153–166.

Patton, W., & McMahon, M. (2014). *Career development and systems theory: Connecting theory and practice* (3rd ed.). Rotterdam, The Netherlands: Sense.

Watson, M., McMahon, M., Mkhize, N., Schweitzer, R., & Mpofu, E. (2011). Career counselling people of African ancestry. In E. Mpofu & L. Blokland (Eds.), *Counselling people of African ancestry* (pp. 281–293). Cambridge, England: Cambridge University Press.

Yim, A., Wong, S., & Yuen, M. (2015). Qualitative career assessment approaches in Hong Kong: Reflections from a Confucian cultural heritage perspective. In M. McMahon & M. Watson (Eds.), *Career assessment: Qualitative approaches* (pp. 239–246). Rotterdam, The Netherlands: Sense.

Chapter 21

Action Theory of Career Assessment for Clients With Chronic Illness and Disability

Tina Anctil

People with disabilities represent a significant percentage (12.3% of working-age adults) of the U.S. population (Houtenville, 2013), and their need for quality comprehensive career services is increasing. Career demands are particularly salient for people with chronic illness and disability (CID) due to physical or mental limitations that affect work tasks. Clients who have recently become disabled or begun dealing with an illness may be at different stages of adjustment and transition. They often have financial concerns due to job loss and medical bills, as well as a range of other circumstances such as family adjustment or chronic pain. The construction of career goals after acquiring a disability can be further challenged by fears of workplace discrimination or ignorance of appropriate workplace accommodations.

In this chapter, I describe an action theory (AT) approach to the career assessment of clients with disabilities, including the role of psychosocial adjustment for clients with a disability. A case study of a man with a traumatic brain injury and physical impairments illustrates how the Career Style Interview (CSI) can construct social meaning from the client's behaviors, thoughts, and feelings. Through the integration of AT with the CSI assessment, career counselors can help facilitate clients' adjustment to disability and develop goal-directed behaviors to decrease career distress.

CID

Career counselors without specific training working with clients with disabilities often report feeling overwhelmed by the magnitude of need

of clients with health-related issues. It is helpful to first become familiar with basic definitions and classifications of CID. CID is commonly
classified according to how the impairment affects the body. Physical
disabilities include mobility disabilities (e.g., cerebral palsy, spina bifida,
amputation, stroke, muscular dystrophy, rheumatoid arthritis, multiple
sclerosis, spinal cord injury), visual disabilities and blindness, deafness
and hard of hearing, and other health disorders. Intellectual disabilities
include intellectual disability, mental retardation, Down syndrome, and
autism. Cognitive disabilities include learning disabilities, attention-
deficit/hyperactivity disorder, and traumatic brain injury. Psychiatric
impairments include psychotic reactions, schizophrenia, major depression, and bipolar conditions. In this chapter, I include all disabilities and
impairments under the general term *chronic illness and disability* (CID).
The *Merck Manual* online is an excellent source for more information on
a specific disability or diagnosis.

The International Classification of Functioning, Disability and Health
defines disability as including impairments, activity limitations, and participation restrictions (World Health Organization, 2014). Specifically, the
World Health Organization describes *impairment* as a problem with functioning within the body, whereas an *activity limitation* refers to a problem
performing a specific task, and *participation restriction* broadly means that
a person struggles with a life situation. In the United States, significant
health disparities in racial/ethnic minorities are well established (Mead
et al., 2008), as is the intersection of poverty and disability (U.S. Census
Bureau, 2011). There are various models of disability. In this chapter, I use
the social model of disability, which defines and describes the experience
of disability as an interaction between the impairment itself and the person's environment. The disability experience is a complex phenomenon,
and environments can limit physical access and opportunities for work,
education, and social participation. The social model of disability recognizes that a person's impairment can become much more disabling in an
unresponsive and insensitive environment and much less disabling in an
accessible and accommodating space. The role of the career counselor is to
maximize opportunities for accommodation and accessibility.

Career counseling is almost never a stand-alone activity for the person with
a CID. A routine career counseling approach, such as an interest inventory and
transferrable skills analysis, is often ineffective. Comprehensive career assessment with an individual with CID should recognize the unique characteristics
of the person's life (e.g., cultural identifiers), physical and cognitive limitations
(e.g., functional limitations), and environmental demands. Prior to beginning a
formalized career assessment, the counselor must explore the client's worldview
and his or her experience of disability or impairment, including occurrences of
workplace discrimination and family reactions. If administered appropriately,
career assessment can help the client adjust and move toward psychological
acceptance of the disability, thereby increasing the person's quality of life.

Working with clients of color with CID requires the counselor to
incorporate awareness, knowledge, and skills pertaining to the client's

ethnicity in the counseling process (Sue & Sue, 2016). For example, Jones (1985) described a model with four interactive factors that are important to include with African American clients: reactions to racial oppression, influence of Afro-American culture, influence of majority culture, and personal experiences and endowments. This model remains relevant today because it facilitates discussions of oppression, racism, and personal strengths with the client. The client's response to each of these factors must be considered by the counselor when working with the presenting problem (e.g., career change due to a disability). The task of the career counselor is to help the client determine whether any of these factors are influencing the client's career decision-making process and if any further growth or intervention is necessary to improve career outcomes.

Utilizing an AT approach with qualitative assessment techniques provides an opportunity for the counselor to work with the client in a culturally inclusive manner to identify unresolved problems. Such issues often include functional limitations from the CID, thus allowing for substantial movement toward a realistic employment goal. Clients with a CID may increase their motivation to return to work after gaining awareness of how their emotions and actions are creating barriers to movement along their new career pathway.

AT and Career Counseling

AT applied to career counseling includes an integration of constructionist, contextual, and narrative postmodern approaches. AT demands a practical, individualized style that flows from theory to practice, with special attention offered to the metacognitive goals of *identity* and *adaptability* (Savickas, 2015). AT is conceptualized as evaluating the actions of individuals in daily life through multiple dimensions of perspective and organization (Domene, Valach, & Young, 2015). Conscious and unconscious processes (including emotions) influence actions, and counseling provides an opportunity for counselor and client to collaboratively deconstruct the client's behaviors within the context of his or her daily life. AT provides a framework for the career counseling assessment process through the theoretical constructs of the perspectives of action, the organization of action, and the systems of action. The counselor can help the client understand how the organizations and systems of action in the client's life influence the career decision-making process and outcomes for the client.

Perspectives of Action

AT evaluates an individual's daily actions from three perspectives: manifest behavior, internal process, and social meaning (Young et al., 2010). *Manifest behavior* is "the readily observable sequence of behavior involved in carrying out an activity" (Domene et al., 2015, p. 152). *Internal process* refers to the cognitive and emotional process the person is experiencing during an activity. These thoughts and emotions about the activity inform the manifest behaviors and contribute to the construction of social meaning. *Social meaning* includes explanations about the action that the person tells him- or herself and shares with others. Social meaning encompasses the intentions and purposes of the action that is occurring (Domene et al., 2015).

Organization of Action

Understanding the three tiers of the organization of action allows the career counselor to apply AT. Young et al. (2010) described the three ranked tiers, beginning with the *elements of action* (e.g., verbal phrases) that move toward a *functional step* (e.g., initiating a topic in the counseling session) and finally develop into an *intentional framework* of actions (e.g., developing a goal). Each tier involves increasing levels of action. For example, an injured worker with posttraumatic stress disorder illustrated this progression through her yawning and irritability (elements of action in the session), then by her suggestion that she was tired and irritable because her sleep was disrupted (functional step), and eventually by her decision to seek a psychiatric evaluation (intentional framework).

Systems of Action

These individual and joint actions form the system of action, which AT refers to as projects. Domene et al. (2015) wrote that *projects* "are completely intertwined with specific action, in that people intentionally engage in a variety of actions over time to achieve the joint projects they have constructed with significant individuals in their lives" (p. 154). Within career counseling, this system of action is viewed as a goal-directed adaptation project in which the counselor assists the client in creating actions or behaviors (the projects) that facilitate the transitions necessary to achieve career goals (Savickas, 2015; Young et al., 2011). Savickas (2015) summarized this process by describing action as a set of intentional, goal-directed behaviors that develop into a collection of actions (projects) that form a career.

AT and Career Assessment With CID

Career counselors using AT to assess persons with CID must also integrate contextual factors specific to the CID along with individualized factors such as ethnicity and sexual identity. For career clients with CID, this means working with the client to identify his or her transition projects and to construct the appropriate goal-directed actions that will eventually create a career project. The career assessment process emphasizes the psychosocial experience of CID and acknowledges that experiences depend on the nature of the CID, the prognosis, the interaction of functional limitations and available workplace accommodations, the individual's relationships, and any other factors that make the individual unique. The assessment process must carefully facilitate discussion with the client that includes his or her personal experience with the CID in addition to the more typical career-related concerns of interests, personality, and values.

Psychosocial adaptation refers to the individual's ability to emotionally cope with her or his CID so that the quality of life of the person can be maintained. This adaptation process has been explored through multiple models but generally includes adaption within the functional, psychological, and social aspects of the person's life. Bishop's (2005) disability centrality model incorporates affective and cognitive factors as predictors of a dynamic, interactive quality of life, which is useful in the career counselor's assessment process. The quality of life domains typically assessed include psychological well-being, physical well-being, social and interpersonal well-being, financial and material well-being, employment or productivity, and functional ability (Bishop, 2005). Changes in quality of life following the onset of CID further act to diminish satisfaction with important life domains, decrease perceived personal control over valued life outcomes, or increase the frequency and magnitude of experienced negative emotions (Bishop, Smedema, & Lee, 2009). Thus the client with a CID who seeks career counseling is very likely experiencing a diminished quality of life and dissatisfaction within important life domains, which must be assessed and included in the career counseling process.

Integrating the disability centrality model (Bishop, 2005) with an AT paradigm allows the career counselor to establish rapport and understanding with the client with a CID prior to beginning the formal career assessment. For instance, intentional goal-directed actions may be hindered by blind spots, or unconscious processes, regarding acceptance of the disability. The career counselor who observes the counterproductive actions of a client, such as neglecting an important medical appointment, can use AT to assess the client's adaptation process rather than marching forward with a more career-oriented assessment. If the client is not accepting the need for medical intervention, she may be returning to work with an unrealistic understanding of her impairment and its impact on her ability to perform in the workplace. Furthermore, using the lens of assessing actions through varying perspectives, organizations, and systems of action allows the career counselor to collaboratively evaluate the metacognitive adaptation process as the client works toward the return to work project.

Qualitative Assessment

One of the important goals of career assessment is to provide hope and motivation for the client to pursue his or her new career path or project. Career counselors can use qualitative assessments to foster both self-determination and hope as the client identifies adaptation projects important to the client's life. For example, Savickas (2015) contended that people construct their careers based on vocational behaviors and occupational experiences, wherein the individual's career history creates a personal story counselors may use to create a personal narrative for their clients. The CSI (Savickas, 1989, 1998; Taber, Hartung, Briddick, Briddick, & Rehfuss, 2011) is a didactic counseling tool that empowers the client to share his or her personal narrative. When used with clients with CID, it also can facilitate substantial adjustment processing. The specific questions deal with role models, social environments, interests, and work environments through life stories. In the first session, the career counselor records the responses, listening carefully throughout, while eliciting as much detail as possible from the client. Basic counseling skills of paraphrasing and reflection are imperative because clients with CID often have difficulty with some of the questions, as they may evoke memories about life before and after the CID. The questions deal broadly with the client's ego ideals, person–environment fit, problem-solving style, self-expression and interests, and preferred job tasks and work environment. The interpretation occurs jointly with the client in the next counseling session, and the client receives a typed copy of the interview.

Using the structure of AT, the CSI aims to help clients seek congruence between their current and future actions and identify points of adaptation that are needed to develop their project or career. Using questioning and storytelling, career counselors can help clients identify life themes while facilitating identity discussions. Engaging in this structured storytelling process naturally leads to conversations that include adaptation dialogue, such as "before and after" the disability or diagnosis. People with CID typically struggle with how the CID has changed their identity, and the career assessment process can begin to open windows of hope as clients determine what the "new normal" is and how they will reinvent themselves. In this way, the interview identifies unresolved problems (manifest behaviors, internal processes, social meaning), which leads to creating goal-directed behaviors (organization of actions) toward a realistic employment goal (perspectives of action). Through the collaborative interpretation of clients' stories, counselors can help clients to better understand the process of adjusting to their disability and to develop goal-directed behaviors to decrease their career distress.

The Case of Ryan

Ryan is a 44-year-old African American man referred to a career counselor by his vocational rehabilitation counselor at a state agency for assistance with developing a job goal that includes a community college degree. Ryan is married with two children in elementary school. His wife recently began working as an educational assistant for the school district after years of being a stay-at-home mother. After completing high school, Ryan had a successful career as a barber for about 20 years. He was in the process of retraining to become a journeyman carpenter when he was randomly assaulted on the street on his way home from his work at a construction site. He says he is interested in "working with computers" but is unsure of any specific careers within this area. Ryan can no longer physically perform the tasks of a barber or a carpenter because of his injuries.

Ryan's injuries were extensive and very traumatic for his family. He was in a coma for one week, had several surgeries, received more than 6 months of in-patient care, and spent 1 month at a community rehabilitation facility where he received physical and occupational therapy. He has recovered from his injuries, but he now has lifelong impairments as a result of a traumatic brain injury. His functional limitations include difficulty walking (he uses a motorized scooter outside of his home), impaired use of his right hand (he cannot type or write with it), some impairment in his cognitive processing speed (he needs extra time to complete tasks), and a speech impairment (mostly difficulty with finding words). He has an average IQ and no other cognitive limitations.

Ryan would like help identifying an appropriate college major that will lead to a solid career pathway within his physical and psychological abilities. His primary concern is being able to support his family with a living wage, which he defines as $50,000 a year or better. He is excited about the opportunity to go to college for the first time but wants to make sure he will have a job after he graduates.

Ryan's career counselor uses a culturally inclusive four-session assessment process to help Ryan construct his future career pathway. Session One: establishing a relationship with the client, discussing the client's satisfaction with his quality of life within Bishop's (2005) disability centrality model. Session Two: administering the CSI (Savickas, 1989, 1998). Session Three: interpreting the CSI, identifying elements and structures in work that are important to the individual through conceptualizing the client's actions in daily life. Session Four: integration of assessment and career project planning through the identification of goal-directed behaviors and actions needed to develop (a) the career goal, (b) satisfaction within life domains, and (c) accommodations and resources needed. During these sessions, the career counselor is listening for clues about identity and adaptation to the CID to facilitate Ryan's self-awareness and understanding of how his actions will create his career transition.

Session One

The counselor begins to form a working alliance by asking Ryan what he hopes to discover through career counseling. She also describes her philosophy and approach to career counseling, including the basic tenets of AT, the assessment process (using the CSI), and the expected outcomes (identifying specific goals needed to develop a new career path). Central to developing a rapport is her ability to share with the client how her understanding of his happiness and satisfaction in all aspects of his life is important to her being able to help him construct his life story. She encourages Ryan to talk about his daily life in his roles of father and husband with a newly acquired disability. She also encourages him to talk about his experiences in life as an African American. She is listening intently for emotional responses related to his well-being (psychological well-being, physical well-being, social and interpersonal well-being, financial and material well-being, employment or productivity, and functional ability) and the related behaviors that are affecting his life. Incorporating the A. C. Jones model (1985), she listens and probes for information related to experiences of racial oppression and the influence of Afro-American culture and White majority culture. She uses empathic statements to encourage him to elaborate on his stories to facilitate an increase in his self-awareness and understanding of himself as an African American man with a disability. In this manner, the counselor begins to understand how the life-threatening assault has changed Ryan's identity and how this is critical to identifying his transition projects (returning to college, then to the workplace). She gathers information about his personal history (he was raised in foster care by mostly Caucasian parents) and work history (he was a barber in an African American barber shop) and provides encouraging comments that highlight his strengths, such as his prior ability to maintain a career as a barber for 20 years and then successfully retrain as a carpenter. Ryan has a strong sense of ethnic identity, and though he is able to share experiences of discrimination, he remains positive about his ability to be successful in his future career.

Session Two

The counselor interviews Ryan, using the adapted CSI questions (Savickas, 1989, 1998). The following summaries illustrate Ryan's responses to the CSI:

Role Models. John (African American foster parent): He had a strong work ethic, an authentic person. Mike (karate instructor): He was smart, he was tough, he was compassionate. Grant (teacher): He was a very open guy, he liked and cared about what he was doing. He enjoyed ideas and loved to read books.

Magazines/Websites/TV Shows. YouTube: I like YouTube videos for do-it-yourself. I've learned some tricks about my scooter, like how to fill my tires. *Time* magazine and *U.S. News & World Report*: drawn to what's relevant in the moment. Facebook: I like a combination of news and social, a glimpse inside other people's heads.

Favorite Movie/Favorite Book. Malcolm Gladwell: The way he lays the narrative down is very accessible, anyone can read his books. To me it's entertainment. *The Spook Who Sat By the Door*: The way the token Black guy becomes a leader and revolts against the establishment. He exhibits discipline and leadership.

Hobbies. Exercise: I used to be able to work out with weights and get results in my body. Now, it's the idea of not being stagnant and staying busy. Cooking: I like to feel my way through the recipes. I have a tendency to want to be precise. Golf: I used to golf before my accident. I liked it because it's always played at the best places, it's green and beautiful, it is crazy fun. You may never get good at it, but when I was done I always felt great.

Favorite Subjects in School. Social studies, English, and journalism class: I was learning about the world that I was living in.

Session Three

In the third session, Ryan and the counselor begin to review his answers from the previous week's interview and start identifying meaning in his life stories. From the stories about his role models, it is determined that Ryan values a strong work ethic, intelligence, compassion, and the expression of ideas. The ways in which he was able to satisfy these needs in his previous careers is discussed. His response regarding magazines and websites is interpreted as indicating that he would prefer a work environment that allows him to use information while also being social. His best potential work environment should foster his love of learning. The counselor and Ryan determine that he enjoys complex problems that require him to work within organizational structures. He also does not mind mastering a routine because it makes him feel productive. As a carpenter, he liked adjusting the project as needed to complete it well. His hobbies and interests indicate that he enjoys being active and creating things. Finally, it is determined that an ideal career would involve working with information that is useful to his community.

Based on the CSI interpretation, the counselor and Ryan begin to discuss how his current actions and behaviors are in alignment with his life stories and identity. Ryan offers that he feels stagnant in his life now because he is not working and "isn't really sure who I am anymore." After his wife and kids leave for work and school, he is inactive and feels depressed. He is hoping he can go to college and earn a 2-year degree or certificate that will help him to begin a new career path. Despite these aspirations, he has not visited the community college and instead watches the History Channel all day. In this way, the counselor facilitates Ryan's exploration of how his daily activities and actions are affecting his movement toward his career goals. The counselor is hoping this will lead to the construction of appropriate goal-directed actions (informational interviews, registering for community college classes, etc.) to create a career trajectory.

The session concludes with an online job search in the field of computer science via the Occupational Information Network (O*NET). Ryan and the counselor begin by assessing the job market in terms of positions available to individuals with an associate's degree. Special attention is paid to the skills, abilities, and work context descriptions to determine whether Ryan can physically and mentally perform the primary job tasks with accommodations. The counselor shows Ryan how to use the Job Accommodation Network (askjan.org) to identify common strategies for accommodations for his physical limitations (e.g., only being able to use one hand to type). As a homework assignment, Ryan is instructed to continue this online exploration on his own, including finding computer science community college programs and looking over the classes required for these degrees. A fourth and final session is scheduled for 2 weeks later, allowing Ryan time to complete his homework assignments.

Session Four

The goal of the final career counseling session is to facilitate substantial movement toward a realistic employment goal. The counselor hopes the prior work identifying the incongruence between Ryan's actions and his desire to return to work will have increased his goal-directed actions. Although many clients with less developed adaptation skills might have required a slower and more nuanced counseling approach, Ryan is able to make significant progress in four sessions.

Ryan has explored computer sciences, information security analysis, business administration, and project management. Within each of these fields, he reviewed the day-to-day work requirements, educational requirements, and his level of interest for each. He explored the associate's degree requirements for business management and determined that the math requirements were reasonable and within his ability. Other major degree requirements are focused on applied computer classes, which have many transferrable applications that Ryan likes. The broad employment options for this degree are appealing to him and also well suited to his situation. The accommodations needed for work in this field are variable and depend on the work setting, but in general they appear to be realistic for Ryan's current functional limitations. An internship would be an ideal opportunity for Ryan to explore his specific interests within this field while also getting to experience job site accommodations. The counselor and Ryan conclude that he is best suited for the field of business administration and should seek work as a purchasing agent, which has an excellent labor market and salary. See Table 21.1 for an application guide.

Table 21.1
Practical Application Guide

Topic	Action Theory of Career Assessment With Chronic Illness and Disability
General goals and purposes	1. Promote understanding of the relationship between disability and career distress 2. Explore the ways the client's behaviors, cognitions, and environment are influencing career decision making 3. Identify career themes that emerge in the CSI interpretation 4. Describe how the client's actions in relation to the emergent themes can be used to address career distress
Applicable modality	Individual counseling
Applicable counselor settings	College, university career services/disability services, community agency, school, private practice
Recommended time to complete	Three to five sessions for individual counseling, more time needed if combining with personal adjustment counseling
Materials/equipment needed	Computer to type responses, Internet access to O*NET for action-taking steps
Step-by-step outline of the process	*Session One:* Relationship development/rapport, exploring disability centrality model domains, collecting work and educational history, identifying potential identity and adaptation barriers *Session Two:* Administering the CSI *Session Three:* Interpreting the CSI via analysis of actions and emotions in daily life *Session Four:* Integration of assessment and career project planning through identification of goal-directed behaviors needed for career transition Additional session may be needed to slow down this process, offering more time for individual reflection, relationship building, and career research as needed.

Note. CSI = Career Style Interview. O*NET = Occupational Information Network.

Conclusion

The case study of Ryan illustrated how career demands are particularly salient for people with CID, often requiring the career assessment to be individualized to the unique characteristics of the person's life, functional limitations, and environmental demands. Utilizing an AT approach with qualitative assessment techniques, such as the CSI, provides an opportunity for the career counselor to explore clients' psychosocial adjustment to their disability while incorporating the perspectives of behavior, cognition, and social meaning. The use of questioning and storytelling helps clients identify how their actions may be influenced by their emotions, which can instill hope and facilitate the reinvention of a positive identity as a person with a CID. The goal of the assessment process is to increase clients' awareness of the connections between their emotions, daily actions, and career goals. By identifying barriers to actions through an analysis of the theoretical components of actions described in this chapter (perspectives of action, the organization of action, and systems of action), the career counselor helps clients to better understand their adjustment to their disability while developing goal-directed behaviors to successfully follow a new career pathway.

Recommended Resources

Job Accommodation Network. (2016). *Ask JAN.* Retrieved from https:// askjan.org

Martz, E., & Livneh, H. (Eds.). (2007). *Coping with chronic illness and disability: Theoretical, empirical, and clinical aspects.* New York, NY: Springer Science Business Media.

Merck Manual. (2016). Retrieved from http://www.merckmanuals.com/ home/index.html

O*NET Online. (2016). *Occupation information network.* Retrieved from http://www.onetonline.org

Savickas, M. L. (2015). *Life design counseling manual.* Retrieved from http:// vocopher.com/LifeDesign/LifeDesign.pdf

Young, R. A., Domene, J. F., & Valach, L. (Eds.). (2015). *Counseling and action: Toward life-enhancing work, relationships, and identity.* New York, NY: Springer Science Business Media.

References

Bishop, M. (2005). Quality of life and psychosocial adaptation to chronic illness and disability: A conceptual and theoretical synthesis. *The Journal of Rehabilitation, 71,* 5–14.

Bishop, M., Smedema, S., & Lee, E. (2009). Quality of life and adaptation to chronic illness and disability. In F. Chan, E. da Silva Cardoso, & J. Chronister (Eds.), *Understanding psychosocial adjustment to chronic illness and disability: A handbook for evidence-based practitioners in rehabilitation* (pp. 521–550). New York, NY: Springer.

Domene, J. F., Valach, L., & Young R. A. (2015). Action in counseling: A contextual action theory perspective. In R. A. Young, J. D. Domene, & L. Valach (Eds.), *Counseling and action: Toward life-enhancing work, relationships, and identity* (pp. 151–166). New York, NY: Springer.

Houtenville, A. J. (2013). *2013 annual compendium of disability statistics.* Durham: University of New Hampshire, Institute on Disability.

Jones, A. C. (1985). Psychological functioning in Black Americans: A conceptual guide for use in psychotherapy. *Psychotherapy, 22,* 363–369.

Mead, M. A., Cartwright-Smith, L., Jones, K., Ramos, C., Woods, K., & Siegel, B. (2008). *Racial and ethnic disparities in U.S. health care: A chartbook.* Retrieved from http://www.commonwealthfund.org/publications/chartbooks/2008/mar/racial-and-ethnic-disparities-in-u-s--health-care--a-chartbook

Savickas, M. L. (1989). Career style assessment and counseling. In T. Sweeney (Ed.), *Adlerian counseling: A practical approach for a new decade* (3rd ed., pp. 329–359). Muncie, IN: Accelerated Development.

Savickas, M. L. (1998). Career style assessment and counseling. In T. Sweeney (Ed.), *Adlerian counseling: A practical approach for a new decade* (4th ed., pp. 289–320). Muncie, IN: Accelerated Development.

Savickas, M. L. (2015). Designing projects for career construction In R. A. Young, J. D. Domene, & L. Valach (Eds.), *Counseling and action: Toward life-enhancing work, relationships, and identity* (pp. 13–31). New York, NY: Springer.

Sue, D. W., & Sue, D. (2016). *Counseling the culturally diverse: Theory and practice* (7th ed.). New York, NY: Wiley.

Taber, B. J., Hartung, P. J., Briddick, H., Briddick W. C., & Rehfuss, M. C. (2011). Career style interview: A contextualized approach to career counseling. *The Career Development Quarterly 59,* 274. doi: 10.1002/j.2161-0045.2011.tb00069.x

U.S. Census Bureau. (2011). *Income, poverty and health insurance coverage in the United States: 2010.* Retrieved from http://www.census.gov/prod/2011pubs/p60-239.pdf

World Health Organization. (Ed.). (2014, December 1). *Disability and health: Factsheet No. 353.* Retrieved from http://www.who.int/mediacentre/factsheets/fs352/en/

Young, R. A., Valach, L., Marshall, S. K., Domene, J. F., Graham, M. D., & Zaidman-Zait, A. (2010). *Transition to adulthood: Action, projects, and counseling.* New York, NY: Springer.

Chapter 22

Using Chaos Theory of Careers as a Counseling Framework With a Female African American College Student

Delila Lashelle Owens

Historically, career development literature has had a tendency to base traditional theories and evidence on the experiences of White middle-class individuals (Blustein, 2001; Hartung, 2002). The increased awareness and acknowledgment of diversity in America has called for career theories that address the lived experiences of people of color as well as those from other underserved populations (Blustein, 2001; D. Brown, 2002; Chung, 2003; Hartung, 2002). Some career development theories suggest that career choice and development are contingent on multiple factors. These factors include self-concept, personality, sexism, racism, and resources (Duffy & Sedlacek, 2007; Holland, 1985, 1997; Sharf, 2010). The chaos theory of careers (CTC) provides new ways for counselors to conceptualize career choice and development. The theory moves away from the linear career development process and toward disequilibrium and diversity (Parker, Schaller, & Hansmann, 2003). For career counseling to be successful with African American women, career counselors must have a keen awareness of clients' double minority status (D. K. King, 1988; M. King, 1975; Lorber, 1998; Neufeld, Harrison, Steward, & Hughes 2008; Schneider, Hitlan, & Radhakrishnan, 2000). African American women have to deal with the complex interplay between being both a woman and a person of color. Chaos theory gives greater attention to cultural context, which helps to inform case conceptualization and to set appropriate career interventions. McAuliffe and Associates (2008) defined culture as the "attitudes, habits, norms, beliefs, customs, rituals, styles, and artifacts that express a group's adaption to its environment" (p. 8).

Many traditional theories are lacking in that they do not adequately capture the lived experiences of African American women in the United States. New formulations are required. In this chapter, I present an overview of the CTC and then apply it to working with a female African American college student. The case study features an assessment and possible interventions for this client, broadening the traditional career development literature by considering in detail the unique career development needs of African American women.

CTC

Traditional theories of career development do not seem to capture the realities of individuals in the world of work. Many career theories miss the context in which career development decisions are made by failing to consider factors such as family, school, and community. Some argue that CTC is a more realistic career development model because it is more flexible and adaptable (Bland & Roberts-Pittman, 2014). CTC asserts that we ourselves are complex and are embedded in other complex dynamical systems and that our career behavior cannot be captured adequately using interests and personality codes alone. CTC is vital because it emphasizes the complexity of career development and multiple perspectives (Bright & Pryor, 2011).

The CTC was developed because there was no comprehensive framework to conceptualize a person's career process. It recognizes that human lives can be complex and unpredictable (Bright, Pryor, & Harpham, 2005). The core components of the theory include change, chance, fractal patterns, complexity, and meaning making or contribution. The counseling outcomes for the chaos theory include creativity and open-mindedness, spiritual development, pattern identification, luck readiness, and dealing with uncertainty (Bright & Pryor, 2011).

The CTC characterizes individuals as complex, open, dynamic systems that are embedded in other complex dynamic systems. The human systems include cardiovascular, physiological, neuronal, and cognitive systems. At the same time, humans also are embedded in social systems, political systems, environmental systems, and legal systems, to name but a few. These complex systems are subject to a large number of influences; they are open because the systems can be influenced by "external" factors; and they are dynamic because they are living, moving, and ever evolving. Systems such as these are unpredictable in the medium to long term because it is impossible to gauge the impact of all the variables in any one system on all the other variables. To illustrate the impossibility of prediction in complex systems, consider the relatively simple system of a cosmetics sales team made up of five members. Suppose they can each visit five different stores, and sell one of five different products, depending on how effectively they are operating on a given day (which ranges on a 5-point scale from very poorly to very well). They are making sales at five different price points (from large discount to large markup) resulting in five possible customer service ratings, five different warranty outcomes, five different product recommendations on social media, and five different sales bonuses. This simple system has 5 (team members) × 5 (stores) × 5 (products) × 5 (sales outcomes) × 5 (prices) × 5 (ratings) × 5 (warranty) × 5 (recommendations) x 5 (bonuses) variables—resulting in 1.95 million different outcomes. Careers are influenced by a much greater range of variables and are not constrained to five outcomes. Consequently, it is simply not possible to compute all of the possible scenarios. We cannot predict with precision, and there is always uncertainty. Sometimes unexpected combinations of factors are experienced as chance events. The massive interconnectedness of influences leads to nonlinearity in the system; small changes in one variable can have a disproportionate impact on other variables in the system. This phenomenon is commonly referred to as the *butterfly effect*, which explores the idea that if a butterfly flaps its wings in the Amazon, it can eventually cause a tornado in Texas.

The CTC proposes that our careers are subject to change, open to many external influences, and generally nonlinear. CTC states that the career development process has many components, including but not limited to: change, which is for the most part nonlinear (Bright & Pryor, 2008; Jepson & Choudhury, 2001); chance, which includes unplanned, unpredictable, and unacknowledged events (Krumboltz & Levin, 2004); fractal patterns (Bright & Pryor, 2011); complexity, which is defined as connectedness among systems (Patton & McMahon, 2006); and meaning making or contribution, which is the individual's ability to define identity, motivation, thoughts, and actions. These components are defined by an individual's priorities, meaning, purpose, commitment, spiritual aspirations, and desire to contribute (Zander & Zander, 2000).

The CTC considers four attractors when describing a system's functioning: *point attractor* (which is goal-directed thinking and behavior), *pendulum attractor* (which describes the motion of the system characterized by periods of swing), *torus attractor* (which recognizes that the motion of the system is complex but predictable and repeats cycles over and over—such as our disciplined and organized thought patterns, or locked in pattern of thinking), and *strange attractor* (which is characterized by a complex motion system that is sensitive to change; although the behavior may be self-repeating, it is not necessarily in the same motion).

The career development of African American women, in particular, can be negatively influenced by the glass ceiling as metaphor, which describes a work environment in which mobility is nearly impossible because of systematic racism and sexism, sabotage by colleagues, and unstable employment patterns. African American women also are more likely to experience careers on the edge of chaos because they are often in the circle or a part of a team but out of the loop or excluded from key business decisions (Bell, 1990). For example, African American women are more likely to be excluded from golf club gatherings or other important networks where major critical decisions are made. Thus, major decisions about their careers are often made before they enter the room. They also may psychologically limit themselves to certain career possibilities and fail to pursue upward career mobility.

African American Women and Career Development

Despite advances in both the African American history and women's history movements, scholarship on the career development process of African American women is scarce. The intersectionality of race, gender, and socioeconomic status in the lives of African American women must be considered. Determining the most significant identity to confront can be challenging (Hine-Clark, 1994; hooks, 1981, 1993; Pack-Brown, Whittington-Clark, & Parker, 2002; Reid, 1988). Literature examining African American women is relatively new and often linked to writings focused on the larger African American community (Annunziata, Hogue, Faw, & Liddle, 2006; T. L. Brown, Linver, Evans, & DeGennaro, 2009; Frey, Ruchkin, Martin, & Schwab-Stone, 2008; hooks, 1993). Historically this literature has been written from a nonaffirming perspective (hooks, 1994; Ladson-Billings, 2005). Hooks (1993) asserted that it is impossible for African American women to maintain healthy emotional well-being in high stress, low-satisfaction employment.

Author Marsha Sinetar (1989) wrote that when considering the world of work, African American women should view work from the standpoint of a concept she called "right livelihood." At the heart of Sinetar's message is that work should be both meaningful and purposeful. It should embody components such as conscious choice, self-expression, commitment, and mindfulness. Sinetar wrote that individuals who consciously choose work of this nature are more self-actualized and have higher self-esteem. Individuals must consciously choose work that is purposeful, meaningful, and enjoyable.

Being a woman of color can affect both identity and self-esteem (Bell, 1990; hooks, 1993, 2002; Jackson & Greene, 2000). African American women have to effectively manage their double jeopardy status. Gloria Ladson-Billings, Kumea Shorter-Gooden, bell hooks, Charisse Jones, and Harriett McAdoo all emphasize the positive aspects African American life and womanhood. Accurate information about the unique lived experiences of African American women will aid helping professionals in understanding life from their frame of reference and in developing effective career counseling interventions and strategies. Regardless of various within-group differences, African American women share an interconnected reality of being both a woman and a person of color (Bell, 1990; Hine-Clark, 1994; hooks, 1993; Jackson & Greene, 2000; Jones & Shorter-Gooden, 2003).

It is imperative that career development literature on the lived experiences of African American women be frequently and thoroughly updated. When this does not happen, reliance on limited literature leads to premature generalizations about the career development process of African American women, and possible counseling interventions can become vague, with limited applicability. To illustrate, I present the case of a young African

American female college student (Cree) and discuss her experiences in relation to traditional career development theories and CTC.

The Case of Cree

Cree is 19 years old and is currently a sophomore at a predominantly White university in the South. Cree enters career counseling and reports feelings of social alienation. She wants to choose a meaningful career and is unsure about being a math major. She chose math because of her mom's suggestion but feels her passion is working with children. She also reports that her relationship with her boyfriend is unstable, she feels isolated from her family, and she feels spiritually disconnected. Three of her four jobs during adolescence were working with elementary age children. In her final year of high school, she held a position as an assistant for a math professor at a local university, but this position was the least satisfying. She has maintained a 3.0 cumulative college grade point average.

Cree is a first-generation college student. She resides with her mother in a modest income neighborhood in a small town in the Midwest. She lost contact with her father when she was 10 years old. She is close with her extended family and church community. She reports being reluctant to speak to a career counselor because she is fearful of what they will do with personal information she discloses. However, the urgency of her need to find a congruent major prompted her to seek career counseling. Cree presents with irritability and persistent headaches.

Assessment Phase

Effective cross-cultural service delivery is essential. Cross-cultural counseling has been defined by scholars as having a set of congruent behaviors, attitudes, and policies that professionals combine to effectively service the needs of diverse populations (Dillard, 1992; McAuliffe & Associates, 2008; Sue & Sue, 2013). To begin the process, counselors must be aware of their own internal biases and how they might affect the counseling process and client case conceptualization. Counselors also must be aware of the client population they will serve and have the necessary skills to effectively serve that population (McAuliffe & Associates, 2008; Sue & Sue, 2013). It is *impossible* to live in the United States and not be subconsciously exposed to misinformation about various cultural groups. Counselors must be aware that clients present with different symptoms when entering therapy.

Counselors must address both individual concerns and systemic challenges for a more holistic or wellness-centered approach. Cree presents with concerns about choosing a major, social alienation, relationships, and being a first-generation college student. There are countless interventions and strategies that career counselors could use to address Cree's concerns.

In general, the focus of the career counseling sessions should be on assisting Cree with finding a congruent academic area of study. The career counselor would seek to develop culturally congruent treatment goals for Cree. These would include administering career assessments that measure her interests, aptitudes, and abilities; giving her homework such as interviewing and job shadowing; getting her to volunteer for a local organization such as a homeless shelter, an organization for adolescents, or an organization that fit her interests; and supporting her in feeling more connected in her current community.

It is imperative that counselors understand the cultural dimensions of religion in the lives of African American women. Cree mentioned feeling spiritually disconnected. Historically, religion has provided both political leadership and moral development (Frederick, 2003). It was through the efforts of Christian African American women such as Rosa Parks, Sarah Jane Woodson Early, Fannie Lou Hamer, and Mary Mason that a greater understanding of gender equity and justice in America was achieved (Collier-Thomas, 2010; Frederick, 2003). Although some religious scholars would argue that spirituality has more to do with individualism than with affiliation (Burkhardt, 1989; Tanyi, 2001), Cree's feelings of spiritual disconnection may stem directly from nonaffiliation with a congregation. Connecting Cree with a mentor also would be beneficial. A mentor could act as a tangible person to be accountable to and also be part of a support system in the local community.

Effective case conceptualization considers the impact of environment, race, ethnicity, religion, and gender in the lives of individuals. A thorough and comprehensive case conceptualization informs treatment planning and therapeutic outcomes (Leach & Aten, 2010; Sue & Sue, 2013). A detailed guide developed by Prieto and Scheel (2002) consists of five major sections (represented by the acronym STIPS): signs and symptoms (client's present level of functioning), topics of discussion (this section also details new developments since the previous session), interventions (strategies used to address identified concerns), progress and plan (treatment targets), and special issues (e.g., abuse, threat of harm to self or others, or anything that warrants the therapist's immediate attention).

Intervention Phase

The interventions and strategies used when working with Cree are grounded in both the CTC and more traditional career development techniques. It is essential for counselors to understand how culture shapes the lived experiences of African American women. Culture includes the customs and values of a given society: socioeconomic systems, political structures, science, religion, and education are all components of culture (Sue & Sue, 2013; Wolma, 1989). Scholars have noted that historical cultural mistrust for formal systems (agencies, schools, etc.) contributes to lower levels of help-seeking behaviors in African Americans (Snowden, 1999; Sue & Sue, 2013; Whaley, 2001). Cree may unconsciously be sticking to a psychological routine (torus attractor) that serves as a protector. Exploring whether she is caught in "us versus them" thinking is beneficial; this kind of thinking could be tied to race or to geographical location (pendulum attractor thinking). Cree should be encouraged to take risks and explore additional ways of overcoming self-limiting behaviors. In addition, she should be encouraged to view her failures as learning endeavors rather than lifetime stains.

To understand Cree's cultural perspective, the career counselor asks Cree specific questions about her upbringing, focusing specifically on family and community. These questions might include asking her to describe ways in which she stays connected to her family and social circle, discussing her religious or spiritual upbringing, and discovering her cultural ideals related to counseling and career development (Leach & Aten, 2010; McAuliffe & Associates, 2008). This discussion allows the counselor to understand Cree's emergent pattern of behavior in a holistic way. The counselor is attempting to understand Cree's fractal patterns.

Productive career counseling explores cultural differences such as Cree's being from a midwestern town yet attending a predominantly White institution in the South. This evaluation allows the career counselor to accurately evaluate Cree's experiences. Engaging Cree in a dialogue related to race and gender also can be beneficial (hooks, 1993; McAuliffe & Associates, 2008; Sue & Sue, 2013). Specific discussions tied to micro-aggressions that include microassaults, mircoinvalidations, and racial microaggressions are warranted. Career counselors must pay particular attention to goal-directed thinking (point attractor). Given that Cree is a woman of color and very accustomed to daily microaggressions, it would be very easy to interpret neutral gestures as potential threats and violations. The counselor can help Cree develop open system connections to supportive people and assist her with developing resilience and coping mechanisms in the face of systemic racism and oppression. However, caution must be used not to negate Cree's experiences and fall into the illusion of a postracial era.

Ethnocentric monocultural bias is a reality in most formal systems in the United States. African American women have become accustomed to the unfairness in these systems (Schmader, Major, & Gramzow, 2001; Sue & Sue, 2013). A discussion on stereotype threat and optimal participation is also warranted (Steele, Spencer, & Aronson, 2002). Given that Cree does not have peer group connections, the career counselor must explore ways to help her feel more connected. Getting Cree involved with campus and community organizations will help her to feel connected and give her a sense of *family* away from home. This will mitigate her feelings of isolation (contribution). The concept of "fictive kin" (individuals who are not related by blood or marriage but are still considered family) has historically been used in the African American community.

Inventories to assess Cree's interests, aptitudes, and abilities also are administered. The counselor begins with an exploration of Cree's interests and self-estimates of her ability. This can be done both formally and informally. To formally understand Cree's abilities, the career counselor chooses from a number of reliable instruments and assessments. The most widely used interest inventory is the Strong Interest Inventory. Another interest inventory to consider is the Kuder DD. Cree could benefit from a career development self-assessment as well. The counselor might consider giving Cree the SIGI, formerly called the SIGI-Plus (Valpar International, 2007) and the DISCOVER (Act, Inc., 2007). These assessments will be coupled with job shadowing and interviewing.

The field of counseling is beginning to recognize the prevalence of spirituality and religion in the lives of some individuals and the role it can play in life-altering decisions (Frame, 2003; Hickson, Housley, & Wages, 2000). An effective counselor will address Cree's concerns about feeling spirituality disconnected. The career counselor can offer several recommendations, including becoming involved in campus Bible study groups and campus Christian organizations, participating in local Christian outreach activities, and exploring churches in her new community (contribution, meaning making, and complexity).

The counselor discusses Cree's goals and sense of meaning (point attractors). Cree is engaged in a discussion about any competing roles such as student, daughter, and girlfriend (pendulum attractors); beneficial study routines (torus attractors); and finally being creative and open to new experiences (strange attractors). The counselor must keep in mind that valuing work is tied to career maturity for African American adolescents (Sharf, 2013). See Table 22.1 for an application guide.

Conclusion

Several historical factors must be considered when working with a client who is a female person of color. Experiences of prejudice and social exclusion are common for people of color, and the cultural community must be considered in both the assessment and intervention phases of career development. Codifying in writing the counselor's commitment to cultural sensitivity is essential. This acknowledgment should be a part of the counselor's professional disclosure statement.

Although the term *race* is fluid and contextual, effective counseling addresses issues related to race and to individuals' lived experiences. It is vital that counselors recognize the importance of cultural identity and community framework when assisting African American clients. Information gathered during the assessment phase can be used to conceptualize the client's concerns and develop culturally and developmentally appropriate interventions.

It is imperative that career counselors use a holistic framework when conceptualizing the career development realities of clients of color. Counselors must also be mindful of the major attractors and how they can assist with formulating case conceptualizations and, thus, appropriate interventions. Counselors must keep in mind the cultural context and the sociopolitical realities in which many career development decisions are made (Leach & Aten, 2010; Sharf, 2013). Incorporating culture into case conceptualizations requires taking into consideration cultural norms, extended family, the race/the ethnicity of the client, impact of discrimination, social contexts, and family patterns and perspectives. The counselor's first approach should be a fairly accurate multicultural

Table 22.1

Practical Application Guide

Topic	Using Chaos Theory of Careers as a Counseling Framework
General goals and purposes	1. Understand the history of the chaos theory of careers 2. Describe how chaos theory can be applied to an actual client 3. Explain components of the double jeopardy status and how it influences the career choice and development of African American women
Applicable modality	Individual and dyadic
Applicable counselor settings	College/university career services, community agency, school, private practice
Recommended time to complete	Five to seven sessions for individual counseling. More if needed.
Materials/equipment needed	Flip chart/poster-size paper, different color markers/crayons, and conceptualization wheel
Step-by-step outline of the process	1. Discuss career decision makers being part of complex dynamic systems. Introduce the client to order and randomness of human lives. 2. Discuss the concepts of connection, content, complexity, change, and chance in the lives of individuals. Also, discuss the four attractors. 3. Invite the client to write all concerns in the Parmer conceptualization wheel. 4. Explore the components of contribution, meaning making, managing expectations, and complexity during the career development process. 5. Administer career inventories such as SIGI, Self-Directed Search, and DISCOVER. Facilitate the client's career exploration and decision-making process. 6. Review career inventories for accuracy. Particular focus is given to contribution and meaning making. The client selects three careers and contacts professionals in those areas for an informal interview or job shadowing. 7. Combine it all together. Narrow career majors down to the top three. The client makes the final selection based on all of the information gathered. Follow-up sessions as needed.

case conceptualization. The STIPS treatment plan can be used to develop a thorough case conceptualization.

Interventions for clients can include learning new skills through activities associated with occupational engagement, gaining self-understanding through the career development assessment process, and informal processing. Numerous career development instruments are available to assess clients' interests, abilities, and aptitudes. Finally, clients can reduce psychological symptoms by managing the expectations of others. Interventions used in this chapter's case study were culturally congruent and were connected with the four attractors of the CTC.

Recommended Resources

Bright, J. (2013, November 3). *Chaos theory of careers explained—Interview with Dr. Jim Bright at Vanderbilt University* [Video]. Available from https://www.youtube.com/watch?v=BL2wTkgBEyk

Lindskoog, D. (2011, October 1). *Applying chaos theory to career development.* Retrieved from http://www.careeroptionsmagazine.com/articles/applying-chaos-theory-to-career-development/

Pryor, R., & Bright, J. (2011). *The chaos theory of careers: A new perspective on working in the twenty-first century.* New York, NY: Routledge.

References

Act, Inc. (2007). *DISCOVER.* Retrieved from https://actapps.act.org/eDISCOVER/Index.jsp

Annunziata, D., Hogue, A., Faw, L., & Liddle, H. A. (2006). Family functioning and school success in at-risk inner-city adolescents. *Journal of Youth and Adolescence, 55,* 105–113.

Bell, E. (1990). The bicultural life experience of career-oriented Black women. *Journal of Organizational Behavior, 11,* 459–477.

Bland, A. M., & Roberts-Pittman, B. J. (2014). Existential and chaos theory: "Calling" for adaptability in career decision-making. *Journal of Career Development, 41,* 382–401.

Blustein, D. (2001). Extending the reach of vocational psychology. Toward an inclusive and integrative psychology of working. *Journal of Vocational Behavior, 59,* 171–182.

Bright, J., & Pryor, R. (2008). Shiftwork: A chaos theory of careers agenda for change in career counselling. *Australian Journal of Career Development, 17,* 63–72.

Bright, J., & Pryor, R. (2011). The chaos theory of careers. *Journal of Employment Counseling, 48,* 163–166.

Bright, J., Pryor, R., & Harpham, L. (2005). The role of chance events in career decision making. *Journal of Vocational Behavior, 66,* 561–576.

Brown, D. (2002). The role of work and cultural values in occupational choice, satisfaction, and success: A theoretical statement. *Journal of Counseling & Development, 80,* 48–56.

Brown, T. L., Linver, M. R., Evans, M., & DeGennaro, D. (2009). African American parent's racial and ethnic socialization and adolescent academic grades: Teasing out the role of gender. *Journal of Youth Adolescence, 38,* 214–227.

Burkhardt, M. A. (1989). Spirituality: An analysis of the concept. *Holistic Nursing Practice, 3,* 69–77.

Chung, Y. B. (2003). Career counseling with lesbian, gay, bisexual, and transgendered persons: The next decade. *The Career Development Quarterly, 52,* 78–86.

Collier-Thomas, B. (2010). *Jesus, jobs, and justice: African American women and religion.* New York, NY: Knopf.

Dillard, M. (1992). Culturally competent occupational therapy in a diversely populated mental health setting. *American Journal of Occupational Therapy, 46,* 721–726.

Duffy, R. D., & Sedlacek, W. E. (2007). The work values of first-year college students: Exploring group differences. *The Career Development Quarterly, 55,* 359–364.

Frame, M. (2003). *Incorporating religion and spirituality into counseling: A comprehensive approach.* Pacific Grove, CA: Brooks/Cole.

Frederick, M. F. (2003). *Between Sundays: Black women and everyday struggles of faith.* Berkeley: University of California Press.

Frey, A., Ruchkin, V., Martin, A., & Schwab-Stone, M. (2008). Adolescents in transition: School and family characteristics in the development of violent behaviors entering high school. *Child Psychiatry Human Development, 40,* 1–13.

Hartung, P. J. (2002). Cultural context in career theory and practice: Role salience and values. *The Career Development Quarterly, 51,* 12–25.

Hickson, J., Housley, W., & Wages, D. (2000). Counselors' perception of spirituality in the counseling process. *Counseling and Values, 45,* 58–66.

Hine-Clark, D. (1994). *Hine sight: Black women and the reconstruction of American history.* Brooklyn, NY: Carlson.

Holland, J. L. (1985). *Making vocational choices: A theory of vocational personalities and work environments* (2nd ed.). Englewood Cliffs, NJ: Prentice-Hall.

Holland, J. L. (1997). *Making vocational choices: A theory of vocational personalities and work environments* (3rd ed.). Odessa, FL: Psychological Assessment Resources.

hooks, b. (1981). *Ain't I a woman? Black women and feminism.* Boston, MA: South End Press.

hooks, b. (1993). *Sisters of the yam: Black women and self-recovery.* Boston, MA: South End Press.

hooks, b. (1994). *Teaching to transgress. Education as the practice of freedom.* London, England: Routledge Press.

hooks, b. (2002). *Communion: The female search for love.* London, England: Women's Press.

Jackson, L. C., & Greene, B. (2000). *Psychotherapy with African American women: Innovations psychodynamic perspectives and practice.* New York, NY: Guilford Press.

Jepson, D. A., & Choudhury, E. (2001). Stability and change in 25-year occupational career patterns. *The Career Development Quarterly, 50,* 3–19.

Jones, C., & Shorter-Gooden, K. (2003). *Shifting: The double lives of Black women in America.* New York, NY: HarperCollins.

King, D. K. (1988). Multiple jeopardy, multiple consciousness: The context of a Black feminist ideology. *Signs, 14,* 42–72.

King, M. (1975). Oppression and power: The unique status of the Black woman in the American political system. *Social Science Quarterly, 56,* 123–133.

Krumboltz, J. D., & Levin, A. S. (2004). *Luck is no accident: Making the most of happenstance in your life and career.* Atascadero, CA: Impact.

Ladson-Billings, G. (2005). *Beyond the big house: African American educators on teacher education.* New York, NY: Teachers College Press.

Leach, M. M., & Aten, J. D. (2010). *Culture and the therapeutic process.* London, England: Routledge Press.

Lorber, J. (1998). *Gender inequality: Feminist theories and politics.* Los Angeles, CA: Roxbury.

McAuliffe, G., & Associates (2008). *Culturally alert counseling.* Thousand Oaks, CA: Sage.

Neufeld, A., Harrison, M. J., Steward, M., & Hughes, K. (2008). Advocacy of women family caregivers: Response to nonsupportive interactions with professionals. *Qualitative Health Research, 18,* 301–310.

Pack-Brown, S. P., Whittington-Clark, L. E., & Parker, W. M. (2002). *Images of me: A guide to group work with African Americans.* Boston, MA: Allyn & Bacon.

Parker, R., Schaller, J., & Hansmann, S. (2003). Catastrophe, chaos, and complexity models and psychosocial adjustment to disability. *Rehabilitation Counseling Bulletin, 46,* 234–241.

Patton, W., & McMahon, M. (2006). *Career development and systems theory: Connecting theory and practice.* Rotterdam, The Netherlands: Sense.

Prieto, L., & Scheel, K. (2002). Using case documentation to strengthen counselor trainees' case conceptualization skills. *Journal of Counseling & Development, 80,* 11–21.

Reid, P. T. (1988). Racism and sexism. Comparisons and conflicts. In P. A. Katz & D. Taylor (Eds.), *Eliminating racism: Profiles in controversy* (pp. 203–221). New York, NY: Plenum Press.

Schmader, T., Major, B., & Gramzow, R. H. (2001). Coping with ethnic stereotypes in the academic domain: Perceived injustice and psychological disengagement. *Journal of Social Issues, 57,* 93–111.

Schneider, K. T., Hitlan, R.T., & Radhakrishnan, P. (2000). The nature and correlates of ethnic harassment experiences in multiple contexts. *Journal of Applied Psychology, 85,* 3–12.

Sharf, R. S. (2010). *Applying career development theory to counseling* (5th ed.). Belmont, CA: Brooks/Cole, Cengage.

Sharf, R. S. (2013). *Applying career development theory to counseling* (6th ed.). Belmont, CA: Brooks/Cole, Cengage.

Sinetar, M. (1989). *Do what you love, the money will follow.* New York, NY: Paulist Press.

Snowden, L. (1999). African American service use for mental health problems. *Journal of Community Psychology, 27,* 303–313.

Steele, C. M., Spencer, S. J., & Aronson, J. (2002). Contending with group image: The psychology of stereotype and social identity threat. *Advances in Experimental Social Psychology, 34*, 379–440.

Sue, D. W., & Sue, D. (2012). *Counseling the culturally diverse. Theory and practice* (6th ed.). Hoboken, NJ: Wiley.

Tanyi, R. A. (2001). Toward clarification of the meaning of spirituality. *Journal of Advanced Nursing, 39*, 500–509.

Valpar International. (2007). *SIGI* (Computer program). Tucson, AZ: Author.

Whaley, A. L. (2001). Cultural mistrust of White mental health clinicians among African Americans with severe mental illness. *American Journal of Orthopsychiatry, 71*, 252–256.

Wolma, B. B. (Ed.). (1989). *Dictionary of behavioral sciences* (2nd ed.). San Diego, CA: Academic Press.

Zander, R. S., & Zander, B. (2000). *The art of possibility.* New York, NY: Penguin Books.

Conclusion

Postmodern Principles and Teaching Considerations for 21st-Century Career Counseling

Louis A. Busacca and Mark C. Rehfuss

"We inhabit the great stories of our culture. We live through stories.
We are lived by the stories of our race and place. . . . We are, each of us,
locations where the stories of our place and time become partially tellable."
—Miller Mair, 1989

In a world in which career planning has become precarious and work more contingent, career counselors must now help clients to define the self, create meaning, and live within their sociocultural context. In a new social organization of work, employees feel more anxious, discouraged, and frustrated because of perceived job insecurity, coping with multiple transitions, and multicultural imperatives. Career counseling in a postmodern era requires more counselors who are trained to help clients shape their stories and supply a sense of continuity, coherence, and commitment as they confront career tasks, occupational transitions, and work traumas. The models and methods of postmodern career counseling in this book are demonstrated by discussing how a client's career world is made through the lens of psychological constructivism and social constructionism. This concluding chapter summarizes the central themes and principles of postmodern career counseling discussed throughout this book. We leave educators with recommendations for teaching career counseling courses using this book and provide practical guidelines for integrating this text into career counseling courses.

The paradigms of postmodern career counseling are philosophical and psychological frameworks rather than a set of techniques from which to apply career counseling and intervention. Career counseling becomes not so much a procedure as an orientation for guiding the work of counselor and client. It differs from modernist or positivist thinking. On a philosophical level, the movement from logical-positivism to constructivism mirrors the earlier shift from a static to a more dynamic approach to career counseling. We recommend that career counselors new to this perspective who want to apply the models and methods in this book begin by reflecting on the six fundamental dimensions of postmodern thinking.

The six dimensions embodied in constructivist and constructionist perspectives include agency, meaning making, identity reconstruction, and relationship (as adapted by Peavy, 1992) and the sociocultural and sociopolitical contexts (as advocated by Gonzalez, Biever, & Gardner, 1994). These six assumptions also can be stated as questions for students and counselors to keep in mind when working with clients.

The six dimensions are depicted in Table C.1 and range on a continuum from constructivist (intrapersonal) to constructionist (interpersonal) thought. As mentioned in the Introduction, we do not recommend viewing these perspectives as mutually exclusive because various forms of constructivism and constructionism exist. That is, constructivist thought is not a single approach but rather a continuum of beliefs that range from radical to more socially based orientations (Sexton, 1997). If you are new to this perspective, you will benefit from viewing the postmodern perspectives on a continuum.

Table C.1

Six Fundamental Dimensions for Applying Postmodern Career Counseling

Fundamental Dimension	Central Concept	Postmodern Perspective Continuum
Encourage the client to actively engage in constructing her or his life.	Active agency	Constructivist Intrapersonal
Help the client to reconstruct a personally meaningful and coherent identity.	Identity reconstruction	↑
Help the client to elaborate and evaluate her or his self-organizing constructions and meanings useful to the client's decisions.	Meaning making	
Help the client recognize the value of relational connection.	Relationship	
View the client as embedded in the social and symbolic systems or contexts within which she or he lives.	Sociocultural context	
Acknowledge that clients from marginalized cultures can have narratives that are significantly influenced by the dominant discourses of society.	Sociopolitical context	Constructionist Interpersonal

Essential Principles for Postmodern Career Counseling

Key elements are unique to postmodern career counseling. We identified 12 essential principles when introducing postmodern career counseling to students and for practitioners new to this perspective. These elements are discussed throughout this book and appear in Table I.1 of the Introduction. Fostering these principles may take time and focus for educators, counselors, and students grounded in the positivist tradition, but the principles are essential for helping clients move forward in their lives and careers during the 21st century. The 12 principles are summarized here.

Epistemology

Two epistemological foundations, realism and constructivism, validate the source of knowledge or what we know about career issues, counseling orientations, and interventions. Realism, as applied to counseling, denotes that counselors can objectively observe clients and come to know particular truths about them. Constructivism denotes that individuals construct meaning or perceive their own reality or truth (R. A. Neimeyer & Stewart, 2000). This contrasts with the modernist assumption that an external and objective meaning can be discovered. Constructivism focuses on meaning making and construing the social and psychological worlds through individual cognitive processes, or how we develop meaning. Constructivism posits a highly individualistic approach with minimal reference to social interaction, context, and discourse, which Young and Collin (2004) asserted are important factors that make self-reflection and meaning making possible. This limitation is being addressed by social constructionism, which emphasizes that the social and psychological worlds are made real (constructed) through social processes and interaction. It may be useful to think of psychological constructivism and social constructionism as windows or perspectives for how counselors view and approach a client's experience and reality.

Core Facets of Counseling

A particular feature of postmodern career counseling concerns a focus on managing one's own career rather than adhering to a linear model of occupational fit or developing a career in a single organization. The goal of vocational guidance is to promote the adjustment outcomes of success, satisfaction, and stability. In career education, the goal is to orient students, young adults, and groups to imminent tasks of vocational development and introduce ways to cope with them. Modernist career interventions, however, have proved insufficient as social, technological, and global changes affect people's working lives. Career counseling becomes a distinct service area for career services. The turn to postmodern career counseling involves a complementary view that concerns the interpersonal process of helping individuals construct their careers. Career counseling requires advanced skills and training and begins with understanding the distinction between career service areas and career content and process (Busacca, 2002). In particular, postmodern career counseling focuses on the subjective process and emotional domain of clients' career problems and the characteristics of a quality counseling relationship. Thus, counselors work with aspects of postmodern career theory and intervention such as adaptability, life stories, themes, usefulness, identities, reflexivity, and active agency.

Cultural Stance

Career counselors embrace a context-sensitive or culture-centered approach when applying postmodern career counseling. Counselors focus on a client's meaning and interpretation of her or his culture and keep in mind that a client's experience is not tied to one cultural identity bounded by group membership but is unconfined by intersecting identities. In addition, counselors should not assume that there is one real truth or "grand narrative" that can explain career development for all people. Counseling becomes a process of liberation from oppressive cultural values. Although many of the career counseling paradigms are intrinsically cultural models because of their epistemological foundation, counselors should be culturally alert to the infusion of cultural models when using career counseling methods that privilege the interpersonal dimension of postmodern career counseling.

Nature of Assessment

Career counselors use qualitative career assessments to assist individuals in increasing self-awareness and meaning making while attending to the contextual dimensions of their life. The criteria for adequacy of assessment are "primarily interpretive and phenomenological" (G. T. Neimeyer & Neimeyer, 1993, p. 23). The postmodern career counselor relies more on clinical judgment, does not compare the client with some norm or reference group, remains flexible and adaptable when working with clients from diverse backgrounds, uses open-ended questions, and takes a holistic approach to understanding the client's problem.

Phases of Counseling

Career counselors are open to a counseling process that is overlapping and integrative. In contrast with being linear or in phases, the career assessment process becomes fully integrated into the intervention process (Whiston & Rahardja, 2005). Goldman (1992) suggested that this intimate connection between the assessment and counseling processes offers greater adaptability for ethnic, cultural, age, gender, and other individual differences. Assessment is introduced in the course of counseling at points when it has the potential to be clarifying and change generating (R. A. Neimeyer, 2009). This allows the client to express her or his unique story and necessary language to make sense of who she or he is and wishes to become.

Use of Language

The strategic use of language to elicit new meanings, expand perspectives, and encourage change is central to the postmodern perspective. Language is not viewed as a tool for uncovering a client's true self or solely as a reflection of clients' subjective perceptions. Language is used in an active way in constructing identity and meaning in therapeutic conversations (Watson, 2011). Thus, language is viewed in a relational rather than a conventional sense (Bird, 2004). The power of language in constructing meaning is an important contribution to postmodern career counseling.

Identity

The construct of identity for postmodern career counseling places a focus on interpersonal relations rather than intrapersonal possession. This move toward the social constructionist dimension is different from the modernist perspective, which views identity as individualistic and not tied to social roles. Identity is constructed and reconstructed within relationships and across multiple contexts (Collin & Young, 2000). Each person has multiple identities. That is, multiple stories or truths are formed through relationships and internalized through experience within various cultural contexts (Stead, 2004). Individuals must adapt by repeatedly revising their identity to integrate new experiences into their ongoing life story (Savickas, 2011). This occurs when individuals find that their story—who they are and where they fit in relation to occupation and work—loses continuity. Consequently, individuals often seek career counseling when the content of their identity is unable to support them when confronting a new set of demands imposed by work.

Motivational Process

As career counselors work with clients to establish counseling goals, they also are establishing a working alliance by eliciting emotions to help clarify the problem clients wish to change. What motivates clients toward change is emotion rather than reason. As Hartung (2011) eloquently noted, emotions "may benefit the motivational process of goal striving whereby people seek to 'move out' from a place of tension (experienced anger, fear, guilt, sadness, inferiority, confusion, and passivity) to a place of intention (purposefulness and goal directedness) and ultimately to a place of retention (self-reintegration and new meaning)" (p. 302). Career counselors are encouraged to explore and express emotions with clients when meaning is fragmented by a developmental task, occupational transition, or work trauma.

Counselor Role

Career counselors are aware that their role in the counseling process is that of shared meaning. A counselor's main interest is to establish dialogue to create the opportunity for self-agency, personal freedom, and possibilities that are unique to the client and her or his situation. This view requires counselors to position themselves in a different manner. Anderson (1997) noted that this altered position or philosophical stance is characterized by an authentic, natural, spontaneous, and sustained position that is unique to each relationship and each discourse. Such a stance, according to Anderson, shifts the counselor away from thinking in terms of her or his roles and functions and toward considering the relationship the counselor has with the client.

Client Role

Career counselors view the role of the client as a collaborator in creating solutions and new perspectives of problems. The client becomes a conversational partner as the counselor combines the client's expertise on her or his self with the counselor's expertise of the process, creating new knowledge, meanings, and perspectives (Anderson, 1997). Clients can author their own stories that are in process instead of being subject to the received messages of others.

Therapeutic Relationship

Postmodern career counseling places considerable emphasis on the therapeutic relationship. Counselors attend to process in the counseling relationship rather than content or outcomes. As with other qualitative approaches to counseling, the position of the client moves from passive responder to active participant, and the position of the counselor moves from that of expert to one of an interested, curious, and tentative inquirer and observer (McMahon & Patton, 2002).

Ethical Decision Making

A postmodern career counselor would likely approach ethical decision making from a context-centered, meaning-making, and relationship-oriented perspective. Counselors operating from a modernist perspective tend to seek a single, correct interpretation of any given ethics code, whereas counselors who adhere to a postmodern perspective tend to see information in ethics codes as intersubjective, changeable, and open to interpretation (Guterman & Rudes, 2008). Some postmodern career counselors rely on ethical decision making through a process of dialogue between counselor and client (supervisors, others in the client's world) and view a code of ethics as essential but fluid and a socially constructed document.

Teaching Considerations

The primary goal for teaching postmodern career counseling is to foster in students a way of thinking or a value orientation aligned with postmodern thought. Patton and McMahon (1999) believed that constructivist approaches in career theory represent a significant challenge for career counselors trained in positivist approaches. Consistent with constructivist principles of education, instructors should keep in mind that movement toward new epistemological perspectives involves a process of cognitive development in counselor trainees (see Lovell & McAuliffe, 1997, for a review). Because the process of learning is embedded within discussion and reflection, taking this perspective requires students and educators to challenge their assumptions about objectivity, reality, and the very nature of knowledge. The focus is on developing a dialogue in which the students become participants rather than solely teaching fixed and static knowledge. The role of the educator resembles that of introducing new perspectives and alternative meaning systems along with didactic preparation.

There are some challenges when fostering a postmodern worldview in students. Postmodernism in counseling and psychology can often appear vague and abstract to the student and novice counselor. The emphasis is on the process, not the step-by-step strategies to direct the counseling process. Consequently, the abstract and vague feel of meaning making can be frustrating for a linear, task-oriented student, counselor, or even educator. In addition, traditional students coming into counseling programs directly from undergraduate studies may not have had enough life experiences to be able to recognize patterns in their lives or their choices. It also may be difficult for them to recognize all the contextual influences on those choices (Emmett & McAuliffe, 2011).

It is beyond the scope of this chapter to fully outline a curriculum that would embody constructivist principles and practices. Nevertheless, we offer 12 selected learning activities that we believe make up the foundation for teaching a postmodern perspective in career counseling. Educators can begin with these activities and processes when using this book and modify their instruction accordingly. This book concludes with Table C.2, which takes the 12 principles previously described and positions them into suggested course objectives, along with content, activities, and the relevant terms and concepts represented throughout this book.

Conclusion

This concluding chapter identified and summarized the essential principles that permeate the literature on postmodern career counseling. Career counseling for the 21st century, much like feminist theory and the social justice movement, acknowledges the role of culture in human problems. Furthermore, because a person's life course today depends less on the normatively imposed life course and more on an individually shaped life, "career," derived from the Latin *carrus*, which means chariot, seems appropriate in the 21st century. This book addressed how social constructionist ideals in particular address the limitations of modernist paradigms. It fits nicely with counseling's multicultural foundation and the underlying philosophy of counseling as a diversity-embracing, inclusive, and health-enhancing profession. Postmodern career counseling does not replace but rather takes its place among the interventions of vocational guidance, developmental career counseling, career education, and other career service areas. Ultimately, career counseling embedded in psychological constructivism and social constructionism offers a unique and potentially valuable paradigm for practice, research, and training. At the dawn of the 21st century, when career paths have become ambiguous and the institutionalized life story has disappeared, counselors can help clients create their own chariots to carry them through their careers.

Table C.2

Course Objectives, Content, Lessons and Activities, and Postmodern Career Counseling Terms and Concepts

Learning Objective	Content	Lessons and Activities	Postmodern Terms and Concepts
Understand the philosophical contrast between modernist and postmodernist perspectives.	Epistemology	• Read and discuss Introduction and Chapter 2. • Define psychological constructivist from the social constructionist perspective. • Select a case from one of the chapters in Part III. Referring to Table C.1 (p. 326), discuss how these perspectives are reflected in the approach and interactions of the case.	Epistemology, paradigm Realism Psychological constructivist, social constructionist, narrative
View the client as embedded in the social and symbolic systems or contexts within which she or he lives and intersecting identities.	Cultural stance	• Read and discuss Chapter 4. • Referring to Table C.1 (p. 326), select a chapter in Part III and determine to what degree the model or method incorporates context and environmental issues in its conceptualization and if the infusion of cultural models may be useful. • Write a one-page reflective paper identifying the narratives by the dominant discourse of society that have influenced	Contextual, dominant discourse, power relations, social justice, metanarratives, intersecting identities

(Continued)

Course Objectives, Content, Lessons and Activities, and Postmodern Career Counseling Terms and Concepts

Learning Objective	Content	Lessons and Activities	Postmodern Terms and Concepts
View the client as embedded in the social and symbolic systems or contexts within which she or he lives and intersecting identities. (*Continued*)	Cultural stance	• you positively or negatively throughout your life. • Reflect on intersections of identity through group activity. Draw a web diagram ("Identity Web") to depict the different ways you identify yourself. Refer to multiple influences of culture on your personal identity (e.g., sex, age, race, nationality, sexual orientation, class, religion/spirituality, disability). Discuss how these identities are interconnected and interdependent for you. Write dominant identities in uppercase letters and nondominant identities in lowercase letters.	Contextual, dominant discourse, power relations, social justice, metanarratives, intersecting identities
Understand the applied distinction between modernist and postmodernist career theory and intervention.	Core facets of counseling	• Read and discuss the "The Postmodern Turn in Career Counseling" in the Introduction. • In small groups, highlight several ways in which postmodern career counseling assists individuals in making meaning of work in their lives and managing their careers.	Adaptability, life stories, themes, usefulness, identities, reflexivity, active agency

(Continued)

Table C.2 (*Continued*)

Course Objectives, Content, Lessons and Activities, and Postmodern Career Counseling Terms and Concepts

Learning Objective	Content	Lessons and Activities	Postmodern Terms and Concepts
Understand the applied distinction between modernist and postmodernist career theory and intervention. (*Continued*)	Core facets of counseling	• List and contrast the core facets of counseling in vocational guidance, career development, career education, and career counseling.	Adaptability, life stories, themes, usefulness, identities, reflexivity, active agency
Demonstrate skills in using open-ended questions and relationship building and selecting qualitative assessments that relate to the story told by the client.	Nature of assessment	• Read and discuss Chapter 4. • Discuss how assessments can be tailored to meet a client's unique needs and life circumstances. • Reflect on this statement: "Qualitative assessment places emphasis on the counseling relationship rather than on the delivery of the service" (McMahon & Patton, 2002, p. 55). How does qualitative career assessment define the counseling relationship differently? • Discuss how qualitative assessment can foster expansion of language and narrative, and how quantitative measures can create a jumping off point for this expression.	Subjective, qualitative, contextual, holistic, flexible, collaborative, active agency

(*Continued*)

Table C.2 (*Continued*)

Course Objectives, Content, Lessons and Activities, and Postmodern Career Counseling Terms and Concepts

Learning Objective	Content	Lessons and Activities	Postmodern Terms and Concepts
Recognize the integration of assessment in the intervention process.	Phases of counseling	• In small groups, identify phases and overlap in assessment and intervention using a chapter in Part III (e.g., Chapter 9).	Integrative Process oriented: construction, co-construction, deconstruction, and reconstruction
Demonstrate the relational use of language to elicit new meanings, expand perspectives, and encourage change.	Use of language	• Read "Use of Language" in the Introduction. • Practice Bird's approach to relational language making. • Describe yourself in five words only. Identify from whom or where you first heard those words.	Social constructionist Relational language making Dialogical voice versus authoritative voice
Understand methods used to help the client reconstruct a personally meaningful identity; develop identity of career counselor.	Identity	• Read and discuss "Toward a Postmodern Conception of Identity" in Chapter 1. • Discuss how using narrative, card sorts, life design, and Possible Selves Mapping help clients construct meaningful identity. • Practice the StoryTech activity in Chapter 2.	Reflexivity Identity constructed through language

(*Continued*)

Table C.2 (Continued)

Course Objectives, Content, Lessons and Activities, and Postmodern Career Counseling Terms and Concepts

Learning Objective	Content	Lessons and Activities	Postmodern Terms and Concepts
Understand emotion as a motivational factor.	Motivational process	• Contrast responding to content with feelings/emotions. Choose a case from Part III (e.g., Chapter 6 or 8) that demonstrates this stance, and identify how this was achieved. • Effectively demonstrate responding skills and strategies for meaning-making facilitation. • Reflect on and discuss this statement: "Emotion is a way in which people imbue the world with meaning" (Leach & Tiedens, 2004, p. 1).	Discovery of themes, patterns, and meaning
Understand the counselor's roles and functions when considering the relationship with the client.	Counselor role	• Distinguish counselor's position from an expert to a facilitator of dialogue. • In small groups, choose a case from Part III that demonstrates this stance and identify how this was achieved. • Reflect on and discuss this statement: From the modernist perspective, the counselor may be viewed as a representative of a dominant social and cultural discourse.	Tentative observer and inquirer

(Continued)

Table C.2 *(Continued)*

Course Objectives, Content, Lessons and Activities, and Postmodern Career Counseling Terms and Concepts

Learning Objective	Content	Lessons and Activities	Postmodern Terms and Concepts
Understand the client's expertise of self and the counselor's expertise of the process in creating new knowledge, meanings, and perspectives.	Client role	• Practice using "what if" and "exception" questions in dyads. • Discuss how some clients may be reluctant to view themselves as experts. • Choose a case from Part III that demonstrates the client as expert, and identify how this was achieved.	Active participant, client as expert, self-authoring
Develop skills to form a cooperative alliance with the client.	Therapeutic relationship	• Practice active listening with a partner. • Discuss how clients may doubt the helpfulness of a counselor who assumes a "not-knowing position." • In small groups, choose a case from Part III that demonstrates the counselor assuming a not-knowing stance, and identify how this was achieved.	Collaborative, interactive, conversational partners
Develop awareness and responsibility for professional codes of ethics while valuing counselor–client dialogue in the ethical decision-making process.	Ethical decision making	• Discuss ethical decision making as the responsibility of the counselor or as a dialogue between counselor and client.	Social construction Dialogue, power, social justice

References

Anderson, H. (1997). *Conversation, language, and possibilities: A postmodern approach to therapy*. New York, NY: Basic Books.

Bird, J. (2004). *Talk that sings: Therapy in a new linguistic key*. Auckland, New Zealand: Edge Press.

Busacca, L. A. (2002). Career problem assessment: A conceptual schema for counselor training. *Journal of Career Development, 29*, 129–146.

Collin, A., & Young, R. A. (2000). The future of career. In A. Collin & R. A. Young (Eds.), *The future of career* (pp. 276–300). Cambridge, UK: Cambridge University Press.

Emmett, J., & McAuliffe, G. J. (2011). Teaching career development. In G. McAuliffe & K. Eriksen (Eds.), *Handbook of counselor preparation: Constructivist, developmental, and experiential approaches* (pp. 209–227). Thousand Oaks, CA: Sage.

Goldman, L. (1992). Qualitative assessment: An approach for counselors. *Journal of Counseling & Development, 70*, 616–621.

Gonzalez, R., Biever, J. L., & Gardner, G. T. (1994). The multicultural perspective in therapy: A social constructionist approach. *Psychotherapy, 31*, 515–524.

Guterman, J. T., & Rudes, J. (2008). Social constructionism and ethics: Implications for counseling. *Counseling and Values, 52*, 136–144.

Hartung, P. J. (2011). Barrier of benefit? Emotion in life-career design. *Journal of Career Assessment, 19*, 296–305.

Leach, C. W., & Tiedens, L. Z. (2004). Introduction: A world of emotion. In L. Z. Tiedens & C. W. Leach (Eds.), *The social life of emotions* (pp. 1–18). New York, NY: Cambridge University Press.

Lovell, C., & McAuliffe, G. J. (1997). Principles of constructivist training and education. In T. L. Sexton & B. L. Griffin (Eds.), *Constructivist thinking in counseling practice, research, and training* (pp. 211–228). New York, NY: Teachers College Press.

Mair, M. (1989). *Between psychology and psychotherapy: A poetics of experience*. London, England: Routledge.

McMahon, M., & Patton, W. (2002). Using qualitative assessment in career counseling. *International Journal of Educational and Vocational Guidance, 2*, 51–66.

Neimeyer, G. T., & Neimeyer, R. A. (1993). Defining the boundaries of constructivist assessment. In G. J. Neimeyer (Ed.), *Constructivist assessment: A casebook* (p. 130). Newbury Park, CA: Sage.

Neimeyer, R. A. (2009). *Constructivist psychotherapy*. New York, NY: Routledge.

Neimeyer, R. A., & Stewart, A. E. (2000). Constructivist and narrative psychotherapies. In C. R. Snyder & R. E. Ingram (Eds.), *Handbook of psychological change: Psychotherapy processes and practices for the 21st century* (pp. 337–357). New York, NY: Wiley.

Patton, W., & McMahon, M. (1999). *Career development and systems theory: A new relationship*. Pacific Grove, CA: Brooks/Cole.

Peavy, R. V. (1992). A constructivist model of training for career counselors. *Journal of Career Development, 18,* 215–229.

Savickas, M. L. (2011). *Career counseling.* Washington, DC: American Psychological Association.

Sexton, T. L. (1997). Constructivist thinking within the history of ideas: The challenge of a new paradigm. In T. L. Sexton & B. L. Griffin (Eds.), *Constructivist thinking in counseling practice, research, and training* (pp. 3–18). New York, NY: Teachers College Press.

Stead, G. B. (2004). Culture and career psychology: A social constructionist perspective. *Journal of Vocational Behavior, 64,* 389–406.

Watson, M. B. (2011). Postmodern career counseling and beyond. In K. Maree (Ed.), *Shaping the story: A guide to facilitating career counseling* (pp. 73–86). Pretoria, South Africa: Van Schaik.

Whiston, S. C., & Rahardja, D. (2005). Qualitative career assessment: An overview and analysis. *Journal of Career Assessment, 13,* 371–380.

Young, R. A., & Collin, A. (2004). Introduction: Constructivism and social constructionism in the career field. *Journal of Vocational Behavior, 64,* 373–388.

Glossary

active agency–Derived from constructivism, it implies that individuals are actively engaged in constructing lives characterized by independence, autonomy, and initiative.

at-will employment contract–An employer can terminate an employee at any time for any reason, except an illegal one, or for no reason without incurring legal liability and can change the terms of the employment relationship with no notice and no consequences.

career adaptability–The psychological resources for coping with current and anticipated career developmental tasks, occupational transitions, and work traumas.

career counseling–Career interventions that use psychological methods to foster self-exploration to help clients choose and adjust to occupations.

career education–A career service area that rests on a predictable trajectory of developmental tasks. Educational methods orient students, young adults, and groups to imminent tasks of vocational development and ways to cope with them.

context–The influences and interactions that make and remake the individual, such as socioeconomic status, workplace, employment market, educational institutions, geographical location, peers, political decisions, family, historical trends, media, globalization, and community groups.

contextualism–A worldview reflected in social constructionism that considers knowledge about ourselves, development, and change as a result of an ongoing process of interaction between the client and his or her environment.

culture–The personal meaning and interpretations clients ascribe to characteristics such as race, ethnicity, age, sex, sexual orientation, disability, religion, and socioeconomic status along with their intersecting identities.

deinstitutionalization of the life course–The current narratives about work life that have become less useful in today's society because of loss of stable structures and predictable trajectories resulting from life in a postmodern world.

discourse analysis–A social constructionist approach that underscores how language is ruled by the hierarchies of discourse, including structures of power, ideology, and knowledge, and moves from the dominant social discourse concerned with power relations to more contextual processes concerned with local occurrences of behavior.

globalization–The process by which goods, information, labor, services, business, finance, natural resources, and cultural products move across national boundaries.

holding environment–In the context of work, the interpersonal or group-based relationships that enable people to cope with situations that trigger anxiety.

identity–From a postmodernist view, identity is the self that is invested in a social role and co-constructed by the individual and her or his social context. Identity is communicated to others through language and is historically and socially embedded in and shaped by culture.

individualization–The responsibility people have for shaping their own lives as a result of nonstandard work arrangements in organizations. A person's life course today depends less on the normatively imposed life course and more on an individually shaped life.

intersecting identities–Drawing on feminist and multicultural perspectives, the assumption that an individual's identities must be considered in combination and not in isolation. Cultural variables such as age, gender, race, class, sexuality, religion/spirituality, and disability simultaneously affect the perceptions, experiences, and opportunities of the individual.

mechanism–A philosophical position or the assumption that psychological processes and behaviors can be explained the same way that mechanical or physiological processes are explained.

metanarratives–The dominant societal scripts that include the collective norms and values of family and social institutions that intentionally shape and state expectations for how people live their lives.

micronarratives–Short stories individuals embed within their social role and local context that give metanarratives their context. Through dialogue, clients define their own micronarratives to give new meaning to their lives.

modernism–The foundational assumption of realism; belief that an actual reality, with particular enduring properties, exists independently from those who observe it and represents what we know.

narrative career counseling–Exemplifies a constructivist-based approach to career counseling in which the counselor supports the client in constructing a personal story (or stories) in a contextual manner that enables the person to make sense of his or her problems and that promotes meaningful career decisions and actions.

narrative identity–A personalized interpretation of the self in a social world, elicited through narrative expression, that confers meaning and purpose and helps individuals achieve a genuine and integrated sense of self.

narrative theory–A conceptual system that enables individuals to give meaning to their actions and existence. Narratives give shape to meaning and mattering in life and provide the constructive tale that links together everyday events and actions into a short episode. It can provide the picture through which to gain insight into the past and to plan for the future.

nonstandardized employment–A form of flexibility that advocates a small group of core workers in managerial positions augmented by an adjustable number of peripheral workers who make up a contingent, part-time, and temporary workforce.

postmodern career counseling–An umbrella term that denotes the career counseling paradigms and processes derived from the epistemologies of contemporary psychological constructivism and social constructionism.

postmodernism–An intellectual movement that has its center in art, architecture, literature, and cultural studies. Rejects the fundamental assumptions of modernism regarding objective truths, and in general asserts that individuals construct meaning or perceive their own reality or truth.

precarious work–Employment that is uncertain and unpredictable from the point of view of the employee.

psychological constructivism–A perspective that arose in developmental and cognitive psychology that focuses on meaning making and how people interpret their social and psychological worlds through individual cognitive processes.

psychological employment contract–The long-term implicit contract between employee and employer in which workers trade their work hours, labor, and commitment for a lifetime job or at least a steady income and job security geared to seniority.

realism–A philosophical position or the assumption that objects have an existence independent of the observer.

reflexivity–In contemporary social theory, a position that views identity as something that is routinely created and sustained in the reflexive activities of the individual to respond to rapid social change.

relational context–People learn about themselves, their social world, and culture through relationships; acknowledges the potential adaptive function of interpersonal connection in approaching career transitions, career choice, and work traumas.

self-reliance–Characteristics necessary to actively plan and implement self-management behaviors in the work environment. Necessary qualities for self-realization require people to acquire active agency and relational interdependence.

social constructionism–A perspective derived from multidisciplinary sources such as sociology, literary studies, and postmodern approaches in which it is believed the social and psychological worlds are made real (constructed) through social processes and interaction.

standardized employment–Individuals who work full time, within the boundaries of a single employer, and have opportunities to advance gradually in responsibility and pay.

transactional employment contract–A short-term explicit contract between employee and employer; workers cannot depend on guaranteed job security, regardless of their occupational status.

vocational guidance–A career service area that rests on enhancing self-knowledge, increasing occupational information, and securing occupational fit. The overriding goal of vocational guidance is to promote the adjustment outcomes of career success, satisfaction, and stability.

Index

Figures and tables are indicated by "f" and "t" following page numbers.

B

C

(Continued)

(Continued)

Y